Table of Contents

Readings

1. **Geoffrey Chaucer**

   The Canterbury Tales..3

      The General Prologue...................................3

      The Prioress's Prologue and Tale....................29

2. **Isaac Barrow**

   From *The Duty and Reward of Bounty to the Poor*...................39

3. **Bernard Mandeville**

   An Essay on Charity and Charity-Schools...................57

4. **Richard Steele**

   The Conscious Lovers...................................89

5. **Jonathan Swift**

   A Modest Proposal....................................139

6. **Samuel Johnson**

   The Rambler...145

      Number 60...145

      Number 149.......................................147

7. **Samuel Johnson**

   The Life of Savage...................................151

8. **William Wordsworth**

   From *Preface to Lyrical Ballads*....................203

9. **William Wordsworth**

   The Old Cumberland Beggar...........................215

10. **Samuel Taylor Coleridge**

    This Lime-Tree Bower My Prison.....................221

11. **Edward Bulwer Lytton**

    Money..225

12. **Robert Browning**

    Fra Lippo Lippi....................................279

13. **General William Booth**

    From *In Darkest England*............................291

Information and Terms

1. Information for Anglo-Saxon and Middle English 328

2. Terms for Chaucer 329

3. Terms for Shakespeare 330

4. Dates of Reigns (and Other Matters) 331

5. Terms for the 18th Century and Barrow 332

6. Terms for Mandeville and Steele 333

7. Terms for Swift 334

8. Cicero and *A Modest Proposal* 335

9. Terms for Johnson 336

10. Terms for Sterne 337

11. Terms for Bentham and Malthus 338

12. Terms for Wordsworth and Coleridge 339

13. Terms for Bulwer Lytton and Dickens 340

14. Terms for Browning 341

15. Terms for Booth and Stead 342

16. Terms for Shaw 343

Readings

Reading

Geoffrey Chaucer

The Canterbury Tales

THE GENERAL PROLOGUE

Whan that Aprill with his shoures sote°	*sweet showers*
The droghte° of Marche hath perced to the rote,°	*dryness /root*
And bathed every veyne° in swich licour,°	*vein /such moisture*
Of which vertu° engendred is the flour;	*By power of which*
5 Whan Zephirus° eek with his swete breeth	*the west wind*
Inspired° hath in every holt° and heeth°	*Breathed into / wood / heath*
The tendre croppes,° and the yonge sonne	*sprouts*
Hath in the Ram his halfe cours y-ronne;[1]	
And smale fowles° maken melodye,	*birds*
10 That slepen al the night with open yë°—	*eye(s)*
So priketh hem Nature in hir corages[2]—	
Than longen° folk to goon° on pilgrimages,	*Then long / go*
And palmeres for to seken straunge strondes,[3]	
To fern halwes,° couthe° in sondry londes;	*far-off shrines / known*
15 And specially, from every shires ende	
Of Engelond to Caunterbury they wende,	
The holy blisful martir[4] for to seke,°	*seek*
That hem hath holpen,° whan that they were seke.°	*helped / sick*
Bifel° that, in that seson on a day,	*It befell*
20 In Southwerk at the Tabard° as I lay°	*(an inn) / lodged*
Redy to wenden° on my pilgrimage	*depart*
To Caunterbury with ful devout corage,°	*heart*
At night was come into that hostelrye°	*inn*
Wel nyne and twenty, in a companye	
25 Of sondry folk, by aventure° y-falle°	*chance / fallen*
In felawshipe, and pilgrims were they alle,	
That toward Caunterbury wolden° ryde.	*wished to*
The chambres° and the stables weren wyde,°	*bedrooms / spacious*
And wel we weren esed° atte beste.°	*made comfortable / in the best (ways)*

From *The Canterbury Tales: Fifteen Tales and General Prologue*, 2nd Edition by Geoffrey Chaucer, edited by V. A. Kolve and Glending Olson. Copyright © 2005, 1989 by W. W. Norton & Company, Inc. Used by permission of W. W. Norton & Company, Inc.

30 And shortly, whan the sonne was to° reste,	*at*
So hadde I spoken with hem everichon°	*everyone*
That I was of hir felawshipe anon,	
And made forward° erly for to ryse,	*agreement*
To take oure wey, ther as I yow devyse.°	*(will) tell*
35 But natheles,° whyl I have tyme and space,	*nevertheless*
Er that I ferther in this tale pace,°	*pass on*
Me thinketh it acordaunt to resound[5]	
To telle yow al the condicioun[6]	
Of ech of hem, so as it semed me,°	*seemed to me*
40 And whiche° they weren, and of what degree,°	*what / status*
And eek in what array° that they were inne;	*clothing*
And at a knight than wol° I first beginne.	*will*
A KNIGHT ther was, and that a worthy man,	
That fro° the tyme that he first bigan	*from*
45 To ryden out,° he loved chivalrye,	*ride (on expeditions)*
Trouthe and honour, fredom and curteisye.[7]	
Ful worthy was he in his lordes werre,°	*war(s)*
And therto° hadde he riden, no man ferre,°	*in such / further*
As wel in Cristendom as in hethenesse,°	*in pagan lands*
50 And evere honoured for his worthinesse.	
At Alisaundre° he was whan it was wonne;	*Alexandria*
Ful ofte tyme he hadde the bord bigonne°	*headed the table*
Aboven alle naciouns in Pruce.°	*Prussia*
In Lettow hadde he reysed and in Ruce,[8]	
55 No Cristen man so ofte of his degree.°	*rank*
In Gernade° at the sege° eek hadde he be°	*Granada / siege / been*
Of Algezir,° and riden in Belmarye.°	*Algeciras / Benmarin (in Morocco)*
At Lyeys° was he and at Satalye,°	*Ayas / Adalia (both in Asia Minor)*
Whan they were wonne; and in the Grete See°	*Mediterranean*
60 At many a noble armee° hadde he be.	*armed expedition*
At mortal batailles[9] hadde he been fiftene,	
And foughten for oure feith at Tramissene°	*Tlemcen (in Algeria)*
In listes° thryes,° and ay slayn his foo.°	*tournaments / thrice / foe*
This ilke° worthy knight hadde been also	*same*
65 Somtyme with the lord of Palatye,°	*Palatia*
Ageyn° another hethen in Turkye;	*Against*
And everemore he hadde a sovereyn prys.°	*reputation*
And though that he were worthy,° he was wys,°	*i.e., valiant/prudent*
And of his port° as meke as is a mayde.	*deportment*

4

70 He nevere yet no vileinye° ne sayde	*rudeness*
In al his lyf, unto no maner wight.°	*any sort of person*
He was a verray,° parfit,° gentill knight.	*true / perfect / noble*
But for to tellen yow of his array,	
His hors° were gode, but he was nat gay.°	*horses / brightly dressed*
75 Of fustian° he wered° a gipoun°	*rough cloth / wore / tunic*
Al bismotered with° his habergeoun,°	*stained by / coat of mail*
For he was late y-come° from his viage,°	*recently come / expedition*
And wente for to doon° his pilgrimage.	*make*
With him ther was his sone, a young SQUYER,	
80 A lovyere, and a lusty bacheler,[10]	
With lokkes crulle, as they were leyd in presse.[11]	
Of twenty yeer of age he was, I gesse.	
Of° his stature he was of evene lengthe,°	*In / average height*
And wonderly delivere,° and of greet strengthe.	*agile*
85 And he hadde been somtyme in chivachye°	*on expeditions*
In Flaundres,° in Artoys,° and Picardye,°	*Flanders / Artois / Picardy*
And born him wel, as of so litel space,[12]	
In hope to stonden° in his lady° grace.	*stand / lady's*
Embrouded° was he, as it were a mede°	*Embroidered / meadow*
90 Al ful of fresshe floures, whyte and rede.	
Singinge he was, or floytinge,° al the day;	*fluting (whistling?)*
He was as fresh as is the month of May.	
Short was his gowne, with sieves longe and wyde.	
Wei coude° he sitte on hors, and faire ryde.	*knew how to*
95 He coude songes make and wel endyte,°	*compose verse*
Juste° and eek daunce, and wel purtreye° and wryte,	*Joust / draw*
So hote° he lovede that by nightertale	*hotly / at night*
He sleep° namore° than dooth a nightingale.	*slept/no more*
Curteys he was, lowly, and servisable,[13]	
100 And carf° biforn his fader at the table.	*carved (meat)*
A YEMAN hadde he, and servaunts namo[14]	
At that tyme, for him, liste° ryde so;	*it pleased him to*
And he was clad in cote and hood of grene.	
A sheef of pecok arwes° brighte and kene	*arrows*
105 Under his belt he bar° ful thriftily.°	*bore / carefully*
Wel coude he dresse° his takel° yemanly:	*keep in order / equipment*
His arwes drouped noght with fetheres lowe,	
And in his hand he bar a mighty bowe.	
A not-heed° hadde he, with a broun visage.°	*closely cropped head / face*

110	Of wodecraft wel coude° he al the usage.	knew
	Upon his arm he bar a gay bracer,°	fine wrist guard
	And by his syde a swerd and a bokeler,°	shield
	And on that other syde a gay daggere,	
	Harneised° wel, and sharp as point of spere;	mounted
115	A Cristofre° on his brest of silver shene.°	St. Christopher medal / bright
	An horn he bar, the bawdrik° was of grene;	shoulder strap
	A forster° was he, soothly, as I gesse.	forester
	Ther was also a Nonne, a PRIORESEE,	
	That of hir smyling was ful simple and coy°—	modest
120	Hir gretteste ooth was but by Seynte Loy°—	Eligius (Fr. Eloi)
	And she was cleped° madame Eglentyne.	called
	Ful wel she song° the service divyne,	sang
	Entuned° in hir nose ful semely;°	Intoned / becomingly
	And Frensh she spak ful faire and fetisly,°	elegantly
125	After the scole of Stratford atte Bowe,[15]	
	For Frensh of Paris was to hire unknowe.	
	At mete° wel y-taught was she with alle:	i.e., at table
	She leet° no morsel from hir lippes falle,	let
	Ne wette hir fingres in hir sauce depe.°	(too) deeply
130	Wel coude she cane a morsel, and wel kepe[16]	
	That no drope ne fille° upon hire brest.	fell
	In curteisye° was set ful muchel° hir lest.°	etiquette / much / delight
	Hir over°-lippe wyped she so clene,	upper
	That in hir coppe was no ferthing° sene°	small drop / seen
135	Of grece° whan she dronken hadde hir draughte.	grease
	Ful semely after hir mete she raughte,°	reached
	And sikerly° she was of greet disport,°	certainly / cheerfulness
	And ful plesaunt, and amiable of port,°	deportment
	And peyned hire° to countrefete chere°	took pains / imitate behavior
140	Of court, and to been estatlich° of manere,	stately
	And to ben holden digne° of reverence.	considered worthy
	But, for to speken of hire conscience,°	sensibility
	She was so charitable and so pitous,°	compassionate
	She wolde wepe, if that she sawe a mous°	mouse
145	Caught in a trappe, if it were deed or bledde.	
	Of° smale houndes hadde she, that she fedde	i.e., some
	With rosted flesh, or milk and wastel-breed.°	fine white bread
	But sore° wepte she if oon of hem were deed,	sorely
	Or if men° smoot it with a yerde° smerte;°	(some)one / stick / sharply

150 And al was conscience and tendre herte.

Ful semely hir wimpel° pinched° was, — *headdress / pleated*

Hir nose tretys,° hir eyen° greye as glas, — *graceful / eyes*

Hir mouth ful smal, and therto softe and reed.

But sikerly° she hadde a fair forheed— — *certainly*

155 It was almost a spanne° brood, I trowe°— — *span / believe*

For hardily° she was nat undergrowe.° — *certainly / undersized*

Ful fetis° was hir cloke, as I was war.° — *elegant / aware*

Of smal coral° aboute hire arm she bar — *i.e., small coral beads*

A peire of bedes, gauded al with grene;[17]

160 And theron heng a broche° of gold ful shene,° — *ornament / bright*

On which ther was first write° a crowned A,[18] — *written*

And after, *Amor vincit omnia.*° — *Love conquers all*

Another NONNE with hire hadde she,

That was hir chapeleyne,° and PREESTES three. — *chaplain, assistant*

165 A MONK ther was, a fair for the maistrye,° — *a very fine one*

An outrydere° that lovede venerye:° — *estate supervisor / hunting*

A manly man, to been an abbot able.

Ful many a deyntee° hors hadde he in stable, — *valuable*

And when he rood, men mighte his brydel here° — *hear*

170 Ginglen° in a whistling wind als° clere — *Jingling / as*

And eek° as loude as dooth the chapel belle, — *also*

Ther as° this lord was kepere of the celle.[19] — *Where*

The reule of Seint Maure° or of Seint Beneit,° — *Maurus / Benedict*

By cause that it was old and somdel streit,° — *somewhat strict*

175 This ilke° monk leet olde thinges pace,° — *same/pass away*

And held after the newe world the space.° — *course (i.e., custom)*

He yaf° nat of° that text a pulled° hen, — *gave / for / plucked*

That seith that hunters ben° nat holy men, — *are*

Ne that a monk, whan he is reccheless,° — *negligent of his vows*

180 Is lykned til° a fish that is waterlees° — *likened to / out of water*

(This is to seyn,° a monk out of his cloistre); — *say*

But thilke° text held he nat worth an oistre.° — *that same / oyster*

And I seyde his opinioun was good:

What° sholde he studie, and make himselven wood,° — *Why / mad*

185 Upon a book in cloistre alwey to poure,° — *pore over*

Or swinken° with his handes and laboure — *work*

As Austin bit?° How shal the world be served? — *Augustine bids*

Lat Austin have his swink° to him reserved! — *work*

Therfore he was a pricasour° aright° — *hard rider / truly*

7

190   Grehoundes he hadde, as swifte as fowel° in flight;   *bird*

        Of priking° and of hunting for the hare   *riding*

        Was al his lust,° for no cost wolde he spare.   *pleasure*

        I seigh° his sieves purfiled° at the hond   *saw / trimmed*

        With grys,° and that the fyneste of a lond;°   *gray fur / land*

195   And, for to festne° his hood under his chin,   *fastens*

        He hadde of gold y-wroght° a ful curious pin: *made*

        A love-knotte[20] in the gretter° ende ther was.   *larger*

        His heed was balled,° that shoon as any glas,   *bald*

        And eek his face, as° he had been anoint.°   *as if / anointed*

200   He was a lord ful fat and in good point°   *condition*

        His eyen° stepe,° and rollinge in his heed,   *eyes / prominent*

        That stemed as a forneys of a leed;[21]

        His bootes souple,° his hors in greet estat°—   *supple / condition*

        Now certeinly he was a fair prelat.

205   He was nat pale as a forpyned goost°   *tormented spirit*

        A fat swan loved he best of any roost.

        His palfrey° was as broun as is a berye.°   *horse / berry*

           A FRERE° ther was, a wantowne° and a merye,   *Friar / gay (one)*

        A limitour,[22] a ful solempne° man.   *distinguished*

210   In alle the ordres foure[23] is noon that can°   *knows*

        So muchel of daliaunce and fair langage.

        He hadde maad° ful many a manage   *arranged*

        Of yonge wommen, at his owne cost.[24]

        Unto his ordre he was a noble post.°   *pillar*

215   Ful wel biloved and famulier was he

        With frankeleyns over al in his contree,[25]

        And eek with worthy wommen of the toun;

        For he hadde power of confessioun,

        As seyde himself, more than a curat,°   *parish priest*

220   For of his ordre he was licentiat.°   *licensed to hear confessions*

        Ful swetely herde he confessioun,

        And plesaunt was his absolucioun;

        He was an esy man to yeve° penaunce   *give*

        Ther as he wiste to have a good pitaunce.[26]

225   For unto a povre° ordre for to yive°   *poor / give*

        Is signe that a man is wel y-shrive°—   *shriven*

        For if he yaf,° he dorste make avaunt,°   *gave / (the Friar) dared assert*

        He wiste° that a man was repentaunt.   *knew*

        For many a man so hard is of his herte,

230   He may flat wepe althogh hym sore smerte:°   *it sorely pain him*

Therfore, in stede of wepinge and preyeres,

Men moot° yeve silver to the povre° freres.   *may / poor*

His tipet° was ay farsed° ful of knyves   *scarf / always stuffed*

And pinnes, for to yeven° faire wyves.   *give to*

235   And certeinly he hadde a murye note;°   *pleasant voice*

Wel coude he singe and pleyen on a rote;°   *stringed instrument*

Of yeddinges he bar outrely the prys.[27]

His nekke whyt was as the flour-de-lys;°   *lily*

Therto° he strong was as a champioun.   *moreover*

240   He knew the tavernes wel in every toun,

And everich hostiler° and tappestere°   *innkeeper / barmaid*

Bet than a lazar or a beggestere,[28]

For unto swich° a worthy man as he   *such*

Acorded nat, as by his facultee,[29]

245   To have with seke lazars° aqueyntaunce: *sick lepers*

It is nat honest,° it may nat avaunce°   *respectable / be profitable*

For to delen with no swich poraille,°   *such poor people*

But al with riche and selleres of vitaille.°   *victuals*

And over al,° ther as° profit sholde aryse,   *everywhere / wherever*

250   Curteys he was, and lowely of° servyse.   *humble in*

Ther nas° no man nowher so vertuous.°   *was not / capable*

He was the beste beggere in his hous,

252a   [And yaf° a certeyn ferme° for the graunt: *gave / payment*

252b   Noon of his bretheren cam ther in his haunt.]°   *area of begging*

For thogh a widwe° hadde noght a sho,°   *widow / shoe*

So plesaunt was his *In principio,*°   *"In the beginning"*

255   Yet wolde he have a ferthing,° er he wente.   *farthing*

His purchas was wel bettre than his rente.[30]

And rage he coude, as it were right a whelpe;[31]

In love-dayes° ther coude he muchel° helpe,   *legal arbitrations / much*

For there he was nat lyk a cloisterer,[32]

260   With a thredbare cope,° as is a povre scoler.   *cape*

But he was lyk a mister° or a pope: *Master of Arts*

Of double worsted was his semi-cope,°   *half cape*

That rounded as a belle out of the presse.°   *mould*

Somwhat he lipsed, for his wantownesse,[33]

265   To make his English swete upon his tonge;

And in his harping, whan that he hadde songe,

His eyen° twinkled in his heed aright   *eyes*

As doon° the sterres° in the frosty night. — *do / stars*
This worthy limitour was cleped° Huberd. — *called*
270   A MARCHANT was ther with a forked berd,° — *beard*
In mottelee,° and hye[34] on horse he sat; — *figured cloth*
Upon his heed a Flaundrish° bever° hat, — *Flemish / beaver fur*
His bootes clasped° faire and fetisly.° — *tied / neatly*
His resons° he spak ful solempnely,° — *opinions / impressively*
275   Souninge° alway th'encrees° of his winning.° — *Proclaiming / increase / profit*
He wolde the see were kept for any thing[35]
Bitwixe Middleburgh° and Orewelle.° — *(in Holland) / (in England)*
Wel coude he in eschaunge° sheeldes° selle. — *foreign exchange / French coins*
This worthy man ful wel his wit bisette:° — *used*
280   Ther wiste no wight° that he was in dette, — *no person knew*
So estatly° was he of his governaunce,° — *dignified / conduct*
With his bargaynes and with his chevisaunce.° — *(possibly illegal) lending*
For sothe he was a worthy man with alle,
But sooth to seyn, I noot° how men him calle. — *know not*
285   A CLERK° ther was of Oxenford° also, — *student / Oxford*
That unto logik hadde longe y-go.[36]
As leene° was his hors as is a rake, — *lean*
And he nas° nat right fat, I undertake,° — *was not / declare*
But loked holwe,° and therto° soberly. — *hollow / also*
290   Ful thredbar was his overest courtepy,° — *outer short cloak*
For he hadde geten him° yet no benefyce, — *obtained for himself*
Ne was so worldly for to have offyce;° — *secular employment*
For him was levere° have at his beddes heed — *he would rather*
Twenty bokes, clad° in blak or reed, — *bound*
295   Of Aristotle and his philosophye,
Than robes riche, or fithele,° or gay sautrye.° — *fiddle / psaltery, harp*
But al be that° he was a philosophre,[37] — *although*
Yet hadde he but litel gold in cofre;° — *coffer*
But al that he mighte of his freendes hente,° — *get*
300   On bokes and on lerninge he it spente,
And bisily gan for the soules preye[38]
Of hem that yaf him wherwith° to scoleye.° — *i.e., the means / study*
Of studie took he most cure° and most hede.° — *care / heed*
Noght o° word spak he more than was nede, — *Not one*
305   And that was seyd in forme° and reverence,° — *properly / respectfully*
And short and quik, and ful of hy sentence.° — *serious meaning*
Souninge° in moral vertu was his speche, — *Resounding*

And gladly wolde he lerne, and gladly teche.

A SERGEANT OF THE LAWE,° war° and wys,   *eminent lawyer / alert*

310 That often hadde been at the Parvys,[39]

Ther was also, ful riche of excellence.

Discreet he was and of greet reverence:°   *worthy of great respect*

He semed swich,° his wordes weren so wyse.   *such*

Justyce° he was ful often in assyse,°   *Judge / local courts*

315 By patente° and by pleyn° commissioun;   *letter of appointment / full*

For his science° and for his heigh renoun,   *knowledge*

Of fees and robes hadde he many oon.°   *a one*

So greet a purchasour° was nowher noon:°   *speculator in land/some*

Al was fee simple to him in effect;[40]

320 His purchasing mighte flat been infect.°   *invalidated*

Nowher so bisy a man as he ther nas;

And yet he semed bisier than he was.

In termes hadde he caas and domes alle,[41]

That from the tyme of King William[42] were falle.°   *had taken place*

325 Therto he coude endyte,° and make a thing;°   *write / draw up papers*

Ther coude no wight pinche at° his wryting,   *no one find fault with*

And every statut coude° he pleyn by rote.°   *knew / completely by heart*

He rood but hoomly° in a medlee° cote,   *informally / I figured*

Girt with a ceint° of silk, with barres° smale;   *girdle / metal bars*

330 Of his array telle I no lenger tale.

A FRANKELEYN° was in his companye.   *wealthy landowner*

Whyt was his berd as is the dayesye;°   *daisy*

Of his complexioun° he was sangwyn.°   *temperament / sanguine*

Wel loved he by the morwe a sop in wyn.[43]

335 To liven in delyt was evere his wone,°   *custom*

For he was Epicurus[44] owene sone,

That heeld opinioun that pleyn° delyt   *complete*

Was verray° felicitee parfyt.°   *true / perfect*

An housholdere, and that a greet,° was he;   *a great one*

340 Seint Julian[45] he was in his contree.°   *region*

His breed, his ale, was alweys after oon;°   *of uniform good quality*

A bettre envyned° man was nowher noon.   *stocked with wine*

Withoute bake mete° was nevere his hous,   *meat pies*

Of fish and flesh,° and that so plentevous°   *meat / plentiful*

345 It snewed° in his hous of mete° and drinke.   *snowed / food*

Of alle deyntees° that men coude thinke,   *delicacies*

After° the sondry sesons of the yeer,   *According to*

So chaunged° he his mete° and his soper. — *varied / dinner*

Ful many a fat partrich° hadde he in mewe,° — *partridge / coop*

350 And many a breem° and many a luce° in stewe.° — *carp / pike / fishpond*

Wo° was his cook, but if° his sauce were — *(Made) sorry / unless*

Poynaunt° and sharp, and redy al his gere.° — *Pungent / utensils*

His table dormant[46] in his halle° alway — *main room*

Stood redy covered° al the longe day. — *set*

355 At sessiouns ther was he lord and sire;[47]

Ful ofte tyme he was knight of the shire.[48]

An anlas° and a gipser° al of silk — *dagger / purse*

Heng° at his girdel, whyt as morne° milk. — *Hung / morning*

A shirreve° hadde he been, and a countour;° — *sheriff / auditor*

360 Was nowher such a worthy vavasour.° — *landholder*

    An HABERDASSHER and a CARPENTER,

A WEBBE,° a DYERE, and a TAPICER,° — *weaver / tapestry maker*

Were with us eek, clothed in o liveree° — *one livery (uniform)*

Of a solempne° and greet fraternitee.° — *distinguished / (parish) guild*

365 Ful fresh and newe hir gere° apyked° was; — *equipment / adorned*

Hir knyves were chaped° noght with bras, — *mounted*

But al with silver; wroght ful clene and wee!

Hire girdles° and hire pouches° everydeel.° — *belts / purses / altogether*

Wel semed ech of hem a fair burgeys° — *citizen / burgher*

370 To sitten in a yeldhalle° on a deys.[49] — *guildhall*

Everich,° for the wisdom that he can,° — *Each one / knows*

Was shaply° for to been an alderman. — *fit*

For catel° hadde they ynogh and rente,° — *property / income*

And eek° hir wyves wolde it wel assente;° — *also / assent to*

375 And elles° certein were they to blame.° — *otherwise / deserving of blame*

It is ful fair to been y-clept° "Madame,"° — *called / "my lady"*

And goon to vigilyës al bifore,[50]

And have a mantel royalliche y-bore.° — *royally carried*

    A COOK they hadde with hem for the nones,° — *occasion*

380 To boille the chiknes° with the mary-bones° — *chickens / marrowbones*

And poudre-marchant tart and galingale.[51]

Wel coude he knowe° a draughte of London ale. — *recognize*

He coude° roste, and sethe,° and broille, and frye, — *knew how to / boil*

Maken mortreux,° and wel bake a pye. — *stews*

385 But greet harm° was it, as it thoughte° me, — *misfortune / seemed to*

That on his shine° a mormal° hadde he. — *shin / ulcerous sore*

For blankmanger,[52] that made he with the beste.

A SHIPMAN was ther, woninge fer by weste:[53]
For aught I woot,° he was of Dertemouthe.°   *know / Dartmouth (in Devon)*
390   He rood upon a rouncy, as he couthe,[54]
In a gowne of falding° to the knee.   *heavy wool*
A daggere hanginge on a laas° hadde he   *cord*
Aboute his nekke, under his arm adoun.
The hote somer° hadde maad his hewe al broun;   *summer*
395   And certeinly he was a good felawe.°   *cheerful companion*
Ful many a draughte of wyn had he y-drawe°   *drawn off*
Fro Burdeux-ward, whyl that the chapman sleep.[55]
Of nyce° conscience took he no keep:°   *scrupulous / heed*
If that he faught, and hadde the hyer hond,°   *upper hand*
400   By water he sente hem hoom° to every lond.   *i.e., drowned them*
But of his craft, to rekene wel his tydes,[56]
His stremes° and his daungers him bisydes,°   *currents / close to him*
His herberwe° and his mone,° his lodemenage,°   *harbor / moon / pilotage*
Ther nas noon swich° from Hulle to Cartage.[57]   *such*
405   Hardy he was, and wys to undertake;[58]
With many a tempest hadde his berd been shake.
He knew wel alle the havenes,° as they were,   *harbors*
From Gootlond to the cape of Finistere,[59]
And every cryke° in Britayne° and in Spayne;   *creek / Brittany*
410   His barge y-cleped° was the Maudelayne.°   *called / Magdalen*
    With us ther was a DOCTOUR OF PHISYK;°   *a physician*
In al this world ne was ther noon him lyk
To speke of phisik° and of surgerye,   *In regard to medicine*
For he was grounded in astronomye.°   *astrology*
415   He kepte° his pacient a ful greet deel   *watched*
In houres, by his magik naturel.[60]
Wel coude he fortunen the ascendent
Of his images for his pacient.[61]
He knew the cause of everich maladye,
420   Were it of hoot or cold, or moiste, or drye,[62]
And where engendred,° and of what humour;   *originated*
He was a verrey° parfit practisour.°   *true / practitioner*
The cause y-knowe,° and of his harm° the roote,°   *known / malady / cause*
Anon° he yaf° the seke man his boote.°   *Quickly / gave / remedy*
425   Ful redy hadde he his apothecaries[63]
To sende him drogges and his letuaries,°   *medicinal syrups*
For ech of hem made other for to winne;°   *profit*

Hir° frendschipe nas nat newe to biginne.° *Their / recently begun*
Wel knew he the olde Esculapius,
430 And Deiscorides, and eek Rufus,
Old Ypocras, Haly, and Galien,
Serapion, Razis, and Avicen,
Averrois, Damascien, and Constantyn,
Bernard, and Gatesden, and Gilbertyn.[64]
435 Of his diete mesurable° was he, *moderate*
For it was of no superfluitee
But of greet norissing° and digestible. *nourishment*
His studie was but litel on the Bible.[65]
In sangwin° and in pers° he clad was al, *bloodred / blue*
440 Lyned with taffata and with sendal;[66]
And yet he was but esy of dispence.° *slow to spend*
He kepte that he wan in pestilence,
For gold in phisik is a cordial;[67]
Therefore he lovede gold in special.° *particularly*
445 A good WYF was ther of bisyde BATHE,° *from near Bath*
But she was somdel° deef, and that was scathe.° *somewhat / a pity*
Of clooth-making she hadde swiche an haunt,° *such practiced skill*
She passed° hem of Ypres and of Gaunt.[68] *surpassed*
In at the parisshe wyf ne was ther noon
450 That to the offringe° bifore hir sholde goon;° *offering in church / go*
And if ther dide, certeyn so wrooth° was she, *angry*
That she was out of alle charitee.
Hir coverchiefs° ful fyne were of ground; *kerchiefs / texture*
I dorste° swere they weyeden° ten pound *would dare / weighed*
455 That on a Sonday weren upon hir heed.
Hir hosen° weren of fyn scarlet reed, *hose*
Ful streite y-teyd,° and shoos ful moiste° and newe. *tightly tied/soft*
Bold was hir face, and fair, and reed of hewe.° *hue*
She was a worthy womman al hir lyve:
460 Housbondes at chirche dore[69] she hadde fyve,
Withouten° other companye in youthe— *Not to mention*
But therof nedeth nat to speke as nouthe°— *at present*
And thryes° hadde she been at Jerusalem. *thrice*
She hadde passed many a straunge streem:[70]
465 At Rome she hadde been, and at Boloigne,° *Boulogne (France)*
In Galice at Seint Jame, and at Coloigne;[71]
She coude° muchel of wandringe by the weye.° *knew/along the road(s)*

14

Gat-tothed° was she, soothly for to seye. — *Gap-toothed*
Upon an amblere° esily° she sat, — *saddle horse / comfortably*
470 Y-wimpled° wel, and on hir heed an hat — *Covered with a wimple*
As brood as is a bokeler° or a targe;° — *shields*
A foot-mantel° aboute hir hipes large, — *outer skirt*
And on hir feet a paire of spores° sharpe. — *spurs*
In felawschipe wel coude she laughe and carpe.° — *talk*
475 Of remedyes of love she knew per chaunce,° — *as it happened*
For she coude° of that art the olde daunce.° — *knew (steps of the) dance*

    A good man was ther of religioun,
And was a povre PERSOUN° of a toun, — *poor parson*
But riche he was of holy thoght and werk.
480 He was also a lerned man, a clerk,° — *scholar*
That Cristes gospel trewely wolde preche;
His parisshens° devoutly wolde he teche. — *parishioners*
Benigne° he was, and wonder° diligent, — *Kindly / very*
And in adversitee ful pacient,
485 And swich he was y-preved ofte sythes.[72]
Ful looth° were him to cursen° for his tithes, — *loath / excommunicate*
But rather wolde he yeven,° out of doute,° — *give / there is no doubt*
Unto his povre parisshens aboute
Of° his offring, and eek of his substaunce.° — *From / income*
490 He coude in litel thing han suffisaunce.[73]
Wyd was his parisshe, and houses fer asonder,
But he ne lafte° nat, for reyn ne° thonder, — *ceased / nor*
In siknes nor in meschief° to visyte — *misfortune*
The ferreste in his parisshe, muche and lyte,[74]
495 Upon his feet, and in his hand a staf.
This noble ensample° to his sheep he yaf,° — *example / gave*
That first he wroghte,° and afterward he taughte. — *did (what was right)*
Out of the gospel he tho° wordes caughte,° — *those / took*
And this figure° he added eek therto, — *metaphor, image*
500 That if gold ruste, what shal iren° do? — *iron*
For if a preest be foul,° on whom we truste, — *corrupted*
No wonder is a lewed man to ruste;[75]
And shame it is, if a preest take keep,° — *heed (it)*
A shiten° shepherde and a clene sheep. — *i.e., covered with excrement*
505 Wel oghte a preest ensample for to yive,° — *give*
By his clennesse, how that his sheep sholde live.
He sette nat his benefice to hyre,[76]

And leet° his sheep encombred in the myre, — left
And ran to London unto Seynte Poules° — St. Paul's cathedral
510 To seken him a chaunterie for soules,
Or with a bretherhed to been withholde,[77]
But dwelte at hoom, and kepte° wel his folde, — took care of
So that the wolf ne made it nat miscarie;° — come to harm
He was a shepherde and noght a mercenarie.
515 And though he holy were, and vertuous,
He was to sinful men nat despitous,° — scornful
Ne of his speche daungerous ne digne,° — haughty nor disdainful
But in his teching discreet and benigne.
520 To drawen folk to heven by fairnesse,
By good ensample, this was his bisinesse;° — endeavor
But it were° any persone obstinat, — were there
What so° he were, of heigh or lough estat,° — Whatever / condition, class
Him wolde he snibben° sharply for the nones.° — rebuke / on such an occasion
A bettre preest I trowe° that nowher noon is. — believe
525 He wayted after° no pompe and reverence, — looked for
Ne maked him a spyced conscience,[78]
But Cristes lore,° and his apostles twelve, — teaching
He taughte, and first he folwed it himselve.
With him ther was a PLOWMAN, was his brother,
530 That hadde y-lad° of dong° many a fother.° — hauled / dung / cartload
A trewe swinkere° and a good was he, — worker
Livinge in pees° and parfit charitee. — peace
God loved he best with al his hole° herte — whole
At alle tymes, thogh him gamed or smerte,[79]
535 And thanne his neighebour right as himselve.
He wolde thresshe, and therto dyke° and delve,° — make ditches / dig
For Cristes sake, for every povre wight,° — poor man
Withouten hyre,° if it lay in his might.° — wages / power
His tythes° payed he ful faire and wel, — tithes
540 Bothe of his propre swink° and his catel.° — own work / possessions
In a tabard° he rood upon a mere.° — smock / mare
Ther was also a Reve° and a Millere, — Reeve
A Somnour° and a Pardoner also, — Summoner
A Maunciple,° and myself—ther were namo.° — Manciple / no more
545 The MILLERE was a stout carl° for the nones;[80] — exceedingly strong man
Ful big he was of brawn, and eek of bones—
That proved wel, for over al ther he cam,

At wrastling he wolde have alwey the ram.[81]

He was short-sholdred, brood, a thikke knarre:°   *knotty fellow*

550   Ther nas no dore that he nolde heve of harre,[82]

Or breke it at a renning° with his heed.   *(by butting it)*

His berd as any sowe or fox was reed,

And therto brood, as though it were a spade.

Upon the cop right° of his nose he hade   *very top*

555   A werte,° and theron stood a tuft of herys,   *wart*

Reed as the bristles of a sowes erys;°   *ears*

His nosethirles° blake were and wyde.   *nostrils*

A swerd and a bokeler° bar he by his syde.   *small shield*

His mouth as greet° was as a greet forneys;°   *large / furnace*

560   He was a janglere° and a goliardeys,°   *chatterer / teller of jests*

And that was most of sinne and harlotryes.°   *vulgarities*

Wel coude he stelen corn, and tollen thryes,[83]

And yet he hadde a thombe of gold, pardee.[84]

A whyt cote and a blew hood wered° he.   *wore*

565   A baggepype wel coude he blowe and sowne,°   *play*

And therwithal° he broghte us out of towne.   *with it*

    A gentil° MAUNCIPLE was ther of a temple,[85]   *worthy, proper*

Of which° achatours° mighte take exemple   *From whom / buyers*

For to be wyse in bying of vitaille,°   *provisions*

570   For whether that he payde, or took by taille,°   *on account*

Algate he wayted so in his achat[86]

That he was ay biforn° and in good stat.   *always ahead*

Now is nat that of God a ful fair grace,

That swich a lewed° mannes wit shal pace°   *unlearned / surpass*

575   The wisdom of an heep of lerned men?

Of maistres hadde he mo° than thryes ten   *more*

That weren of° lawe expert and curious,°   *in / skillful*

Of which° ther were a doseyn° in that hous   *Among whom / dozen*

Worthy to been stiwardes of rente° and lond   *income*

580   Of any lord that is in Engelond,

To make him live by his propre good°   *within his own income*

In honour, dettelees,° but° he were wood,°   *debtless / unless / mad*

Or live as scarsly as him list desire,[87]

And[88] able for to helpen al a shire°   *an entire county*

585   In any cas° that mighte falle° or happe;   *eventually / befall*

And yit this maunciple sette hir aller cappe.°   *made fools of them all*

    The REVE was a sclendre colerik man.[89]

His berd was shave as ny° as ever he can;   *close*

His heer was by his eres° ful round y-shorn,°   *ears / cut off*

590 His top was dokked° lyk a preest biforn.°   *cut short / in front*

Ful longe were his legges, and ful lene,

Ylyk° a staf; ther was no calf y-sene.°   *Like / to be seen*

Wel coude he kepe a gerner° and a binne—   *granary*

Ther was noon auditour coude on him winne.°   *catch him short*

595 Wel wiste° he by the droghte and by the reyn   *knew*

The yeldinge of his seed and of his greyn.

His lordes sheep, his neet,° his dayerye,°   *cattle / dairy cows*

His swyn, his hors, his stoor,° and his pultrye,°   *livestock / poultry*

Was hoolly° in this reves governinge,   *wholly*

600 And by his covenaunt° yaf° the rekeninge,   *contract / (he) gave*

Sin that° his lord was twenty yeer of age.   *Since*

Ther coude no man bringe him in arrerage.°   *arrears*

Ther nas bailiff, ne herder, ne other hyne,[90]

That he ne knew his sleighte° and his covyne;°   *cunning / deceit*

605 They were adrad° of him as of the deeth.[91]   *afraid*

His woning° was ful fair upon an heeth;   *dwelling*

With grene trees shadwed was his place.

He coude bettre than his lord purchase.[92]

Ful riche he was astored prively;°   *privately stocked*

610 His lord wel coude he plesen subtilly,

To yeve and lene him of his owne good,

And have a thank, and yet a cote and hood.[93]

In youthe he hadde lerned a good mister:°   *trade*

He was a wel good wrighte,° a carpenter.   *craftsman*

615 This reve sat upon a ful good stot°   *farm horse*

That was al pomely° grey and highte° Scot.   *dappled / named*

A long surcote° of pers° upon he hade,   *outer coat/blue cloth*

And by his syde he bar° a rusty blade.   *bore*

Of Northfolk° was this reve of which I tell,   *Norfolk*

620 Bisyde° a toun men clepen° Baldeswelle.   *(From) near / call*

Tukked° he was as is a frere° aboute;   *Belted / friar*

And evere he rood the hindreste° of oure route.°   *hindmost / company*

A SOMONOUR[94] was ther with us in that place,

That hadde a fyr-reed cherubinnes face,[95]

625 For sawcefleem° he was, with eyen° narwe.   *pimpled / eyes*

As hoot° he was and lecherous as a sparwe,°   *passionate / sparrow*

With scalled° browes blake, and piled berd;°   *scabby / scraggy beard*

Of his visage° children were aferd.° — *face / afraid*
Ther nas quiksilver, litarge,° ne brimstoon, — *lead oxide*
630 Boras,° ceruce,° ne oille° of tartre noon, — *Borax / white lead / cream*
Ne oynement that wolde dense and byte,° — *sting*
That him mighte helpen of° his whelkes° whyte, — *cure / pimples*
Nor of the knobbes° sittinge on his chekes. — *lumps*
Wel loved he garleek, oynons, and eek lekes,° — *leeks*
635 And for to drinken strong wyn, reed as blood.
Thanne wolde he speke, and crye° as° he were wood;° — *shout / as if / mad*
And whan that he wel dronken hadde the wyn,
Thanne wolde he speke no word but Latyn.° — *(in) Latin*
A fewe termes° hadde he, two or three, — *technical phrases*
640 That he had lerned out of som decree—
No wonder is,° he herde it al the day; — *it is*
And eek ye knowen wel how that a jay° — *a chattering bird*
Can clepen "Watte" as well as can the Pope.[96]
But whoso coude in other thing him grope,° — *question*
645 Thanne hadde he spent° al his philosophye; — *exhausted*
Ay *"Questio quid iuris"* wolde he crye;[97]
was a gentil° harlot° and a kinde;° — *worthy / rascal / natural one*
A bettre felawe° sholde men noght finde: — *companion*
He wolde suffre,° for a quart of wyn, — *allow*
650 A good felawe to have his concubyn
A° twelf-month, and excuse him atte fulle;° — *(For) a / fully*
Ful prively a finch eek coude he pulle.[98]
And if he fond° owher° a good felawe, — *found / anywhere*
He wolde techen him to have non awe° — *fear*
655 In swich cas of the erchedeknes curs,[99]
But-if° a mannes soule were in his purs, — *Unless*
For in his purs he sholde y-punisshed be.
"Purs is the erchedeknes helle," seyde he.
But wel I woot° he lyed right in dede: — *know*
660 Of cursing oghte ech gilty man him drede—
For curs wol slee, right as assoilling saveth—
and also war him of a significavit.[100]
In daunger° hadde he at° his owene gyse° — *his power / in / way*
The yonge girles° of the diocyse, — *wenches*
665 And knew his counseil° and was al hir reed.° — *their secrets / adviser to them all*
A gerland° hadde he set upon his heed, — *garland*
As greet as it were for an ale-stake;° — *tavern sign*

19

A bokeler° hadde he maad him of a cake.° — *shield / round bread*
    With him ther rood a gentil PARDONER[101]

670 Of Rouncival,[102] his freend and his compeer,° — *companion*
That streight was comen fro the court of Rome.
Ful loude he song,° "Com hider,° love, to me." — *sang / hither*
This somnour bar to° him a stif burdoun,° — *accompanied / sturdy bass*
Was nevere trompe° of half so greet a soun.° — *trumpet / sound*

675 This pardoner hadde heer° as yelow as wex,° — *hair / wax*
But smothe it heng,° as dooth a strike of flex;° — *hung / bunch of flax*
By ounces° henge his lokkes that he hadde, — *In thin strands*
And therwith° he his shuldres overspradde;° — *with it / covered*
But thinne it lay, by colpons° oon and oon; — *in small bunches*

680 But hood, for jolitee,° wered° he noon, — *sportiveness / wore*
For it was trussed° up in his walet.° — *packed / pouch*
Him thoughte he rood al of the newe jet;
Dischevele, save his cappe, he rood al bare.[103]
Swiche glaringe eyen° hadde he as an hare. — *staring eyes*

685 A vernicle[104] hadde he sowed on his cappe.
His walet lay biforn° him in his lappe, — *in front of*
Bretful of pardoun comen from Rome al hoot.[105]
A voys he hadde as smal as hath a goot.° — *goat*
No berd hadde he, ne nevere sholde have,

690 As smothe it was as it were late shave:° — *recently shaved*
I trowe° he were a gelding or a mare. — *believe*
But of his craft, fro Berwik into Ware,° — *i.e., from north to south*
Ne was ther swich another pardoner.
For in his male° he hadde a pilwe-beer,° — *bag / pillowcase*

695 Which that he seyde was Oure Lady veyl.° — *Our Lady's veil*
He seyde he hadde a gobet° of the seyl° — *piece / sail*
That seynt Peter hadde, whan that he wente° — *walked*
Upon the see, til Jesu Christ him hente.° — *took hold of*
He hadde a croys° of latoun,° ful of stones,° — *cross / metal / gems*

700 And in a glas° he hadde pigges bones. — *glass container*
But with thise relikes,° whan that he fond — *relics*
A povre person dwellinge upon lond,[106]
Upon a° day he gat him more moneye — *In one*
Than that the person gat in monthes tweye.° — *two*

705 And thus, with feyned flaterye and japes,° — *tricks*
He made the person and the peple his apes.° — *fools*
But trewely to tellen, atte laste,° — *after all*

He was in chirche a noble ecclesiaste.° *preacher*
Wel coude he rede a lessoun or a storie,° *religious tale*
710 But alderbest° he song° an offertorie; *best of all / sang*
For wel he wiste,° whan that song was songe, *knew*
He moste preche, and wel affyle° his tonge *make smooth*
To winne silver, as he ful wel coude—
Therefore he song the murierly° and loude. *more merrily*
715   Now have I told you soothly, in a clause,° *briefly*
Th'estaat, th'array, the nombre, and eek the cause
Why that assembled was this compaignye
In Southwerk, at this gentil° hostelrye, *worthy*
That highte° the Tabard, faste° by the Belle.° *was called / close / Bell Inn*
720 But now is tyme to yow for to telle
How that we baren us° that ilke° night, *conducted ourselves / same*
Whan we were in that hostelrye alight;° *alighted*
And after wol I telle of our viage,° *journey*
And al the remenaunt° of oure pilgrimage. *remainder*
725 But first I pray yow, of youre curteisye,
That ye n'arette it nat my vileinye,[107]
Thogh that° I pleynly speke in this matere, *Even though*
To tell yow hir° wordes and hir chere,° *their / behavior*
Ne thogh I speke hir wordes properly.° *exactly*
730 For this ye knowen al so wel as I:
Whoso shal telle a tale after a man,[108]
He moot reherce° as ny° as evere he can *must repeat / closely*
Everich a word, if it be in his charge,
Al speke he never so rudeliche and large;[109]
735 Or elles° he moot° telle his tale untrewe,
Or feyne thing,° or finde wordes newe.
He may nat spare,° althogh he[110] were his brother;
He moot° as wel seye o° word as another.
Crist spak himself ful brode° in Holy Writ,
740 And wel ye woot,° no vileinye° is it,
Eek Plato seith, whoso can him rede,
The wordes mote be cosin° to the dede.
Also I prey yow to foryeve° it me,
Al have I nat set folk in hir degree[111]
745 Here in this tale, as that they sholde stonde;
My wit is short, ye may wel understonde.
Greet there made oure Hoste us everichon,[112]

21

And to the soper sette he us anon;°	
He served us with vitaille° at the beste.	
750 Strong was the wyn, and wel to drinke us leste.°	
A semely° man oure hoste was withalle	
For to been a marshal in an halle;[113]	
A large man he was with eyen stepe°—	
A fairer burgeys° was ther noon in Chepe.°	
755 Bold of his speche, and wys, and wel y-taught,	
And of manhod him lakkede° right naught.	*he lacked*
Eek therto he was right° a mery man,	*truly*
And after soper pleyen° he bigan,	*to jest*
And spak of mirthe amonges othere thinges—	
760 Whan that we hadde maad oure rekeninges°—	*paid our bills*
And seyde thus: "Now, lordinges, trewely,	
Ye been° to me right welcome hertely.°	*are / heartily*
For by my trouthe, if that I shal nat lye,	
I saugh nat this yeer so mery a compaignye	
765 Atones° in this herberwe° as is now.	*At one time / inn*
Fayn wolde I doon yow mirthe, wiste I how,	
And of a mirthe I am right now bithoght,[114]	
To doon yow ese,° and it shal coste noght.	*give you pleasure*
Ye goon° to Caunterbury—God yow spede;	*are going*
770 The blisful martir quyte° yow your mede.°	*pay / reward*
And wel I woot, as ye goon by the weye,	
Ye shapen yow to talen and to pleye;[115]	
For trewely, confort° ne mirthe is noon°	*pleasure / (there) is none*
To ryde by the weye doumb as a stoon;	
775 And therfore wol I maken yow disport,°	*amusement*
As I seyde erst,° and doon yow som confort.	*before*
And if yow lyketh° alle, by oon° assent,	*it pleases you / one*
Now for to stonden at° my jugement,	*abide by*
And for to werken° as I shal yow seye,	*do*
780 To-morwe, whim ye ryden by the weye—	
Now by my fader° soule that is deed—	*father's*
But° ye be merye, I wol yeve° yow myn heed.°	*Unless / give / head*
Hold up youre hondes, withouten more speche."	
Oure counseil° was nat longe for to seche;°	*decision / seek*
785 Us thoughte it was noght worth to make it wys,[116]	
And graunted him withouten more avys,°	*further consideration*
And bad him seye his voirdit° as him leste.°	*verdict / it pleased him*

"Lordinges," quod° he, "now herkneth° for the beste,   *said / listen*
But tak it nought, I prey yow, in desdeyn.°   *disdain*
790   This is the poynt, to speken short and pleyn:
That ech of yow, to shorte with° oure weye,   *with which to shorten*
In this viage° shal telle tales tweye,°   *journey / two*
To Caunterbury-ward,° I mene° it so,   *toward Canterbury / intend*
And homeward he shal tellen othere two,
795   Of aventures that whylom° han bifalle.   *once upon a time*
And which° of yow that bereth° him best of alle,   *whichever / conducts*
That is to seyn, that telleth in this cas°   *on this occasion*
Tales of best sentence° and most solas,°   *wisdom, instruction / delight*
Shal have a soper at oure tiller cost°   *the expense of us all*
800   Here in this place, sittinge by this post,°   *column*
Whan that we come agayn fro Caunterbury.
And for to make yow the more mery,°   *merry*
I wol myselven goodly° with yow ryde,   *gladly*
Right at myn owne cost, and be youre gyde.
805   And whoso wole my jugement withseye°   *oppose*
Shal paye al that we spenden by the weye.
And if ye vouchesauf° that it be so,   *grant*
Tel me anon,° withouten wordes mo,°   *immediately / more*
And I wol erly shape me° therfore."   *prepare myself*
810   This thing was graunted, and oure othes° swore°   *oaths / sworn*
With ful glad herte, and preyden° him also   *we begged*
That he wolde vouchesauf for° to do so,   *grant*
And that he wolde been oure governour
And of oure tales juge and reportour,°   *referee(?)*
815   And sette a soper at a certeyn prys;°   *price*
And we wol reuled been at his devys°   *desire, will*
In heigh and lowe;° and thus, by oon assent,   *In all respects*
We been acorded to his jugement.
And therupon the wyn was fet° anon;°   *fetched / at once*
820   We dronken, and to reste wente echon,°   *each one*
Withouten any lenger taryinge.
    Amorwe,° whan that day bigan to springe,   *In the morning*
Up roos oure Host and was oure aller cok,[117]
And gadrede° us togidre,° alle in a flok;   *gathered / together*
825   And forth we riden,° a° litel more than pas,°   *rode / at a / walking speed*
Unto the watering of Seint Thomas,[118]
And there oure Host bigan his hors areste,°   *stopped his horse*

And seyde, "Lordinges, herkneth, if yow leste.°   *it may please*
Ye woot° youre forward,° and I it yow recorde.°   *know / agreement / recall*
830   If even-song and morwe-song° acorde,   *morning song*
Lat se° now who shal telle the firste tale.   *Let us see*
As evere mote° I drinke wyn or ale,   *may*
Whoso be rebel to my jugement
Shal paye for al that by the weye is spent.
835   Now draweth cut,° er that we ferrer twinne;°   *lots, cut straws / go farther*
He which that hath the shortest shal biginne.
Sire Knight," quod he; "my maister and my lord,
Now draweth cut for that is myn acord.°   *decision*
Cometh neer,"° quod he, "my lady Prioresse;   *nearer*
840   And ye, sire Clerk, lat be° youre shamfastnesse,°   *leave off / shyness*
Ne studieth° noght. Ley hond to, every man!"   *deliberate*
Anon° to drawen every wight° bigan,   *At once / person*
And shortly for to tellen as it was,
Were it by aventure,° or sort,° or cas,°   *chance / fate / fortune*
845   The sothe° is this, the cut fit° to the Knight,   *truth / fell*
Of which ful blythe and glad was every wight;
And telle he moste° his tale, as was resoun,°   *must / right*
By forward° and by composicioun,°   *agreement / arrangement*
As ye han herd. What nedeth wordes mor   *more*
850   And whan this gode man saugh it was so,
As he that wys was and obedient
To kepe his forward by his free assent,
He seyde: "Sin° I shal biginne the game,   *Since*
What,° welcome be the cut, a Goddes° name!   *Why / in God's*
855   Now lat us ryde, and herkneth what I seye."
And with that word we riden° forth oure weye;   *rode*
And he bigan with right a mery chere°   *in a very merry mood*
His tale anon, and seyde as ye may heere.

Endnotes

1. Has run his half-course in the Ram; i.e., has passed through half the zodiacal sign of Aries (the Ram), a course completed on April 11. A rhetorically decorative way of indicating the time of year.
2. Nature so spurs them in their hearts.
3. And pilgrims to seek foreign shores.
4. Thomas Becket, archbishop of Canterbury murdered in 1170 and canonized shortly thereafter. The place of his martyrdom was the greatest shrine in England and much visited by pilgrims.

5. It seems to me reasonable (proper).

6. Character, estate, condition.

7. Fidelity, honor, generosity of spirit, and courtesy (the central, chivalric virtues).

8. He had been on campaigns in Lithuania and in Russia.

9. Tournaments fought to the death.

10. A lover and a vigorous young man, one preparing to become a knight.

11. With locks as curly as if they'd been pressed (by a curling iron).

12. And conducted himself well, considering his inexperience.

13. He was courteous, humble, and willing to be of service.

14. He [the Knight] had a Yeoman [a servant one step above a groom in rank; this one seems to be a forester] with him, and no other servants.

15. i.e., in the English fashion, as it was spoken at Stratford at the Bow—a suburb some two miles east of London and home of the Benedictine nunnery of St. Leonard's.

16. She knew well how to raise a portion (to her lips) and take care.

17. A string of beads (a rosary), its groups marked off by special stones, called "gauds," of green.

18. The letter A with a symbolic crown fashioned above it.

19. A priory or dependent house.

20. An elaborate knot symbolizing true love.

21. That gleamed like a furnace (a fire) under a cauldron.

22. One licensed to beg within a certain region or limit.

23. The four orders of friars (Franciscan, Dominican, Carmelite, and Augustinian).

24. i.e., he gave them dowries out of his own funds, perhaps after having first seduced them himself.

25. With rich landholders everywhere in his region.

26. Wherever he knew (that he could expect) to have a good gift in return.

27. At narrative songs, he absolutely took the prize.

28. Better than a leper or beggar woman.

29. It was not fitting, considering his position.

30. His profit from begging was much greater than "his regular income," or "the fee he paid for his exclusive begging rights." (Meaning uncertain.)

31. And he knew how to play and flirt as if he were a puppy.

32. A religious who knows only the enclosed life of the cloister.

33. He lisped a little, out of affectation.

34. On a high saddle.

35. He wanted the sea to be guarded (against pirates) at any cost. (His profits depended on it.)

36. Who had long since proceeded to (the study of) logic in the university curriculum.

37. With a pun on alchemist, another meaning of the word.

38. And busily did pray for the souls.

39. The porch of St. Paul's Cathedral, a favorite gathering place for lawyers.

40. i.e., he always got unrestricted possession ("fee simple") of the property.

41. He knew the exact terms (details) of all the cases and decisions.

42. i.e., since the Norman Conquest (1066).

43. In the morning he dearly loved a sop (a piece of bread or cake) in wine.

44. A Greek philosopher who held that pleasure was the highest good.

45. The patron saint of hospitality.

46. Most tables were made of boards laid on trestles and were taken down after each meal; this one seems to have been permanent.

47. i.e., he presided over meetings of local justices of the peace when they gathered to hear cases.

48. Member of Parliament for his county.

49. The dais (a raised platform) on which the mayor or alderman of a city sat.

50. And go to church vigils at the head of the procession.

51. Both are spices, one tart and one sweet.

52. An elaborate dish of chicken in a sweet milk-and-rice sauce.

53. There was a shipmaster, dwelling far off to the west.

54. He rode on a small sturdy horse, as (well as) he knew how. (A man more used to ships than horses.)

55. On the way from Bordeaux, while the (wine-) merchant slept.

56. But at his craft, in calculating well the tides.

57. From Hull (in England) to Carthage (in northern Africa) or possibly Cartagena (in Spain).

58. Prudent in the risks he undertook.

59. From Gotland (an island in the Baltic Sea) to Cape Finisterre (in Spain).

60. During those hours (best for treatment) through his knowledge of natural magic (i.e., astrology).

61. He knew well how to determine the most favorable position of the stars for (making astrological) images for his patient.

62. The four fundamental qualities which were thought to combine in pairs to form the four elements and the four humors (melancholia, cholera, phlegm, and blood); bodily health depended upon the existence of a proper equilibrium among them.

63. i.e., pharmacists.

64. A list of the best medical authorities, ancient and modern (e.g., John of Gaddesden, an Englishman, died ca. 1349).

65. Doctors were often held to be skeptical in religious matters.

66. With linings of taffeta and fine silk.

67. He kept what he had earned during time of plague, for gold in medicine is good for the heart. (An ironic reference to *aurum potabile*, a liquid medicine compounded of gold and held to be a sovereign remedy for disease.)

68. Cloth-making in the Low Countries (here represented by Ypres and Ghent) was of high repute.

69. The medieval marriage ceremony was customarily performed by the priest on the church porch. Afterward the company entered the church to hear the nuptial mass.

70. She had crossed many a foreign river.

71. In Galicia (in Spain) at (the shrine of) St. James of Compostella, and at Cologne.

72. And he was proved (to be) such many times.

73. He knew how to have enough in very little.

74. The furthest (members) of his parish, great and humble.

75. It is no wonder that an unlearned man (should go) to rust.

76. He did not hire out (i.e., engage a substitute for) his benefice (church appointment).

77. To seek for himself an appointment as a chantry-priest singing masses for the souls of the dead or to be retained (as a chaplain) by a guild. (Both sorts of positions were relatively undemanding and paid enough for such a priest to retain a curate at home and have money to spare.)

78. Nor affected an overly scrupulous nature.

79. At all times, whether he was glad or in distress.

80. A tag-ending, useful to fill out the line metrically but almost wholly devoid of meaning (cf. 1. 523).

81. That (was) well proved for everywhere he went, at wrestling contests he would always win the ram (a usual prize).

82. There was no door he wasn't willing to heave off (its) hinges.

83. He knew well how to steal corn (grain) and take his toll (his percentage for grinding it) three times over.

84. The proverb "An honest miller hath a golden thumb" implies there are no honest millers; "pardee" is a weak form of "by God" (Fr. *par Dieu*), perhaps best translated simply as "I swear."

85. A manciple was in charge of purchasing provisions for a college or (as here) for an inn of court, where law was studied.

86. He was always so watchful in his purchasing.

87. Or live as frugally as it pleases him to wish.

88. The subject is again the "doseyn" men of 1. 578 worthy to be stewards.

89. A reeve was manager and accountant of an estate or manor and was chosen from among the serfs. This one is choleric, i.e., dominated by the humor called choler (or yellow bile), and thus hot-tempered by nature.

90. There was no overseer, nor herdsman, nor (any) other servant.

91. Death in general, or perhaps the Black Death (plague).

92. He knew, better than his lord, how to increase one's possessions.

93. He knew well how to please his lord in sly ways, giving and lending to him from his (the lord's) own resources, and earn thanks (for it) and a coat and hood besides.

94. A summoner was an officer who cited ("summoned") malefactors to appear before an ecclesiastical court: in this case, an archdeacon's, having jurisdiction over matrimonial cases, adultery, and fornication.

95. Cherubim, the second order of angels, were sometimes painted brilliant red ("fire-red") in medieval art. The summoner resembles them, not through beatitude but through a skin disease.

96. Knows how to say "Walter" as well as does the Pope.

97. He would always cry, "The question is, what point of law applies?"

98. He was skilled in secretly seducing girls. ("To pull a finch," i.e., to pluck a bird, was an obscene expression.)

99. Curse, the power of excommunication.

100. Every guilty man ought to be fearful of excommunication, for it will slay (the soul eternally), just as absolution (the forgiveness granted through the sacrament of penance) saves—and (he ought) also beware a *significavit* (a writ of arrest).

101. A pardoner was a seller of papal indulgences (remissions of punishment for sin), whose proceeds were often intended to build or support a religious house. Many pardoners were fraudulent, and their abuses were much criticized.

102. Near Charing Cross in London.

103. It seemed to him he rode in the very latest fashion; (his hair) loose, he rode bareheaded except for his cap.

104. A copy of the veil St. Veronica gave to Christ when He was carrying the cross, that He might wipe His brow; it received the imprint of Christ's face.

105. Brimful of pardons, come all hot (fresh) from Rome.

106. A poor parson living in the country.

107. That you do not attribute it to my churlishness.

108. I.e., repeats another man's story.

109. Every word, if that be the responsibility he's charged with, however roughly and broadly he (may) speak.

110. I.e., the original teller.

111. Although I haven't described (these) people in (the order of) their social rank.

112. Our host made great welcome to every one of us.

113. i.e., the officer in charge of the serving of meals and banquets in a great hall.

114 I would gladly make you (some) amusement if I knew how, and I have just now thought of some fun.

115. You plan to tell tales and to play.

116. It seemed to us (that) it was not worth pondering over.

117. The rooster who wakened us all.

118. St. Thomas a Watering was a brook two miles from London on the Canterbury road.

THE PRIORESS'S PROLOGUE AND TALE

The Introduction

435   "Well seyd, by *corpus dominus,*°" quod° oure Hoste,   *the Lord's body / said*

    "Now longe moot° thou sayle by the coste,°   *may / sail along the coast*

    Sire gentil maister, gentil mariner[1]

    God yeve this monk a thousand last quad yeer![2]

    A ha! felawes!° beth ware of swiche° a jape!°   *companions / such / trick*

440   The monk putte in the mannes hood an ape,[3]

    And in his wyves eek,° by Seint Austin!°   *as well / Augustine*

    Draweth° no monkes more unto youre in.°   *Take / lodging*

    But now passe over,° and lat us seke aboute,   *on*

    Who shal now telle first, of al this route,°   *company*

445   Another tale;" and with that word he sayde,

    As curteisly as it had been a mayde,[4]

    "My lady Prioresse, by your leve,

    So that I wiste° I sholde yow nat greve,°   *knew / vex*

    I wolde demen° that ye tellen sholde   *would decide*

450   A tale next, if so were that ye wolde.°   *were willing*

    Now wol ye vouche saut° my lady dere?"   *agree*

        "Gladly," quod she, and seyde as ye shal here.

The Prologue

        Domine, dominus noster.°   *Oh Lord, our lord*

      O Lord, oure Lord, thy name hew merveillous°   *marvelously*

    Is in this large world y-sprad°—quod° she—   *spread / said*

455   For noght only thy laude° precious   *praise*

    Parfourned° is by men of dignitee,   *Celebrated, performed*

    But by the mouth of children thy bountee°   *goodness*

    Parfourned is, for on the brest soukinge°   *sucking*

    Somtyme shewen° they thyn heryinge.°   *show forth / praise*

460   Wherfore in laude,° as I best can or may,   *praise*

    Of thee, and o the whyte lily flour°   *i.e., the Virgin*

    Which that thee bar,° and is a mayde° alway,   *Who bore thee/virgin*

    To telle a stone I wol do my labour;

    Not that I may encresen° hir honour,   *increase*

465   For she hirself is honour, and the rote°   *root*
         Of bountee, next° hir sone, and soules bote.°   *next (to) / help*

         O moder mayde! o mayde moder free!°   *gracious, bountiful*
         O bush unbrent, brenninge in Moyses sighte,[5]
         That ravysedest° doun fro the deitee,   *ravished*
470   Thurgh thyn humblesse, the goost° that in th'alighte,°   *(Holy) Spirit / alighted in thee*
         Of whos vertu, whan he thyn herte lighte,
         Conceived was the Fadres sapience,[6]
         Help me to telle it in thy reverence!
         Lady, thy bountee, thy magnificence,
475   Thy vertu, and thy grete humilitee,
         Ther may° no tonge expresse in no science;°   *can / whatever its learning*
         For somtyme, lady, er° men praye to thee,   *before*
         Thou goost biforn° of thy benignitee,   *proceedest*
         And getest us the light, of° thy preyere,   *by means of*
480   To gyden° us unto thy Sone so dere.   *guide*

         My conning° is so wayk,° o blisful Quene,   *skill / weak*
         For to declare thy grete worthinesse,
         That I ne may the weighte nat sustene;
         But as a child of twelf monthe old, or lesse,
485   That can unnethes° any word expresse,   *hardly*
         Right so fare I, and therfor I yow preye,
         Gydeth° my song that I shal of yow seye.   *Guide*

The Tale

         Ther was in Asie,° in a greet citee,   *Asia (Minor)*
         Amonges Cristen folk, a Jewerye°   *Jews' quarter*
490   Sustened by a lord of that contree
         For foule usure° and lucre of vileynye,°   *usury / wicked financial gain*
         Hateful to Crist and to his compaignye;°   *i.e., Christians*
         And thurgh° the strete men mighte ryde or wende,°   *through / go*
         For it was free, and open at either ende.

495   A litel scole° of Cristen° folk ther stood   *school / Christian*
         Doun at the ferther ende, in which ther were
         Children an heep,° y-comen° of Cristen blood,   *many, a crowd / come*
         That lerned in that scole yeer by yere

Swich manere doctrine as men used there—[7]
500 This is to seyn,° to singen and to rede,°   *say / read*
As smale children doon in hire childhede.

Among thise children was a widwes° sone,   *widow's*
A litel clergeoun,° seven yeer of age,   *schoolboy*
That day by day to° scole was his wone,°   *i.e., to go to / custom*
505 And eek also, where as° he saugh° th'ymage   *wherever / saw*
Of Cristes moder, hadde he in usage,°   *he was accustomed*
As him was taught, to knele adoun and seye
His *Ave Marie,*° as he goth by the weye.   *Hail, Mary*

Thus hath this widwe hir litel sone y-taught
510 Our blisful Lady, Cristes moder dere,
To worshipe ay;° and he forgat it naught,   *always*
For sely child wol alday sone lere.[8]
But ay,° whan I remembre° on this matere,   *ever / i.e., think, mediate*
Seint Nicholas[9] stant° evere in my presence,   *stands*
515 For he so yong to Crist did reverence.°   *honored*
This litel child, his litel book lerninge,
As he sat in the scole at his prymer,[10]
He *Alma redemptoris*[11] herde singe,
As children lerned hire antiphoner,°   *their anthem-book*
520 And, as he dorste, he drough him ner and ner,[12]
And herkned ay° the wordes and the note,°   *ever / music*
Til he the firste vers coude° al by rote.°   *knew / by heart*

Noght wiste° he what this Latin was to seye,°   *knew / meant*
For he so yong and tendre was of age;
525 But on a day his felaw gan he preye[13]
T'ex-pounden him this song in his langage,°   *his own language*
Or telle him why this song was in usage;°   *used*
This preyde he him to construe° and declare   *interpret*
Ful ofte tyme upon his knowes° bare.   *knees*

530 His felawe, which that elder was than he,
Answerde him thus: "This song, I have herd seye,
Was maked of° our blisful Lady free,°   *about / generous*
Hire to salue,° and eek° hire for to preye   *salute, greet / also*
To been oure help and socour° when we dye.°   *succor, aid / die*

31

535   I can no more expounde in this matere:

I lerne song, I can° but smal° grammere."   *know / little*

"And is this song maked in reverence

Of Cristes moder?" seyde this innocent.

"Now certes,° I wol do my diligence   *certainly*

540   To conne° it al, er° Cristemasse be went.°   *learn / before / is passed*

Though that I for my prymer[14] shal be shent,°   *scolded*

And shal be beten thryes° in an houre,   *thrice*

I wol it conne, oure Lady for to honoure."

His felaw taughte him homward prively,[15]

545   Fro day to day, til he coude° it by rote,   *knew*

And thanne he song° it wel and boldely°   *sang / forcefully*

Fro word to word, according with the note;

Twyes° a day it passed thurgh his throte,   *Twice*

To scoleward° and homward whan he wente.   *Toward school*

550   On Cristes moder set was his entente.°   *(heart's) intent*

As I have seyd, thurghout the Jewerye

This litel child, as he cam to and fro,

Ful merily than wolde he singe and crye°   *cry out*

O *Alma redemptoris* everemo.

555   The swetnesse his herte perced° so   *pierced*

Of Cristes moder, that, to hire to preye,

He can nat stinte of° singing by° the weye.   *cease from / along*

Oure firste fo,° the serpent Sathanas,°   *foe / Satan*

That hath in Jewes herte his waspes nest,

560   Up swal° and seide, "O Hebraik peple, alias!   *swelled*

Is this to yow a thing that is honest,°   *honorable, seemly*

That swich° a boy shal walken as him lest°   *such / it pleases him*

In youre despyt, and singe of swich sentence,[16]

Which is agayn° oure lawes reverence?"[17]   *against*

565   Fro thennes forth° the Jewes han° conspyred   *thenceforth / have*

This innocent out of this world to chace:°   *drive*

An homicyde° therto han they hyred,°   *murderer / hired*

That in an aley° hadde a privee° place;   *alley / secret*

And as the child gan forby for to pace,°   *was walking by*

570   This cursed Jew him hente° and heeld him faste,   *seized*
        And kitte° his throte, and in a pit him caste.   *cut*

        I seye that in a wardrobe° they him threwe   *privy*
        Where as these Jewes purgen hir entraille.[18]
        O cursed folk of Herodes° al newe,°   *Herod / always renewed*
575   What may youre yvel entente° yow availle?   *evil plan*
        Mordre° wol out, certein, it wol nat faille,   *Murder*

        And namely there° th'onour of God shal sprede,   *there where*
        The blood out cryeth on your cursed dede.

        O martir souded to° virginitee,   *made fast in*
580   Now maystou° singen, folwinge evere in oon°   *mayest thou / forever*
        The Whyte Lamb celestial—quod she—
        Of which the grete evangelist Seint John
        In Pathmos[19] wroot, which seith that they that goon°   *walk*
        Biforn° this Lamb and singe a song al newe,°   *Before / wholly new*
585   That nevere, fleshly,° wommen they ne knewe.   *carnally*

        This povre widwe° awaiteth al that night   *poor widow*
        After hir litel child, but he cam noght;
        For which, as sone as it was dayes light,
        With face pale of drede° and bisy thoght,°   *fear / anxiety*
590   She hath at scole and elleswhere him soght,
        Til finally she gan so fer espye°   *found out this much*
        That he last seyn° was in the Jewerye.   *seen*

        With modres pitee in hir brest enclosed,
        She gooth, as° she were half out of hir minde,   *as if*
595   To every place wher she hath supposed
        By lyklihede hir litel child to finde.
        And evere on Cristes moder meke and kinde
        She cryde, and atte laste thus she wroghte:[20]
        Among the cursed Jewes she him soghte.

600   She frayneth° and she preyeth° pitously   *inquires / begs*
        To every Jew that dwelte in thilke° place,   *that same*
        To telle hire if hir child wente oght forby.°   *by at all*
        They seyde "Nay"; but Jesu, of° his grace,   *by*

Yaf in hir thought, inwith a litel space,[21]

605   That° in that place after hir sone she cryde°   *So that / called*

Where he was casten in a pit bisyde.°   *nearby*

O grete God, that parfournest thy laude[22]

By mouth of innocents, lo heer° thy might!   *behold here*

This gemme of chas-titee, this emeraude,°   *emerald*

610   And eek° of martirdom the ruby bright,   *also*

Ther he with throte y-corven lay upright,[23]

He *Alma redemptoris* gan° to singe   *began*

So loude that al the place gan to ringe.°   *resounded*

The Cristen folk, that thurgh the strete wente,

615   In coomen° for to wondre upon this thing,   *came*

And hastily they for the provost° sente;   *magistrate*

He cam anon withouten tarying,

And herieth° Grist that is of heven king,   *praises*

And eek° his moder, honour of mankinde,   *also*

620   And after that the Jewes leet he binde.°   *he had bound*

This child with pitous lamentacioun

Up taken was, singing his song alway;

And with honour of greet processioun

They carien him unto the nexte abbay.°   *nearest abbey*

625   His moder swowning° by his bere° lay.   *swooning / bier*

Unnethe° might the peple that was there   *Scarcely*

This newe Rachel[24] bringe fro his bere.

With torment° and with shamful deth echon°   *torture / each one*

This provost dooth° thise Jewes for to sterve°   *causes / die*

630   That of this mordre wiste,° and that anon;°   *knew / immediately*

He nolde no swich cursednesse observe.[25]

"Yvel shal have that yvel wol deserve:"[26]

Therfore with wilde hors° he dide hem drawe,°   *horses / had them drawn, dragged*

And after that he heng° hem by the lawe.   *hanged (probably on pikes)*

635   Upon his bere al lyth° this innocent   *still lies*

Biforn the chief auter,° whyl the masse° laste,   *altar / the mass*

And after that, the abbot with his covent°   *monks*

Han sped hem° for to burien him ful faste;   *have hastened*
And whan they holy water on him caste,
640   Yet spak this child, whan spreynd° was holy water,   *sprinkled*
And song° *O Alma redemptoris mater!*   *sang*

This abbot, which that was an holy man
As monkes been°—or elks oghten° be—   *are / else ought to*
This yonge child to conjure° he bigan,   *entreat*
645   And seyde, "O dere child, I halse° thee,   *beg*
In vertu of the Holy Trinitee,
Tel me what is thy cause for to singe,
Sith that° thy throte is cut, to my seminge?"°   *Since / it seems to me*

"My throte is cut unto my nekke-boon,"
650   Seyde this child, "and, as by wey of kinde,°   *nature*
I sholde have deyed, ye,° longe tyme agoon,°   *yea, yes / ago*
But Jesu Crist, as ye in bokes finde,
Wil° that his glorie laste and be in minde;   *Wills*

And for the worship of his moder dere
655   Yet° mat I singe *O Alma* loude and clere.   *Still*

This welle° of mercy, Cristes moder swete,   *spring*
I lovede alwey as after my conninge;°   *as best I could*
And whan that I my lyf sholde forlete,°   *was to leave*
To me she cam, and bad me for to singe
660   This antem° verraily° in my deyinge,   *hymn / truly*
As ye han herd; and whan that I had songe,
Me thoughte she leyde a greyn° upon my tonge.   *seed*

Wherfore I singe, and singe moot certeyn,°   *indeed must*
In honour of that blisful mayden free,°   *generous*
665   Til fro my tonge of° taken is the greyn;   *off*
And afterward thus seyde she to me,
'My litel child now wol I fecche° thee   *fetch*
Whan that the greyn is fro thy tongue y-take;
Be nat agast,° I wol thee nat forsake.'"   *afraid*

670   This holy monk, this abbot, him mene I,
His tongue out caughte and took awey the greyn,

And he yaf° up the goost ful softely.   *gave*

And whan this abbot had this wonder seyn,°   *seen*

His salte teres° trikled doun as reyn,°   *tears / like rain*

675   And gruf° he fil al plat° upon the grounde,   *face downward / flat*

And stille° he lay as° he had been y-bounde.   *(as) quietly / as if*

The covent° eek° lay on the pavement,   *monks / also*

Weping and herying° Cristes moder dere,   *praising*

And after that they ryse, and forth ben went,°   *have gone*

680   And toke awey this martir fro his bere,°   *bier*

And in a tombe of marbulstones clere°   *bright, splendid*

Enclosen they his litel body swete.

Ther° he is now, God leve° us for to mete.°   *where / grant / meet*

O yonge Hugh of Lincoln,[27] slayn also

685   With° cursed Jewes, as it is notable°—   *By / well known*

For it nis° but a litel whyle ago—   *is not*

Preye eek° for us, we sinful folk unstable,°   *also / unsteadfast*

That, of his mercy, God so merciable°   *merciful*

On us his grete mercy multiplye,

690   For reverence of his moder Marye. Amen.

Endnotes

1. The Shipman has just told his tale of a merchant, his wife, and a lecherous monk.

2. God give this monk a thousand cartloads of bad years.

3. The monk put an ape in the man's hood, i.e., made a fool of him.

4. As courteously as if it had been a maiden (speaking).

5. Oh, bush unburned, burning in Moses's sight (a common figure for the miracle of Mary's virginity, preserved even in her motherhood of Christ; ultimately based on Exodus 3:1-5).

6. Through whose power, when he illumined thy heart, was conceived the Wisdom of the Father, i.e., Christ, the Logos.

7. Such kinds of subjects as were usual there.

8. For a good child will always learn quickly.

9. St. Nicholas is said to have fasted even as an infant; he took the breast only once on Wednesdays and Fridays. He is also the patron saint of schoolboys.

10. A prayerbook used as an elementary school text.

11. For text and translation of this anthem, see Norton critical edition of the Canterbury Tales, p. 448.

12. And, as (much as) he dared, he drew nearer and nearer.

13. But one day he begged his companion.

14. i.e., for failing to study my primer.
15. His companion taught him (on the way) homeward, privately.
16. In scorn of you, and sing of such a subject.
17. The best manuscripts read "oure," as here; some read "youre."
18. Where these Jews empty their bowels.
19. The isle of Patmos in Greece, where St. John wrote the Book of Revelation.
20. She called, and in the end she did thus.
21. Gave her an idea, within a little while.
22. Oh, great God, that (hast) thy praise performed.
23. There where he lay face-up, with his throat cut.
24. This second Rachel (a grieving Jewish mother, in Jeremiah 31:15, who was said to prefigure the grieving mothers of the innocents slain by command of Herod, in Matthew 2:18).
25. He would not tolerate such evil doings.
26. "He who will deserve evil shall have evil."
27. Hugh of Lincoln was thought to have been murdered by Jews in a similar fashion in 1255.

Isaac Barrow

From *The Duty and Reward of Bounty to the Poor*

Farther, before we deny our relief to our poor Neighbour, let us with the eyes of our mind look on him, and attentively consider who he is; what he is in himself, and what he is in relation unto us.

1. He whose need craves our bounty, whose misery demands our mercy, what is he? He is not truly so mean and sorry a thing, as the disguise of misfortune, under which he appears, doth represent him. He who looks so deformedly and dismally, who to outward sight is so ill bestead, and so pitifully accoustred, hath latent in him much of admirable beauty and glory; he within himself containeth a nature very excellent; an immortal soul, and an intelligent mind, by which he nearly resembleth God himself, and is comparable to Angels; he invisibly is owner of endowments, rendring him capable of the greatest and best things: What are Money and Lands? what are Silk and fine Linen? what are Horses and Hounds in comparison to Reason, to Wisdom, to Vertue, to Religion, which he hath, or (in despite of all misfortune) he may have, if he please? He whom you behold so dejectedly sneaking, in so despicable a garb, so destitute of all convenience and comfort, (lying in the dust, naked or clad with rags, meagre with hunger or pain) he comes of a most high and heavenly extraction; he was born a Prince, the Son of the greatest King Eternal; he can truly call the Sovereign Lord of all the World his Father; having derived his soul from the mouth, having had his body formed by the hands of God himself: (in this, *The rich and poor*, as the Wise-man faith, *do meet together; the Lord is the Maker of them all.*) That fame forlorn Wretch, whom we are so apt to despise and trample upon, was framed and constituted Lord of the visible World; had all the goodly brightnesses of Heaven, and all the costly furnitures of Earth created to serve him: *(Thou madest him,* saith the *Psalmist* of man) *to have dominion over the works of thine hands; thou hast put all things under his feet:)* Yea, he was made an inhabitant of Paradise, and Possessour of felicities superlative; had immortal life, and endless joy in his hand; did enjoy the entire favour and friendship of the most High: such in worth of Nature, and nobleness of Birth he is, as a man; and highly more considerable he is, as a Christian: for as vile and contemptible as he looks, God hath so regarded and prized him, as for his sake to descend from Heaven, to cloath himself with flesh, to assume the form of a servant; for his good to undertake and undergo the greatest inconveniencies, infirmities, wants and disgraces; the most grievous troubles, and most sharp pains incident to mortal nature; God hath adopted him to be his Child; the Son of God hath deigned to call him Brother; he is a Member of Christ, a Temple of the Holy Ghost, a free Denizon of the heavenly City; an Heir of Salvation, and Candidate of eternal Glory; the greatest and richest Personage is not capable of better priviledges, than God hath granted him, or of higher preferments, than God hath deigned him to: He equally with the mightiest Prince is the object of Gods especial Providence and Grace, of his continual regard and care, of his fatherly love and affection; who, as good *Elihu* saith, *accepteth not the persons of Princes, nor regardeth the rich more than the poor; for they are all the work of his hands.* In fine, this poor Creature whom thou seest, is a man, and a Christian, thine equal, whoever thou art, in

Published 1671, printed by Andrew Clark for Barabazon Aylmer, London.

nature, and thy peer in condition; I say not in the uncertain and unstable gifts of fortune, not in this worldly state, which is very inconsiderable; but in gifts vastly more precious, in title to an estate infinitely more rich and excellent: yea, if thou art vain and proud, he sober and humble, he is thy better, in true dignity much to be preferred before thee, far in real wealth surpassing thee: for, *better is the poor that walketh in his uprightness, than he that is perverse in his ways, though he be rich.*

2. That distinction, which thou standeth upon, and which seemeth so vast between thy poor Neighbour and thee, what is it? whence did it come? whither tends it? It is not any wise natural, or according to primitive design: for as all men are in faculties and endowments of nature equal, so were they all originally equal in condition, all wealthy and happy, all constituted in a most prosperous and plentiful estate; all things at first were promiscuously exposed to the use and enjoyment of all; every one from the common flock assuming as his own what he needed. Inequality and private interest in things, (together with sicknesses and pains, together with all other infelicities and inconveniences) were the by-blows of our fall; sin introduced these degrees and distances; it devised the names of rich and poor; it begot these ingrossings and enclosures of things; it forged those two small pestilent Words, *meum* and *tuum,* which have engendred so much strife among men, and created so much mischief in the world: these preternatural distinctions were (I say) brooded by our fault, and are in great part fostered and maintained thereby; for were we generally so good, so just, so charitable as we should be, they could hardly subsist, especially in that measure they do. God indeed (for promoting some good ends, and for prevention of some mischiefs, apt to spring from our ill nature in this our lapsed state; particularly to prevent the strife and disorder which scrambling would cause among men, presuming on equal right, and parity of force) doth suffer them in some manner to continue, and enjoins us a contented submission to them; but we mistake, if we think that natural equality and community are in effect quite taken away; or that all the world is so cantonized among some few, that the rest have no share therein; No, every man hath still a competent patrimony due to him, and a sufficient provision made for his tolerable subsistence; God hath brought no man hither to be necessarily starved, or pinched with extream want; but hath assigned to every one a Childs portion, in some fair way to be obtained by him, either by legal right, or by humble request, which according to Conscience ought to have effect. No man therefore is allowed to detain, or to destroy superfluously what another man apparently wants, but is obliged to impart it to him: so that rich men are indeed but the Treasurers, the Stewards, the Caterers of God for the rest of men, having a strict charge to *dispense unto every one his meat in due season,* and no just priviledge to withhold it from any: the honour of distribution is conferred on them, as a reward of their fidelity and care; the right of enjoyment is reserved to the poor, as a provision for their necessity. Thus hath God wisely projected, that all his Children should both effectually, and quietly be provided for; and that none of them should be oppressed with penury; so that (as St. Paul hath it) *One mans abundance should supply another mans want, that there may be an equality:* for since no man can enjoy more than he needs, and every every man should have so much as he needs, there can be really no great inequality among men; the distinction will scarce remain other where than in fancy. What the Philosopher said of himself, *What I have, is so mine, that it is every mans,* is according to the practice of each man, who is truly and in due measure charitable; whereby that seemingly enormous discrimination among men is well moderated, and the equity of Divine Providence is vindicated: But he that ravenously grasps far more than he can well use, and gripes it fast in his clutches, so that the needy in their distress cannot come by it, doth pervert that equity which God hath established in things, defeats his good intention, (so far as he can) and brings a scandal on his Providence and so doing is highly both injurious and impious.

3. It was also (which we should consider) even one main end of this difference among us, permitted and ordered by Gods Providence, that as some mens industry and patience might be exercised by their poverty, so other men by their wealth should have ability of practicing justice and charity; that so both rich and poor might thence become capable of recompences, suitable to the worth of such vertuous performances. Why *art thou rich,* (saith St. Basil) *and he poor? Surely for this; That thou mayst attain the reward of benignity, and faithful dispensation; and that he may be honoured with the great prize of patience.* God in making thee rich, would have thee to be a double benefactor, not only to thy poor Neighbour, but also to thy self; whilst thou bestowest relief on him, purchasing a reward to thy self. God also by this order of things designs, a charitable entercourse should be maintained among men, mutually pleasant and beneficial; the rich kindly obliging the poor, and the poor gratefully serving the rich. Wherefore by neglecting these duties, we unadvisedly cross the good purpose of God toward us, depriving ourselves of the chief advantages our wealth may afford.

4. We should also do well to consider, that a poor man, even as such, is not to be disregarded, and that poverty it self is no such contemptible thing as we may be prone to imagine: there are Considerations, which may qualifie Poverty even to dispute the place with Wealth, and to claim precedence to it: If the world vulgarly doth account, and call the rich man happy, a better Author hath pronounced the poor man such: *Blessed are the poor,* doth march in the van of the Beatitudes, and a reason goeth along therewith which asserteth its right to the place; *for theirs is the Kingdom of Heaven;* for that they are not only in an equal capacity as men, but in a nearer disposition as poor to the acquisition of that blissful state; for that poverty (the Mistress of Sobriety and honest Industry, the Mother of Humility and Patience, the Nurse of all Vertue) renders men more willing to go, and more expedite in the way toward Heaven: by it also we conform unto the Son of God himself, the Heir of Eternal Majesty, the Saviour of the World, *who for our sake became poor, (...) that we through his poverty* (or beggery) *might become rich:* he willingly chose, he especially dignified and sanctified that depth of poverty, which we so proudly slight and loath. The greatest Princes and Potentates in the World, the most wealthy and haughty of us all, but for one poor Beggar had been irrecoverably miserable: to Poverty it is, that every one of us doth owe all the possibility there is; all the hopes we can have of our Salvation; and shall we then ingratefully requite it with scorn, or with pitiless neglect? Shall we presume in the person of any poor man, to abhor or contemn the very poor, but most holy and most happy Jesus, our Lord and Redeemer? No; if we will do Poverty right, we must rather for his dear sake and memory defer an especial respect and veneration thereto.

5. Thus a due reflection on the poor man himself, his nature and state, will induce us to succour; but let us also consider him as related unto ourselves: Every such person is our near Kinsman, is our Brother, is by indissoluble bands of cognation in blood, and agreement in Nature knit and united to us. We are all but several streams issuing from one source, several twigs sprouting from one flock; *One blood,* derived through several channels; one substance, by miraculous efficacy of the Divine Benediction, multiplied or dilated unto several times and places. We are all fashioned according to the same original Idea, resembling God our common Father; we are all endewed with the same faculties, inclinations and affections; we all conspire in the same essential ingredients of our constitution, and in the more notable adjuncts thereof; it is only some inconsiderable accidents, (such as age, place, figure, stature, colour, garb) which diversifie and distinguish us; in which, according to successions of time and chance, we commonly no less differ from ourselves, than we do at present from them: so that in effect, and reasonable esteem, everyman is not only our Brother, but (as *Aristotle* faith of a Friend) ... *another ones self;* is not only our most lively image, but in a manner our very substance; another our self under a small variation of present circumstances: the most of distinction between us and our poor Neighbour, consists in exteriour shew, in moveable attire, in casual appendages to the nature of man; so that really when we use him well, we are kind to our selves, when we yield him courteous regard, we bear respect to our own nature; when we feed and comfort him, we do sustain and cherish a member of our own body: but when we are cruel or harsh to him, we abuse our selves; when we scorn him, we lay disparagement and disgrace on mankind it self; when we withhold succour or sustenance from him, we do (as the Prophet speaketh) *hide our selves from our own flesh;* we starve a part of our own body, and wither a branch of our flock: immoderate selfishness so blindeth us, that we oversee and forget our selves: it is in this, it is in other good senses true what the Wise-man saith, *The merciful man doth good to his own soul; but he that is cruel, troubleth his own flesh.*

6. Farther, as the poor man is so nearly allied to us by society of common nature, so is he more strictly joined to us by the bands of spiritual Consanguinity. All Christians (high and low, rich and poor) are children of the same heavenly Father, spring from the same incorruptible seed, are regenerated to the same lively hope, are Co-heirs of the same heavenly inheritance; are all members of one body, *(members, saith St. Paul, one of another)* and animated by one holy Spirit; which relation, as it is the most noble, and the most close that can be, so it should breed the greatest endearments, and should express itself in correspondent effects; it should render us full of affection and sympathy one toward another; it should make us to tender the needs, and feel the sufferings of any Christian as our own; it should dispose us freely to communicate whatever we have, how pretious soever, to any of our brethren: this holy friendship should establish a charitable equality and community among us, both in point of honour and of estate: for since all things considerable are common unto us, since we are all purchased and purified by the same precious blood, since we all partake of the same precious faith, of the same high calling, of the same honourable priviledges, of the same glorious promises and hopes since we all have the same Lord and Saviour; why should these secular trifles be so private and particular among us? Why should not so huge a parity in those only valuable things not wholly (I say not in worldly state, or outward appearance, such as the preservation of order in secular affairs requireth, but) in our opinion and affection extinguish that slight distinction of *rich* and *poor,* in concernments temporal? How can we slight so noble, so great a Personage as a Christian, for wanting a little dross? How can we deem our selves much his superiour, upon so petty an advantage, for having that, which is not worth speaking or thinking of, in comparison to what he enjoyeth? Our Lord himself is not ashamed to call the least among us his Brother, and his Friend; and shall we then disdain to yield to such an one the regard, and treatment suitable to such a Quality? Shall we not honour any Brother of our Lord? Shall we not be civil and kind to any Friend of his? If we do not, how can we pretend to bear any true respect or affection unto himself? It is his express precept, that the greatest among us should, in imitation of his most humble and charitable Self, be ready to serve the meanest; and, that we should *in honour prefer one another, and in lowliness of mind esteem others better than our selves,* are Apostolical Rules, extending indifferently to rich and poor, which are plainly violated by disregarding the poor. Yea, this relation should, according to *St. johns* Doctrine, dispose us not only freely to impart these temporal goods, but even, if occasion be, willingly to expose our very lives for our brethren: *Hereby,* saith he, *we perceive the love of God, because he laid down his life for us; and we ought to lay down our lives for our brethren.* How greatly then are they deficient from their duty, how little in truth are they Christians, who are unwilling to part with the very superfluities and excrements of their fortune for the relief of a poor Christian? Thus considering our Brother may breed in us charitable dispositions toward him, and induce us to the practice of these duties. Moreover, if we reflect upon our selves, and consider either our nature, or our state here, we cannot but observe many strong engagements to the same practice.

1. The very constitution, frame and temper of our nature, directeth and inclineth us thereto; whence by observing those duties, we observe our own nature, we improve it, we advance it to the best perfection it is capable of; by neglecting them, we thwart, we impair, we debase the same ...; The best of our natural inclinations (those sacred reliques of Gods image originally stamped on our minds) do sensibly prompt, and vehemently urge us to mercy and pity: the very same bowels, which in our own want do by a lively sense of pain inform us thereof, and instigate us to provide for its relief, do also grievously resent the distresses of another, admonishing us thereby, and provoking us to yield him succour. Such is the natural sympathy between men, (discernable in all, but appearing most vigorous in the best natures) that we cannot see, cannot hear of, yea can hardly imagine the calamities of other men, without being somewhat disturbed, and afflicted our selves. As also nature to the acts requisite toward preservation of our life, hath annexed a sensible pleasure forcibly enticing us to the performance of them: so hath she made the communication of benefits to others, to be accompanied with a very delicious relish upon the mind of him that practices it; nothing indeed carrying with it a more pure and savoury delight than beneficence. A man may be vertuously voluptuous and a laudable Epicure by doing much good; for to receive good, even in the judgment of *Epicurus* himself, (the great Patron of Pleasure) is no wise so pleasant as to do it: God and Nature therefore within us do sollicite the poor mans case; even our own ease and satisfaction demand from us compassion and kindness toward him; by exercising them, we hearken to Natures wise Disciplines, and comply with her kindly Instincts; we cherish good humour, and sweeten our complexion; so ennobling our minds, we become not only more like to God, but more perfectly men; by the contrary practice we rebel against the Laws, and pervert the due course of our Nature; we do weaken, corrupt and stifle that which is best in us; we harden and stupifie our souls; so monstrously degenerating from the perfection of our kind, and becoming rather like savage beasts, than sociable men; yea, somewhat worse perhaps than many beasts; for commonly bruits will combine to the succour of one another; they will defend and help those of the same kind.

2. And if the sensitive part within us doth suggest so much, the rational dictates more unto us; that heavenly faculty, having capacities so wide, and so mighty energies; was surely not created to serve mean or narrow designs; it was not given us to scrape eternally in earth, or to amass heaps of clay for private enjoyment; for the service of one puny creature, for the sustenance or satisfaction of a single carcase: 'tis much below an intelligent person to weary himself with servile toils, to distract his mind with ignoble cares for concernments so low and scanty; but to regard and pursue the common good of men; to dispense advise and aid, where needs requires; to diffuse its virtue all about in beneficial effects; these are Operations worthy of Reason, these are Imployments, congruous to the native excellency of that Divine Power implanted in us; such performances declare indeed what a man is, whence he sprang, and whither he tends.

3. Farther, examining our selves, we may also observe, that we are in reality, what our poor Neighbour appears to be, in many respects no less indigent and impotent than he: we no less, yea far more, for our subsistance depend upon the arbitrary bounty of another, than he seemeth to relie upon ours. We as delectible creatures do continually want support; we as grievous sinners do always need mercy; every moment we are contracting huge debts, far beyond our ability to discharge; debts of gratitude for benefits received, debts of guilt for offences committed; we therefore perpetually stand obliged to be craving for mercy and relief at the Gates of Heaven. We all, from Prince to Peasant, live meerly upon alms, and are most really in condition Beggars: *to pray always,* is a duty incumbent on us from the condition of our nature, as well as by the command of God. Such a likeness in state should therefore dispose us to succour our fellows, and ... *to lend mercy to God, who need mercy from him,* as the good Father speaketh. We should (as the Apostle advises and argues) *Remember them that are in bonds, as bound with them; and them which suffer adversity, as being our selves also in the body;* as being companions in necessity, or subject to the like distress. If we daily receive mercy and relief, yet unmindful of our obligation to God, refuse them to others, shall we not deserve to hear that dreadful exprobration, *O thou wicked servent, I forgave thee all that debt because thou desiredst me; shouldest not thou also have had compassion on thy fellow-servant, even as I had pity on thee?*

4. The great incertainty, and instability of our condition, doth also require our consideration. We that now flourish in a fair and full estate, may soon be in the case of that poor creature, who now sues for our relief; we that to this day enjoy the wealth of *Job,* may the morrow need his patience; there are *Sabeans,* which may come and drive away our cattel; there are tempests, which may arise, and smite down our houses; there is a fire of God, which may fall from Heaven, and consume our substance; a messenger of all these mischiefs may, for all we know, be presently at our doors; it happened so to a better man than we, as unexpectedly and with as small ground to fear it, as it can arrive to us: all our wealth is surrounded with dangers, and exposed to casualties innumerable; Violence may snatch it from us, Treachery may cheat us of it; Mischance may seize thereon, a secret Moth may devour it; the wisdom of Providence for our trial, or its justice for our punishment, may bereave us thereof; its own light and fluid nature (if no other accomptable causes were apparent) might easily serve to waft it from us; for, *Riches* (saith the Wise-man) *make themselves wings,* (they it seems do need no help for that) *and fly away like as an Eagle toward Heaven;* that is, of their own accord they do swiftly convey themselves away, out of our sight, and beyond our reach: they are but wind, *What profit* (says the Preacher) *hath he that laboreth for the wind?* for wind, that is, for a thing which can no wise be fixed or setled in one corner; which therefore 'tis a vanity to conceive, that we can surely appropriate, or long retain. How then can we think to stand firm upon a place so slippery? How can we build any confidence on a bottom so loose and brittle? How can we suffer our minds to be swell'd up, like bubbles, with vain conceit, by the breath of such things, more fleeting and vertiginous than any Air? against the precepts of the wisest and best men: *If riches increase,* saith the Psalmist, *set not your heart* on them: *Wilt thou set thine eyes upon that which is not?* saith the Wise man: (that is, wilt thou regard that which is so transitory and evanid, that it hardly may be deemed real; which we can scarce look on, before it is gone) and *charge them* (saith St. Paul) *that are rich in this world,* *that they be not high minded, nor trust in uncertain riches:* (... in the obscurity, or inevidence of riches; things which we can never plainly discern how long we shall keep them, how much we can enjoy them) what should make us unwilling with certain advantage to our selves, freely to let that go, which presently without our leave may forsake us? How can we reasonably judge our case much different from that of the poorest body, whenas in a trice we may perhaps change places and persons; when the scene turning, he may be advanced unto our wealth, we may be depressed into his want? since every Age yieldeth instances of some *Croesus,* some *Polycrates,* some *Pompey,* some *Job,* some *Nebuchodonosor,* who within a small compass of time doth appear to all men the object both of admiration and pity; is to the less wise the mark both of envy and scorn; seeing every day presenteth unexpected vicissitudes, the Sea of Humane Affairs continually ebbing and flowing, now rolling on this, now on the other shore its restless waves of profit and credit; since especially there is a God, who arbitrarily disposeth things, and with a turn of his hand changeth the state of men; who as the Scripture saith, *Maketh rich and poor, bringeth to low and lifteth up; poureth contempt upon Princes; raiseth the poor out of the dust, and lifteth the beggar from the dunghil, to set them among Princes, and to make them inherit the throne of glory:* seeing, I say, apparently such is the condition of things here, that we may soon need his pity and help, who now requesteth ours, why should we not be very ready to afford them to him? why should we not gladly embrace our opportunity, and use our turn well; becoming aforehand with others, and preventing their reciprocal contempt or neglect of us hereafter? *Cast thy bread upon the waters, for thou shalt find it after many days; give a portion to seven, and also unto eight, for thou knowest not what evil shall be upon the earth:* that is, considering the inconstancy & uncertainty of affairs here, and what adversity may befall thee, be liberal upon all occasions, and thou shalt (even a good while after) find returns of thy liberality upon thee: so the Wise man advises, and so Wisdom certainly dictates that we should do;

5. And equity doth exact no less: for were any of us in the needy mans plight, (as easily we may be reduced thereto) we should believe our case deserved commiseration; we should importunately demand relief, we should be grievously displeased at a repulse; we should apprehend our selves very hardly dealt with, and sadly we should complain of inhumanity and cruelty, if succour were refused to us. In all equity therefore we should be apt to minister the same to others; for nothing can be more unreasonable or unjust, than to require or expect that from another, which in a like case we are unwilling to render unto him; it is a plain deviation from that Fundamental Rule, which is the Base of all Justice; and virtually the sum (as our Saviour telleth us) of whatever is prescribed us: *All things whatsoever ye would that men should do to you, do ye even so to them; for this is the Law and the Prophets. I* add, that upon these Considerations, by unmerciful dealing, we put our selves into a very bad and ticklish condition; wholly depending upon the constancy of that which is most inconstant; so that if our fortune do fail, we can neither reasonably hope for, nor justly pretend to any relief or comfort from others.

6. We should also remember concerning our selves, that we are mortal and frail. Were we immortal, or could we probably retain our Possessions for ever in our hands; yea, could we forsee some definite space of time, considerably long, in which we might assuredly enjoy our stores, it might seem somewhat excusable to scrape hard, and to hold fast; to do so might look like rational Providence: but since *Riches are not forever, nor doth the Crown endure to all generations,* (as the Wise-man speaketh) since they must infallibly be soon left, and there is no certainty of keeping them for any time; 'tis very unaccomptable why

we should so greedily seek them, and hug them so fondly. *The rich man,* saith St. *James, as the flower of the grass shall pass away:* it is his special doom *to fade away* suddenly; it is obvious why in many respects he is somewhat more than others obnoxious to the fatal stroke, and upon special accompts of justice he may be farther more exposed thereto; considering the case of the rich fool in the Gospel, we may easily discern them; we should reckon, that it may happen to us, as it did there to him; that after we have reared great Barns, and *stored up much goods for many years,* our *soul this very night* may be *required of us;* however, if it be uncertain when, it is most certain, that after a very short time our thred will be spun out; then shall we be rifled, and quite stript of all; becoming stark naked, as when we came into the world: we shall not carry with us one grain of our glistering Metals, or one rag of our gaudy Stuff; our stately Houses, our fine Gardens, and our spatious Walks, must all be exchanged for a close Hole under ground; we must for ever bid farewell to our Pomps and Magnificences, to our Feasts and Jollities, to our Sports and Pastimes; not one of all our numerous and splendid retinue; no Companion of our Pleasure, no Admirer of our Fortune, no Flatterer of our Vices can wait upon us; desolate and unattended we must go down into the Chambers of Darkness; then shall we find, that to die rich (as men are wont improperly to speak) is really to die most poor; that to have carefully kept our Money, is to have lost it utterly; that by leaving much, we do indeed leave worse than nothing: To have been wealthy, if we have been illiberal and unmerciful, will be no advantage or satisfaction to us after we are gone hence; yea, it will be the cause of huge damage, and bitter regret unto us: All our Treasures will not procure us any favour, or purchase one Advocate for us in that impartial World; yea, it shall be they which will there prosecute us with clamorous accusations, will bear sore testimony against us, *(The rust of them,* saith St. *James, shall be a witness against us,* signifying our unjust or uncharitable detention of them) will obtain a most heavy sentence upon us; they will render our audit more difficult, and enflame our reckoning; they will aggravate the guilt of our sins with imputations of unfaithfulness and ingratitude; so with their load they will press us deeper into perdition; to omit, that having so ill managed them, we shall leave them behind us as marks of obloquy, and monuments of infamy upon our memories; for ordinarily of such a rich person it is true, that *Job* says of him, *Men shall clap their hands at him, and shall hiss him out of his place;* like one, who departs from off this stage, after having very ill acted his part. Is it not therefore infinitely better to prevent this being necessarily and unprofitably deprived of our goods, by seasonably disposing them so, as may conduce to our benefit, and our comfort, and our honour; being very indifferent and unconcerned in our affection toward them; modest and humble in our conceits about them; moderate and sober in our enjoyments of them; contented upon any reasonable occasion to loose or leave them; and especially most ready to dispense them in that best way; which God hath prescribed, according to the exigencies of Humanity and Charity? By thus ordering our Riches, we shall render them benefits and blessings to us; we shall by them procure sure friendship and favour, great worship and respect in the other world; having so lived (in the exercise of bounty and mercy) we shall truly die rich, and in effect carry all our goods along with us, or rather we have thereby sent them before us; having, like wise Merchants, transmitted and drawn them by a most safe conveyance into our Country and Home; where infallibly we shall find them, and with everlasting content enjoy them. So considering our selves, and our state will dispose us to the practice of these duties.

Furthermore, if we contemplate our Wealth it self, we may therein descry great motives to bounty. **1.** Thus to employ our Riches, is really the best use they are capable of; not only the most innocent, most worthy, most plausible; but the most safe, most pleasant, most advantagious, and consequently in all respects most prudent way of disposing them. To keep them close without using or enjoying them at all, is a most sottish extravagance, or a strange kind of madness; a man thence affecting to be rich, quite impoverisheth himself, dispossesseth himself of all, & alienateth from himself his Estate: his Gold is no more his, than when it was in the *Indies,* or lay hid in the Mines; his Corn is no more his, than if it stood growing in *Arabia* or *China;* he is no more owner of his Lands, than he is Master of *Jerusalem,* or *Grand-Cairo;* for what difference is there, whether distance of place or baseness of mind sever things from him? whether his own heart, or another mans hand detain them from his use? whether he hath them not at all, or hath them to no purpose? whether one is a beggar out of necessity, or by choice? is pressed to want, or a Volunteer thereto? Such an one may fancy himself rich, and others, wise as himself, may repute him so; but so distracted persons to themselves and to one another do seem great Princes, and stile themselves such; with as much reason almost he might pretend to be wise, or to be good. Riches are … things whose nature consists in usefulness; abstract that, they become nothing, things of no consideration or value; he that hath them, is no more concerned in them, than he that hath them not: it is the heart and skill to use affluence of things wisely and nobly, which makes it Wealth, and constitutes him rich that hath it; otherwise the Chests may be cramm'd, and the Barns stuffed full, while the man is miserably poor and beggarly; 'tis in this sense true, which the Wise-man says, *There is that maketh himself rich, yet hath nothing.* But the very having Riches (will such a man say) is matter of Reputation; men do esteem and honour him that hath them; true, if he knows how, and hath the mind to use them well, otherwise all the credit they yield consists in making their Master ridiculous to wise men, and infamous among all men: but, putting safe that any should be so foolish as to respect us merely for seeming rich, why should we accommodate our practice to their vain opinion, or be base our selves because others are not wise? But however, (may he say again) it is a pleasant thing to see them; a heap of Gold is the most lovely spectacle that one can behold; it does a mans heart good to view an abundance of good things about him; for this plea indeed he hath a good Author; this it should seem was all the benefit the Wise-man observed in them, accruing to such persons: *What good,* saith he, *is there to the owners thereof, saving the beholding of them with their eyes?* But if this be all they are good for, it is, one would think, a very slim benefit they afford, little able to balance the pain and care requisite to the acquist and custody of them; a benefit indeed not proper to the possessour, for any one may look on them as well as he, or on the like; any one at pleasure may enjoy better sights; all the Riches and Ornaments of Nature, the glorious splendours of Heaven, and the sweet beauties of the Field, are exposed to common view; the choicest Magnificencies and Gallantries of the World, do studiously present themselves to every mans eye; these in part every man truly may appropriate to himself; and by imagination any man can as well take all that he sees for his own, as the tenacious Miser doth fancy his dear self to be his.

But mine Heir (perhaps he will farther say) will thank me, will praise me, will bless me for my great care and providence: If he doth, what is that to thee? Nothing of that will concern thee, or can reach thee; thou shalt not hear what he says, or feel any good from what he does: And most probably thou art mistaken in thy opinion concerning him; as thou *knowest not who* he shall be, *that shall gather all thou heapest up, or shall rule over all thy labour, (whither he shall be a wise man or a fool,* a kinsman or a stranger, a friend or a foe) so thou canst as little guess what he will think or say: If he hath wit, he may sweetly laugh at thee for thy fond wisdom; if he hath none, his commendations will little adorn thy memory; he will to thy disgrace spend what thou leavest, as vainly, as thou didst get or keep it. But (this to be sure he will in the end say for himself) Money is a good reserve against necessary occasions, or bad times, that may come; against the time of old age, of sickness, of adversity; 'tis the surest friend a man can have in such cases, which, when all fails, will be ready to help him: *The rich mans Wealth is his strong City,* the Wise-man ... never spake more wisely; he therefore will not dismantle this fortress, but will keep it Well stored, letting therefore his wealth lie dead and useless by him: but (to let pass now the prophane infidelity of this plea, excluding all hope in God, and substituting our Providence in the room of his) what a folly is it, thus to anticipate evil, and to create to our selves a present adversity from a suspicion of one future; to pinch our selves now, lest we should suffer hereafter; to pine to day, because we can imagine it possible that we may starve to morrow; to forego certain occasions of enjoying our goods, for that perchance the like occasions may happen one day, we know not when; not to use things now, when reason bids us, because they may be useful at another time? Not considering also, that many intervenient accidents, more probably than a moderate and handsome use of our Wealth, may crop the excrescencies thereof.

2. But setting aside these absurd excuses of penuriousness, we may consider, that secluding the good use of them in beneficence, Riches are very impertinent, very cumbersome, very dangerous, very mischievous things; either superfluous toys, or troublesome clogs, or treacherous snares, or rather all these in combination, productive of trouble, sorrow, and sin. A small pittance will, and must suffice to all reasonable purposes, to satisfie our necessities, to procure conveniencies, to yield innocent delight and ease: our nature doth not require, nor cannot bear much: *(Take heed and beware of covetousness,* saith our Lord, *for a mans life consisteth not in the abundance of the things which he possesseth:* that is, a man may live well without it) all the rest, setting beneficence apart, can only serve vanity or vice, will make us really fools or slaves. *(They that will be rich,* (saith the Apostle) *fall into temptation, and a snare, and into many foolish and hurtful lusts, which drown men into destruction and perdition.)* They puff up our minds with vain and false conceits; making us, as if we were in a dream or frenzy, to take our selves for other persons, more great, more wise, more good, more happy than we are: for constantly, as the Wise-man observed, *The rich man is wise in his own conceit;* and *Agur* thus intimates in his prayer, *Remove far from me vanity and lyes, give me neither poverty nor riches.* They render us insensible and forgetful of God, of our selves, of piety and vertue, of all that is good and worthy of us: *(Lest I be full,* said that good man again, assigning a reason why he deprecated being rich, *and deny thee, and say, Who is the Lord?)* they swallow up our thoughts, our affections, our endeavours, our time and leisure; possessing our hearts with a doting love unto them, (excluding other good affections) distracting our minds with anxious cares about them, (choaking other good thoughts) encumbring all our life with business about them, (inconsistent with due attention to our other more weighty and necessary concernments) filling our heads with suspicions, and fears, piercing our hearts with troubles and sorrows; they immerse our souls in all the follies of pride, in all the filths of luxury, in all the mischiefs emergent from sloth and stupidity; they are *the root of all evils* unto us, and the greatest obstructions of our true happiness, rendring Salvation almost impossible, and Heaven in a manner inaccessible to us: so that to be rich, (if severed from a sober mind, and free heart) is a great disease, and the source of many grievous distempers both of body and mind; from which we cannot otherwise, well otherwise, secure or rescue our selves, than by liberally spending them in works of bounty and mercy: so shall we ease our selves of the burdens, so shall we elude the temptations, so shall we abandon the vices, and so shall we escape all the sad mischiefs incident to them: Thus to use wealth, shall turn it into a convenience, and an ornament of our lives, into a considerable blessing, and a ground of much comfort to us. Exclusing this use of wealth, or abstracting a capacity of doing good therewith, nothing is more pitiful and despicable than it; it is but like the load, or the trappings of an Ass; a wise man on that condition would not chuse it, or endure to be pestered with it; but would serve it, as those Philosophers did, who flung it away, that it might not disturb their contemplations: 'tis the power it affords of benefiting men, which only can reason, and ingratiate it to the relish of such a person; otherwise it is evidently true, which the Wise-man affirms, *Better is a little with the fear of the Lord, than great treasure, and trouble therewith.*

3. Again, we may consider, that to dispense our Wealth liberally, is the best way to preserve it, and continue Masters thereof; what we give, is not thrown away, but saved from danger; while we detain it at home (as it seems to us) it really is abroad, and at adventures; it is out at Sea, sailing perilously in storms, near rocks and shelves, among Pirates; nor can it ever be safe, till it is brought into this port, or ensured this way; when we have bestowed it on the poor, then have we lodged it in unquestionable safety; in a place where no rapine, no deceit, no mishap, no corruption can ever by any means come at it. All our Doors and Bars, all our Forces and Guards, all the circumspection and vigilancy we can use, are no defence or security at all in comparison to this disposal thereof: The poor man's stomach is a Granary for our Corn, which never can be exhausted; the poor man's back is a Wardrobe for our Clothes, which never can be pillaged; the poor man's Pocket is a Bank for our Money, which never can disappoint or deceive us; all the rich Traders in the World may decay and break, but the Poor can never fail, except God himself turn Bankrupt; for what we give to the poor, we deliver and entrust in his hands, out of which no force can wring it, no craft can filch it; it is laid up in Heaven, whither no thief can climb, where no moth or rust do abide. In despite of all the fortune, of all the might, of all the malice in the world, the liberal man will ever be rich; for God's Providence is his Estate; God's Wisdom and Power are his Defence; God's Love and Favour are his Reward; God's Word is his Assurance; who hath said it, that *He which giveth to the poor, shall not lack:* no vicissitude therefore of things can surprise him, or find him unfurnished; no disaster can impoverish him, no adversity can overwhelm him; he hath a certain reserve against all times and occasions: He that *deviseth liberal things, by liberal things shall he stand,* (saith the Prophet.) But on the other hand, being niggardly is the likeliest course we can take to lose our Wealth and Estate; we thereby expose them to danger, and leave them defenceless; we subject them to the envious eye, to the slanderous tongue, to the ravenous and insidious hand; we deprive them of Divine protection, which if it be away, *The watch-man waketh but in vain:* We provoke God irrecoverably to take it from us, as he did the Talent from that unprofitable servant, who did not use it well. We do indeed thereby yield God just cause of war, and enmity against us: which being, *Omnia dat qui justa negat;* we do forfeit all to Divine Justice, by denying that portion which belongs to him, and which he claims. Can we hope to live in quiet possession of any thing, if we refuse to pay our due Tributes and Taxes imposed upon us by our Almighty Sovereign; if we live in such rebellion against his Authority, such violation of his right, such diffidence to his Word? No: *He that trusteth in his riches, shall fall, but the righteous shall flourish as a branch:* such is the difference between the covetous and the liberal in point of security and success concerning their Estate.

Even according to the humane and ordinary way of esteeming things, (abstracting from the special Providence of God) the liberal person hath in consequence of his bounty, more real security for his Wealth, than this world hath any other: He thereby gets an interest in the gratitude and affection of those, whom he obligeth, together with the good will and respect of all men, who are spectators of his vertuous and generous dealing: the hearts and memories of men are repositories to him of a treasure, which nothing can extort from him, or defraud him of. If any mischance should arrive, or any want come near him, all men would be ready to commiserate him, every man would hasten to his succour. As when a haughty, a greedy, or a gripple man do fall into calamity or disgrace, scarce any one regardeth or pitieth him; Fortune deserting such a person, carries all with it, few or none stick to him, his most zealous flatterers are commonly the first that forsake him, contempt and neglect are the only adherents to his condition; that of the Wise-man appears verified, *He that hideth his eyes from the poor, shall have many a curse:* so the courteous and bountiful person, when Fortune seems to frown on him, hath a sure refuge in the good will and esteem of men; all men, upon accompts of honour and honesty, take themselves to be concerned in his case, and engaged to favour him; even those, who before were strangers, become then his friends, and in effect discover their affection to him: it, in the common judgment of people, appears an indignity and a disgrace to mankind, that such a man should want or suffer.

4. Nay farther we may consider, that exercising bounty is the most advantageous method of improving and increasing an Estate; but that being tenacious and illiberal, doth tend to the diminution and decay thereof. The way to obtain a great encrease, is to sow much: he that sows little, how can he expect a good Crop? It is as true in spiritual Husbandry, as in the other, that *what a man soweth, that he shall reap,* both in kind, and according to proportion; so that great Husband-man St. *Paul* assureth us, *He that soweth sparingly, shall reap sparingly; but he that soweth bountifully, shall also reap bountifully:* and *Salomon* means the same, when he saith, *To him that soweth righteousness, shall be a sure reward.* The way to gain abundantly is, you know well, to trade boldly; he that will not adventure any thing considerable, how can he think of a large return? 'Tis so likewise in the Evangelical Negotiations; if we put out much upon score of Conscience or Charity, we shall be sure to profit much. Liberality is the most beneficial Traffick that can be; it is bringing our Wares to the best Market; it is letting out our Money into the best hands; we thereby lend our Money to God, who repays with vast Usury; an hundred to one is the rate he allows at present, and above hundred millions to one he will render hereafter; so that if you will be Merchants this way, you shall be sure to thrive, you cannot fail to grow rich most easily and speedily: *The liberal soul shall be made fat, and he that watereth shall be watered himself:* This is that which S. *Paul* again argues upon, when commending the *Philippians* free kindness toward him, he says, *Not because I desire a gift, but I desire fruit that may abound to your accompt.* Bounty yields ... a fruit that multiplies and abundantly turns to good accompt; it indeed procuring Gods benediction, the fountain of all desirable plenty and prosperity, for, *The blessing of the Lord it maketh rich, and he addeth no sorrow with it.* It is therefore the greatest want of policy, the worst ill-husbandry and unthriftiness that can be, to be sparing this way; he that uses it, cannot be thriving; he must spend upon the main stock, and may be sure to get nothing considerable. God ordinarily so proceeds, as to recompence, and retaliate men in the same kind, wherein they endeavour to please him, or presume to offend him; so that for them who freely offer him their goods, he in regard thereto will prosper their dealings, and bless their estates: *(For this very thing the Lord thy*

God shall bless thee in all thy works, and in all that thou puttest thine hand unto, says *Moses)* but they who will not lay out any thing for him, he will not concern himself in their success otherwise than to cross it, or (which is worse) to curse it: for if he seem to favour them for a time with some prosperity in their affairs, their condition is much worse thereby, their accompt will be more grievous, and their fate more disastrous in the end.

5. Farther, the contributing part of our goods to the poor, will qualifie us to enjoy the rest with satisfaction and comfort: The Oblation of these Firstfruits, as it will sanctifie the whole lump of our Estate, so it will sweeten it; having offered this well-pleasing sacrifice of piety, having discharged this debt of justice, having paid this tribute of gratitude, our hearts being at rest, and our conscience will satisfied, we shall, like those good people in the Acts, *eat our meat with gladness, and singleness of heart;* to see the poor man by our means accommodated, eased, and refreshed, will give a delicious relish to all our enjoyments. But withholding his portion from the poor, as it will pollute and profane all our Estate, so it will render the fruition thereof sowre or unsavoury to us: for, can we with any content taste our dainties, or view our plenties, while the poor man stands in sight pining with hunger? Can we without regret see our Walls cloathed with Tapestry, our Horses deckt with Golden Trappings, our Attendants strutting in wanton Gaiety, while our honest poor Brother appears half naked, and trembling with cold? Can we carry on one finger enough to furnish ten poor people with necessaries, and have the heart within us, without shame and displeasure, to see them want? No; the sense of our impiety and ingratitude toward God, of our inhumanity and unworthiness toward our Neighbour, will not fail (if ever we considerately reflect on our behaviour) to sting us with cruel remorse and self-condemnation; the clamours of want and misery surrounding us, will pierce our ears, and wound our hearts; the frequent objects of pity and mercy, do what we can to banish them from our prospect or regard, will so assail, and so pursue us, as to disturb the freedom of our enjoyments, to quash the briskness of our mirth, to allay the sweetness of our pleasure; yea rather, if stupidity and obduration have not seized on us, to imbitter all unto us; we shall feel that true, which *Zophar* speaks of the cruel and covetous Oppessour, *Surely he shal not feel quietness in his belly—he shall not rejoice in his substance—in the fullness of his sufficiency he shall be in straits.*

6. I shall touch but one consideration more, persuasive of this practice; it is this: The peculiar nature of our Religion specially requires it, and the honour thereof exacts it from us; nothing better suits Christianity, nothing more graces it, than liberality; nothing is more inconsistent therewith, or more disparageth it, than being miserable and sordid. A Christian Niggard is the veriest nonsense that can be; for, What is a Christian? What, but a man, who adores God alone, who loves God above all things, who reposes all his trust and confidence in God? What is he, but one who undertaketh to imitate the most good and bountiful God, to follow, as the best pattern of his practice, the most benign and charitable Jesus, the Son of God; to obey the Laws of God, and his Christ, the sum and substance of which is Charity; half whose Religion doth consist in loving his Neighbor as himself? What is he farther, but one who hath renounced this world, with all the vain pomps and pleasures of it; who professes himself in disposition and affection of mind to forsake all things for Christs sake; who pretends little to value, affect, or care for any thing under Heaven; having all his main concernments and treasures, his heart, his hopes, and his happiness in another world? Such is a Christian; and what is a Niggard? All things quite contrary: One whose practice manifestly shews him to worship another thing beside, and before God; to love Mammon above God, and more to confide in it, than in him; One, who bears small good will, kindness or pity toward his Brother; who is little affected or concerned with things future or celestial; whose mind and heart are riveted to this world; whose hopes and happinesses are settled here below; whose soul is deeply immersed and buried in earth: One who, according to constant habit, notoriously breaketh the two great heads of Christian duty, *Loving God with all his heart, and his Neighbour as himself* It is therefore, by comparing those things, very plain, that we pretend to reconcile gross contradictions and inconsistencies, if we profess our selves to be Christians, and are illiberal. It is indeed the special grace and glory of our Religion, that it consisteth not in barren speculations, or empty formalities, or forward professions; not in fancying curiously, or speaking zealously, or looking demurely; but in really producing sensible fruits of goodness; in doing (as St. *Paul* signifies) *things good and profitable unto men,* such as those chiefly are, of which we speak. The most gracious wisdom of God hath so modeled our Religion, that according to it Piety and Charity are the same thing; that we can never express our selves more dutiful toward him, or better please him, or more truly glorifie him, than when we are kind and good to our poor Brother. We grosly mistake, if we take giving of Alms to be a Jewish or Popish practice, suitable to Children and Dullards in Religion, beneath so refined, so improved, so loftily spiritual Gallants as we: No, 'tis a duty most properly, and most highly Christian, as none more, a most goodly fruit of grace, and a most faithful mark thereof: *By the experiment of this ministration, we* (as St. *Paul* saith) *glorifie God for our professed subjection unto the Gospel of Christ, and for our liberal distribution unto our brethren, and unto all men:* without it our faith is dead and senseless; our high attainments are fond presumptions, our fine notions and delicate spiritualities are in truth but silly dreams, the issues of a proud and ignorant fancy: he that appears hard-hearted and close-fisted toward his needy Brother, let him think or call himself what he pleaseth, he plainly is no Christian, but a blemish, a reproach, and a scandal to that honourable Name.

7. To all these Considerations and Reasons inducing to the practice of this kind of Charity, I might subjoin examples, and set before you the fairest Copies that can be imagined thereof. We have for it the pattern of God himself, who is infinitely munificent and merciful; *from whom every good and perfect gift descendeth; who giveth life, and breath, and all things unto all; who giveth liberally and upbraideth not.* We have the example of the Son of God, who out of pure charity did freely part with the riches and glories of Eternity, voluntarily embracing extream poverty and want for our sake, that we who were poor, might be enriched; we that were miserable, might become happy; who *went about doing good;* spent all his life in painful dispensation of beneficence, and relieving the needs of men in every kind. We have the blessed Patriarchs to follow, who at Gods pleasure and call did readily leave their Country, their Friends, their Goods, and all they had. We have the practice of the holy Apostles, who freely *let go all to follow their Lord;* who chearfully sustained all sorts of losses, disgraces, and pains for promoting the honour of God, and procuring good unto men; we have to move and encourage us hereto the first and best Christians, most full of grace and holy zeal, who *so many as were possessours of lands and houses, did sell them,* and did impart the price of them to the community, *so that there was none poor among them,* and that *distribution was made to every one as he had need.* We have all the saints and eminent servants of God in all times, who have been high and wonderful in the performance of these duties, (I could tell you of the blessed Martyr St. *Cyprian,* who was liberal by whole-sale, bestowing all at once, a fair Estate, on God and the poor; of the renowned Bishop St. *Basil,* who constantly waited on the sick, and kissed their sores;

of the most pious Confessour St. *Martin,* who having but one Coat left, and seeing a poor man that wanted cloaths, tore it in two pieces, and gave one to that *poor man;* and many like instances out of authentick History might be produced, apt to provoke our imitation: I might also, to beget emulation and shame in us, represent exemplary practices of Humanity and Charity even in Jews, Mahometans and Pagans, such as in these cold days might pass for more than ordinary among us) but I shall only propound one present and sensible example, that of this Noble City, whose publick bounty and charity in all kinds, (in education of Orphans, in curing the Diseased, both in body and mind, in provision for the poor, in relieving all sorts of necessities and miseries) let me earnestly intreat, and exhort us all for Gods sake, as we are able, by our private charity to imitate, to encourage, and to affect; let us do this so much the more willingly and freely, as the sad circumstances of things, by Gods judgments brought upon us, do plainly require, that the Publick Charity it self (lying under so great impediments, discouragements and distresses) should be supported, supplied, and relieved by particular liberality. No words that I can devise will be so apt to affect and move you, as the case it self, if you please to consider it: hear it therefore speaking, and, I pray, with a pious and charitable disposition of mind attend there to:

A true Report, &c.

For this excellent Pattern of pious bounty and mercy, let us heartily thank Almighty God; let us humbly implore Gods blessing on the future management of it; let us pay due respect to the worthy Promoters thereof, and pray for rewards upon them answerable to their charitable care and industry employed therein; let us also according to our ability perform our duty in following and furthering it: for encouragement to which practise, give me leave briefly to reflect upon the latter part of my Text; which represents some instances of the felicity proper to a bountiful person, or some rewards peculiar to the exercising the duties of bounty and mercy.

The first is, *His righteousness endureth for ever.* These words are capable of various senses, or of divers respects; they may import that the fame and remembrance of his bounty is very durable, or that the effects thereof do lastingly continue, or that eternal rewards are designed thereto; they may respect the bountiful man himself, or his posterity here; they may simply relate to an endurance in Gods regard and care; or they may with that also comprehend a continuance in the good memory, and honourable mention of men. Now in truth according to all these interpretations, the bountiful mans righteousness doth endure for ever, that is, very lastingly (or so long as the special nature of the case doth bear) in any sense; or for an absolute perpetuity, in some sense: the words in their plenitude do naturally and without straining involve so many truths, none which therefore we think fit to exclude, but shall briefly touch them all.

1. As for future reputation and fame, (which that it in part is intended here, that which precedes, *The righteous shall be had in everlasting remembrance,* doth argue) it is evident, that it peculiarly attends upon this practice: the bountiful person is especially that *just* man, whose *memory is blessed, (...* that is, is prosecuted with commendations and praises.) No Spices can so embalm a man, no Monument can so preserve his Name and Memory, as works of beneficence; no other fame is comparably so precious, or truly glorious, as that which grows from thence: The Renown of Power and Prowess, of Wit or Learning, of any Wisdom or Skill, may dwell in the fancies of men with some admiration; but the remembrance of Bounty reigns in their hearts with cordial esteem and affection; there erecting immoveable Trophies over Death and Oblivion, and it thence spreading it self through the tongues of men with sincere and sprightly Commendations. The bountiful mans very Dust is fragrant, and his Grave venerable; his Name is never mentioned without respect; his Actions have always these best Ecchoes, with innumerable iterations resounding after them: This was a true Friend to Mankind; This was a real Benefactour to the World; This was a Man good in earnest, and pious to good purpose.

2. The effects of his righteousness are likewise very durable: When he is departed hence, and in person is no more seen, he remains visible and sensible in the footsteps and fruits of his goodness; the Poor still beholds him present in the subsistence of himself, and his Family; the Sick-man feels him in the refreshment, which he yet enjoys by his provision; he supervives in the heart of the Afflicted, which still resents the comfort, and rejoices in the ease which he procured him; all the World percieves benefit from him by the edification it receiveth from his example; Religion obtaineth profit and ornament, God himself enjoyeth glory and praise from his righteousness.

3. His righteousness also endureth in respect to his posterity. It is an usual plea for tenacity and parsimony, that care must be had of posterity, that enough must be provided and laid up for the Family: But in truth this is a very absurd excuse, and doing according thereto, is a very preposterous method of proceeding toward that end; it is really the greatest improvidence in that respect, and the truest neglect that can be of our Children: for so doing, together with a seeming Estate, we entail a real Curse upon them; we devest them of Gods protection and benediction, (the only sure preservatives of an Estate) we leave them Heirs of nothing so much as of punishments due to our ingratitude, our infidelity, our impiety and injustice both toward God and man: whereas by liberally bestowing on the poor, we demise unto them Gods blessing, which is the best inheritance; we recommend them to Gods especial care, which is the best tuition; we leave them Gods protection and providence, which are a Wealth indefectible and inexhaustible; we constitute God their Guardian, who will most faithfully manage, and most wisely improve their substance, both that which we leave to them, and that which we gave for them to the poor; we thereby in good part entitle them unto the rewards appropriate to our pious Charity, our Faith, our Gratitude, our Self-denial, our Justice, to whatever good is virtually contained in our acts of bounty; to omit the honour and the good will of men, which constantly adhere to the bountiful mans House and Family. It is therefore expressly mentioned in Scripture as a recompence peculiar to this vertue, that security from want, and all happiness do attend the posterity of the bountiful person: *He is ever merciful and lendeth, and his seed is blessed,* saith *David* of him generally; and *David* also particularly observed, that in all the course of his long life, he could find no exception to the Rule: *I have been young, and now am old, yet have I not seen the righteous forsaken, nor his seed begging their bread.*

4. His righteousness also endureth for ever in the perpetual favour of God, and in the eternal rewards which God will confer upon him, who out of Conscience and reverence toward God, out of good will and kindness toward his Brother hath dispersed, and given to the poor. *God will not* (as the Apostle saith) *be unjust to forget his labour of charity in ministring* to his poor Brother: from the seed, which he *hath sown to the Spirit,* he shall assuredly reap a most plentiful Crop of blessings spiritual; he shall effectually enjoy *the good foundation* that he hath *stored up:* for the goods he hath sold and delivered, he shall *bonâ fide* receive his Bargain, *the hidden treasure,* and *precious pearl* of eternal life; for this best improvement of his Talent of worldly Riches, he shall hear the *Euge bone serve, Well done good and faithful servant, enter into thy Masters joy:* he shall at last find God infinitely more bountiful to him, than he hath been unto the poor.

Thus when all the flashes of sensual pleasure are quite extinct; when all the flowers of secular glory are withered away; when all earthly glories are buried in darkness; when this world, and all the fashion of it, are utterly vanished and gone, the bountiful mans state will be still firm and flourishing, and *His righteousness shall endure for ever.*

It follows, *His horn shall be exalted with honour:* A Horn is an Emblem of Power; for in it the Beasts strength, offensive and defensive, doth consist; and of Plenty, for it hath within it a capacity apt to contain what is put into it; and of Sanctity, for that in it was put the holy Oyl, with which Kings were Consecrated; and of Dignity, both in consequence upon the Reasons mentioned, (as denoting might, and affluence, and sacredness accompanying Soveraign Dignity) and because also it is an especial beauty and ornament to the Creature which hath it; so that this expression *(His Horn shall be exalted with honour)* may be supposed to import, that an abundance of high, and holy, of firm and solid honour shall attend upon the bountiful person. And that so it truly shall, may from many Considerations appear.

1. Honour is inseparably annexed thereto as its natural Companion and shadow. God hath impressed upon all Vertue a Majesty and a Beauty, which do command respect, and with a kindly violence extort Veneration from men; such is the natural Constitution of our Souls, that as our sense necessarily liketh what is fair and sweet, so our mind unavoidably will esteem what is vertuous and worthy; all good Actions as such are honourable, but of all Vertues Beneficence doth with most unquestionable right claim honour, and with irrestistible force procures it; as it is indeed the most divine of Vertues, so men are most apt to venerate them, whom they observe eminently to practice it. Other Vertues men see, and approve as goodly to the sight, but this they taste and feel; this by most sensible experience they find to be pleasant and profitable, and cannot therefore but highly prize it. They, who *do their alms before men,* although out of unworthy vain glorious design, *have* yet, as our Saviour intimates, *their reward;* they fail not to get Honour thereby; and even so have no bad penny-worth; for, in the Wise-mans judgment, *A good name is rather to be chosen than great riches,* they receive at least fine air for gross earth; and things very spiritual, for things most material; they obtain that which every man doth naturally desire and prize, for that which only fashion in some places endeareth, and commandeth: they get the end for the means, for scarce any man seeketh wealth for it self, but either for Honour, or for Vertues sake, that he may live creditably, or may do good therewith: Necessity is served with a little, Pleasure may be satisfied with a competence, Abundance is required only to support Honour, or promote good; and Honour by a natural connexion adhereth to Bounty.

2. But farther, an accession of Honour according to gracious promise, (grounded upon somewhat of special reason, of equity, and decency in the thing it self) is due from God unto the bountiful person, and is by special Providence surely conferred on him. There is no kind of piety, or instance of obedience, whereby God himself is more signally honoured, than by this. These are chiefly those *good works,* the which *men seeing,* are apt to *glorifie our Father which is in Heaven;* to these fruits that is most applicable, which our Lord saith, *Hereby is my Father glorified, if you bear much fruit:* for, as, *He that oppresseth the poor, reproacheth his Maker;* so *he honoureth him, that hath mercy on the poor.* The comfortable experience of good in this sort of actions, will most readily dispose men to admire and commend the excellency, the wisdom, the goodness of the Divine Laws, will therefore procure God hearty praise, and thanks for them: For, as St. *Paul* teacheth us, *The administration of this service not only supplyeth the want of the Saints, but is abundant also by many thanksgivings unto God; whilst by experiment of this ministration, they glorifie God for your professed subjection unto the Gospel of Christ, and for your liberal distribution unto them, and unto all men.* Since then God is so peculiarly honoured by this practice, it is but equal and fit, that God should remunerate it with honour; Gods noble goodness will not let him seem defective in any sort of beneficial correspondence toward us, we shall never be able to yield him any kind of good thing in duty, which he will not be more apt to render us in Grace; they who (as *Salomon* speaketh) *honour God with their substance,* shall by God certainly be honoured with his blessing: Reason intimates so much, and we beside have Gods express Word for it; *Them* (saith he) *who honour me, I will honour.* He that absolutely and independently is the Fountain of all Honour; *from whom* (as good King *David* saith) *riches and honour cometh,* for that *he reigneth over all,* he will assuredly prefer and dignifie those, who have been at special care and cost to advance his Honour. He that hath the *hearts of all men in his hands,* and *fashioneth them* as he pleaseth, will raise the bountiful man in the judgments and affections of men. He that ordereth all the events of things, and disposeth success as he thinks fit, will cause the bountiful persons Enterprizes to prosper, and come off with credit. He will not suffer the reputation of so real an Honourer of himself to be extreamly slurr'd by disaster, to be blasted by slander, to be supplanted by envy or malice; but will *bring forth his righteousness as the light, and his judgment as the noonday.*

3. God will thus exalt the bountiful Man's Horn even here in this World, and to an infinitely higher pitch he will advance it in the future state: He shall there be set at the right hand, in a most honourable place and rank; among the chief Friends and Favourites of the Heavenly King; in happy Comfortship with the holy Angels, and blessed Saints; where, in recompence of his pious Bounty, he shall from the bountiful hands of his most gracious Lord receive *an incorruptible Crown of Righteousness,* and *an unfading Crown of glory:* The which God of his infinite mercy grant unto us all, through Jesus Christ our Lord; to whom for ever be all praise.

AMEN.

Now the God of peace, that brought again from the dead our Lord Jesus, that great Shepherd of the sheep, through the Blood of the Everlasting Covenant, make us perfect in every good Work to do his Will, working in us that which is well-pleasing in his sight, through Jesus Christ: to whom be Glory for ever and ever. Amen.

FINIS.

Bernard Mandeville

An Essay on Charity and Charity-Schools

Charity is that Virtue by which part of that sincere Love we have for our selves is transferr'd pure and unmix'd to others, not tyed to us by the Bonds of Friendship or Consanguinity, and even meer Strangers, whom we have no Obligation to, nor hope or expect any thing from. If we lessen any ways the Rigour of this Definition, part of the Virtue must be lost. What we do for our Friends and Kindred, we do partly for our selves: When a Man acts in behalf of Nephews or Nieces, and says they are my Brother's Children, I do it out of Charity; he deceives you; for if he is capable, it is expected from him, and he does it partly for his own Sake: If he values the Esteem of the World, and is nice as to Honour and Reputation, he is obliged to have a greater Regard to them than for Strangers, or else he must suffer in his Character.

The Exercise of this Virtue relates either to Opinion, or to Action, and is manifested in what we think of others, or what we do for them. To be charitable then in the first Place, we ought to put the best Construction on all that others do or say, that the Things are capable of. If a Man builds a fine House, tho' he has not one Symptom of Humility, furnishes it richly, and lays out a good Estate in Plate and Pictures, we ought not to think that he does it out of Vanity, but to encourage Artists, employ Hands, and set the Poor to work for the Good of his Country: And if, a Man sleeps at Church, so he does not snore, we ought to think he shuts his Eyes to increase his Attention. The Reason is, because in our Turn we desire that our utmost Avarice should pass for Frugality; and that for Religion, which we know to be Hypocrisy. Secondly, That Virtue is conspicuous in us, when we bestow our Time and Labour for nothing, or employ our Credit with others in behalf of those who stand in need of it, and yet could not expect such an Assistance from our Friendship or Nearness of Blood. The last Branch of Charity consists in giving away (whilst we are alive) what we value our selves, to such as I have already named; being contented rather to have and enjoy less, than not relieve those who want, and shall be the Objects of our Choice.

This Virtue is often counterfeited by a Passion of ours call'd *Pity* or *Compassion*, which consists in a Fellowfeeling and Condolance for the Misfortunes and Calamities of others; all Mankind are more or less affected with it; but the weakest Minds generally the most. It is raised in us, when the Sufferings and Misery of other Creatures make so forcible an Impression upon us, as to make us uneasy. It comes in either at the Eye or Ear, or both, and the nearer, and more violently the Object of Compassion strikes those Senses, the greater Disturbance it causes in us, often to such a Degree as to occasion great Pain and Anxiety.

Should any one of us be lock'd up in a Ground-Room, where in a Yard joining to it, there was a thriving good-humour'd Child at play of two or three Years old, so near us that through the Grates of the Window we could almost touch it with our Hand; and if whilst we took delight in the harmless Diversion, and imperfect Prittle-Prattle of the innocent Babe, a nasty over-grown Sow should come in upon the Child, set it a screaming, and frighten it out of its Wits; it is natural to think, that this would make us uneasy, and that with crying out, and making all the menacing Noise we could, we should endeavour to

From *The Fable of the Bees* by Bernard Mandeville.

drive the Sow away. But if this should happen to be an half-starv'd Creature, that mad with Hunger went roaming about in quest of Food, and we should behold the ravenous Brute in spite of our Cries, and all the threatning Gestures we could think of, actually lay hold of the helpless Infant, destroy and devour it: To see her widely open her destructive Jaws, and the poor Lamb beat down with greedy Haste; to look on the defenceless Posture of tender Limbs first trampled on, then tore asunder; to see the filthy Snout digging in the yet living Entrails, suck up the smoking Blood, and now and then to hear the Crackling of the Bones, and the cruel Animal with Savage Pleasure grunt o'er the horrid Banquet; to hear and see all this, what Tortures would it give the Soul beyond Expression! Let me see the most shining Virtue the Moralists have to boast of so manifest either to the Person possess'd of it, or those who behold his Actions: Let me see Courage, or the Love of one's Country so apparent without any Mixture, clear'd and distinct, the first from Pride and Anger, the other from the Love of Glory, and every Shadow of Self-Interest, as this Pity would be clear'd and distinct from all other Passions. There would be no need of Virtue or Self-Denial to be moved at such a Scene, and not only a Man of Humanity of good Morals and Commiseration, but likewise an Highwayman, an House-Breaker, or a Murderer could feel Anxieties on such an Occasion; how calamitous soever a Man's Circumstances might be, he would forget his Misfortunes for the time, and the most troublesome Passion would give way to Pity, and not one of the Species has a Heart so obdurate or engaged, that it would not ake at such a sight, as no Language has an Epithet to fit it.

Many will wonder at what I have said of Pity, that it comes in at the Eye or Ear, but the Truth of this will be known when we consider that the nearer the Object is the more we suffer, and the more remote it is the less we are troubled with it. To see People Executed for Crimes, if it is a great way off, moves us but little, in comparison to what it does when we are near enough to see the Motion of the Soul in their Eyes, observe their Fears and Agonies, and are able to read the Pangs in every Feature of the Face. When the Object is quite removed from our Senses, the Relation of the Calamities or the reading of them can never raise in us the Passion call'd Pity. We may be concern'd at bad News, the Loss and Misfortunes of Friends and those whose Cause we espouse; but this is not Pity, but Grief or Sorrow; the same as we feel for the Death of those we love, or the Destruction of what we value.

When we hear that three or four thousand Men, all Strangers to us, are kill'd with the Sword, or forc'd into some River where they are drown'd, we say and perhaps believe that we pity them. It is Humanity bids us have Compassion with the Sufferings of others, and Reason tells us, that whether a thing be far off or done in our sight our Sentiments concerning it ought to be the same, and we should be asham'd to own that we felt no Commiseration in us when any thing requires it. He is a cruel Man, he has no Bowels of Compassion: all these things are the Effects of Reason and Humanity, but Nature makes no Compliments, when the Object does not strike, the body does not feel it; and when Men talk of pitying People out of sight, they are to be believed in the same manner as when they say, that they are our humble Servants. In paying the usual Civilities at first meeting those who do not see one another every Day, are often very glad and very sorry alternately for five or six times together in less than two Minutes, and yet at parting carry away not a jot more of Grief or Joy than they met with. The same it is with Pity, and it is a thing of choice no more than fear or anger. Those who have a strong and lively Imagination, and can make Representations of things in their Minds, as they would be if they were actually before them, may work themselves up into something that resembles Compassion; but this is done by Art, and often the help of a little Enthusiasm, and is only an imitation of Pity: the Heart feels little of it, and it is as faint as what we suffer at the acting of a Tragedy; where our Judgment leaves part of the mind uninform'd, and to indulge a lazy Wantonness suffers it to be led into an Errour, which is necessary to have a Passion rais'd, the slight strokes of which are not unpleasant to us when the Soul is in an idle unactive Humour.

As Pity is often by our selves and in our own cases mistaken for Charity, so it assumes the shape, and borrows the very name of it; a Beggar asks you to exert that Vertue for Jesus Christ's sake, but all the while his great design is to raise your Pity. He represents to your View the worst side of his Ailments and bodily Infirmities; in chosen words he gives you an Epitome of his Calamities real or fictitious; and whilst he seems to pray God that he will open your Heart, he is actually at work upon your Ears: the greatest Profligate of them flys to Religion for aid, and assists his Cant with a doleful Tone and a study'd dismality of Gestures: But he trusts not to one Passion only, he flatters your Pride with Titles and Names of Honour and Distinction: your Avarice he sooths with often repeating to you the smallness of the Gift he sues for, and conditional promises of future returns with an Interest extravagant beyond the Statute of Usury tho' out of the reach of it. People not used to great Cities, being thus attack'd on all sides, are commonly forc'd to yield, and can't help giving something tho' they can hardly spare it themselves. How oddly are we manag'd by Self-love! It is ever watching in our Defence, and yet, to sooth a predominant Passion, obliges us to Act against our Interest: For when Pity seizes us, if we can but imagine that we contribute to the Relief of him we have Compassion with, and are Instrumental to the lessening of his Sorrows it eases us, and therefore pitiful People often give an Alms when they really feel that they would rather not.

When Sores are very bare or seem otherwise afflicting in an extraordinary manner, and the Beggar can bear to have them expos'd to the Cold Air, it is very shocking to some People; 'tis a shame they cry such Sights should be suffer'd; the main reason is, it touches their Pity feelingly, and at the same time they are resolv'd, either because they are Covetous, or count it an idle Expence, to give nothing, which makes them more uneasy. They turn their Eyes, and where the Cries are dismal, some would willingly stop their Ears if they were not ashamed. What they can do is to mend their Pace, and be very angry in their Hearts that Beggars should be about the Streets. But it is with Pity as it is with Fear, the more we are conversant with Objects that excite either Passion, the less we are disturb'd by them, and those to whom all these scenes and tones are by custom made familiar, they make little Impression upon. The only thing the Industrious Beggar has left to conquer those fortified Hearts, if he can walk either with or without Crutches, is to follow close and with uninterrupted Noise, teaze and importune them, to try if he can make them buy their Peace. Thus thousands give Money to Beggars from the same motive as they pay their Corn-cutter, to walk Easy. And many a Halfpenny is given to impudent and designedly persecuting Rascals, whom, if it could be done handsomly, a man would cane with much greater Satisfaction. Yet all this by the courtesy of the Country is call'd Charity.

The Reverse of Pity is Malice: I have spoke of it where I treat of Envy. Those who know what it is to examine themselves, will soon own that it is very difficult to trace the Root and origin of this Passion. It is one of those we are most ashamed of, and therefore the hurtful part of it is easily subdued and corrected by a Judicious Education. When any body near us stumbles, it is natural even before reflection to stretch out our Hands to hinder or at least break the fall, which shews that whilst we are Calm we are rather bent to Pity. But tho' Malice by it self is little to be fear'd, yet assisted with Pride, it is often mischievous, and becomes most terrible when egg'd on and heighten'd by Anger. There is nothing that more readily or more effectually extinguishes Pity than this mixture, which is call'd Cruelty: From whence we may learn that to perform a meritorious Action, it is not sufficient barely to conquer a Passion unless it likewise be done from a laudable Principle, and consequently how necessary that Clause was in the Definition of Vertue, that our Endeavours were to proceed from *a rational Ambition of being Good.*

Pity, as I have said somewhere else, is the most amiable of all our Passions, and there are not many occasions on which we ought to conquer or curb it. A Surgeon may be as compassionate as he pleases so it does not make him omit or forbear to perform what he ought to do. Judges likewise and Juries may be influenc'd with Pity, if they take care that plain Laws and Justice it self are not infringed and do not suffer by it. No Pity does more Mischief in the World than what is excited by the Tenderness of Parents, and hinders them from managing their Children as their rational Love to them would require, and themselves could wish it. The Sway likewise which this Passion bears in the Affections of Women is more considerable than is commonly imagined, and they daily commit Faults that are altogether ascribed to Lust, and yet are in a great measure owing to Pity.

What I named last is not the only Passion that mocks and resembles Charity; Pride and Vanity have built more Hospitals than all the Virtues together. Men are so tenacious of their Possessions, and Selfishness is so rivited in our Nature, that whoever can but any ways conquer it shall have the Applause of the Publick, and all the Encouragement imaginable to conceal his Frailty and sooth any other Appetite he shall have a mind to indulge. The Man that supplies with his private Fortune, what the whole must otherwise have provided for, obliges every Member of the Society, and therefore all the World are ready to pay him their Acknowledgment, and think themselves in Duty bound to pronounce all such Actions virtuous, without examining or so much as looking into the Motives from which they were perform'd. Nothing is more destructive to Virtue or Religion it self, than to make Men believe that giving Money to the Poor, tho' they should not part with it till after Death, will make a full Atonement in the next World, for the Sins they have committed in this. A Villain who has been guilty of a barbarous Murder may by the help of false Witnesses escape the Punishment he deserv'd: He prospers, we'll say, heaps up great Wealth, and by the Advice of his Father Confessor leaves all his Estate to a Monastery, and his Children Beggars. What fine Amends has this good Christian made for his Crime, and what an honest Man was the Priest who directed his Conscience? He who parts with all he has in his Life-time, whatever Principle he acts from, only gives away what was his own; but the rich Miser who refuses to assist his nearest Relations whilst he is alive, tho' they never designedly disobliged him, and disposes of his Money for what we call Charitable uses after his Death, may imagine of his Goodness what he pleases, but he robbs his Posterity. I am now thinking of a late Instance of Charity, a prodigious Gift, that has made a great Noise in the World: I have a mind to set it in the Light I think it deserves, and beg leave, for once to please Pedants, to treat it somewhat Rhetorically.

That a Man[1] with small Skill in Physick and hardly any Learning, should by vile Arts get into Practice and lay up great Wealth is no mighty wonder; but that he should so deeply work himself into the good Opinion of the World as to gain the general Esteem of a Nation, and establish a Reputation beyond all his contemporaries with no other qualities but a perfect Knowledge of Mankind, and a capacity of making the most of it, is something extraordinary. If a Man arrived to such a height of Glory should be almost distracted with Pride, sometimes give his attendance on a Servant or any mean Person for nothing, and at the same time neglect a Nobleman that gives exorbitant Fees, at other times refuse to leave his Bottle for his Business without any regard to the quality of the Persons that sent for him, or the Danger they are in: If he should be surly and morose, affect to be an Humorist, treat his patients like Dogs, tho' People of distinction, and value no Man but what would deify him, and never call in question the certainty of his Oracles: If he should insult all the World, affront the first Nobility, and extend his insolence even to the Royal Family: If to maintain as well as to increase the Fame of his sufficiency, he should scorn to consult with his Betters on what emergency soever, look down with contempt on the most deserving of his Profession, and never confer with any other Physician but what will pay homage to his Superiour Genius, creep to his Humour and never approach him but with all the slavish Obsequiousness a Court Flaterer can treat a Prince with: If a Man in his life time should discover on the one hand such manifest Symptoms of Superlative Pride, and an insatiable greediness after Wealth at the same time, and on the other no regard to Religion or Affection to his Kindred, no Compassion to the Poor, and hardly any Humanity to his Fellow Creatures; if he gave no proofs that he lov'd his Country, had a Publick Spirit or was a lover of Arts, of Books or of Literature, what must we Judge of his motive, the principle he acted from, when after his Death we find that he has left a Trifle among his Relations who stood in need of it, and an immense Treasure to an University that did not want it.

Let a Man be as charitable as it is possible for him to be without forfeiting his Reason or good Sense; can he think otherwise, but that this famous Physician did in the making of his Will, as in every thing else, indulge his darling Passion, entertaining his Vanity with the Happiness of the Contrivance? When he thought on the Monuments and Inscriptions, with all the Sacrifices of Praise that would be made to him, and above all the yearly Tribute of Thanks, of Reverence and Veneration that would be paid to his Memory with so much Pomp and Solemnity; when he consider'd, how in all these Performances Wit and Invention would be rack'd, Art and Eloquence ransack'd to find out Encomiums suitable to the Publick Spirit, the Munificence and the Dignity of the Benefactor, and the artful Gratitude of the Receivers; when he thought on, I say, and consider'd these Things, it must have thrown his ambitious Soul into vast Extasies of Pleasure, especially when he ruminated on the Duration of his Glory, and the Perpetuity he would by this Means procure to his Name. Charitable Opinions are often stupidly false; when Men are dead and gone, we ought to judge of their Actions, as we do of Books, and neither wrong their Understanding nor our own. The *British Esculapius* was undeniably a Man of Sense, and if he had been influenc'd by Charity, a Publick Spirit, or the Love of Learning, and had aim'd at the Good of Mankind in general, or that of his own Profession in particular, and acted from any of these Principles, he could never have made such a Will; because so much Wealth might have been better managed, and a Man of much less Capacity would have found out several better Ways of laying out the Money. But if we consider, that he was as undeniably a Man of vast Pride, as he was a Man of Sense, and give our selves leave only to surmise, that this extraordinary Gift might have proceeded from such a Motive, we shall presently discover the Excellency of his Parts, and his consummate Knowledge of the World; for, if a Man would render himself immortal, be ever prais'd and deify'd after his Death, and have all the Acknowledgment, the Honours, and Compliments paid to his Memory, that Vain-Glory herself could wish for, I don't think it in human Skill to invent a more effectual Method. Had he follow'd Arms, behaved himself in five and twenty Sieges, and as many Battles, with the Bravery of an *Alexander,* and exposed his Life and Limbs to all the Fatigues and

Dangers of War for fifty Campaigns together; or devoting himself to the *Muses,* sacrific'd his Pleasure, his Rest, and his Health to Literature, and spent all his Days in a laborious Study, and the Toils of Learning; or else abandoning all worldly Interest, excell'd in Probity, Temperance, and Austerity of Life, and ever trod in the strictest Path of Virtue, he would not so effectually have provided for the Eternity of his Name, as after a voluptuous Life, and the luxurious Gratification of his Passions, he has now done without any Trouble or Self-Denial, only by the Choice in the Disposal of his Money, when he was forc'd to leave it.

A rich Miser, who is thorowly selfish, and would receive the Interest of his Money even after his Death, has nothing else to do than to defraud his Relations, and leave his Estate to some famous University: they are the best Markets to buy Immortality at with little Merit; in them Knowledge, Wit, and Penetration are the Growth, I had almost said, the Manufacture of the Place: There Men are profoundly skill'd in Human Nature, and know what it is their Benefactors want; and there extraordinary Bounties shall always meet with an extraordinary Recompence, and the Measure of the Gift is ever the Standard of their Praises, whether the Donor be a Physician or a Tinker, when once the living Witnesses that might laugh at them are extinct. I can never think on the Anniversary of the Thanksgiving-Day decreed to a great Man, but it puts me in mind of the miraculous Cures, and other surprising Things that will be said of him a hundred Years hence, and I dare prognosticate, that before the End of the present Century, he will have Stories forg'd in his Favour, (for Rhetoricians are never upon Oath) that shall be as fabulous at least as any Legends of the Saints.

Of all this our subtle Benefactor was not ignorant, he understood Universities, their Genius, and their Politicks, and from thence foresaw and knew that the Incense to be offer'd to him would not cease with the present or a few succeeding Generations, and that it would not only last for the trifling Space of three or four hundred Years, but that it would continue to be paid to him through all Changes and Revolutions of Government and Religion, as long as the Nation subsists, and the Island it self remains.

It is deplorable that the Proud should have such Temptations to wrong their Lawful Heirs: For when a Man in ease and affluence, brimfull of Vain Glory and humour'd in his Pride by the greatest of a Polite Nation, has such an infallible Security in Petto for an Everlasting Homage and Adoration to his *Manes* to be paid in such an extraordinary manner, he is like a Hero in Battle, who in feasting on his own Imagination tastes all the Felicity of Enthusiasm. It buoys him up in Sickness, relieves him in Pain, and either Guards him against or keeps from his view all the Terrours of Death, and the most dismal Apprehensions of Futurity.

Should it be said that to be thus Censorious, and look into matters, and Mens Consciences with that nicety will discourage People from laying out their Money this way; and that let the Money and the Motive of the Donour be what they will, he that receives the Benefit is the Gainer, I would not disown the charge, but am of Opinion, that it is no Injury to the Publick, should one prevent Men from crowding too much Treasure into the Dead Stock of the Kingdom. There ought to be a vast disproportion between the Active and Unactive part of the Society to make it Happy, and where this is not regarded the multitude of Gifts and Endowments may soon be excessive and detrimental to a Nation. Charity, where it is too extensive, seldom fails of promoting Sloth and Idleness, and is good for little in the Common Wealth but to breed Drones and destroy Industry. The more Colleges and Alms-houses you Build the more you may. The first Founders and Benafactors may have just and good Intentions, and would perhaps for their own Reputations seem to Labour for the most laudable purposes, but the Executors of those Wills, the Governours that come after them have quite other views, and we seldom see Charities long applied as it was first intended they should be. I have no design that is Cruel, nor the least aim that Savours of Inhumanity. To have sufficient Hospitals for Sick and Wounded I look upon as an indispensible Duty both in Peace and War: Young Children without Parents, Old Age without Support, and all that are disabled from Working ought to be taken care of with Tenderness and Alacrity. But as on the one hand I would have none neglected that are helpless, and really necessitous without being wanting to themselves, so on the other I would not encourage Beggary or Laziness in the Poor: All should be set to Work that are any ways able, and Scrutinies should be made even among the Infirm: Employments might be found out for most of our Lame, and many that are unfit for hard Labour, as well as the Blind, as long as their Health and Strength would allow of it. What I have now under consideration leads me naturally to that kind of Distraction the Nation has labour'd under for some time, the Enthusiastick Passion for Charity-Schools.

The generality are so bewitch'd with the Usefulness and Excellency of them, that whoever dares openly oppose them is in danger of being Stoned by the Rabble. Children that are taught the Principles of Religion and can read the Word of God, have a greater opportunity to improve in Virtue and good Morality, and must certainly be more civilis'd than others, that are suffer'd to run at random and have no body to look after them. How perverse must be the Judgment of those, who would not rather see Children decently dress'd, with clean Linnen at least a Week, that in an orderly manner follow their Master to Church, than in every open place meet with a Company of Black-Guards without Shirts or any thing whole about them, that insensible of their Misery are continually encreasing it with Oaths and Imprecations! can any one doubt but these are the great nursery of Thieves and Pick-pockets? What Numbers of Felons and other Criminals have we Tried and Convicted every Sessions! This will be prevented by Charity-Schools, and when the Children of the Poor receive a better Education, the Society will in a few Years reap the Benefit of it, and the Nation be clear'd of so many Miscreants as now this great City and all the Country about it are fill'd with.

This is the General Cry, and he that speaks the least Word against it, an Uncharitable, hard Hearted, and Inhuman if not a Wicked, Prophane and Atheistical Wretch. As to the comliness of the sight, no body disputes it, but I would not have a Nation pay too dear for so transient a Pleasure, and if we might set aside the finery of the Shew, every thing that is material in this Popular Oration might soon be answer'd.

As to Religion, the most knowing and polite Part of a Nation have every where the least of it; Craft has a greater Hand in making Rogues than Stupidity, and Vice in general is no where more predominant than where Arts and Sciences flourish. Ignorance is, to a Proverb, counted to be the Mother of Devotion, and it is certain that we shall find Innocence and Honesty no where more general than among the most illiterate, the poor silly Country People. The next to be consider'd, are the Manners and Civility that by Charity-Schools are to be grafted into the Poor of the Nation. I confess that in my Opinion to be in any degree possess'd of what I named is a frivolous if not a hurtful Quality, at least nothing is less requisite in the Labourious Poor. It is not Compliments we want of them but their Work and Assiduity. But I give up this Article with all my Heart, good manners we'll say are necessary to all People, but which way will they be furnish'd with them in a Charity-School. Boys there may be taught to pull off their Caps promiscuously to all they meet, unless it be a Beggar: But that they should acquire in it any Civility beyond that I can't conceive.

The Master is not greatly qualify'd, as may be guess'd by his Salary, and if he could teach them Manners, he has not time for it: Whilst they are at School they are either learning or saying their Lesson to him, or employ'd in Writing or Arithmetick, and as soon as School is done, they are as much at Liberty as other Poor Peoples Children. It is precept and the example of Parents, and those they Eat, Drink and Converse with, that have an Influence upon the Minds of Children: Reprobate Parents that take Ill Courses and are regardless of their Children, won't have a mannerly civiliz'd Offspring tho' they went to a Charity-School till they were Married. The honest pains-taking People, be they never so poor, if they have any notion of Goodness and Decency themselves, will keep their Children in awe, and never suffer them to rake about the Streets, and lie out a-Nights. Those who will work themselves, and have any command over their Children, will make them do something or other that turns to Profit as soon as they are able, be it never so little; and such as are so Ungovernable, that neither Words or Blows can work upon them, no Charity-School will mend: Nay, Experience teaches us, that among the Charity-Boys there are abundance of bad ones that Swear and Curse about, and, bar the Cloaths, are as much Blackguard as ever *Tower-Hill* or *St. James's* produced.

I am now come to the enormous Crimes, and vast Multitude of Malefactors that are all laid upon the want of this notable Education. That abundance of Thefts and Robberies are daily committed in and about the City, and great numbers Yearly suffer Death for those Crimes, is undeniable: But because this is ever hook'd in when the Usefulness of Charity-Schools is call'd in Question, as if there was no dispute, but they would in a great measure remedy, and in time prevent those Disorders, I intend to examine into the real Causes of those Mischiefs so justly complain'd of, and doubt not but to make it appear that Charity-Schools, and every thing else that promotes Idleness, and keeps the Poor from Working, are more Accessary to the growth of Villainy, than the want of Reading and Writing, or even the grossest Ignorance and Stupidity.

Here I must interrupt my self to obviate the Clamours of some impatient People, who upon Reading of what I said last will cry out that, far from encouraging Idleness, they bring up their Charity-Children to Handicrafts, as well as Trades, and all manner of Honest Labour. I promise them that I shall take notice of that hereafter, and answer it without stifling the least thing that can be said in their Behalf.

In a populous City it is not difficult for a young Rascal, that has push'd himself into a Crowd, with a small Hand and nimble Fingers to whip away a Handkerchief or Snuff Box from a Man who is thinking on Business, and regardless of his Pocket. Success in small Crimes seldom fails of ushering in greater, and he, that picks Pockets with impunity at Twelve, is likely to be a House-breaker at Sixteen, and a thorough paced Villain long before he is Twenty. Those, who are Cautious as well as Bold, and no Drunkards, may do a world of Mischief before they are discover'd; and this is one of the greatest Inconveniencies of such vast overgrown Cities as *London* or *Paris,* that they harbour Rogues and Villains as Granaries do Vermin; they afford a perpetual shelter to the worst of People, and are places of Safety to Thousands of Criminals, who daily commit Thefts and Burglaries, and yet by often changing their places of Abode, may conceal themselves for many Years, and will perhaps for ever escape the hands of Justice unless by chance they are apprehended in a Fact. And when they are taken, the Evidences perhaps want clearness or are otherwise insufficient, the Depositions are not strong enough, Juries and often Judges are touch'd with Compassion; Prosecutors tho' vigorous at first often relent before the time of Trial comes on: Few Men prefer the publick Safety to their own Ease; a Man of Good Nature is not easily reconcil'd with the taking away of another Man's Life, tho' he has deserv'd the Gallows. To be the cause of any one's Death, tho' Justice requires it, is what most People are startled at, especially Men of Conscience and Probity, when they want Judgment or Resolution; as this is the reason that Thousands escape that deserve to be Capitally Punish'd, so it is likewise the cause that there are so many Offenders, who boldly venture in hopes, that if they are taken they shall have the same good Fortune of getting off.

But if Men did imagine and were fully persuaded, that as surely as they committed a Fact that deserv'd Hanging, so surely they would be Hang'd, Executions would be very rare, and the most desperate Felon would almost as soon hang himself as he would break open a House. To be Stupid and Ignorant is seldom the Character of a Thief. Robberies on the High-way and other bold Crimes are generally perpetrated by Rogues of Spirit and a Genius, and Villains of any Fame are commonly subtle cunning Fellows, that are well vers'd in the Method of Trials, and acquainted with every Quirk in the Law, that can be of Use to them, that overlook not the smallest Flaw in an Indictment, and know how to make an Advantage of the least slip of an Evidence and every thing else, that can serve their turn to bring 'em off.

It is a mighty Saying, that it is better that Five Hundred Guilty People should escape, than that one Innocent Person should suffer: This Maxim is only true as to Futurity, and in relation to another World; but it is very false in regard to the Temporal Welfare of the Society. It is a terrible thing a Man should be put to Death for a Crime he is not Guilty of; yet so oddly Circumstances may meet in the infinite variety of Accidents, that it is possible it should Come to pass, all the Wisdom that Judges, and Conscientiousness that Juries may be possess'd of, notwithstanding. But where Men endeavour to avoid this with all the Care and Precaution human prudence is able to take, should such a Misfortune happen perhaps once or twice in Half a Score Years, on Condition that all that time Justice should be Administered with all the Strictness and Severity, and not one Guilty Person suffer'd to Escape with Impunity; it would be a vast Advantage to a Nation, not only as to the securing of every ones Property and the peace of the Society in General, but it would likewise save the Lives of Hundreds, if not Thousands, of Necessitous Wretches, that are daily hang'd for Trifles, and who would never have attempted any thing against the Law, or at least not have ventured on Capital Crimes, if the hopes of getting off should they be taken, had not been one of the Motives that animated their Resolution. Therefore where the Laws are plain and severe all the remisness in the Execution of them, Lenity of Juries and frequency of Pardons are in the main a much greater Cruelty to a populous State or Kingdom, than the use of Racks and the most exquisite Torments.

Another great Cause of those Evils is to be look'd for in the want of Precaution in those that are robb'd, and the many Temptations that are given. Abundance of Families are very remiss in looking after the Safety of their Houses, some are Robb'd by the carelessness of Servants, others for having grudg'd the price of Bars and Shutters. Brass and Pewter are ready Money, they are every where about the House; Plate perhaps and Money are better secured, but an ordinary Lock is soon open'd, when once a Rogue is got in.

It is manifest then that many different Causes concur, and several scarce avoidable Evils contribute to the misfortune of being pester'd with Pilferers, Thieves, and Robbers, which all Countries ever were and ever will be, more or less, in and near considerable Towns, more especially vast and overgrown Cities. 'Tis Opportunity makes the Thief; carelesness and neglect in Fastning Doors and Windows, the excessive Tenderness of Juries and Prosecutors, the small difficulty of getting a Reprieve and frequency of Pardons, but above all the many Examples of those, who are known to be Guilty, are destitute both of Friends and Money, and yet by imposing on the Jury, Baffling the Witnesses or other Tricks and Stratagems, find out means to escape the Gallows. These are all strong Temptations that conspire to draw in the Necessitous, who want Principle and Education.

To these you may add as Auxiliaries to mischief, an habit of Sloth and Idleness and strong aversion to Labour and Assiduity, which all Young People will contract that are not brought up to down right Working, or at least kept employ'd most Days in the Week, and the greatest part of the Day. All Children that are Idle, even the best of either Sex, are bad Company to one another whenever they meet.

It is not then the want of Reading and Writing, but the concurrence and a complication of more Substantial Evils that are the perpetual nursery of abandon'd Profligates in great and opulent Nations; and whoever would accuse Ignorance, Stupidity and Dastardness, as the first, and what Physicians call the Procatartic Cause,[2] let him examine into the Lives, and narrowly inspect the Conversations and Actions of ordinary Rogues and our common Felons, and he will find the reverse to be true, and that the blame ought rather to be laid on the excessive Cunning and Subtlety, and too much Knowledge in general, which the worst of Miscreants and the Scum of the Nation are possess'd of.

Human Nature is every where the same: Genius, Wit and Natural Parts are always sharpen'd by Application, and may be as much improv'd in the practice of the meanest Villainy, as they can in the exercise of Industry or the most Heroic Virtue. There is no Station of Life, where Pride, Emulation and the love of Glory may not be display'd. A Young Pick-pocket that makes a Jest of his Angry Prosecutor, and dextrously wheedles the Old Justice into an Opinion of his Innocence, is envied by his Equals and admired by all the Fraternity. Rogues have the same Passions to gratify as other Men, and value themselves on their Honour and Faithfulness to one another, their Courage, Intrepidity and other Manly Virtues as well as People of better Professions; and in daring Enterprizes the Resolution of a Robber may be as much supported by his Pride, as that of an Honest Soldier, who Fights for his Country.

The Evils then we complain of are owing to quite other Causes than what we assign for them. Men must be very wavering in their Sentiments, if not inconsistent with themselves, that at one time will uphold Knowledge and Learning to be the most proper means to promote Religion, and defend at another that Ignorance is the Mother of Devotion.

But of the Reasons alledg'd for this general Education are not the true ones, whence comes it that the whole Kingdom both great and small are so Unanimously Fond of it? There is no miraculous conversion to be perceiv'd among us, no Universal Bent to Goodness and Morality that has on a sudden overspread the Island: there is as much Wickedness as ever, Charity is as Cold, and real Virtue as Scarce: The Year Seventeen Hundred and Twenty has been as Prolifick in deep Villainy, and remarkable for Selfish Crimes and premeditated Mischief, as can be pick'd out of any Century whatever; not committed by Poor Ignorant Rogues that could neither Read nor Write, but the better sort of People as to Wealth and Education, that most of them were great Masters in Arithmetick, and lived in Reputation and Splendour.[3] To say that when a thing is once in Vogue, the multitude follows the common cry, that Charity Schools are in Fashion in the same manner as Hoop'd Petticoats, by Caprice, and that no more Reason can be given for the one than the other, I am afraid will not be Satisfactory to the Curious, and at the same time I doubt much, whether it will be thought of great Weight by many of my Readers, what I can advance besides.

The real Source of this present Folly is certainly very abstruse and remote from sight, but he that affords the least light in matters of great obscurity does a kind office to the Enquirers. I am willing to allow, that in the Beginning the first Design of those Schools was Good and Charitable, but to know what encreases them so extravagantly, and who are the chief Promoters of them now, we must make our search another way, and address our selves to the rigid Party-men that are zealous for their Cause, either Episcopacy or Presbytery; but as the latter are but the Poor Mimicks of the first, tho' equally pernicious, we shall confine our selves to the National Church, and take a turn through a Parish that is not bless'd yet with a Charity School.

But here I think my self obliged in conscience to ask pardon of my Reader for the tiresom Dance I am going to lead him if he intends to follow me, and therefore I desire that he would either throw away the Book and leave me, or else arm himself with the Patience of *Job* to endure all the Impertinencies of Low Life, the Cant and Tittle Tattle he is like to meet with before he can go half a Street's length.

First we must look out among the young Shop-keepers, that have not half the Business they could wish for, and consequently Time to spare. If such a New-beginner has but a little Pride more than ordinary, and loves to be medling, he is soon mortify'd in the Vestry, where Men of Substance and long standing, or else your pert litigious or opinionated Bawlers, that have obtained the Title of Notable Men, commonly bear the sway. His Stock and perhaps Credit are but inconsiderable, and yet he finds within himself a strong Inclination to Govern. A Man thus qualified thinks it a thousand pities there is no Charity-School in the Parish: he communicates his Thoughts to two or three of his Acquaintance first; they do the same to others, and in a Month's time there is nothing else talk'd of in the Parish. Every body invents Discourses and Arguments to the Purpose according to his Abilities.—It is an errant Shame, says one, to see so many Poor that are not able to educate their Children, and no provision made for them where we have so many Rich People. What d'ye talk of Rich, answers another, they are the worst: they must have so many Servants, Coaches and Horses: They can lay out Hundreds, and some of them Thousands of Pounds for Jewels and Furniture, but not spare a Shilling to a poor Creature that wants it: When Modes and Fashions are discours'd of they can hearken with great Attention, but are willfully deaf to the Cries of the Poor. Indeed Neighbour, replies the first, you are very right, I don't believe there is a worse Parish in England for Charity than ours: 'Tis such as you and I that would do good if it was in our power, but of those that are able there's very few that are willing.

Others more violent fall upon particular Persons, and fasten Slander on every Man of Substance they dislike, and a thousand idle Stories in behalf of Charity are rais'd and handed about to defame their Betters. Whilst this is doing throughout the Neighbourhood, he that first broach'd the pious Thought rejoices to hear so many come in to it, and places no small Merit in being the first cause of so much Talk and Bustle: But neither himself nor his Intimates being considerable enough to set such a thing on foot, some body must be found out who has greater Interest: he is to be address'd to, and shew'd the Necessity, the Goodness, the Usefulness and Christianity of such a Design: next he is to be flatter'd.—Indeed Sir, if you would espouse it, no body has a greater Influence over the best of the Parish than your self: One Word of you I am sure would engage such a one: If you once would take it to heart, Sir, I would look upon the thing as done, Sir—If by this kind of Rhetorick they can draw in some old Fool or conceited Busy-body that is rich, or at least reputed to be such, the thing begins to be feasible, and is discours'd of among the better sort. The parson, or his Curate, and the Lecturer are every where extolling the Pious Project. The first Promoters mean while are indefatigable: If they were Guilty of any open Vice they either Sacrifice it to the love of Reputation or at least grow more cautious and learn to play the Hypocrite, well knowing that to be flagitious or noted for Enormities is inconsistent with the Zeal which they pretend to for Works of Supererrogation and Excessive Piety.

The number of these diminutive Patriots encreasing, they form themselves into a Society, and appoint stated Meetings, where every one concealing his Vices has liberty to display his Talents. Religion is the Theme, or else the Misery of the Times occasion'd by Atheism and Prophaneness. Men of Worth, who live in Splendor, and thriving People that have a great deal of Business of their own, are seldom seen among them. Men of Sense and Education likewise, if they have nothing to do, generally look out for better diversion. All those who have a higher aim, shall have their attendance easily excus'd, but contribute they must or else lead a weary Life in the Parish. Two sorts of People come in voluntarily, Stanch Churchmen, who have good reasons for it in Petto, and your sly Sinners that look upon it as meritorious, and hope that it will expiate their Guilt, and Satan be Nonsuited by it at a small Expence. Some come in to it to save their Credit, others to retrieve it, according as they have either lost or are afraid of losing it; others again do it Prudentially to encrease their Trade and get Acquaintance, and many would own to you, if they dared to be sincere and speak the Truth, that they would never have been concern'd in it, but to be better known in the Parish. Men of Sense that see the Folly of it and have no body to Fear, are persuaded into it not to be thought singular or to run Counter to all the World; even those who are resolute at first in denying, it is ten to one but at last they are teaz'd and importun'd into a Compliance. The Charge being calculated for most of the Inhabitants, the Insignificancy of it is another Argument that prevails much, and many are drawn in to be Contributors, who without that would have stood out and strenuously opposed the whole Scheme.

The Governours are made of the midling People, and many inferiour to that Class are made use of, if the forwardness of their Zeal can but over-ballance the meanness of their Condition. If you should ask these Worthy Rulers, why they take upon them so much Trouble to the detriment of their own Affairs and loss of Time, either singly or the whole body of them, they would all Unanimously Answer, that it is the regard they have for Religion and the Church, and the Pleasure they take in Contributing to the Good, and Eternal Welfare of so many Poor Innocents that in all probability would run into Perdition in these Wicked Times of Scoffers and Free-thinkers. They have no Thought of Interest even those who deal in and provide these Children with what they want, have not the least design of getting by what they sell for their Use, and tho' in every thing else their Avarice and Greediness after Lucre be glaringly conspicuous, in this Affair they are wholly divested from Selfishness, and have no Worldly Ends. One Motive above all, which is none of the least with most of them, is to be carefully conceal'd, I mean the Satisfaction there is in Ordering and Directing: There is a Melodious Sound in the word Governour that is charming to mean People: Every Body admires Sway and Superiority, even *Imperium in Belluas*[4] has its Delights, there is a Pleasure in Ruling over any thing, and it is this chiefly that supports Human Nature in the Tedious Slavery of School-masters. But if there be the least Satisfaction in governing the Children, it must be ravishing to govern the School-master himself. What fine things are said and perhaps Wrote to a Governour, when a School-master is to be Chosen! How the Praises tickle, and how Pleasant it is not to find out the Fulsomness of the Flattery, the Stifness of the Expressions, or the Pedantry of the Stile!

Those who can examine Nature will always find, that what these People most pretend to is the least, and what they utterly deny their greatest Motive. No Habit or Quality is more easily acquired than Hypocrisy, nor any thing sooner learn'd than to deny the Sentiments of our Hearts and the Principle we Act from: But the Seeds of every Passion are innate to us, and no body comes into the World without them. If we will mind the Pastimes and Recreations of Young Children, we shall observe nothing more general in them, than that all who are suffer'd to do it, take delight in playing with Kittens and little Puppy Dogs. What makes them always lugging and pulling the poor Creatures about the House proceeds from nothing else but that they can do with them what they please, and put them into what posture and shape they list, and the Pleasure they receive from this is originally owing to the love of Dominion and that Usurping Temper all Mankind are Born with.

When this great Work is brought to bear, and actually accomplish'd, Joy and Serenity seem to overspread the Face of every Inhabitant, which likewise to account for I must make a short digression. There are every where slovenly sorry Fellows that are used to be seen always Ragged and Dirty: These People we look upon as miserable Creatures in General, and unless they are very remarkable we take little Notice of them, and yet among these there are handsome and well shaped Men as well as among their Betters. But if one of these turns Soldier, what a vast Alteration is there observ'd in him for the better, as soon as he is put in his Red Coat, and we see him look smart with his Granadiers Cap and a great Ammunition Sword! All who knew him before are struck with other Ideas of his Qualities, and the Judgment which both Men and Women form of him in their Minds is very different from what it was. There is some thing Analogous to this in the Sight of Charity Children; there is a natural Beauty in Uniformity which most People delight in. It is diverting to the Eye to see Children well match'd, either Boys or Girls, march two and two in good Order; and to have them all whole and tight in the same Cloaths and Trimming must add to the Comliness of the Sight; and what makes it still more generally entertaining is the imaginary Share which even Servants and the meanest in the Parish have in it, to whom it costs nothing: our Parish Church, our Charity Children. In all this there is a Shadow of property that tickles every Body that has a Right to make Use of the Words, but more especially those who actually contribute and had a great Hand in advancing the pious Work.

It is hardly conceivable that Men should so little know their own Hearts and be so ignorant of their inward Condition, as to mistake Frailty, Passion and Enthusiasm for Goodness, Virtue and Charity; yet nothing is more true than that the Satisfaction, the Joy and Transports they feel on the accounts I named pass with these miserable Judges for principles of Piety and Religion. Whoever will consider what I have said for two or three Pages, and suffer his Imagination to rove a little further on what he has heard and seen concerning this Subject, will be furnished with sufficient Reasons abstract from the love of God and true Christianity, why Charity-Schools are in such uncommon Vogue, and so unanimously approv'd of and admired among all sorts and conditions of People. It is a Theme which every Body can talk of and understands thoroughly, there is not a more inexhaustible fund for Tittle Tattle, and a variety of low conversation in Hoy-boats and Stage-coaches. If a Governour that in Behalf of the School or the Sermon exerted himself more than ordinary, happens to be in Company, how he is commended by the Women, and his Zeal and Charitable Disposition extoll'd to the Skies! Upon my word, Sir, says an Old Lady we are all very much obliged to you, I don't think any of the other Governours could have made Interest enough to procure us a Bishop; 'twas on your Account I am told that his Lordship came, tho' he was not very well: To which the other replies very gravely, that it is his Duty, but that he values no Trouble nor Fatigue so he can be but serviceable to the Children, poor Lambs: Indeed, says he, I was resolv'd to get a pair of Lawn Sleeves tho' I rid all Night for it, and I am very glad I was not disappointed.

Sometimes the School it self is discours'd of, and of whom in all the Parish it is most expected he should Build one: The old Room where it is now kept is ready to drop down: Such a one had a vast Estate left him by his Uncle, and a great deal of Money besides; a Thousand Pounds would be nothing in his Pocket.

At others the great Crowds are talk'd of that are seen at some Churches, and the considerable Sums that are gather'd; from whence by an easy transition they go over to the Abilities, the different Talents and Orthodoxy of Clergymen. Dr.—is a Man of great Parts and Learning, and I believe he is very hearty for the Church, but I don't like him for a Charity-Sermon. There is no better Man in the World than—; he forces the Money out of their Pockets. When he Preach'd last for our Children I am sure there was abundance of People that gave more than they intended when they came to Church. I could see it in their Faces and rejoyc'd at it Heartily.

Another Charm that renders Charity-Schools so bewitching to the Multitude is the general Opinion Establish'd among them, that they are not only actually Beneficial to Society as to Temporal Happiness, but likewise that Christianity enjoyns and requires of us, we should erect them for our Future Welfare. They are earnestly and fervently recommended by the whole body of the Clergy, and have more Labour and Eloquence laid out upon them than any other Christian Duty; not by young Parsons or poor Scholars of little Credit, but the most Learned of our Prelates and the most Eminent for Orthodoxy, even those who do not often fatigue themselves on any other Occasion. As to Religion, there is no doubt but they know what is chiefly required of us, and consequently the most necessary to Salvation: and as to the World, who should understand the Interest of the Kingdom better than the Wisdom of the Nation, of which the Lords Spiritual are so considerable a Branch? The consequence of this Sanction is first, that those, who with their Purses or Power are Instrumental to the encrease or maintenance of these Schools, are tempted to place a greater merit in what they do than otherwise they could suppose it deserv'd. Secondly, that all the rest, who either cannot or will not any ways contribute towards them, have still a very good reason why they should speak well of them; for tho' it be difficult, in things that interfere with our Passions, to act well, it is always in our power to wish well, because it is perform'd with little Cost. There is hardly a Person so Wicked among the Superstitious Vulgar, but in the liking he has for Charity-Schools, he imagines to see a Glimmering Hope that it will make an Atonement for his Sins, from the same Principle as the most Vicious comfort themselves with the Love and Veneration they bear to the Church, and the greatest Profligates find an Opportunity in it to shew the Rectitude of their Inclinations at no Expence.

But if all these were not inducements sufficient to make Men stand up in Defence of the Idol I speak of, there is another that will infallibly Bribe most People to be Advocates for it. We all naturally love Triumph, and whoever engages in this Cause is sure of Conquest at least in Nine Companies out of Ten. Let him dispute with whom he will, considering the Speciousness of the pretence, and the Majority he has on his side, it is a Castle, an impregnable Fortress he can never be beat out of, and was the most Sober, Virtuous Man alive to produce all the Arguments, to prove the detriment Charity-Schools, at least the Multiplicity of them, do to Society, which I shall give hereafter, and such as are yet stronger, against the greatest Scoundrel in the World, who should only make use of the common Cant of Charity and Religion, the Vogue would be against the first, and himself lose his Cause in the Opinion of the Vulgar.

The Rise then and Original of all the Bustle and Clamour that is made throughout the Kingdom in Behalf of Charity-Schools is chiefly Built on Frailty and Human Passion, at least it is more than possible that a Nation should have the same Fondness and feel the same Zeal for them as are shewn in ours, and yet not be prompted to it by any principle of Virtue or Religion. Encouraged by this Consideration, I shall with the greater Liberty attack this Vulgar Error, and endeavour to make it evident, that far from being Beneficial, this forc'd Education is pernicious to the Publick, the Welfare whereof as it demands of us a regard Superiour to all other Laws and considerations, so it shall be the only Apology I intend to make for differing from the present Sentiments of the Learned and Reverend Body of our Divines, and venturing plainly to deny, what I have just now own'd to be openly asserted by most of our Bishops as well as Inferior Clergy. As our Church pretends to no Infallibility even in Spirituals, her proper Province, so it cannot be an Affront to her to Imagine that she may err in Temporals which are not so much under her immediate care.—But to my Task.

The whole Earth being Curs'd and no Bread to be had but what we eat in the sweat of our Brows, vast Toil must be undergone before Man can provide himself with Necessaries for his Sustenance and the bare support of his corrupt and defective Nature as he is a single Creature; but infinitely more to make Life comfortable in a Civil Society, where Men are become taught Animals and great numbers of them have by mutual compact framed themselves into a Body Politick; and the more Man's Knowledge encreases in this State, the greater will be the variety of Labour required to make him easy. It is impossible that a Society can long subsist and suffer many of its Members to live in Idleness, and enjoy all the Ease and Pleasure they can invent, without having at the same time great multitudes of People that to make good this defect, will condescend to be quite the Reverse, and by use and patience inure their Bodies to Work for others and themselves besides.

The plenty and cheapness of Provisions depends in a great measure on the Price and Value that is set upon this Labour, and consequently the Welfare of all Societies even before they are tainted with Foreign Luxury, requires that it should be perform'd by such of their Members as in the first place are sturdy and robust and never used to Ease or Idleness, and in the second, soon contented as to the necessaries of Life; such as are glad to take up with the coursest Manufacture in every thing they wear, and in their Diet have no other aim than to feed their Bodies when their Stomachs prompt them to Eat, and, with little regard to Taste or Relish, refuse no Wholesome Nourishment that can be swallow'd when Men are Hungry, or ask any thing for their Thirst but to quench it.

As the greatest part of the Drudgery is to be done by Daylight, so it is by this only that they actually measure the time of their Labour, without any thought of the Hours they are employ'd, or the Weariness they feel; and the Hireling in the Country must get up in the Morning, not because he has rested enough, but because the Sun is going to rise. This last Article alone would be an intollerable hardship to Grown People under Thirty, who during nonage had been used to lye a Bed as long as they could sleep; but all three together make up such a Condition of Life as a Man more mildly Educated would hardly chuse; tho' it should deliver him from a Goal or a Shrew.

If such People there must be, as no great Nation can be happy without vast Numbers of them, would not a Wise Legislature cultivate the Breed of them with all imaginable Care, and provide against their Scarcity as he would prevent the Scarcity of Provision it self? No Man would be Poor and Fatigue himself for a Livelihood if he could help it: The absolute necessity all stand in for Victuals and Drink, and in cold

Climates for Cloaths and Lodging, makes them submit to any thing that can be bore with. If no body did Want no body would Work; but the greatest Hardships are look'd upon as Solid Pleasures when they keep a Man from Starving.

From what has been said it is manifest, that in a Free Nation where Slaves are not allow'd of, the surest wealth consists in a multitude of Laborious Poor; for besides that they are the never failing Nursery of Fleets and Armies, without them there could be no enjoyment, and no Product of any Country could be valuable. To make the Society Happy and People Easy under the meanest Circumstances, it is requisite that great numbers of them should be Ignorant as well as Poor. Knowledge both enlarges and multiplies our Desires, and the fewer things a Man Wishes for, the more easily his Necessities may be supply'd.

The Welfare and Felicity therefore of every State and Kingdom, require that the Knowledge of the Working Poor should be confin'd within the Verge of their Occupations, and never extended (as to things visible) beyond what relates to their Calling. The more a Shepherd, a Plowman or any other Peasant knows of the World, and the things that are Foreign to his Labour or Employment, the less fit he'll be to go through the Fatigues and Hardships of it with Chearfulness and Content.

Reading, Writing and Arithmetick are very necessary to those, whose Business require such Qualifications, but where Peoples Livelihood has no dependance on these Arts, they are very pernicious to the Poor, who are forc'd to get their Daily Bread by their Daily Labour. Few Children make any progress at School, but at the same time they are capable of being employ'd in some Business or other, so that every Hour those of poor People spend at their Book is so much time lost to the Society. Going to School in comparison to Working is Idleness, and the longer Boys continue in this easy sort of Life, the more unfit they'll be when grown up for downright Labour, both as to Strength and Inclination. Men who are to remain and end their Days in a Labourious, Tiresome and Painful Station of Life, the sooner they are put upon it at first, the more patiently they'll submit to it for ever after. Hard Labour and the coursest Diet are a proper Punishment to several kinds of Malefactors, but to impose either on those that have not been used and brought up to both is the greatest Cruelty, when there is no Crime you can charge them with.

Reading and Writing are not attain'd to without some labour of the Brain and assiduity, and before People are tollerably vers'd in either, they esteem themselves infinitely above those who are wholly Ignorant of them, often with so little Justice and Moderation as if they were of another Species. As all Mortals have naturally an Aversion to trouble and pains-taking, so we are all fond of, and apt to overvalue those Qualifications we have purchas'd at the Expence of our ease and quiet for Years together. Those who spent a great part of their Youth in Learning to Read, Write and Cypher, expect and not unjustly to be employ'd where those Qualifications may be of use to them; the generality of them will look upon downright Labour with the utmost contempt, I mean labour perform'd in the service of others, in the lowest Station of Life, and for the meanest consideration. A Man who has had some Education, may follow Husbandry by choice, and be diligent at the dirtiest and most laborious Work; but then the concern must be his own, and Avarice, the care of a Family, or some other pressing Motive must put him upon it, but he wont make a good Hireling and serve a Farmer for a pitiful Reward, at least he is not so fit for it as a Day Labourer that has always been employ'd about the Plow and Dung Cart, and remembers not that ever he has lived otherwise.

When Obsequiousness and mean Services are required, we shall always observe that they are never so chearfully nor so heartily perform'd as from Inferiours to Superiours; I mean Inferiours not only in Riches and Quality, but like wise in Knowledge and Understanding. A Servant can have no unfeign'd Respect for his Master, as soon as he has Sense enough to find out that he serves a Fool. When we are to learn or to obey we shall experience in our selves, that the greater Opinion we have of the Wisdom and Capacity of those that are either to Teach or Command us, the greater deference we pay to their Laws and Instructions. No Creatures submit contentedly to their Equals, and should a Horse know as much as a Man, I should not desire to be his Rider.

Here I am obliged again to make a Digression, tho' I declare I never had a less mind to it than I have at this Minute; but I see a Thousand Rods in Piss,[5] and the whole Posse of diminutive Pedants against me for Assaulting the Christ-cross-row,[6] and opposing the very Elements of Literature.

This is no Panick Fear, and the Reader will not imagine my apprehensions ill Grounded, if he considers what an Army of petty Tyrants I have to Cope with, that all either actually persecute with Birch or else are solliciting for such a Preferment. For if I had no other Adversaries than the starving Wretches of both Sexes, throughout the Kingdom of *Great Britain,* that from a natural antipathy to Working, have a great Dislike to their present Employment, and perceiving within a much stronger Inclination to Command than ever they felt to Obey others, think themselves qualify'd, and wish from their Hearts to be Masters and Mistresses of Charity-Schools, the Number of my Enemies would by the most modest Computation, amount to One Hundred Thousand at Least.

Methinks I hear them cry out that a more dangerous Doctrine never was broach'd, and Popery's a Fool to it, and ask what Brute of a *Saracen it* is that draws his ugly Weapon for the Destruction of Learning. It is ten to one but they'll indict me for endeavouring by Instigation of the Prince of Darkness, to introduce into these Realms greater Ignorance and Barbarity than ever Nation was plunged into by *Goths* and *Vandals* since the Light of the Gospel first appeared in the World. Whoever labours under the Publick Odium has always Crimes laid to his charge he never was guilty of, and it will be suspected that I have had a hand in obliterating the Holy Scriptures, and perhaps affirm'd that it was at my Request that the small Bibles publish'd by Patent in the Year 1721, and chiefly made use of in Charity Schools, were through badness of Print and Paper render'd illegible: which yet I protest I am as innocent of as the Child unborn. But I am in a thousand Fears; the more I consider my Case the worse I like it, and the greatest Comfort I have is in my sincere Belief, that hardly any body will mind a word of what I say; or else if ever the People suspected that what I write would be of any weight to any considerable part of the Society, I should not have the Courage barely to think on all the Trades I should disoblige; and I cannot but smile When I reflect on the Variety of uncouth Sufferings that would be prepar'd for me, if the Punishment they would differently inflict upon me, was Emblematically to point at my Crime. For if I was not suddenly stuck full of useless Penknives up to the Hilts, the Company of Stationers would certainly take me in hand, and either have me buried alive in their Hall under a great heap of Primers and Spelling-books, they would not be able to sell; or else send me up against Tide to be bruised to Death in a Paper Mill that Would be obliged to stand still a Week upon my account. The Inkmakers at the same time would for the Publick Good offer to choak me with Astringents, or drown me in the black Liquor that would be left upon their Hands; which, if they joyn'd stock, might easily be perform'd in less than a Month; and if I should escape the Cruelty of these united Bodies the Resentment of a private Monopolist would be as fatal to me, and I should soon find my self pelted and knock'd o' the head with little squat Bibles clasp'd in Brass and ready arm'd for Mischief, that, Charitable Learning ceasing, would be fit for nothing but unopen'd to fight with, and Exercises truly Polemick.

The Digression I spoke of just now is not the foolish Trifle that ended with the last Paragraph, and which the grave Critick, to whom all Mirth is unseasonable, will think very impertinent; but a serious Apologetical one I am going to make out of hand, to clear my self from having any Design against Arts and Sciences, as some Heads of Colleges and other careful Preservers of Human Learning might have apprehended upon seeing Ignorance recommended as a necessary Ingredient in the mixture of Civil Society.

In the first place I would have near double the number of Professors in every University of what there is now. Theology with us is generally well provided, but the two other Faculties have very little to boast of, especially Physick. Every Branch of that Art ought to have two or three Professors, that would take pains to communicate their Skill and Knowledge to others. In Publick Lectures a vain Man has great Opportunities to set off his Parts, but private Instructions are more useful to Students. Pharmacy and the Knowledge of the Simples are as necessary as Anatomy or the History of Diseases: It is a shame that when Men have taken their Degree, and are by Authority entrusted with the Lives of the Subject, they should be forc'd to come to *London* to be acquainted with the *Materia Medica* and the Composition of Medicines, and receive Instructions from others that never had University Education themselves; it is certain that in the City I named there is ten times more Opportunity for a Man to improve himself in Anatomy, Botany, Pharmacy and the Practice of Physick than at both our Universities together. What has an Oyl-shop to do with Silks; or who would look for Hams and Pickles at a Mercers? Where things are well managed, Hospitals are made as subservient to the Advancement of Students in the Art of Physick as they are to the Recovery of Health in the Poor.

Good Sense ought to govern Men in Learning as well as in Trade: No Man ever bound his Son Prentice to a Goldsmith to make him a Linnendraper; then why should he have a Divine for his Tutor to become a Lawyer or a Physician? It is true that the Languages, Logick and Philosophy should be the first Studies in all the Learned Professions; but there is so little Help for Physick in our Universities that are so rich, and where so many idle People are well paid for eating and drinking, and being magnificently as well as commodiously lodg'd, that bar Books and what is common to all the Three Faculties, a Man may as well qualify himself at *Oxford* or *Cambridge* to be a Turky-Merchant as he can to be a Physician: Which is in my Humble Opinion a great sign that some part of the great Wealth they are possess'd of is not so well applied as it might be.

Professors should besides their Stipends allow'd them by the Publick, have Gratifications from every Student they Teach, that Self-Interest as well as Emulation and the Love of Glory might spur them on to Labour and Assiduity. When a Man excels in any one study or part of Learning, and is qualify'd to teach others, he ought to be procured if Money will purchase him, without regarding what Party, or indeed what Country or Nation he is of, whether Black or White. Universities should be publick Marts for all manner of Literature, as your Annual Fairs, that are kept at *Leipsich, Francfort,* and other places in *Germany,* are for different Wares and Merchandizes, where no difference is made between Natives and Foreigners, and which Men resort to from all Parts of the World with equal Freedom and equal Privilege.

From paying the Gratifications I spoke of I would excuse all Students design'd for the Ministry of the Gospel. There is no Faculty so immediately necessary to the Government of a Nation as that of Theology, and as we ought to have great numbers of Divines for the Service of this Island, I would not have the meaner People discouraged from bringing up their Children to that Function. For tho' Wealthy Men, if they have many Sons, sometimes make one of them a Clergyman, as we see even Persons of Quality take up Holy Orders, and there are likewise People of good Sense, especially Divines, that from a Principle of Prudence bring up their Children to that Profession, when they are morally assured that they have Friends or Interest enough, and shall be able either by a good Fellowship at the University, Advowsons or other means to procure 'em a Livelihood: But these produce not the large Number of Divines that are Yearly Ordain'd, and for the Bulk of the Clergy we are indebted to another Original.

Among the midling People of all Trades there are Bigots who have a Superstitious Awe for a Gown and Cassock: of these there are Multitudes that feel an ardent Desire of having a Son promoted to the Ministry of the Gospel, without considering what is to become of them afterwards, and many a kind Mother in this Kingdom, without consulting her own Circumstances or her Child's Capacity, transported with this laudable Wish is Daily Feasting on this pleasing Thought, and often before her Son is Twelve Years Old, mixing Maternal Love with Devotion, throws her self into Extasies and Tears of Satisfaction, by reflecting on the Future Enjoyment she is to receive from seeing him stand in a Pulpit, and with her own Ears hearing him Preach the Word of God. It is to this Religious Zeal, or at least the Human Frailties that pass for and represent it, that we owe the great plenty of poor Scholars the Nation enjoys. For considering the inequality of Livings, and the smalness of Benefices up and down the Kingdom, without this happy Disposition in Parents of small Fortune, we could not possibly be furnish'd from any other Quarter with proper Persons for the Ministry, to attend all the Cures of Souls, so pitifully provided for, that no Mortal could Live upon them that had been Educated in any Tolerable Plenty, unless he was possess'd of real Virtue, which it is Foolish and indeed Injurious, we should more expect from the Clergy than we generally find it in the Laity.

The great Care I would take to promote that part of Learning which is more immediately useful to Society, should not make me neglect the more Curious and Polite, but all the Liberal Arts and every Branch of Literature should be encouraged throughout the Kingdom, more than they are, if my wishing could do it. In every County there should be one or more Large Schools Erected at the Publick Charge, for Latin and Greek that should be divided into Six or more Classes, with particular Masters in each of them. The whole should be under the Care and Inspection of some Men of Letters in Authority, who would not only be Titular Governours, but actually take pains at least Twice a Year, in hearing every Class thoroughly examin'd by the Master of it, and not content themselves with Judging of the Progress the Scholars had made from Themes and other Exercises that had been made out of their Sight.

At the same time I would discourage and hinder the multiplicity of those petty Schools, that never would have had any Existence had the Masters of them not been extremely indigent. It is a Vulgar Error that no body can spell or write *English* well without a little smatch of *Latin*. This is upheld by Pedants for their own Interest, and by none more strenuously maintain'd than such of 'em as are poor Scholars in more than one Sense: in the mean time it is an abominable Falshood. I have known, and am still acquainted with several, and some of the Fair Sex, that never learn'd any *Latin*, and yet keep to strict Orthography, and write admirable good Sense; whereas on the other hand every body may meet with the Scriblings of pretended Scholars at least, such as went to a Grammar School for several Years, that have Grammar Faults and are ill-spelt. The understanding of *Latin* thoroughly is highly necessary to all that are design'd for any of the Learned Professions, and I would have no Gentleman without Literature; even those who are to be brought up Attorneys, Surgeons and Apothecaries, should be much better vers'd in that Language than generally they are; but to Youth who afterwards are to get a Livelihood in Trades and Callings, in which *Latin* is not daily wanted, it is of no Use, and the learning of it an evident Loss of just so much Time and Money as are bestowed upon it. When Men come into Business, what was taught them of it in those petty Schools is either soon forgot, or only fit to make them impertinent, and often very troublesome in Company. Few Men can forbear valuing themselves on any Knowledge they had once acquired, even after they have lost it; and unless they are very modest and discreet, the undigested scraps, which such People commonly remember of *Latin,* seldom fail of rendering them at one time or other ridiculous to those who understand it.

Reading and Writing I would Treat as we do Musick and Dancing, I would not hinder them nor force them upon the Society: As long as there was any thing to be got by them, there would be Masters enough to Teach them; but nothing should be taught for nothing but at Church: And here I would exclude even those who might be design'd for the Ministry of the Gospel; for if Parents are so miserably Poor that they can't afford their Children these first Elements of Learning, it is Impudence in them to aspire any further.

It would Encourage likewise the lower sort of People to give their Children this part of Education, if they could see them preferr'd to those of idle Sots or sorry Rake-hells, that never knew what it was to provide a Rag for their Brats but by Begging. But now when a Boy or a Girl are wanted for any small Service, we reckon it a Duty to employ our Charity Children before any other. The Education of them looks like a Reward for being Vicious and Unactive, a Benefit commonly bestow'd on Parents, who deserve to be punish'd for shamefully neglecting their Families. In one Place you may hear a Rascal Half-drunk, Damning himself, call for th' other Pot, and as a good Reason for it add, that his Boy is provided for in Cloaths and has his Schooling for nothing: In another you shall see a poor Woman in great Necessity, whose Child is to be taken care of, because herself is a Lazy Slut, and never did any thing to remedy her Wants in good earnest, but bewailing them at a Gin-shop.

If every Body's Children are well taught, who by their own Industry can Educate them at our Universities, there will be Men of Learning enough to supply this Nation and such another; and Reading, Writing or Arithmetick would never be wanting in the Business that requires them, tho' none were to learn them but such whose Parents could be at the Charge of it. It is not with Letters as it is with the Gifts of the Holy Ghost, that they may not be purchased with Money; and bought Wit, if we believe the Proverb, is none of the Worst.

I thought it necessary to say thus much of Learning, to obviate the Clamours of the Enemies to Truth and fair Dealing, who had I not so amply explain'd my self on this Head, would have represented me as a Mortal Foe to all literature and useful Knowledge, and a wicked Advocate for Universal Ignorance and Stupidity. I shall now make good my promise of answering what I knew the Well-wishers to Charity-Schools would object against me, by saying that they brought up the Children under their care to Warrantable and Laborious Trades, and not to Idleness as I did insinuate.

I have sufficiently shew'd already, why going to School was Idleness if compared to Working, and exploded this sort of Education in the Children of the Poor, because it Incapacitates them ever after for down right Labour, which is their proper Province, and in every Civil Society a Portion they ought not to repine or grumble at, if exacted from them with Discretion and Humanity. What remains is that I should speak as to their putting them out to Trades, which I shall endeavour to demonstrate to be destructive to the Harmony of a Nation, and an impertinent Intermedling with what few of these Governours know any thing of.

In order to this let us examine into the Nature of Societies, and what the Compound ought to consist of if we would raise it to as high a degree of Strength, Beauty and Perfection, as the Ground we are to do it upon will let us. The Variety of Services that are required to supply the Luxurious and Wanton Desires as well as real Necessities of Man, with all their subordinate Callings, is in such a Nation as ours prodigious; yet it is certain that, tho' the number of those several Occupations be excessively great, it is far from being infinite; if you add one more than is required it must be superfluous. If a Man had a good Stock and the best Shop in *Cheapside* to sell Turbands in, he would be ruin'd, and if *Demetrius* or any other Silversmith made nothing but *Diana's* Shrines he would not get his Bread, now the Worship of that Goddess is out of Fashion. As it is Folly to set up Trades that are not wanted, so what is next to it is to encrease in any one Trade the Numbers beyond what are required. As things are managed with us, it would be preposterous to have as many Brewers as there are Bakers, or as many Woollendrapers as there are Shoemakers. This Proportion as to Numbers in every Trade finds it self, and is never better kept than when no body meddles or interferes with it.

People that have Children to educate that must get their Livelihood, are always consulting and deliberating what Trade or Calling they are to bring them up to, till they are fix'd, and thousands think on this that hardly think at all on any thing else. First they confine themselves to their Circumstances, and he that can give but Ten Pounds with his Son must not look out for a Trade where they ask an Hundred with an Apprentice: but the next they think on is always which will be the most advantageous: if there be a Calling where at that time People are more generally employ'd than they are in any other in the same Reach, there are presently half a score Fathers ready to supply it with their Sons. Therefore the greatest Care most Companies have is about the Regulation of the Number of Prentices. Now when all Trades complain, and perhaps justly, that they are overstock'd, you manifestly injure that Trade, to which you add one Member more than would flow from the Nature of Society. Besides that the Governors of Charity Schools don't deliberate so much what Trade is the best, but what Tradesmen they can get that will take the Boys with such a Sum; and few Men of Substance and Experience will have any thing to do with these Children: they are afraid of a hundred Inconveniencies from the necessitous Parents of them: So that they are bound at least most commonly, either to Sots and neglectful Masters, or else as are very needy and don't care what becomes of their Prentices, after they have received the Money: by which it seems as if we study'd nothing more than to have a perpetual Nursery for Charity Schools.

When all Trades and Handicrafts are overstock'd, it is a certain sign there is a Fault in the management of the Whole; for it is impossible there should be too many People if the Country is able to Feed them. Are Provisions Dear? whose Fault is that, as long as you have Ground Untill'd and Hands Unemploy'd? But I shall be answer'd, that to encrease Plenty, must at long run undo the Farmer or lessen the Rents all over *England*. To which I reply, that what the Husbandman complains of most is what I would redress: The greatest Grievance of Farmers, Gardiners and others, where hard Labour is required, and dirty Work to be done, is that they can't get Servants for the same Wages they used to have them at. The Day Labourer grumbles at Sixteen Pence to do no other Drudgery than what Thirty Years ago his Grandfather did chearfully for half the Money. As to the Rents, it is impossible they should fall whilst you encrease your Numbers, but the price of Provisions and all Labour in general must fall with them if not before; and a Man of a Hundred and Fifty Pounds a Year, has no reason to complain that his Income is reduced to One Hundred, if he can Buy as much for that One Hundred as before he could have done for Two.

There is no Intrinsick Worth in Money but what is alterable with the Times, and whether a Guinea goes for Twenty Pounds or for a Shilling, it is (as I have already hinted before) the Labour of the Poor and not the high and low value that is set on Gold or Silver, which all the comforts of Life must arise from. It is in our Power to have a much greater Plenty than we enjoy, if Agriculture and Fishery were taken care of, as they might be; but we are so little capable of encreasing our Labour, that we have hardly Poor enough to do what is necessary to make us subsist. The proportion of the Society is spoil'd, and the Bulk of the Nation which should every where consist of Labouring Poor, that are unacquainted with every thing but their Work, is too little for the other parts. In all Business where downright Labour is shun'd or over-paid, there is plenty of People. To One Merchant you have Ten Book-keepers, or at least Pretenders; and every where in the Country the Farmer wants Hands. Ask for a Footman that for some time has been in Gentlemens Families and you'll get a Dozen that are all Butlers. You may have Chamber-maids by the Score, but you can't get a Cook under Extravagant Wages.

No Body will do the Dirty Slavish Work, that can help it. I don't discommend them, but all these things shew that the People of the meanest Rank know too much to be Serviceable to us. Servants require more than Masters and Mistresses can afford, and what madness is it to Encourage them in this, by industriously encreasing at our Cost that Knowledge which they will be sure to make us pay for over again! And it is not only that those who are Educated at our own Expence encroach upon us, but the Raw Ignorant Country Wenches and Boobily Fellows that can do, and are good for, nothing impose upon us likewise. The scarcity of Servants occasion'd by the Education of the first, gives a Handle to the latter of advancing their Price, and demanding what ought only to be given to Servants that understand their Business, and have most of the good Qualities that can be required in them.

There is no place in the World where there are more Clever Fellows to look at or to do an Errand than some of our Footmen; but what are they good for in the main? The greatest part of them are Rogues and not to be trusted; and if they are Honest half of them are Sots, and will get Drunk three or four times a Week. The surly ones are generally Quarrelsome, and valuing their Manhood beyond all other considerations, care not what Cloaths they spoyl, or what Disappointments they may occasion, when their Prowess is in Question. Those who are Good-natured, are generally sad Whoremasters that are ever running after the Wenches, and spoyl all Maid Servants they come near. Many of them are Guilty of all these Vices, Whoring, Drinking, Quarrelling, and yet shall have all their Faults over-look'd and bore with, because they are Men of good Mien and humble Address that know how to wait on Gentlemen; which is an unpardonable Folly in Masters, and generally ends in the Ruin of Servants.

Some few there are that are not addicted to any of these Failings, and understand their Duty besides; but as these are Rarities so there is not one in Fifty but what over-rates himself; his Wages must be extravagant and you can never have done giving him; every thing in the House is his Perquisite, and he won't stay with you unless his Vails[7] are sufficient to maintain a midling Family; and tho' you had taken him from the Dunghill, out of an Hospital, or a Prison, you shall never keep him longer than he can make of his

Place what in his high Estimation of himself he shall think he deserves; Nay, the best and most civilis'd, that never were Saucy or Impertinent, will leave the most indulgent Master, and, to get handsomely away, frame Fifty Excuses, and tell downright Lyes as soon as they can mend themselves. A Man, who keeps an Half-Crown or Twelve-penny Ordinary, looks not more for Money from his Customers than a Footman does from every Guest that Dines or Sups with his Master; and I question whether the one does not often think a Shilling or Half a Crown, according to the Quality of the Person, his due as much as the other.

A Housekeeper who cannot afford to make many Entertainments, and does not often invite People to his Table can have no creditable Man-Servant; and is forc'd to take up with some Country Booby or other Awkward Fellow, who will likewise give him the Slip as soon as he imagines himself fit for any other Service, and is made wiser by his rascally Companions. All noted Eating Houses and Places that many Gentlemen resort to for Diversion or Business, more especially the Precincts of *Westminster-Hall,* are the great Schools for Servants, where the dullest Fellows may have their Understandings improved; and get rid at once of their Stupidity and their Innocence. They are the Accademies for Footmen where Publick Lectures are daily read on all Sciences of low Debauchery by the experience'd Professors of them, and Students are instructed in above Seven Hundred illiberal Arts, how to Cheat, Impose upon, and find out the blind side of their Masters, with so much Application that in few Years they become Graduates in Inquity. Young Gentlemen and others that are not thoroughly vers'd in the World, when they get such knowing Sharpers in their Service, are commonly indulging above measure; and for Fear of discovering their want of Experience hardly dare to contradict or deny them any thing which is often the Reason that by allowing them unreasonable Privileges they expose their Ignorance when they are most endeavouring to conceal it.

Some perhaps will lay the things I complain of to the charge of Luxury, of which I said that it could do no Hurt to a Rich Nation, if the Imports never did exceed the Exports; but I don't think this imputation Just, and nothing ought to be scored on the Account of Luxury, that is downright the Effect of Folly. A Man may be very extravagant in indulging his Ease and his Pleasure, and render the Enjoyment of the World as Operose and Expensive as they can be made, if he can afford it, and at the same time shew his good Sense in every thing about him: This he cannot be said to do if he industriously renders his People incapable of doing him that Service he expects from them. 'Tis too much Money, excessive Wages, and unreasonable Vails that spoil Servants in *England.* A Man may have Five and Twenty Horses in his Stables without being Guilty of Folly, if it suits with the rest of his Circumstances, but if he keeps but one and over feeds it to shew his Wealth he is a fool for his Pains. Is it not Madness to suffer that Servants should take three and others five *per Cent.* of what they pay to Tradesmen for their Masters, as is so well known to Watchmakers and others that sell Toys, superfluous Nicknacks, and other Curiosities, if they deal with People of Quality, and Fashionable Gentlemen that are above telling their own Money? If they should accept of a present when offer'd, it might be conniv'd at, but it is an unpardonable Impudence that they should claim it as their due, and contend for it if refused. Those who have all the Necessaries of Life provided for, can have no occasion for Money but what does them hurt as Servants, unless they were to hoard it up for Age or Sickness, which among our *Skip-kennels*[8] is not very common, and even then it makes them Saucy and Insupportable.

I am credibly inform'd that a parcel of Footmen are arriv'd to that height of Insolence as to have enter'd into a Society together, and made Laws by which they oblige themselves not to serve for less than such a Sum, nor carry Burdens or any Bundle or Parcel above a certain Weight, not exceeding Two or Three Pounds, with other regulations directly opposite to the Interest of those they Serve, and altogether destructive to the use they were design'd for. If any of them be turn'd away for strictly adhearing to the Orders of this Honourable Corporation, he is taken care of till another Service is provided for him, and there is no Money wanting at any time to commence and maintain a Law-suit against any Master that shall pretend to strike or offer any other Injury to his Gentleman Footman, contrary to the Statutes of their Society. If this be true, as I have reason to believe it is, and they are suffer'd to go on in Consulting and Providing for their own Ease and Coveniency any further, we may expect quickly to see the *French* Comedy *Le Maitre Le Valet*[9] Acted in good earnst in most Families, which if not redress'd in a little time, and those Footmen encrease their Company to the Number it is possible they may, as well as Assemble when they please with Impunity, it will be in their Power to make a Tragedy of it whenever they have a mind to 't.

But suppose those Apprehensions frivolous and groundless, it is undeniable that Servants in general are daily encroaching upon Masters and Mistresses, and endeavouring to be more upon the Level with them. They not only seem sollicitous to abolish the low dignity of their Condition, but have already considerably rais'd it in the common Estimation from the Original meanness which the Publick Welfare requires it should always remain in. I don't say that these things are altogether owing to Charity Schools, there are other Evils they may be partly ascrib'd to. *London* is too big for the Country, and in several Respects we are wanting to our selves. But if a Thousand Faults were to concur before the Inconveniencies could be produced we Labour under, can any Man doubt who will consider what I have said, that Charity Schools are Accessary, or at least that they are more likely, to Create and Encrease than to lessen or redress those Complaints.

The only thing of Weight then that can be said in their behalf is, that so many Thousand Children are Educated by them in the Christian Faith and the Principles of the Church of *England*. To demonstrate that this is not a sufficient Plea for them, I must desire the Reader, as I hate Repetitions, to look back on what I have said before, to which I shall add, that whatever is necessary to Salvation and requisite for Poor Labouring People to know concerning Religion, that Children learn at School, may fully as well either by Preaching or Catechizing, be taught at Church, from which or some other Place of Worship I would not have the meanest of a Parish that is able to walk to it be absent on *Sundays*. It is the Sabbath the most useful Day in Seven that is set apart for Divine Service and Religious Exercise as well as resting from Bodily Labour, and it is a Duty incumbent on all Magistrates to take particular Care of that Day. The Poor more especially and their Children should be made to go to Church on it both in the Fore and Afternoon, because they have no Time on any other. By Precept and Example they ought to be encouraged and used to it from their very Infancy; the wilful Neglect of it ought to be counted Scandalous, and if down right Compulsion to what I urge might seem too Harsh and perhaps impracticable, all Diversions at least ought strictly to be prohibited, and the Poor hindred from every Amusement Abroad that might allure or draw them from it.

Where this Care is taken by the Magistrates as far as it lies in their Power, Ministers of the Gospel may instill into the smallest Capacities, more Piety and Devotion, and better Principles of Virtue and Religion than Charity-Schools ever did or ever will produce, and those, who complain, when they have such Opportunities that they cannot imbue their Parishioners with sufficient Knowledge of what they stand in need of as Christians, without the assistance of Reading and Writing, are either very Lazy or very Ignorant and undeserving themselves.

That the most Knowing are not the most Religious, will be evident if we make a Trial between People of different Abilities even in this Juncture, where going to Church is not made such an Obligation on the Poor and Illiterate, as it might be. Let us pitch upon a Hundred Poor Men the first we can light on, that are above Forty, and were brought up to hard Labour from their Infancy, such as never went to School at all, and always lived remote from Knowledge and Great Towns: Let us compare to these an equal number of very good Scholars, that shall all have had University Education; and be, if you will, half of them Divines, well versed in Philology and Polemick Learning; then let us impartially examine into the Lives and Conversations of both, and I dare engage that among the first who can neither Read nor Write, we shall meet with more Union and Neighbourly Love, less Wickedness and Attachment to the World, more Content of Mind, more Innocence, Sincerity, and other good Qualities that conduce to the Publick Peace and Real Felicity, than we shall find among the latter, where on the contrary, we may be assured of the height of Pride and Insolence, eternal Quarrels and Dissentions, Irreconcilable Hatreds, Strife, Envy, Calumny and other Vices destructive to mutual Concord which the illiterate labouring Poor are hardly ever tainted with to any considerable Degree.

I am very well persuaded, that what I have said in the last Paragraph will be no News to most of my Readers; but if it be Truth, why should it be stifled, and why must our concern for Religion be eternally made a Cloak to hide our real Drifts and worldly Intentions? Would both Parties agree to pull off the Masque, we should soon discover that whatever they pretend to, they aim at nothing so much in Charity-Schools as to strengthen their Party, and that the great Sticklers for the Church, by Educating Children in the Principles of Religion, mean, inspiring them with a Superlative Veneration for the Clergy of the Church of *England,* and a strong Aversion and immortal Animosity against all that dissent from it. To be assured of this, we are but to mind on the one hand, what Divines are most admired for their Charity Sermons and most fond to Preach them, and on the other; whether of late Years we have had any Riots or Party Scuffles among the Mob, in which the Youth of a Famous Hospital in this City, were not always the most forward Ring-leaders.

The Grand Asserters of Liberty, who are ever guarding themselves and Skirmishing against Arbitrary Power, often when they are in no danger of it, are generally speaking, not very Superstitious, nor seem to lay great stress on an Modern Apostleship: Yet some of these likewise speak up lowdly for Charity-Schools, but what they expect from 'em has no relation to Religion or Morality: They only look upon them as the proper means to destroy and disappoint the power of the Priests over the Laity. Reading and Writing encrease Knowledge, and the more Men know, the better they can Judge for themselves, and they imagine that, if Knowledge could be rendred Universal, People could not be Priest-rid, which is the thing they fear the most.

The First, I confess, it is very probable will get their Aim. But sure Wise Men that are not Red-hot for a Party or Bigots to the Priests, will not think it worth while to suffer so many Inconveniencies, as Charity-Schools may be the Occasion of, only to promote the Ambition and Power of the Clergy. To the other I would answer, that if all those who are Educated at the Charge of their Parents or Relations, will but think for themselves and refuse to have their reason imposed upon by the Priests, we need not be concerned for what the Clergy will work upon the Ignorant that have no Education at all. Let them make the most of them, considering the Schools we have for those who can and do pay for Learning, it is ridiculous to imagine that the abolishing of Charity-Schools would be a step towards any Ignorance that could be prejudicial to the Nation.

I would not be thought Cruel, and am well assured if I know any thing of my self, that I abhor Inhumanity; but to be Compassionate to excess where Reason forbids it, and the general Interest of the Society requires steadiness of Thought and Resolution, is an unpardonable Weakness. I know it will be ever urged against me, that it is Barbarous the Children of the Poor should have no Opportunity of exerting themselves as long as God has not debarr'd them from Natural Parts and Genius more than the Rich. But I cannot think this is harder than it is, that they should not have Money as long as they have the same Inclinations to spend as others. That Great and Useful Men have sprung from Hospitals, I don't deny, but it is likewise very probable, that when they were first employ'd, many as capable themselves not brought up in Hospitals were neglected, that with the same good Fortune would have done as well as they, if they had been made use of instead of 'em.

There are many examples of Women that have excell'd in Learning, and even in War, but this is no reason we should bring 'em all up to *Latin* and *Greek* or else Military Discipline, instead of Needle-work and Housewifry. But there is no scarcity of Sprightliness or Natural Parts among us, and no Soil or Climate has Human Creatures to boast of, better form'd either inside or outside than this Island generally produces. But it is not Wit, Genius or Docility we want, but Diligence, Application, and Assiduity.

Abundance of hard and dirty Labour is to be done, and course Living is to be complied with: Where shall we find a better Nursery for these Necessities than the Children of the Poor? none certainly are nearer to it or fitter for it. Besides that the things I have call'd Hardships, neither seem nor are such to those, who have been brought up to 'em, and know no better. There is not a more contented People among us, than those who work the hardest and are the least Acquainted with the Pomp and Delicacies of the World.

These are Truths that are undeniable; yet I know few People will be pleas'd to have them divulg'd; what makes them odious is an unreasonable Vein of Petty Reverence for the Poor, that runs through most Multitudes, and more particularly in this Nation, and arises from a mixture of Pity, Folly and Superstition. It is from a lively sense of this Compound that Men cannot endure to hear or see any thing said or acted against the Poor; without considering, how Just the one, or Insolent the other. So a Beggar must not be beat tho' he strikes you first. Journeymen Taylors go to Law with their Masters and are obstinate in a wrong Cause,[10] yet they must be pitied; and Murmuring Weavers must be reliev'd, and have Fifty silly things done to humour them, tho' in the midst of their Poverty they insult their Betters, and on all Occasions appear to be more prone to make Holy Days and Riots than they are to Working or Sobriety.

This puts me in mind of our Wool, which considering the posture of our Affairs, and the Behaviour of the Poor, I sincerely believe ought not upon any Account to be carried abroad: But if we look into the reason, why suffering it to be fetch'd away is so pernicious, our heavy Complaint and Lamentations that it is exported can be no great Credit to us. Considering the mighty and manifold Hazards that must be run before it can be got off the Coast, and safely, Landed beyond Sea; it is manifest that the Foreigners, before they can work our Wool, must pay more for it very considerably, than what we can have it for at Home. Yet notwithstanding this great difference in the Prime Cost, they can afford to sell the Manufactures made of it cheaper at Foreign Markets than our selves. This is the Disaster we groan under, the intollerable Mischief, without which the Exportation of that Commodity could be no greater prejudice to us than that of Tin or Lead, as long as our Hands were fully employ'd, and we had still Wool to spare.

There is no People yet come to higher Perfection in the Woollen Manufacture, either as to dispatch or goodness of Work, at least in the most considerable Branches, than our selves, and therefore what we complain of can only depend on the difference in the Management of the Poor, between other Nations and ours. If the Labouring People in one Country will Work Twelve Hours in a Day, and Six Days in a Week, and in another they are employ'd but Eight Hours in a Day and not above Four Days in a Week, the one is obliged to have Nine Hands for what the other does with Four. But if moreover the Living, the Food and Raiment, and what is consumed by the Workmen of the Industrious costs but half the Money of what is expended among an equal number of the other, the Consequence must be that the first will have the Work of Eighteen Men for the same Price as the other gives for the Work of Four. I would not insinuate neither do I think, that the difference either in diligence or necessaries of Life between us and any Neighbouring Nation is near so great as what I speak of, yet I would have it considered, that half of that difference and much less is sufficient to over-ballance the Disadvantage they labour under as to the Price of Wool.

Nothing to me is more evident than that no Nation in any Manufactory whatever can undersell their Neighbours with whom they are at best but Equals as to Skill and Dispatch, and the conveniency for Working, more especially when the Prime Cost of the thing to be Manufactured is not in their favour, unless they have Provisions, and whatever is relating to their Sustenance Cheaper, or else Workmen that are either more Assiduous and will remain longer at their Work or be content with a meaner and courser way of Living than those of their

Neighbours. This is certain, that where Numbers are Equal, the more Laborious People are, and the fewer Hands the same quantity of Work is perform'd by, the greater Plenty there is in a Country of the Necessaries for Life, the more considerable and the cheaper that Country may render its Exports.

It being granted then, that abundance of Work is to be done, the next thing which I think to be likewise undeniable is, what the more chearfully it is done the better, as well for those that perform it as for the rest of the Society. To be happy is to be pleas'd, and the less Notion a Man has of a better way of Living, the more content he'll be with his own; and on the other hand the greater a Man's Knowledge and Experience is in the World, the more exquisite the Delicacy of his Taste, and the more consummate Judge he is of things in general, certainly the more difficult it will be to please him. I would not advance any thing that is Barbarous or Inhuman: But when a Man enjoys himself, Laughs and Sings, and in his Gesture and Behaviour shews me all the tokens of Content and Satisfaction, I pronounce him happy and have nothing to do with his Wit or Capacity. I never enter into the reasonableness of his Mirth, at least I ought not to judge of it by my own Standard, and Argue from the Effect which the thing that makes him merry would have upon me. At that rate a Man that hates Cheese must call me Fool for loving Blue Mold. *De gustibus non est disputandum*[11] is as true in a Metaphorical as it is in the Literal Sense, and the greater the distance is between People as to their Condition, their Circumstances and manner of Living, the less capable they are of Judging of one anothers Troubles or Pleasures.

Had the meanest and most uncivilis'd Peasant leave *Incognito* to observe the greatest King for a Fortnight: tho' he might pick out several things he would like for himself, yet he would find a great many more, which, if the Monarch and he were to change Conditions, he would wish for his part to have immediately alter'd or redress'd, and which with amazement he sees the King submit to. And again if the Sovereign was to examine the Peasant in the same manner. His Labour would be Insufferable, the Dirt and Squallor, his Diet and Amours, his Pastimes and Recreations would be all abominable; but then what Charms would he find in the other's peace of Mind, the Calmness and Tranquillity, of his Soul. No Necessity for Dissimulation with any of his Family, or feign'd Affection to his Mortal Enemies; no Wife in a Foreign Interest, no Danger to apprehend from his Children; no Plots to unravel, no Poyson to fear; no popular Statesman at Home or cunning Courts Abroad to manage: no seeming Patriots to bribe; no unsatiable Favourite to gratify; no Selfish Ministry to obey, no divided Nation to please, or fickle Mob to humour that would direct and interfere with his Pleasures.

Was impartial reason to be Judge between real Good and real Evil, and a Catalogue made accordingly of the Several Delights and Vexations differently to be met with in both Stations, I question whether the Condition of Kings would be at all preferable to that of Peasants, even as Ignorant and Laborious as I seem to require the latter to be. The reason why the generality of People would rather be Kings than Peasants is first owing to Pride and Ambition, that is deeply riveted in Human Nature, and which to gratify we daily see Men undergo and despise the greatest hazards and difficulties. Secondly to the difference there is in the force with which our Affection is wrought upon as the Objects are either Material or Spiritual. Things that immediately strike our outward senses act more violently upon our Passions than what is the result of Thought and the dictates of the most demonstrative Reason, and there is a much stronger Biass to gain our Liking or Aversion in the first than there is in the latter.

Having thus demonstrated that what I urge could be no Injury or the least diminution of Happiness to the Poor, I leave it to the Judicious Reader, whether it is not more probable we should encrease our Exports by the methods I hint at, than by sitting still and Damning and Sinking our Neighbours for beating us at our own Weapons, some of them out selling us in Manufactures made of our own Product which they dearly purchas'd, others growing Rich in spight of Distance and Trouble, by the same Fish which we neglect, tho' it is ready to jump into our Mouths.

As by discouraging Idleness with Art and Steadiness you may compel the Poor to labour without Force, so by bringing them up in Ignorance you may inure them to real Hardships without being ever sensible themselves that they are such. By bringing them up in Ignorance, I mean no more, as I have hinted long ago, than that as to Worldly Affairs their Knowledge should be confin'd within the Verge of their own Occupations, at least that we should not take pains to extend it beyond those Limits. When by these two Engines we shall have made Provisions, and consequently Labour cheap, we must infallibly out-sell our Neighbours; and at the same time encrease our Numbers. This is the Noble and Manly way of encountring the Rivals of our Trade, and by dint of Merit out-doing them at Foreign Markets.

To allure the Poor we make use of policy in some cases with Success. Why should we be neglectful of it in the most important point, when they make their boast that they will not live as the Poor of other Nations? If we cannot alter their Resolution, why should we applaud the Justness of their Sentiments against the Common Interest. I have often wondred formerly how an *English Man* that pretended to have the Honour and Glory as well as the Welfare of his Country at Heart, could take delight in the Evening to hear an Idle Tenant that owed him above a Years Rent ridicule the *French* for wearing Wooden Shoes, when in the Morning he had had the Mortification of hearing the great King *William,* that Ambitious Monarch as well as able Statesman, openly own to the World and with Grief and Anger in his looks complain of the Exorbitant Power of *France.* Yet I don't recommend Wooden Shoes, nor do the maxims I would introduce require Arbitrary Power in one Person. Liberty and Property I hope may remain secured, and yet the Poor be better employ'd than they are, tho' their Children should wear out their Cloaths by useful Labour, and blacken them with Country Dirt for something, instead of tearing them off their Backs at play, and dawbing 'em with Ink for nothing.

There is above Three or Four Hundred Years Work, for a Hundred Thousand Poor more than we have in this Island. To make every part of it Useful, and the whole thoroughly Inhabited, many Rivers are to be made Navigable, Canals to be cut in Hundreds of Places. Some Lands are to be drain'd and secured from Inundations for the future: Abundance of barren Soil is to be made fertile, and Thousands of Acres rendred more beneficial by being made more accessible. *Dii Laboribus omnia vendunt.*[12] There is no difficulty of this Nature, that Labour and Patience cannot Surmount. The highest Mountains may be thrown into their Valleys that stand ready to receive them, and Bridges might be laid where now we would not dare to think of it. Let us look back on the Stupendious Works of the *Romans,* more especially their Highways and Aqueducts. Let us consider in one view the vast extent of several of their Roads, how substantial they made them, and what duration they have been of, and in another a poor Traveller that at every Ten Miles end is stop'd by a Turnpike, and dunn'd for a Penny for mending the Roads in the Summer, with what every Body knows will be Dirt before the Winter that succeeds it is expired.

The Conveniency of the Publick ought ever to be the Publick Care, and no Private Interest of a Town or a whole County should ever hinder the Execution of a Project or Contrivance that would manifestly tend to the Improvement of the whole; and every Member of the Legislature, who knows his Duty and would chuse, rather to act like a wise Man, than curry Favour with his Neighbours, will prefer the least Benefit accruing to the whole Kingdom to the most visible Advantage of the Place he serves for.

We have Materials of our own, and want neither Stone nor Timber to do any thing, and was the Money that People give uncompell'd to Beggars who don't deserve it, and what every Housekeeper is obliged to pay to the Poor of his Parish that is otherwise employ'd or ill applied, to be put together every Year, it would make a sufficient Fund to keep a great many Thousands at work. I don't say this because I think it practicable, but only to shew that we have Money enough to spare to employ vast multitudes of Labourers: neither should we want so much for it as we perhaps might imagine. When it is taken for granted that a Soldier, whose Strength and Vigour is to be kept up at least as much as any Body's, can Live upon Six Pence a Day, I can't conceive the Necessity of giving the greatest part of the Year Sixteen and Eighteen Pence to a Day Labourer.

The Fearful and Cautious People that are ever Jealous of their Liberty, I know will cry out, that where the Multitudes I speak of should be kept in constant Pay, Property and Privileges would be precarious. But they might be answer'd, that sure means might be found out, and such Regulations made, as to the Hands in which to trust the management and direction of these Labourers; that it would be impossible for the Prince or any Body else to make an ill Use of their numbers.

What I have said in the Four or Five last Paragraphs, I foresee will with abundance of Scorn be Laugh'd at by many of my Readers, and at best be call'd Building Castles in the Air; but whether that is my Fault or theirs is a Question. When the Publick Spirit has left a Nation, they not only lose their Patience with it, and all thoughts of Perseverance, but become likewise so narrow-soul'd, that it is a pain for them even to think of things that are of uncommon extent or require great length of Time; and whatever is Noble or Sublime in such Conjunctures is counted Chimerical. Where deep Ignorance is entirely routed and expell'd, and low Learning promiscuously scatter'd on all the People, Self-Love turns Knowledge into Cunning, and the more this last Qualification prevails in any Country the more the People will fix all their Cares, Concern and Application on the Time present, without regard of what is to come after them, or hardly ever thinking beyond the next Generation.

But as Cunning, according to my Lord *Verulam,* is but Lefthanded Wisdom, so a prudent Legislature ought to provide against this Disorder of the Society as soon as the Symptoms of it appear, among which the following are the most obvious. Imaginary Rewards are generally despised: every body is for turning the Penny and short Bargains: he that is diffident of every thing and believes nothing but what he sees with his own Eyes is counted the most prudent, and in all their Dealings Men seem to Act from no other Principle than that of the Devil take the hindmost. Instead of planting Oaks, that will require a Hundred and Fifty Years before they are fit to be cut down, they Build Houses with a design that they shall not stand above Twelve or Fourteen Years. All Heads run upon the uncertainty of things, and the vicissitudes of human Affairs. The Mathematicks become the only valuable Study, and are made use of in every thing even where it is ridiculous, and Men seem to repose no greater Trust in Providence than they would in a Broken Merchant.

It is the Business of the publick to supply the Defects of the Society, and take that in hand first which is most neglected by private Persons. Contraries are best cured by Contraries, and therefore as Example is of greater efficacy than Precept in the amendment of National Failings, the Legislature ought to resolve upon some great undertakings that must be the Work of Ages as well as vast Labour, and convince the World that they did nothing without an anxious regard to their latest Posterity. This will fix or at least help to settle the volatile Genius and fickle Spirit of the Kingdom, put us in mind that we are not born for our selves only, and be a means of rendring Men less distrustful, and inspiring them with a true love for their Country, and a tender Affection for the Ground it self, than which nothing is more necessary to aggrandize a Nation. Forms of Government may alter, Religions and even Languages may change, but *Great Britain* or at least (if that likewise might lose its Name) the Island it self will remain and in all human probability last as long as any part of the Globe. All Ages have ever paid their kind Acknowledgments to their Ancestors for the Benefits derived from them, and a Christian who enjoys the multitude of Fountains and vast Plenty of Water to be met with in the City of St. *Peter,* is an ungrateful Wretch if he never casts a thankful Remembrance on Old *Pagan Rome,* that took such prodigious Pains to procure it.

When this Island shall be cultivated and every Inch of it made Habitable and Useful, and the whole the most convenient and agreeable Spot upon Earth, all the Cost and Labour laid out upon it, will be gloriously Repaid by the Incense of them that shall come after us; and those who burn with the Noble Zeal and desire after Immortality, and took such Care to improve their Country may rest satisfy'd, that a Thousand and Two Thousand Years hence they shall live in the Memory and everlasting Praises of the future Ages that shall then enjoy it.

Here I should have concluded this Rhapsody of Thoughts but something comes in my Head concerning the main Scope and Design of this Essay, which is to prove the Necessity there is for a certain Portion of Ignorance in a Well-order'd Society, that I must not omit, because by mentioning it I shall make an Argument on my side of what if I had not spoke of it, might easily have appear'd as a strong Objection against me. It is the Opinion of most People, and mine among the rest, that the most commendable Quality of the present Czar of *Muscovy*[13] is his unwearied Application in raising his Subjects from their native Stupidity and Civilizing his Nation: but then we must consider it is what they stood in need of, and that not long ago the greatest part of them were next to Brute Beasts. In proportion to the Extent of his Dominions and the Multitudes he Commands, he had not that Number or Variety of Tradesmen and Artificers which the true Improvement of the Country required, and therefore was in the right in leaving no Stone unturn'd to procure them. But what is that to us who labour under a contrary Disease? Sound Politicks are to the Social Body what the Art of Medicine is to the Natural, and no Physician would treat a Man in a Lethargy as if he was sick for want of Rest, or prescribe in a Dropsy what should be administred in a Diabetes. In short, *Russia* has too few Knowing Men, and *Great Britain* too many.

Endnotes

1. Dr John Radcliffe (1650-1714), the famous physician, who left his large fortune to the University of Oxford. —Ed.
2. The primary cause of a disease.—Ed.
3. Mandeville is referring to the South Sea Bubble.—Ed.
4. 'Rule over beasts', Terence, *Eunuchus,* 415.—Ed.
5. Punishments in waiting.—Ed.
6. The alphabet.—Ed.
7. Gratuities.—Ed.
8. Footmen.—Ed.
9. A play by Scarron.—Ed.
10. In 1720 seven thousand tailors formed a trade union which was outlawed by an act of Parliament later in the year.—Ed.
11. 'There is no disputing tastes', according to the well-known Latin proverb.—Ed.
12. 'The gods sell everything for labour.' Latin proverb.—Ed.
13. Peter the Great, who reigned from 1682 to 1725.—Ed.

Richard Steele
The Conscious Lovers

Illud genus narrationis quod in personis positum est, debet habere sermon is festivitatem,
animorum dissimilitudinem, gravitatem, lenitatem, spem, metum, suspicionem, desiderium,
dissimulationem, misericordiam, rerum varietates, fortunce commlutationem, inspera turn
incommodum, subitam lcetitiam, jucundum exitum rerum.

Cic. Rhetor ad Herenn. Lib. I.[1]

The Preface

This comedy has been received with universal acceptance, for it was in every part excellently performed; and there needs no other applause of the actors but that they excelled according to the dignity and difficulty of the character they represented. But this great favour done to the work in acting renders the expectation still the greater from the author, to keep up the spirit in the representation of the closet, or any other circumstance of the reader, whether alone or in company: to which I can only say that it must be remembered a play is to be seen, and is made to be represented with the advantage of action, nor can appear but with half the spirit without it; for the greatest effect of a play in reading is to excite the reader to go see it; and when he does so, it is then a play has the effect of example and precept.

The chief design of this was to be an innocent performance, and the audience have abundantly showed how ready they are to support what is visibly intended that way; nor do I make any difficulty to acknowledge that the whole was writ for the sake of the scene of the fourth act, wherein Mr. Bevil evades the quarrel with his friend, and hope it may have some effect upon the Goths and Vandals that frequent the theatres, or a more polite audience may supply their absence.

But this incident, and the case of the father and daughter, are esteemed by some people no subjects of comedy; but I cannot be of their mind; for anything that has its foundation in happiness and success must be allowed to be the object of comedy, and sure it must be an improvement of it to introduce a joy too exquisite for laughter, that can have no spring but in delight, which is the case of this young lady. I must, therefore, contend that the tears which were shed on that occasion flowed from reason and good sense, and that men ought not to be laughed at for weeping till we are come to a more clear notion of what is to be imputed to the hardness of the head and the softness of the heart; and I think it was very politely said of Mr. Wilks, to one who told him there was a general weeping for Indiana, "I'll warrant he'll fight ne'er the worse for that." To be apt to give way to the impressions of humanity is the excellence of a right disposition and the natural working of a well-turned spirit. But as I have suffered by critics who are got no farther than to enquire whether they ought to be pleased or not, I would willingly find them properer matter for their employment, and revive here a song which was omitted for want of a performer, and designed for the entertainment of Indiana; Sig.

From *Eighteenth-Century Plays* with introduction by Ricardo Quintana.

Carbonelli, instead of it, played on the fiddle, and it is for want of a singer that such advantageous things are said of an instrument which were designed for a voice. The song is the distress of a love-sick maid, and may be a fit entertainment for some small critics to examine whether the passion is just or the distress male or female.

I.

From place to place forlorn I go,
With downcast eyes a silent shade;
Forbidden to declare my woe;
To speak, till spoken to, afraid.

II.

My *inward pangs, my secret grief,*
My soft consenting looks betray:
He loves, but gives me no relief;
Why speaks not he who may?

It remains to say a word concerning Terence, and I am extremely surprised to find what Mr. Gibber told me prove a truth, that what I valued myself so much upon, the translation of him, should be imputed to me as a reproach. Mr. Cibber's zeal for the work, his care and application in instructing the actors and altering the disposition of the scenes, when I was, through sickness, unable to cultivate such things myself, has been a very obliging favour and friendship to me. For this reason I was very hardly persuaded to throw away Terence's celebrated funeral, and take only the bare authority of the young man's character; and how I have worked it into an Englishman, and made use of the same circumstances of discovering a daughter when we least hoped for one, is humbly submitted to the learned reader.

Prologue

By Mr. Welsted

To win your hearts and to secure your praise,
The comic-writers strive by various ways:
By subtle stratagems they act their game,
And leave untry'd no avenue to fame.
One writes the spouse a beating from his wife,
And says each stroke was copy'd from the life.
Some fix all wit and humour in grimace,
And make a livelihood of Pinkey's face:
Here one gay show and costly habits tries,
Confiding to the judgment of your eyes:
Another smuts his scene (a cunning shaver),
Sure of the rakes' and of the wenches' favour.

Oft have these arts prevail'd; and, one may guess,
If practis'd o'er again, would find success.
But the bold sage, the poet of to-night,
By new and desp'rate rules resolv'd to write;
Fain would he give more just applauses rise,
And please by wit that scorns the aids of vice;
The praise he seeks from worthier motives springs,
Such praise as praise to those that give it brings.

    Your aid, most humbly sought, then, Britons, lend,
And lib'ral mirth like lib'ral men defend:
No more let ribaldry, with licence writ,
Usurp the name of eloquence or wit;
No more let lawless farce uncensur'd go,
The lewd dull gleanings of a Smithfield show.
'Tis yours with breeding to refine the age,
To chasten wit, and moralize the stage.

    Ye modest, wise and good, ye fair, ye brave,
To-night the champion of your virtues save;
Redeem from long contempt the comic name,
And judge politely for your country's fame.

Dramatis Personae

Men:

SIR JOHN BEVIL

MR. SEALAND

JOHN BEVIL JUNIOR, *in love with* INDIANA

CHARLES MYRTLE, *in love with* LUCINDA

CIMBERTON, *a Coxcomb*

HUMPHREY, *an old servant to* SIR JOHN

TOM, *servant to* BEVIL JUNIOR

DANIEL, *a country boy, servant to* INDIANA

Women:

MRS. SEALAND, *second wife to* SEALAND

ISABELLA, *sister to* SEALAND

INDIANA, SEALAND'S daughter by his first wife

LUCINDA, SEALAND'S *daughter by his second wife*

PHILLIS, *maid to* LUCINDA

SCENE: *London*

The Conscious Lovers

ACT I
SCENE I

SCENE: SIR JOHN BEVIL'S house

Enter SIR JOHN BEVIL *and* HUMPHREY

SIR J. BEV.   Have you ordered that I should not be interrupted while I am dressing?

HUMPH.   Yes, Sir: I believed you had something of moment to say to me.

SIR J. BEV.   Let me see, Humphrey; I think it is now full forty years since I first took thee to be about myself.

HUMPH.   I thank you, Sir; it has been an easy forty years, and I have passed 'em without much sickness, care, or labour.

SIR J. BEV.   Thou hast a brave constitution; you are a year or two older than I am, Sirrah.

HUMPH.   You have ever been of that mind, Sir.

SIR J. BEV.   You knave, you know it; I took thee for thy gravity and sobriety, in my wild years.

HUMPH.   Ah, Sir! our manners were formed from our different fortunes, not our different age. Wealth gave a loose to your youth, and poverty put a restraint upon mine.

SIR J. BEV.   Well, Humphrey, you know I have been a kind master to you; I have used you, for the ingenious nature I observed in you from the beginning, more like an humble friend than a servant.

HUMPH.   I humbly beg you'll be so tender of me as to explain your commands, Sir, without any farther preparation.

SIR J. BEV.   I'll tell thee, then. In the first place, this wedding of my son's, in all probability (shut the door) will never be at all.

HUMPH.   How, Sir! not be at all? For what reason is it carried on in appearance?

SIR J. BEV.   Honest Humphrey, have patience, and I'll tell thee all in order. I have myself, in some part of my life, lived, indeed, with freedom, but, I hope, without reproach. Now, I thought liberty would be as little injurious to my son; therefore, as soon as he grew towards man, I indulged him in living after his own manner: I knew not how, otherwise, to judge of his inclination; for what can be concluded from a behaviour under restraint and fear?

But what charms me above all expression is that my son has never, in the least action, the most distant hint or word, valued himself upon that great estate of his mother's, which, according to our marriage settlement, he has had ever since he came to age.

HUMPH.   No, Sir; on the contrary, he seems afraid of appearing to enjoy it before you or any belonging to you. He is as dependent and resigned to your will as if he had not a farthing but what must come from your immediate bounty. You have ever acted like a good and generous father, and he like an obedient and grateful son.

From *Eighteenth-Century Plays* with introduction by Ricardo Quintana.

SIR J. BEV. Nay, his carriage is so easy to all with whom he converses, that he is never assuming, never prefers himself to others, nor ever is guilty of that rough sincerity which a man is not called to and certainly disobliges most of his acquaintance; to be short, Humphrey, his reputation was so fair in the world, that old Sealand, the great India merchant, has offered his only daughter and sole heiress to that vast estate of his, as a wife for him. You may be sure I made no difficulties; the match was agreed on, and this very day named for the wedding.

HUMPH. What hinders the proceeding?

SIR J. BEV. Don't interrupt me. You know I was last Thursday at the masquerade; my son, you may remember, soon found us out. He knew his grandfather's habit, which I then wore; and though it was the mode in the last age, yet the maskers, you know, followed us as if we had been the most monstrous figures in that whole assembly.

HUMPH. I remember, indeed, a young man of quality, in the habit of a clown, that was particularly troublesome.

SIR J. BEV. Right; he was too much what he seemed to be. You remember how impertinently he followed and teased us, and would know who we were.

HUMPH. *(aside)* I know he has a mind to come into that particular.

SIR J. BEV. Ay, he followed us till the gentleman who led the lady in the Indian mantle presented that gay creature to the rustic, and bid him (like Cymon in the fable) grow polite by falling in love, and let that worthy old gentleman alone—meaning me. The clown was not reformed, but rudely persisted, and offered to force off my mask; with that the gentleman, throwing off his own, appeared to be my son, and, in his concern for me, tore off that of the nobleman. At this they seized each other; the company called the guards; and in the surprise the lady swooned away; upon which my son quitted his adversary, and had now no care but of the lady—when, raising her in his arms, "Art thou gone," cried he, "forever?—forbid it, heaven!" She revives at his known voice, and with the most familiar, though modest, gesture, hangs in safety over his shoulder weeping, but wept as in the arms of one before whom she could give herself a loose, were she not under observation. While she hides her face in his neck, he carefully conveys her from the company.

HUMPH. I have observed this accident has dwelt upon you very strongly.

SIR J. BEV. Her uncommon air, her noble modesty, the dignity of her person, and the occasion itself, drew the whole assembly together; and I soon heard it buzzed about, she was the adopted daughter of a famous sea-officer who had served in France. Now this unexpected and public discovery of my son's so deep concern for her—

HUMPH. Was what, I suppose, alarmed Mr. Sealand, in behalf of his daughter, to break off the match?

SIR J. BEV. You are right. He came to me yesterday and said he thought himself disengaged from the bargain, being credibly informed my son was already married, or worse, to the lady at the masquerade. I palliated matters, and insisted on our agreement; but we parted with little less than a direct breach between us.

HUMPH. Well, Sir; and what notice have you taken of all this to my young master?

SIR J. BEV. That's what I wanted to debate with you. I have said nothing to him yet. But look you, Humphrey—if there is so much in this amour of his that he denies upon my summons to marry, I have cause enough to be offended; and then by my insisting upon his marrying to-day I shall know how far he is engaged to this lady in masquerade, and from thence only shall be able to take my measures. In the meantime I would have you find out how far that rogue, his man, is let into his secret. He, I know, will play tricks as much to cross me, as to serve his master.

HUMPH.   Why do you think so of him, Sir? I believe he is no worse than I was for you at your son's age.

SIR J. BEV.   I see it in the rascal's looks. But I have dwelt on these things too long; I'll go to my son immediately, and while I'm gone, your part is to convince his rogue Tom that I am in earnest. I'll leave him to you.   (*Exit* SIR JOHN BEVIL)

HUMPH.   Well, though this father and son live as well together as possible, yet their fear of giving each other pain is attended with constant mutual uneasiness. I'm sure I have enough to do to be honest and yet keep well with them both. But they know I love 'em, and that makes the task less painful, however.—Oh, here's the prince of poor coxcombs, the representative of all the better fed than taught.—Ho! ho! Tom, whither so gay and so airy this morning?

Enter TOM, *singing*

TOM.   Sir, we servants of single gentlemen are another kind of people than you domestic ordinary drudges that do business; we are raised above you. The pleasures of board-wages, tavern dinners, and many a clear gain—vails, alas! you never heard or dreamt of.

HUMPH.   Thou hast follies and vices enough for a man of ten thousand a year, though 'tis but as t'other day that I sent for you to town to put you into Mr. Sealand's family, that you might learn a little before I put you to my young master, who is too gentle for training such a rude thing as you were into proper obedience. You then pulled off your hat to everyone you met in the street, like a bashful great awkward cub as you were. But your great oaken cudgel, when you were a booby, became you much better than that dangling stick at your button, now you are a fop. That's fit for nothing, except it hangs there to be ready for your master's hand when you are impertinent.

TOM.   Uncle Humphrey, you know my master scorns to strike his servants. You talk as if the world was now just as it was when my old master and you were in your youth—when you went to dinner because it was so much o'clock, when the great blow was given in the hall at the pantry door, and all the family came out of their holes in such strange dresses and formal faces as you see in the pictures in our long gallery in the country.

HUMPH.   Why, you wild rogue!

TOM.   You could not fall to your dinner till a formal fellow in a black gown said something over the meat, as if the cook had not made it ready enough.

HUMPH.   Sirrah, who do you prate after? Despising men of sacred characters! I hope you never heard my good young master talk so like a profligate.

TOM.   Sir, I say you put upon me, when I first came to town, about being orderly, and the doctrine of wearing shams to make linen last clean a fortnight, keeping my clothes fresh, and wearing a frock within doors.

HUMPH.   Sirrah, I gave you those lessons because I supposed at that time your master and you might have dined at home every day and cost you nothing; then you might have made a good family servant.

But the gang you have frequented since at chocolate houses and taverns, in a continual round of noise and extravagance—

TOM.   I don't know what you heavy inmates call noise and extravagance; but we gentlemen, who are well fed and cut a figure, Sir, think it a fine life, and that we must be very pretty fellows who are kept only to be looked at.

HUMPH.   Very well, Sir! I hope the fashion of being lewd and extravagant, despising of decency and order, is almost at an end, since it is arrived at persons of your quality.

TOM.   Master Humphrey, ha! ha! you were an unhappy lad to be sent up to town in such queer days as you were. Why now, Sir, the lackeys are the men of pleasure of the age, the top gamesters; and many a laced coat about town have had their education in our parti-coloured regiment. We are false lovers; have a taste of music, poetry, billets-doux, dress, politics; ruin damsels; and when we are weary of this lewd town and have a mind to take up, whip into our masters' wigs and linen, and marry fortunes.

HUMPH.   Hey-day!

TOM.   Nay, Sir, our order is carried up to the highest dignities and distinctions; step but into the Painted Chamber, and by our titles you'd take us all for men of quality. Then, again, come down to the Court of Requests, and you see us all laying our broken heads together for the good of the nation; and though we never carry a question *nemine contradicente,* yet this I can say with a safe conscience (and I wish every gentleman of our cloth could lay his hand upon his heart and say the same), that I never took so much as a single mug of beer for my vote in all my life.

HUMPH.   Sirrah, there is no enduring your extravagance; I'll hear you prate no longer. I wanted to see you to enquire how things go with your master, as far as you understand them; I suppose he knows he is to be married to-day.

TOM.   Ay, Sir, he knows it, and is dressed as gay as the sun; but, between you and I, my dear, he has a very heavy heart under all that gaiety. As soon as he was dressed I retired, but overheard him sigh in the most heavy manner. He walked thoughtfully to and fro in the room, then went into his closet; when he came out he gave me this for his mistress, whose maid, you know—

HUMPH.   Is passionately fond of your fine person.

TOM.   The poor fool is so tender, and loves to hear me talk of the world, and the plays, operas and ridottos for the winter, the parks and Belsize for our summer diversions; and "Lard!" says she, "you are so wild—but you have a world of humour."

HUMPH.   Coxcomb! Well, but why don't you run with your master's letter to Mrs. Lucinda, as he ordered you?

TOM.   Because Mrs. Lucinda is not so easily come at as you think for.

HUMPH.   Not easily come at? Why, Sirrah, are not her father and my old master agreed that she and Mr. Bevil are to be one flesh before to-morrow morning?

TOM.   It's no matter for that; her mother, it seems, Mrs. Sealand, has not agreed to it: and you must know, Mr. Humphrey, that in that family the grey mare is the better horse.

HUMPH.   What dost thou mean?

TOM.   In one word, Mrs. Sealand pretends to have a will of her own, and has provided a relation of hers, a stiff, starched philosopher and a wise fool, for her daughter; for which reason, for these ten days past, she has suffered no message nor letter from my master to come near her.

HUMPH.   And where had you this intelligence?

TOM.   From a foolish, fond soul that can keep nothing from me—one that will deliver this letter too, if she is rightly managed.

HUMPH.   What! her pretty handmaid, Mrs. Phillis?

TOM.   Even she, Sir; this is the very hour, you know, she usually comes hither, under a pretence of a visit to your housekeeper, forsooth, but in reality to have a glance at —

HUMPH.   Your sweet face, I warrant you.

TOM.   Nothing else in nature; you must know, I love to fret and play with the little wanton—

HUMPH.   "Play with the little wanton!" What will this world come to!

TOM.   I met her this morning in a new manteau and petticoat not a bit the worse for her lady's wearing, and she has always new thoughts and new airs with new clothes. Then, she never fails to steal some glance or gesture from every visitant at their house, and is, indeed, the whole town of coquettes at second hand.—But here she comes; in one motion she speaks and describes herself better than all the words in the world can.

HUMPH.   Then I hope, dear Sir, when your own affair is over, you will be so good as to mind your master's with her.

TOM.   Dear Humphrey, you know my master is my friend, and those are people I never forget.

HUMPH.   Sauciness itself! but I'll leave you to do your best for him.   *(Exit)*

Enter PHILLIS

PHIL.   Oh, Mr. Thomas, is Mrs. Sugarkey at home? Lard! one is almost ashamed to pass along the streets. The town is quite empty, and nobody of fashion left in it; and the ordinary people do so stare to see anything dressed like a woman of condition, as it were, on the same floor with them, pass by. Alas! alas! it is a sad thing to walk. O Fortune! Fortune!

TOM.   What! a sad thing to walk? Why, Madam Phillis, do you wish yourself lame?

PHIL.   No, Mr. Tom, but I wish I were generally carried in a coach or chair, and of a fortune neither to stand nor go, but to totter, or slide, to be short-sighted, or stare, to fleer in the face, to look distant, to observe, to overlook, yet all become me; and if I was rich, I could twire and loll as well as the best of them O, Tom! Tom! Is it not a pity that you should be so great a coxcomb, and I so great a coquette, and yet be such poor devils as we are?

TOM.   Mrs. Phillis, I am your humble servant for that—

PHIL.   Yes, Mr. Thomas, I know how much you are my humble servant, and know what you said to Mrs. Judy, upon seeing her in one of her lady's cast manteaus—that any one would have thought her the lady, and that she had ordered the other to wear it till it sat easy, for now only it was becoming—to my lady it was only a covering, to Mrs. Judy it was a habit. This you said, after somebody or other. O Tom! Tom! thou art as false and as base as the best gentleman of them all; but, you wretch, talk to me no more on the old odious subject. Don't, I say.

TOM.   *(in a submissive tone, retiring)* I know not how to resist your commands, Madam.

PHIL.   Commands about parting are grown mighty easy to you of late.

TOM.   *(aside)* Oh, I have her; I have nettled and put her into the right temper to be wrought upon and set a-prating.—Why, truly, to be plain with you, Mrs. Phillis, I can take little comfort of late in frequenting your house.

PHIL.   Pray, Mr. Thomas, what is it all of a sudden offends your nicety at our house?

TOM.   I don't care to speak particulars, but I dislike the whole.

PHIL.   I thank you, Sir, I am a part of that whole.

TOM.   Mistake me not, good Phillis.

PHIL.   Good Phillis! Saucy enough. But however—

TOM.   I say, it is that thou art a part which gives me pain for the disposition of the whole. You must know, Madam, to be serious, I am a man, at the bottom, of prodigious nice honour. You are too much exposed to company at your house. To be plain, I don't like so many, that would be your mistress's lovers, whispering to you.

PHIL.   Don't think to put that upon me. You say this because I wrung you to the heart when I touched your guilty conscience about Judy.

TOM.   Ah, Phillis! Phillis! if you but knew my heart!

PHIL.   I know too much on't.

TOM.   Nay, then, poor Crispo's fate and mine are one. Therefore give me leave to say, or sing at least, as he does upon the same occasion— *(Sings)*

Se vedette, etc.

PHIL.   What, do you think I'm to be fobbed off with a song? I don't question but you have sung the same to Mrs. Judy too.

TOM.   Don't disparage your charms, good Phillis, with jealousy of so worthless an object; besides, she is a poor hussy, and if you doubt the sincerity of my love, you will allow me true to my interest. You are a fortune, Phillis—

PHIL.   What would the fop be at now? In good time, indeed, you shall be setting up for a fortune!

TOM.   Dear Mrs. Phillis, you have such a spirit that we shall never be dull in marriage when we come together. But I tell you, you are a fortune, and you have an estate in my hands. *(He pulls out a purse; she eyes it)*

PHIL.   What pretence have I to what is in your hands, Mr. Tom?

TOM.   As thus: there are hours, you know, when a lady is neither pleased or displeased, neither sick or well; when she lolls or loiters; when she's without desires, from having more of everything than she knows what to do with.

PHIL.   Well, what then?

TOM.   When she has not life enough to keep her bright eyes quite open, to look at her own dear image in the glass.

PHIL.   Explain thyself, and don't be so fond of thy own prating.

TOM.   There are also prosperous and good-natured moments, as when a knot or a patch is happily fixed, when the complexion particularly flourishes.

PHIL.   Well, what then? I have not patience!

TOM.   Why, then—or on the like occasions—we servants who have skill to know how to time business see when such a pretty folded thing as this *(shows a letter)* may be presented, laid, or dropped, as best suits the present humour. And, Madam, because it is a long, wearisome journey to run through all the several stages of a lady's temper, my master, who is the most reasonable man in the world, presents you this to bear your charges on the road. *(Gives her the purse)*

PHIL.   Now you think me a corrupt hussy.

TOM.   Oh, fie! I only think you'll take the letter.

PHIL.   Nay, I know you do, but I know my own innocence; I take it for my mistress's sake.

TOM.   I know it, my pretty one, I know it.

PHIL.   Yes, I say, I do it because I would not have my mistress deluded by one who gives no proof of his passion; but I'll talk more of this as you see me on my way home. No, Tom, I assure thee I take this trash of thy master's, not for the value of the thing, but as it convinces me he has a true respect for my mistress. I remember a verse to the purpose:

> They may be false who languish and complain,
> But they who part with money never feign.   *(Exeunt)*

SCENE II

SCENE: BEVIL JUNIOR'S *lodgings*

BEVIL JUNIOR, *reading*

BEV. JUN.   These moral writers practise virtue after death. This charming Vision of Mirza! Such an author consulted in a morning sets the spirit for the vicissitudes of the day better than the glass does a man's person. But what a day have I to go through! to put on an easy look with an aching heart. If this lady my father urges me to marry should not refuse me, my dilemma is insupportable. But why should I fear it? is not she in equal distress with me? has not the letter I have sent her this morning confessed my inclination to another? Nay, have I not moral assurances of her engagements, too, to my friend Myrtle? It's impossible but she must give in to it: for sure, to be denied is a favour any man may pretend to. It must be so. Well, then, with the assurance of being rejected, I think I may confidently say to my father I am ready to marry her. Then let me resolve upon—what I am not very good at, though it is—an honest dissimulation.

Enter TOM

TOM.   Sir John Bevil, Sir, is in the next room.

BEV. JUN.   Dunce! Why did not you bring him in?

TOM.   I told him, Sir, you were in your closet.

BEV. JUN.   I thought you had known, Sir, it was my duty to see my father anywhere.

(going himself to the door)

TOM.   *(aside)* The devil's in my master! he has always more wit than I have.

BEV. JUN.   *(introducing* SIR JOHN) Sir, you are the most gallant, the most complaisant of all parents. Sure, 'tis not a compliment to say these lodgings are yours. Why would you not walk in, Sir?

SIR J. BEV.   I was loath to interrupt you unseasonably on your wedding-day.

BEV. JUN.   One to whom I am beholden for my birthday might have used less ceremony.

SIR J. BEV.   Well, Son, I have intelligence you have writ to your mistress this morning. It would please my curiosity to know the contents of a wedding-day letter, for courtship must then be over.

BEV. JUN.   I assure you, Sir, there was no insolence in it upon the prospect of such a vast fortune's being added to our family, but much acknowledgment of the lady's greater desert.

SIR J. BEV.   But, dear Jack, are you in earnest in all this? And will you really marry her?

BEV. JUN.   Did I ever disobey any command of yours, Sir? nay, any inclination that I saw you bent upon?

SIR J. BEV.   Why, I can't say you have, Son; but methinks in this whole business you have not been so warm as I could have wished you. You have visited her, it's true, but you have not been particular. Everyone knows you can say and do as handsome things as any man, but you have done nothing but lived in the general—been complaisant only.

BEV. JUN.   As I am ever prepared to marry if you bid me, so I am ready to let it alone if you will have me.

HUMPHREY *enters, unobserved*

SIR J. BEV.   Look you there now! Why, what am I to think of this so absolute and so indifferent a resignation?

BEV. JUN.   Think? that I am still your son, Sir. Sir, you have been married, and I have not. And you have, Sir, found the inconvenience there is when a man weds with too much love in his head. I have been told, Sir, that at the time you married, you made a mighty bustle on the occasion. There was challenging and fighting, scaling walls, locking up the lady, and the gallant under an arrest for fear of killing all his rivals. Now, Sir, I suppose you, having found the ill consequences of these strong passions and prejudices in preference of one woman to another, in case of a man's becoming a widower—

SIR J. BEV.   How is this!

BEV. JUN.   I say, Sir, experience has made you wiser in your care of me; for, Sir, since you lost my dear mother your time has been so heavy, so lonely, and so tasteless, that you are so good as to guard me against the like unhappiness, by marrying me prudentially by way of bargain and sale. For as you well judge, a woman that is espoused for a fortune is yet a better bargain if she dies; for then a man still enjoys what he did marry, the money, and is disencumbered of what he did not marry, the woman.

SIR J. BEV.   But pray, Sir, do you think Lucinda, then, a woman of such little merit?

BEV. JUN.   Pardon me, Sir, I don't carry it so far neither. I am rather afraid I shall like her too well; she has, for one of her fortune, a great many needless and superfluous good qualities.

SIR J. BEV.   I am afraid, Son, there's something I don't see yet, something that's smothered under all this raillery.

BEV. JUN.   Not in the least, Sir. If the lady is dressed and ready, you see I am. I suppose the lawyers are ready too.

HUMPH.   *(aside)* This may grow warm if I don't interpose.—Sir, Mr. Sealand is at the coffeehouse, and has sent to speak with you.

SIR J. BEV.   Oh, that's well! Then I warrant the lawyers are ready. Son, you'll be in the way, you say—

BEV. JUN.   If you please, Sir, I'll take a chair, and go to Mr. Sealand's, where the young lady and I will wait your leisure.

SIR J. BEV.   By no means. The old fellow will be so vain if he sees—

BEV. JUN.   Ay; but the young lady, Sir, will think me so indifferent—

HUMPH.   *(aside to* BEVIL JUNIOR*)* Ay, there you are right; press your readiness to go to the bride— he won't let you.

BEV. JUN.   *(aside to* HUMPHREY*)* Are you sure of that?

HUMPH.   *(aside)* How he likes being prevented!

SIR J. BEV.   *(looking on his watch)* No, no. You are an hour or two too early.

BEV. JUN.   You'll allow me, Sir, to think it too late to visit a beautiful, virtuous young woman, in the pride and bloom of life, ready to give herself to my arms; and to place her happiness or misery, for the future, in being agreeable or displeasing to me, is a—Call a chair!

SIR J. BEV.   No, no, no, dear Jack; this Sealand is a moody old fellow. There's no dealing with some people but by managing with indifference. We must leave to him the conduct of this day. It is the last of his commanding his daughter.

BEV. JUN.   Sir, he can't take it ill that I am impatient to be hers.

SIR J. BEV.   Pray, let me govern in this matter; you can't tell how humoursome old fellows are. There's no offering reason to some of 'em, especially when they are rich.— *(aside)* If my son should see him before I've brought old Sealand into better temper, the match would be impracticable.

HUMPH.   Pray, Sir, let me beg you to let Mr. Bevil *go.—(aside to* SIR JOHN*)* See whether he will or *not—(then to* BEVIL JUNIOR*)* Pray, Sir, command yourself; since you see my master is positive, it is better you should not go.

BEV. JUN.   My father commands me as to the object of my affections, but I hope he will not as to the warmth and height of them.

SIR J. BEV.   *(aside)* So! I must even leave things as I found them, and in the meantime, at least, keep old Sealand out of his sight.—Well, Son, I'll go myself and take orders in your affair. You'll be in the way, I suppose, if I send to you. I'll leave your old friend with you.—Humphrey, don't let him stir, d'ye hear?—Your servant, your servant!

(Exit SIR JOHN BEVIL*)*

HUMPH.   I have a sad time on't, Sir, between you and my master. I see you are unwilling, and I know his violent inclinations for the match.—I must betray neither and yet deceive you both, for your common good.—Heaven grant a good end of this matter! But there is a lady, Sir, that gives your father much trouble and sorrow. You'll pardon me.

BEV. JUN.   Humphrey, I know thou art a friend to both, and in that confidence I dare tell thee—that lady is a woman of honour and virtue. You may assure yourself I never will marry without my father's consent. But give me leave to say, too, this declaration does not come up to a promise that I will take whosoever he pleases.

HUMPH. Come, Sir, I wholly understand you. You would engage my services to free you from this woman whom my master intends you, to make way in time for the woman you have really a mind to.

BEV. JUN. Honest Humphrey, you have always been an useful friend to my father and myself; I beg you, continue your good offices, and don't let us come to the necessity of a dispute; for, if we should dispute, I must either part with more than life, or lose the best of fathers.

HUMPH. My dear master, were I but worthy to know this secret that so near concerns you, my life, my all should be engaged to serve you. This, Sir, I dare promise, that I am sure I will and can be secret. Your trust, at worst, but leaves you where you were; and if I cannot serve you, I will at once be plain and tell you so.

BEV. JUN. That's all I ask. Thou hast made it now my interest to trust thee. Be patient, then, and hear the story of my heart.

HUMPH. I am all attention, Sir.

BEV. JUN. You may remember, Humphrey, that in my last travels my father grew uneasy at my making so long a stay at Toulon.

HUMPH. I remember it; he was apprehensive some woman had laid hold of you.

BEV. JUN. His fears were just, for there I first saw this lady. She is of English birth: her father's name was Danvers, a younger brother of an ancient family, and originally an eminent merchant of Bristol, who, upon repeated misfortunes, was reduced to go privately to the Indies. In this retreat Providence again grew favourable to his industry, and in six years' time restored him to his former fortunes. On this he sent directions over that his wife and little family should follow him to the Indies. His wife, impatient to obey such welcome orders, would not wait the leisure of a convoy, but took the first occasion of a single ship, and, with her husband's sister only, and this daughter, then scarce seven years old, undertook the fatal voyage—for here, poor creature, she lost her liberty and life; she and her family, with all they had, were unfortunately taken by a privateer from Toulon. Being thus made a prisoner, though as such not ill-treated, yet the fright, the shock, and cruel disappointment seized with such violence upon her unhealthy frame, she sickened, pined, and died at sea.

HUMPH. Poor soul! Oh, the helpless infant!

BEV. JUN. Her sister yet survived, and had the care of her. The captain, too, proved to have humanity, and became a father to her; for having himself married an English woman, and being childless, he brought home into Toulon this her little country-woman, presenting her, with all her dead mother's movables of value, to his wife, to be educated as his own adopted daughter.

HUMPH. Fortune here seemed again to smile on her.

BEV. JUN. Only to make her frowns more terrible; for in his height of fortune this captain, too, her benefactor, unfortunately was killed at sea, and, dying intestate, his estate fell wholly to an advocate, his brother, who, coming soon to take possession, there found, among his other riches, this blooming virgin at his mercy.

HUMPH. He durst not, sure, abuse his power!

BEV. JUN. No wonder if his pampered blood was fired at the sight of her—in short, he loved. But when all arts and gentle means had failed to move, he offered, too, his menaces in vain, denouncing vengeance on her cruelty, demanding her to account for all her maintenance from her childhood, seized on her little fortune as his own inheritance, and was dragging her by violence to prison, when Providence at the instant interposed, and sent me, by miracle, to relieve her.

HUMPH.   'Twas Providence, indeed. But pray, Sir, after all this trouble how came this lady at last to England?

BEV. JUN.   The disappointed advocate, finding she had so unexpected a support, on cooler thoughts descended to a composition, which I, without her knowledge, secretly discharged.

HUMPH.   That generous concealment made the obligation double.

BEV. JUN.   Having thus obtained her liberty, I prevailed, not without some difficulty, to see her safe to England, where no sooner arrived but my father, jealous of my being imprudently engaged, immediately proposed this other fatal match that hangs upon my quiet.

HUMPH.   I find, Sir, you are irrecoverably fixed upon this lady.

BEV. JUN.   As my vital life dwells in my heart; and yet you see what I do to please my father: walk in this pageantry of dress, this splendid covering of sorrow. But, Humphrey, you have your lesson.

HUMPH.   Now, Sir, I have but one material question—

BEV. JUN.   Ask it freely.

HUMPH.   Is it, then, your own passion for this secret lady, or hers for you, that gives you this aversion to the match your father has proposed you?

BEV. JUN.   I shall appear, Humphrey, more romantic in my answer than in all the rest of my story; for though I dote on her to death, and have no little reason to believe she has the same thoughts for me, yet in all my acquaintance and utmost privacies with her I never once directly told her that I loved.

HUMPH.   How was it possible to avoid it?

BEV. JUN.   My tender obligations to my father have laid so inviolable a restraint upon my conduct that till I have his consent to speak I am determined, on that subject, to be dumb forever.

HUMPH.   Well, Sir, to your praise be it spoken, you are certainly the most unfashionable lover in Great Britain.

Enter TOM

TOM.   Sir, Mr. Myrtle's at the next door, and, if you are at leisure, will be glad to wait on you.

BEV. JUN.   Whenever he pleases.—Hold, Tom! did you receive no answer to my letter?

TOM.   Sir, I was desired to call again, for I was told her mother would not let her be out of her sight. But about an hour hence, Mrs. Lettice said, I should certainly have one.

BEV. JUN.   Very well.

HUMPH.   Sir, I will take another opportunity: in the meantime, I only think it proper to tell you that, from a secret I know, you may appear to your father as forward as you please to marry Lucinda, without the least hazard of its coming to a conclusion. Sir, your most obedient servant!

BEV. JUN.   Honest Humphrey, continue but my friend in this exigence and you shall always find me yours.

(Exit HUMPHREY)

I long to hear how my letter has succeeded with Lucinda—but I think it cannot fail, for at worst, were it possible she could take it ill, her resentment of my indifference may as probably occasion a delay as her taking it right. Poor Myrtle, what terrors must he be in all this while? Since he knows she is offered to me and refused to him, there is no conversing or taking any measures with him for his own service. But I ought to bear with my friend, and use him as one in adversity:

> All his disquiets by my own I prove;
> The greatest grief's perplexity in love.   *(Exeunt)*

ACT II

SCENE I

Scene continues

Enter BEVIL JUNIOR *and* TOM

TOM.   Sir, Mr. Myrtle.

BEV. JUN.   Very well—do you step again, and wait for an answer to my letter. *(Exit* TOM)

Enter MYRTLE

Well, Charles, why so much care in thy countenance? Is there anything in this world deserves it? You, who used to be so gay, so open, so vacant!

MYRT.   I think we have of late changed complexions. You, who used to be much the graver man, are now all air in your behaviour. But the cause of my concern may, for aught I know, be the same object that gives you all this satisfaction. In a word, I am told that you are this very day—and your dress confirms me in it—to be married to Lucinda.

BEV. JUN.   You are not misinformed. Nay, put not on the terrors of a rival till you hear me out. I shall disoblige the best of fathers if I don't seem ready to marry Lucinda; and you know I have ever told you you might make use of my secret resolution never to marry her, for your own service, as you please. But I am now driven to the extremity of immediately refusing or complying unless you help me to escape the match.

MYRT.   Escape? Sir, neither her merit or her fortune are below your acceptance. Escaping do you call it!

BEV. JUN.   Dear Sir, do you wish I should desire the match?

MYRT.   No, but such is my humourous and sickly state of mind since it has been able to relish nothing but Lucinda, that though I must owe my happiness to your aversion to this marriage, I can't bear to hear her spoken of with levity or unconcern.

BEV. JUN.   Pardon me, Sir; I shall transgress that way no more. She has understanding, beauty, shape, complexion, wit—

103

MYRT.　　　Nay, dear Bevil, don't speak of her as if you loved her, neither.

BEV. JUN.　　Why, then, to give you ease at once, though I allow Lucinda to have good sense, wit, beauty, and virtue, **I** know another in whom these qualities appear to me more amiable than in her.

MYRT.　　　There you spoke like a reasonable and good-natured friend. When you acknowledge her merit and own your prepossession for another, at once you gratify my fondness and cure my jealousy.

BEV. JUN.　　But all this while you take no notice, you have no apprehension, of another man that has twice the fortune of either of us.

MYRT.　　　Cimberton! Hang him, a formal, philosophical, pedantic coxcomb! for the sot, with all these crude notions of divers things, under the direction of great vanity and very little judgment, shows his strongest bias is avarice; which is so predominant in him that he will examine the limbs of his mistress with the caution of a jockey, and pays no more compliment to her personal charms than if she were a mere breeding animal.

BEV. JUN.　　Are you sure that is not affected? I have known some women sooner set on fire by that sort of negligence than by—

MYRT.　　　No, no! hang him, the rogue has no art; it is pure, simple insolence and stupidity.

BEV. JUN.　　Yet with all this, I don't take him for a fool.

MYRT.　　　I own the man is not a natural; he has a very quick sense, though very slow understanding. He says, indeed, many things that want only the circumstances of time and place to be very just and agreeable.

BEV. JUN.　　Well, you may be sure of me if you can disappoint him; but my intelligence says the mother has actually sent for the conveyancer to draw articles for his marriage with Lucinda, though those for mine with her are, by her father's order, ready for signing. But it seems she has not thought fit to consult either him or his daughter in the matter.

MYRT.　　　Pshaw! a poor, troublesome woman. Neither Lucinda nor her father will ever be brought to comply with it; besides, I am sure Cimberton can make no settlement upon her without the concurrence of his great-uncle, Sir Geoffry, in the west.

BEV. JUN.　　Well, Sir, and I can tell you that's the very point that is now laid before her counsel, to know whether a firm settlement can be made without this uncle's actual joining in it. Now pray consider, Sir, when my affair with Lucinda comes, as it soon must, to an open rupture, how are you sure that Cimberton's fortune may not then tempt her father, too, to hear his proposals?

MYRT.　　　There you are right, indeed; that must be provided against. Do you know who are her counsel?

BEV. JUN.　　Yes, for your service I have found out that, too: they are Sergeant Bramble and old Target— by the way, they are neither of 'em known in the family. Now, I was thinking why you might not put a couple of false counsel upon her to delay and confound matters a little; besides, it may probably let you into the bottom of her whole design against you.

MYRT.　　　As how, pray?

BEV. JUN.　　Why, can't you slip on a black wig and a gown, and be old Bramble yourself? MYRT. Ha! I don't dislike it. But what shall I do for a brother in the case?

BEV. JUN.　　What think you of my fellow Tom? The rogue's intelligent, and is a good mimic. All his part will be but to stutter heartily, for that's old Target's case. Nay, it would be an immoral thing to

104

mock him, were it not that his impertinence is the occasion of its breaking out to that degree. The conduct of the scene will chiefly lie upon you.

MYRT.   I like it of all things; if you'll send Tom to my chambers I will give him full instructions. This will certainly give me occasion to raise difficulties, to puzzle or confound her project for awhile at least.

BEV. JUN.   I'll warrant you success: so far we are right, then. And now, Charles, your apprehension of my marrying her is all you have to get over.

MYRT.   Dear Bevil! though I know you are my friend, yet when I abstract myself from my own interest in the thing, I know no objection she can make to you or you to her, and therefore hope—

BEV. JUN.   Dear Myrtle, I am as much obliged to you for the cause of your suspicion as I am offended at the effect: but be assured, I am taking measures for your certain security, and that all things with regard to me will end in your entire satisfaction.

MYRT.   Well, I'll promise you to be as easy and as confident as I can, though I cannot but remember that I have more than life at stake on your fidelity.   *(going)*

BEV. JUN.   Then depend upon it, you have no chance against you.

MYRT.   Nay, no ceremony; you know I must be going.

(Exit MYRTLE*)*

BEV. JUN.   Well! this is another instance of the perplexities which arise, too, in faithful friendship. We must often in this life go on in our good offices even under the displeasure of those to whom we do them, in compassion to their weaknesses and mistakes. But all this while poor Indiana is tortured with the doubt of me! She has no support or comfort but in my fidelity, yet sees me daily pressed to marriage with another! How painful, in such a crisis, must be every hour she thinks on me! I'll let her see at least my conduct to her is not changed. I'll take this opportunity to visit her; for though the religious vow I have made to my father restrains me from ever marrying without his approbation, yet that confines me not from seeing a virtuous woman that is the pure delight of my eyes and the guiltless joy of my heart. But the best condition of human life is but a gentler misery.

To hope for perfect happiness is vain,
And love has ever its allays of pain.   *(Exit)*

SCENE II

Enter ISABELLA *and* INDIANA *in her own lodgings*

ISAB.   Yes, I say 'tis artifice, dear child: I say to thee again and again, 'tis all skill and management.

IND.   Will you persuade me there can be an ill design in supporting me in the condition of a woman of quality? attended, dressed, and lodged like one—in my appearance abroad and my furniture at home, every way in the most sumptuous manner—and he that does it has an artifice, a design in it?

ISAB.   Yes, yes.

IND.   And all this without so much as explaining to me that all about me comes from him!

ISAB.   Ay, ay, the more for that. That keeps the title to all you have the more in him.

IND.   The more in him! He scorns the thought—

ISAB.   Then he—He—He—

IND.   Well, be not so eager. If he is an ill man, let us look into his stratagems. Here is another of them. *(showing a letter)* Here's two hundred and fifty pound in bank notes, with these words: "To pay for the set of dressing-plate which will be brought home, to-morrow." Why, dear Aunt, now here's another piece of skill for you, which I own I cannot comprehend, and it is with a bleeding heart I hear you say anything to the disadvantage of Mr. Bevil. When he is present I look upon him as one to whom I owe my life and the support of it—then again, as the man who loves me with sincerity and honour. When his eyes are cast another way and I dare survey him, my heart is painfully divided between shame and love. Oh! could I tell you—

ISAB.   Ah! you need not: I imagine all this for you.

IND.   This is my state of mind in his presence, and when he is absent, you are ever dinning my ears with notions of the arts of men; that his hidden bounty, his respectful conduct, his careful provision for me, after his preserving me from utmost misery, are certain signs he means nothing but to make I know not what of me.

ISAB.   Oh! You have a sweet opinion of him, truly.

IND.   I have, when I am with him, ten thousand things, besides my sex's natural decency and shame, to suppress my heart, that yearns to thank, to praise, to say it loves him. I say, thus it is with me while I see him; and in his absence I am entertained with nothing but your endeavours to tear this amiable image from my heart and in its stead to place a base dissembler, an artful invader of my happiness, my innocence, my honour.

ISAB.   Ah, poor soul! has not his plot taken? don't you die for him? has not the way he has taken been the most proper with you? Oh! ho! He has sense, and has judged the thing right.

IND.   Go on, then, since nothing can answer you; say what you will of him. Heigh! ho!

ISAB.   Heigh! ho! indeed. It is better to say so, as you are now, than as many others are. There are, among the destroyers of women, the gentle, the generous, the mild, the affable, the humble, who all, soon after their success in their designs, turn to the contrary of those characters. I will own to you, Mr. Bevil carries his hypocrisy the best of any man living, but still he is a man, and therefore a hypocrite. They have usurped an exemption from shame for any baseness, any cruelty towards us. They embrace without love; they make vows without conscience of obligation; they are partners, nay, seducers to the crime wherein they pretend to be less guilty.

IND.   *(aside)* That's truly observed.—But what's all this to Bevil?

ISAB.   This it is to Bevil and all mank

IND.   Trust not those who will think the worse of you for your confidence in them—serpents who lie in wait for doves. Won't you be on your guard against those who would betray you? Won't you doubt those who would contemn you for believing 'em? Take it from me: fair and natural dealing is to invite injuries; 'tis bleating to escape wolves who would devour you! Such is the *world—(aside)* and such (since the behaviour of one man to myself) have I believed all the rest of the sex.

IND.   I will not doubt the truth of Bevil; I will not doubt it. He has not spoke it by an organ that is given to lying; his eyes are all that have ever told me that he was mine. I know his virtue, I know his filial piety, and ought to trust his management with a father to whom he has uncommon obligations. What have I to be concerned for? my lesson is very short. If he takes me forever, my purpose of life is only to please him. If he leaves me (which heaven avert), I know he'll do it nobly, and I shall have nothing to do but to learn to die, after worse than death has happened to me.

ISAB.   Ay do, persist in your credulity! Flatter yourself that a man of his figure and fortune will make himself the jest of the town, and marry a handsome beggar for love.

IND.   The town! I must tell you, Madam, the fools that laugh at Mr. Bevil will but make themselves more ridiculous; his actions are the result of thinking, and he has sense enough to make even virtue fashionable.

ISAB.   O' my conscience, he has turned her head. Come, come; if he were the honest fool you take him for, why has he kept you here these three weeks without sending you to Bristol in search of your father, your family, and your relations?

IND.   I am convinced he still designs it, and that nothing keeps him here but the necessity of not coming to a breach with his father in regard to the match he has proposed him. Beside, has he not writ to Bristol? and has not he advice that my father has not been heard of there almost these twenty years?

ISAB.   All sham, mere evasion; he is afraid if he should carry you hither, your honest relations may take you out of his hands and so blow up all his wicked hopes at once.

IND.   Wicked hopes! did I ever give him any such?

TSAR Has he ever given you any honest ones? Can you say, in your conscience, he has ever once offered to marry you?

IND.   No! but by his behaviour I am convinced he will offer it the moment 'tis in his power, or consistent with his honour, to make such a promise good to me.

ISAB.   His honour!

IND.   I will rely upon it; therefore desire you will not make my life uneasy by these ungrateful jealousies of one to whom I am, and wish to be, obliged, for from his integrity alone I have resolved to hope for happiness.

ISAB.   Nay, I have done my duty; if you won't see, at your peril be it.

IND.   Let it be.—This is his hour of visiting me.

ISAB.   (apart) Oh! to be sure, keep up your form; don't see him in a bed-chamber. This is pure prudence, when she is liable, wherever he meets her, to be conveyed where'er he pleases.

IND.   All the rest of my life is but waiting till he comes: I live only when I'm with him. (Exit)

ISAB.   Well, go thy ways, thou wilful innocent! I once had almost as much love for a man who poorly left me to marry an estate—and I am now, against my will, what they call an old maid: but I will not let the peevishness of that condition grow upon me; only keep up the suspicion of it, to prevent this creature's being any other than a virgin, except upon proper terms. (Exit)

Re-enter INDIANA, *speaking to a Servant*

IND.   Desire Mr. Bevil to walk in.—Design! impossible! A base, designing mind could never think of what he hourly puts in practice. And yet, since the late rumour of his marriage, he seems more reserved than formerly; he sends in, too, before he sees me, to know if I am at leisure. Such new respect may cover coldness in the heart—it certainly makes me thoughtful. I'll know the worst at once; I'll lay such fair occasions in his way that it shall be impossible to avoid an explanation, for these doubts are insupportable.—But see! he comes and clears them all.

Enter BEVIL JUNIOR

BEV. JUN.   Madam, your most obedient! I am afraid I broke in upon your rest last night—'twas very late before we parted, but 'twas your own fault: I never saw you in such agree-able humour.

IND.   I am extremely glad we were both pleased, for I thought I never saw you better company.

BEV. JUN.   Me, Madam! you rally; I said very little.

IND.   But I am afraid you heard me say a great deal; and, when a woman is in the talking vein, the most agreeable thing a man can do, you know, is to have patience to hear her.

BEV. JUN.   Then it's pity, Madam, you should ever be silent, that we might be always agreeable to one another.

IND.   If I had your talent or power to make my actions speak for me, I might indeed be silent, and yet pretend to something more than the agreeable.

BEV. JUN.   If I might be vain of anything in my power, Madam, 'tis that my understanding from all your sex has marked you out as the most deserving object of my esteem.

IND.   Should I think I deserve this, 'twere enough to make my vanity forfeit the very esteem you offer me.

BEV. JUN.   How so, Madam?

IND.   Because esteem is the result of reason, and to deserve it from good sense, the height of human glory. Nay, I had rather a man of honour should pay me that, than all the hom-age of a sincere and humble love.

BEV. JUN.   You certainly distinguish right, Madam; love often kindles from external merit only—

IND.   But esteem arises from a higher source, the merit of the soul.

BEV. JUN.   True, and great souls only can deserve it.

(bowing respectfully)

IND.   Now I think they are greater still that can so charitably part with it.

BEV. JUN.   Now, Madam, you make me vain, since the utmost pride and pleasure of my life is that I esteem you—as I ought.

IND.   *(aside)* As he ought! Still more perplexing! He neither saves nor kills my hope.

BEV. JUN.   But, Madam, we grow grave, methinks. Let's find some other subject. Pray, how did you like the opera last night?

IND.   First give me leave to thank you for my tickets.

BEV. JUN.   Oh, your servant, Madam! But pray tell me; you, now, who are never partial to the fashion, I fancy, must be the properest judge of a mighty dispute among the ladies, that is, whether *Crispo* or *Griselda* is the more agreeable entertainment.

108

IND.   With submission; now, I cannot be a proper judge of this question.

BEV. JUN.   How so, Madam?

IND.   Because I find I have a partiality for one of them.

BEV. JUN.   Pray, which is that?

IND.   I do not know—there's something in that rural cottage of Griselda, her forlorn condition, her poverty, her solitude, her resignation, her innocent slumbers, and that lulling *Dolce sogno* that's sung over her; it had an effect upon me that—in short, I never was so well deceived at any of them.

BEV. JUN.   Oh! Now, then, I can account for the dispute: *Griselda,* it seems, is the distress of an injured, innocent woman; *Crispo,* that only of a man in the same condition; therefore the men are mostly concerned for Crispo, and, by a natural indulgence, both sexes for *Griselda.*

IND.   So that judgment, you think, ought to be for one, though fancy and complaisance have got ground for the other. Well! I believe you will never give me leave to dispute with you on any subject, for I own *Crispo* has its charms for me too, though in the main all the pleasure the best opera gives us is but mere sensation. Methinks it's pity the mind can't have a little more share in the entertainment. The music's certainly fine, but, in my thoughts, there's none of your composers come up to old Shakespeare and Otway.

BEV. JUN.   How, Madam! Why, if a woman of your sense were to say this in the drawing-room—

Enter a Servant

SERV.   Sir, here's Signor Carbonelli says he waits your commands in the next room.

BEV. JUN.   A propos! You were saying yesterday, Madam, you had a mind to hear him; will you give him leave to entertain you now?

IND.   By all means.—Desire the gentleman to walk in.

(Exit Servant)

BEV. JUN.   I fancy you will find something in this hand that is uncommon.

IND.   You are always finding ways, Mr. Bevil, to make life seem less tedious to me.

Enter Music Master

When the gentleman pleases.

(After a sonata is played, BEVIL waits on the Master to the door, etc.)

BEV. JUN.   You smile, Madam, to see me so complaisant to one whom I pay for his visit. Now I own I think it is not enough barely to pay those whose talents are superior to our own (I mean such talents as would become our condition, if we had them). Methinks we ought to do something more than barely gratify them for what they do at our command only because their fortune is below us.

IND.   You say I smile: I assure you it was a smile of approbation; for indeed, I cannot but think it the distinguishing part of a gentleman to make his superiority of fortune as easy to his inferiors as he can.—(aside)—Now once more to try him.—I was saying just now, I believed you would never let the dispute with you, and I daresay it will always be so. However, I must have your opinion upon a subject which created a debate between my aunt and me just before you came hither. She would needs have it that no man ever does any extraordinary kindness or service for a woman but for his own sake.

BEV. JUN.   Well, Madam! Indeed, I can't but be of her mind.

IND.   What, though he should maintain and support her, without demanding anything of her on her part?

BEV. JUN.   Why, Madam, is making an expense in the service of a valuable woman (for such I must suppose her), though she should never do him any favour—nay, though she should never know who did her such service—such a mighty heroic business?

IND.   Certainly! I should think he must be a man of an uncommon mould.

BEV. JUN.   Dear Madam, why so? 'tis but, at best, a better taste in expense. To bestow upon one whom he may think one of the ornaments of the whole creation; to be conscious that from his superfluity an innocent, a virtuous spirit is supported above the temptations and sorrows of life! That he sees satisfaction, health, and gladness in her countenance, while he enjoys the happiness of seeing her (as that I will suppose too, or he must be too abstracted, too insensible)—I say, if he is allowed to delight in that prospect, alas! what mighty matter is there in all this?

IND.   No mighty matter in so disinterested a friendship!

BEV. JUN.   Disinterested! I can't think him so. Your hero, Madam, is no more than what every gentleman ought to be and I believe very many are. He is only one who takes more delight in reflections than in sensations. He is more pleased with thinking than eating; that's the utmost you can say of him. Why, Madam, a greater expense than all this men lay out upon an unnecessary stable of horses.

IND.   Can you be sincere in what you say?

BEV. JUN.   You may depend upon it, if you know any such man, he does not love dogs inordinately.

IND.   No, that he does not.

BEV. JUN.   Nor cards, nor dice.

IND.   No.

BEV. JUN.   Nor bottle companions.

IND.   No.

BEV. JUN.   Nor loose women.

IND.   No, I'm sure he does not.

BEV. JUN.   Take my word, then, if your admired hero is not liable to any of these kind of demands, there's no such preeminence in this as you imagine. Nay, this way of expense you speak of is what exalts and raises him that has a taste for it; and, at the same time, his delight is incapable of satiety, disgust, or penitence.

IND.   But still I insist, his having no private interest in the action makes it prodigious, almost incredible.

BEV. JUN.   Dear Madam, I never knew you more mistaken. Why, who can be more a usurer than he who lays out his money in such valuable purchases? If pleasure be worth purchasing, how great a pleasure is it, to him who has a true taste of life, to ease an aching heart, to see the human countenance lighted up into smiles of joy, on the receipt of a bit of ore which is superfluous and otherwise useless in a man's own pocket? What could a man do better with his cash? This is the effect of a humane disposition where there is only a general tie of nature and common necessity. What then must it be when we serve an object of merit, of admiration!

IND. Well! the more you argue against it, the more I shall admire the generosity.

BEV. JUN. Nay, nay!—then, Madam, 'tis time to fly, after a declaration that my opinion strengthens my adversary's argument. I had best hasten to my appointment with Mr. Myrtle, and be gone while we are friends and—before things are brought to an extremity.

(Exit carelessly)

Enter ISABELLA

ISAB. Well, Madam, what think you of him now, pray?

IND. I protest, I begin to fear he is wholly disinterested in what he does for me. On my heart, he has no other view but the mere pleasure of doing it, and has neither good or bad designs upon me.

ISAB. Oh! dear Niece! Don't be in fear of both! I'll warrant you, you will know time enough that he is not indifferent.

IND. You please me when you tell me so, for if he has any wishes towards me I know he will not pursue them but with honour.

ISAB. I wish I were as confident of one as t'other. I saw the respectful downcast of his eye when you catched him gazing at you during the music. He, I warrant, was surprised, as if he had been taken stealing your watch. Oh, the undissembled, guilty look!

IND. But did you observe any such thing, really? I thought he looked most charmingly graceful! How engaging is modesty in a man when one knows there is a great mind within. So tender a confusion! and yet, in other respects, so much himself, so collected, so dauntless, so determined!

ISAB. Ah, Niece! there is a sort of bashfulness which is the best engine to carry on a shameless purpose: some men's modesty serves their wickedness, as hypocrisy gains the respect due to piety. But I will own to you, there is one hopeful symptom, if there could be such a thing as a distinterested lover. But it's all a perplexity, till—till—till—

IND. Till what?

ISAB. Till I know whether Mr. Myrtle and Mr. Bevil are really friends or foes. And that I will be convinced of before I sleep, for you shall not be deceived.

IND. I'm sure I never shall if your fears can guard me. In the meantime I'll wrap myself up in the integrity of my own heart, nor dare to doubt of his.

> As conscious honour all his actions steers,
> So conscious innocence dispels my fears.   *(Exeunt)*

ACT III

SCENE: SEALAND'S HOUSE

Enter TOM, *meeting* PHILLIS

TOM.   Well, Phillis!—what, with a face as if you had never seen me before!—(aside) What a work have I to do now? She has seen some new visitant at their house, whose airs she has catched, and is resolved to practise them upon me. Numberless are the changes she'll dance through before she'll answer this plain question, videlicet, "Have you delivered my master's letter to your lady?" Nay, I know her too well to ask an account of it in an ordinary way; I'll be in my airs as well as *she—(looking steadfastly at her)* Well, Madam, as unhappy as you are at present pleased to make me, I would not, in the general, be any other than what I am; I would not be a bit wiser, a bit richer, a bit taller, a bit shorter than I am at this instant.

PHIL.   Did ever anybody doubt, Master Thomas, but that you were extremely satisfied with your sweet self?

TOM.   I am, indeed. The thing I have least reason to be satisfied with is my fortune, and I am glad of my poverty. Perhaps if I were rich I should overlook the finest woman in the world, that wants nothing but riches to be thought so.

PHIL.   (aside) How prettily was that said! But I'll have a great deal more before I'll say one word.

TOM.   I should, perhaps, have been stupidly above her, had I not been her equal, and by not being her equal, never had opportunity of being her slave. I am my master's servant for hire; I am my mistress's from choice, would she but approve my passion.

PHIL.   I think it's the first time I ever heard you speak of it with any sense of the anguish, if you really do suffer any.

TOM.   Ah, Phillis! can you doubt, after what you have seen?

PHIL.   I know not what I have seen, nor what I have heard; but since I'm at leisure, you may tell me when you fell in love with me, how you fell in love with me, and what you have suffered or are ready to suffer for me.

TOM.   (aside) Oh, the unmerciful jade! when I'm in haste about my master's letter. But I must go through it.—Ah! too well I remember when, and how, and on what occasion I was first surprised. It was on the first of April, one thousand seven hundred and fifteen, I came into Mr. Sealand's service; I was then a hobbledehoy, and you a pretty little tight girl, a favourite handmaid of the housekeeper. At that time we neither of us knew what was in us. I remember I was ordered to get out the window, one pair of stairs, to rub the sashes clean; the person employed on the inner side was your charming self, whom I had never seen before.

PHIL.   I think I remember the silly accident. What made ye, you oaf, ready to fall down into the street?

TOM.   You know not, I warrant you. You could not guess what surprised me. You took no delight when you immediately grew wanton in your conquest, and put your lips close and breathed upon the glass, and when my lips approached, a dirty cloth you rubbed against my face, and hid your beauteous form; when I again drew near, you spit, and rubbed, and smiled at my undoing.

PHIL. What silly thoughts you men have!

TOM. We were Pyramus and Thisbe—but ten times harder was my fate. Pyramus could peep only through a wall; I saw her, saw my Thisbe in all her beauty, but as much kept from her as if a hundred walls between, for there was more, there was her will against me. Would she but yet relent! O Phillis! Phillis! shorten my torment and declare you pity me.

PHIL. I believe it's very sufferable; the pain is not so exquisite but that you may bear it a little longer.

TOM. Oh, my charming Phillis! if all depended on my fair one's will, I could with glory suffer. But, dearest creature, consider our miserable state.

PHIL. How! Miserable!

TOM. We are miserable to be in love and under the command of others than those we love—with that generous passion in the heart, to be sent to and fro on errands, called, checked, and rated for the meanest trifles. O Phillis! you don't know how many china cups and glasses my passion for you has made me break. You have broke my fortune as well as my heart.

PHIL. Well, Mr. Thomas, I cannot but own to you that I believe your master writes and you speak the best of any men in the world. Never was woman so well pleased with a letter as my young lady was with his, and this is an answer to it.

(Gives him a letter)

TOM. This was well done, my dearest. Consider, we must strike out some pretty livelihood for ourselves by closing their affairs. It will be nothing for them to give us a little being of our own, some small tenement, out of their large possessions: whatever they give us, 'twill be more than what they keep for themselves: one acre with Phillis would be worth a whole county without her.

PHIL. Oh, could I but believe you!

TOM. If not the utterance, believe the touch of my lips.

(Kisses her)

PHIL. There's no contradicting you; how closely you argue, Tom!

TOM. And will closer, in due time. But I must hasten with this letter, to hasten towards the possession of you. Then, Phillis, consider how I must be revenged, look to it, of all your skittishness, shy looks, and at best but coy compliances.

PHIL. O Tom! you grow wanton and sensual, as my lady calls it; I must not endure it. Oh! Foh! you are a man, an odious, filthy male creature; you should behave, if you had a right sense or were a man of sense, like Mr. Cimberton, with distance and indifference, or—let me see—some other becoming hard word, with seeming in-in-inadvertency, and not rush on one as if you were seizing a prey.—But hush! the ladies are coming.—Good Tom, don't kiss me above once, and be gone. Lard! we have been fooling and toying, and not considered the main business of our masters and mistresses.

TOM. Why, their business is to be fooling and toying as soon as the parchments are ready.

PHIL. Well remembered—parchments! My lady, to my knowledge, is preparing writings between her coxcomb cousin, Cimberton, and my mistress, though my master has an eye to the parchments already prepared between your master, Mr. Bevil, and my mistress; and, I believe, my mistress herself has signed and sealed, in her heart, to Mr. Myrtle.—Did I not bid you kiss me but once, and be gone? but I know you won't be satisfied.

TOM.   *(kissing her hand)* No, you smooth creature, how should I!

PHIL.   Well, since you are so humble, or so cool, as to ravish my hand only, I'll take my leave of you like a great lady, and you a man of quality.   *(They salute formally)*

TOM.   Pox of all this state!

(offers to kiss her more closely)

PHIL.   No, prithee, Tom, mind your business! We must follow that interest which will take, but endeavour at that which will be most for us and we like most. Oh, here's my young mistress! *(TOM taps her neck behind, and kisses his fingers.)* Go, ye liquorish fool!   *(Exit Tom)*

Enter LUCINDA

LUC.   Who was that you was hurrying away?

PHIL.   One that I had no mind to part with.

LUC.   Why did you turn him away then?

PHIL.   For your ladyship's service, to carry your ladyship's letter to his master. I could hardly get the rogue away.

LUC.   Why, has he so little love for his master?

PHIL.   No; but he has so much love for his mistress.

LUC.   But I thought I heard him kiss you. Why do you suffer that?

PHIL.   Why, Madam, we vulgar take it to be a sign of love. We servants, we poor people, that have nothing but our persons to bestow or treat for, are forced to deal and bargain by way of sample, and therefore, as we have no parchments or wax necessary in our agreements, we squeeze with our hands and seal with our lips to ratify vows and promises.

LUC.   But can't you trust one another without such earnest down?

PHIL.   We don't think it safe, any more than you gentry, to come together without deeds executed.

LUC.   Thou art a pert, merry hussy.

PHIL.   I wish, Madam, your lover and you were as happy as Tom and your servant are.

LUC.   You grow impertinent.

PHIL.   I have done, Madam; and I won't ask you what you intend to do with Mr. Myrtle, what your father will do with Mr. Bevil, nor what you all, especially my lady, mean by admitting Mr. Cimberton as particularly here as if he were married to you already; nay, you are married actually as far as people of quality are.

LUC.   How's that?

PHIL.   You have different beds in the same house.

LUC.   Pshaw! I have a very great value for Mr. Bevil, but have absolutely put an end to his pretensions in the letter I gave you for him. But my father, in his heart, still has a mind to him, were it not for this woman they talk of; and I am apt to imagine he is married to her, or never designs to marry at all.

PHIL.   Then Mr. Myrtle—

LUC.   He had my parents' leave to apply to me, and by that has won me and my affections: who is to have this body of mine without 'em, it seems, is nothing to me. My mother says it's indecent for me to let my thoughts stray about the person of my husband; nay, she says a maid, rigidly virtuous, though she may have been where her lover was a thousand times, should not have made observations enough to know him from another man when she sees him in a third place.

PHIL.   That is more than the severity of a nun, for not to see when one may is hardly possible; not to see when one can't is very easy. At this rate, Madam, there are a great many whom you have not seen who—

LUC.   Mamma says the first time you see your husband should be at that instant he is made so, when your father, with the help of the minister, gives you to him; then you are to see him, then you are to observe and take notice of him, because then you are to obey him.

PHIL.   But does not my lady remember you are to love as well as obey?

LUC.   To love is a passion, 'tis a desire, and we must have no desires. Oh! I cannot endure the reflection. With what insensibility on my part, with what more than patience, have I been exposed and offered to some awkward booby or other in every county of Great Britain!

PHIL.   Indeed, Madam, I wonder I never heard you speak of it before with this indignation.

LUC.   Every corner of the land has presented me with a wealthy coxcomb. As fast as one treaty has gone off, another has come on, till my name and person have been the tittle-tattle of the whole town. What is this world come to! No shame left! To be bartered for like the beasts of the fields, and that in such an instance as coming together to an entire familiarity and union of soul and body; oh! and this without being so much as well-wishers to each other, but for increase of fortune.

PHIL.   But Madam, all these vexations will end very soon in one for all. Mr. Cimberton is your mother's kinsman, and three hundred years an older gentleman than any lover you ever had; for which reason, with that of his prodigious large estate, she is resolved on him, and has sent to consult the lawyers accordingly—nay, has (whether you know it or no) been in treaty with Sir Geoffry, who, to join in the settlement, has accepted of a sum to do it, and is every moment expected in town for that purpose.

LUC.   How do you get all this intelligence?

PHIL.   By an art I have, I thank my stars, beyond all the waiting-maids in Great Britain; the art of listening, Madam, for your ladyship's service.

LUC.   I shall soon know as much as you do. Leave me, leave me, Phillis, begone! Here, here, I'll turn you out. My mother says I must not converse with my servants, though I must converse with no one else. *(Exit* PHILLIS*)* How unhappy are we who are born to great fortunes! No one looks at us with indifference, or acts towards us on the foot of plain dealing; yet by all I have been heretofore offered to or treated for I have been used with the most agreeable of all abuses, flattery. But now, by this phlegmatic fool I am used as nothing, or a mere thing. He, forsooth! is too wise, too learned, to have any regard to desires, and I know not what the learned oaf calls sentiments of love and passion.—Here he comes with my mother. It's much if he looks at me; or if he does, takes no more notice of me than of any other movable in the room.

Enter MRS. SEALAND *and* MR. CIMBERTON

MRS. SEAL. How do I admire this noble, this learned taste of yours, and the worthy regard you have to our own ancient and honourable house, in consulting a means to keep the blood as pure and as regularly descended as may be.

CIMB. Why, really Madam, the young women of this age are treated with discourses of such a tendency, and their imaginations so bewildered in flesh and blood, that a man of reason can't talk to be understood. They have no ideas of happiness but what are more gross than the gratification of hunger and thirst.

LUC. *(aside)* With how much reflection he is a coxcomb!

CIMB. And in truth, Madam, I have considered it as a most brutal custom that persons of the first character in the world should go as ordinarily and with as little shame to bed as to dinner with one another. They proceed to the propagation of the species as openly as to the preservation of the individual.

LUC. *(aside)* She that willingly goes to bed to thee must have no shame, I'm sure.

MRS. SEAL. O Cousin Cimberton! Cousin Cimberton! how abstracted, how refined is your sense of things! But indeed, it is too true there is nothing so ordinary as to say, in the best governed families, "My master and lady are gone to bed"; one does not know but it might have been said of one's self.

(hiding her face with her fan)

CIMB. Lycurgus, Madam, instituted otherwise; among the Lacedaemonians the whole female world was pregnant, but none but the mothers themselves knew by whom. Their meetings were secret, and the amorous congress always by stealth, and no such professed doings between the sexes as are tolerated among us under the audacious word "marriage."

MRS. SEAL. Oh! had I lived in those days and been a matron of Sparta, one might with less indecency have had ten children, according to that modest institution, than one under the confusion of our modern, barefaced manner.

LUC. *(aside)* And yet, poor woman, she has gone through the whole ceremony, and here I stand a melancholy proof of it.

MRS. SEAL. We will talk then of business. That girl walking about the room there is to be your wife. She has, I confess, no ideas, no sentiments, that speak her born of a thinking mother.

CIMB. I have observed her; her lively look, free air, and disengaged countenance speak her very—

LUC. Very what?

CIMB. If you please, Madam—to set her a little that way.

MRS. SEAL. Lucinda, say nothing to him; you are not a match for him. When you are married, you may speak to such a husband when you're spoken to. But I am disposing of you above yourself every way.

CIMB. Madam, you cannot but observe the inconveniences I expose myself to, in hopes that your ladyship will be the consort of my better part. As for the young woman, she is rather an impediment than a help to a man of letters and speculation. Madam, there is no reflection; no philosophy, can at all times subdue the sensitive life, but the animal shall sometimes carry away the man. Ha! ay, the vermilion of her lips—

LUC. Pray, don't talk of me thus.

CIMB. The pretty enough—Pant of her bosom—

116

LUC.   Sir!—Madam, don't you hear him?

CIMB.   Her forward chest—

LUC.   Intolerable!

CIMB.   High health—

LUC.   The grave, easy impudence of him!

CIMB.   Proud heart—

LUC.   Stupid coxcomb!

CIMB.   I say, Madam, her impatience while we are looking at her, throws out all attractions—her arms—her neck—what a spring in her step!

LUC.   Don't you run me over thus, you strange unaccountable!

CIMB.   What an elasticity in her veins and arteries!

LUC.   I have no veins, no arteries.

MRS. SEAL. O child, hear him; he talks finely; he's a scholar; he knows what you have.

CIMB.   The speaking invitation of her shape, the gathering of herself up, and the indignation you see in the pretty little thing. Now, I am considering her, on this occasion, but as one that is to be pregnant.

LUC.   *(aside)* The familiar, learned, unseasonable puppy!

CIMB.   And pregnant undoubtedly she will be yearly. I fear I shan't, for many years, have discretion enough to give her one fallow season.

LUC.   Monster! There's no bearing it. The hideous sot! there's no enduring it, to be thus surveyed like a steed at sale.

CIMB.   At sale! She's very illiterate—But she's very well limbed too; turn her in; I see what she is.

(Exit LUCINDA, in a rage)

MRS. SEAL. Go, you creature, I am ashamed of you.

CIMB.   No harm done.—you know, Madam, the better sort of people, as I observed to you, treat by their lawyers of weddings *(adjusting himself at the glass)* and the woman in the bargain, like the mansion-house in the sale of the estate, is thrown in, and what that is, whether good or bad, is not at all considered.

MRS. SEAL. I grant it, and therefore make no demand for her youth and beauty, and every other accomplishment, as the common world think 'em, because she is not polite.

CIMB.   Madam, I know your exalted understanding, abstracted as it is from vulgar prejudices, will not be offended when I declare to you, I marry to have an heir to my estate, and not to beget a colony or a plantation. This young woman's beauty and constitution will demand provision for a tenth child at least.

MRS. SEAL. *(aside)* With all that wit and learning, how considerate! What an economist!—Sir, I cannot make her any other than she is, or say she is much better than the other young women of this age, or fit for much besides being a mother; but I have given directions for the marriage settlements, and Sir Geoffry Cimberton's counsel is to meet ours here at this hour, concerning his joining in the deed which, when executed, makes you capable of settling what is due to Lucinda's fortune. Herself, as I told you, I say nothing of.

CIMB.   No, no, no, indeed, Madam, it is not usual; and I must depend upon my own reflection and philosophy not to overstock my family.

MRS. SEAL. I cannot help her, Cousin Cimberton, but she is, for aught I see, as well as the daughter of anybody else.

CIMB.   That is very true, Madam.

Enter a Servant, who whispers MRS. SEALAND

MRS. SEAL. The lawyers are come, and now we are to hear what they have resolved as to the point whether it's necessary that Sir Geoffry should join in the settlement, as being what they call in the remainder. But, good Cousin, you must have patience with 'em. These lawyers, I am told, are of a different kind; one is what they call a chamber counsel, the other a pleader. The conveyancer is slow, from an imperfection in his speech, and therefore shunned the bar, but extremely passionate and impatient of contradiction. The other is as warm as he, but has a tongue so voluble, and a head so conceited, he will suffer nobody to speak but himself.

CIMB.   You mean old Sergeant Target and Counsellor Bramble? I have heard of 'em.

MRS. SEAL. The same.—Show in the gentlemen.

(Exit Servant)

Re-enter Servant, introducing MYRTLE *and* TOM *disguised as* BRAMBLE *and* TARGET

MRS. SEAL. Gentlemen, this is the party concerned, Mr. Cimberton; and I hope you have considered of the matter.

TAR.   Yes, Madam, we have agreed that it must be by in-dent-dent-dent-dent—

BRAM.   Yes, Madam, Mr. Sergeant and myself have agreed, as he is pleased to inform you, that it must be an indenture tripartite, and tripartite let it be, for Sir Geoffry must needs be a party; old Cimberton, in the year 1619, says, in that ancient roll in Mr. Sergeant's hands, as, recourse thereto being had, will more at large appear—

TAR.   Yes, and by the deeds in your hands, it appears that—

BRAM.   Mr. Sergeant, I beg of you to make no inferences upon what is in our custody, but speak to the titles in your own deeds. I shall not show that deed till my client is in town.

CIMB.   You know best your own methods.

MRS. SEAL. The single question is whether the entail is such that my cousin, Sir Geoffry, is necessary in this affair.

BRAM.   Yes, as to the lordship of Tretriplet, but not as to the messuage of Grimgribber.

TAR.   I say that Gr-Gr- that Gr-Gr-Grimgribber, Grimgribber is in us; that is to say, the remainder thereof, as well as that of Tr-Tr-triplet.

BRAM.   You go upon the deed of Sir Ralph, made in the middle of the last century, precedent to that in which old Cimberton made over the remainder, and made it pass to the heirs general, by which your client comes in; and I question whether the remainder even of Tretriplet is in him. But we are willing to waive that, and give him a valuable consideration. But we shall not purchase what is in us forever, as Grimgribber is, at the rate as we guard against the contingent of Mr. Cimberton having no son. Then we know Sir Geoffry is the first of the collateral male line in this family. Yet—

TAR.   Sir, Gr-Gr-ber is—

BRAM.   I apprehend you very well, and your argument might be of force, and we would be inclined to hear that in all its parts. But, Sir, I see very plain what you are going into. I tell you, it is as probable a contingent that Sir Geoffry may die before Mr. Cimberton, as that he may outlive him.

TAR.   Sir, we are not ripe for that yet, but I must say—

BRAM.   Sir, I allow you the whole extent of that argument; but that will go no farther than as to the claimants under old Cimberton. I am of opinion that, according to the instruction of Sir Ralph, he could not dock the entail and then create a new estate for the heirs general.

TAR.   Sir, I have not patience to be told that, when Gr-Gr-ber—

BRAM.   I will allow it you, Mr. Sergeant; but there must be the word "heirs for ever," to make such an estate as you pretend.

CIMB.   I must be impartial, though you are counsel for my side of the question. Were it not that you are so good as to allow him what he has not said, I should think it very hard you should answer him without hearing him. But, gentlemen, I believe you have both considered this matter and are firm in your different opinions. 'Twere better, therefore, you proceeded according to the particular sense of each of you—and gave your thoughts distinctly in writing. And do you see, Sirs, pray let me have a copy of what you say, in English.

BRAM.   Why, what is all we have been saying? In English! Oh! but I forgot myself; you're a wit. But, however, to please you, Sir, you shall have it in as plain terms as the law will admit of.

CIMB.   But I would have it, Sir, without delay.

BRAM.   That, Sir, the law will not admit of: the courts are sitting at Westminster, and I am this moment obliged to be at every one of them, and 'twould be wrong if I should not be in the Hall to attend one of 'em at least; the rest would take it ill else. Therefore I must leave what I have said to Mr. Sergeant's consideration, and I will digest his arguments on my part, and you shall hear from me again, Sir.

(Exit BRAMBLE)

TAR.   Agreed, agreed.

CIMB.   Mr. Bramble is very quick. He parted a little abruptly.

TAR.   He could not bear my argument; I pinched him to the quick about that Gr-Gr-ber.

MRS. SEAL.   I saw that, for he durst not so much as hear you. I shall send to you, Mr. Sergeant, as soon as Sir Geoffry comes to town, and then I hope all may be adjusted. TAR. I shall be at my chambers at my usual hours.

(Exit)

CIMB.   Madam, if you please, I'll now attend you to the tea table, where I shall hear from your ladyship reason and good sense, after all this law and gibberish.

MRS. SEAL.   'Tis a wonderful thing, Sir, that men of professions do not study to talk the substance of what they have to say in the language of the rest of the world. Sure, they'd find their account in it.

CIMB.   They might, perhaps, Madam, with people of your good sense; but with the generality 'twould never do. The vulgar would have no respect for truth and knowledge if they were exposed to naked view.

Truth is too simple, of all art bereav'd:
Since the world will—why, let it be deceiv'd.   *(Exeunt)*

ACT IV
SCENE I

SCENE: BEVIL JUNIOR'S *lodgings*

BEVIL JUNIOR, *with a letter in his hand, followed by* TOM

TOM.   Upon my life, Sir, I know nothing of the matter. I never opened my lips to Mr. Myrtle about anything of your honour's letter to Madam Lucinda.

BEV. JUN.   What's the fool in such a fright for? I don't suppose you did. What I would know is, whether Mr. Myrtle showed any suspicion, or asked you any questions, to lead you to say casually that you had carried any such letter for me this morning.

TOM.   Why, Sir, if he did ask me any questions, how could I help it?

BEV. JUN.   I don't say you could, oaf! I am not questioning you, but him. What did he say to you?

TOM.   Why, Sir, when I came to his chambers, to be dressed for the lawyer's part your honour was pleased to put me upon, he asked me if I had been at Mr. Sealand's this morning. So I told him, Sir, I often went thither—because, Sir, if I had not said that, he might have thought there was something more in my going now than at another time.

BEV. JUN.   Very well!— *(aside)* The fellow's caution, I find, has given him this jealousy.—Did he ask you no other questions?

TOM.   Yes, Sir; now I remember as we came away in the hackney coach from Mr. Sealand's, "Tom," says he, "as I came in to your master this morning, he bade you go for an answer to a letter he had sent. Pray, did you bring him any?" says he. "Ah!" says I, "Sir, your honour is pleased to joke with me; you have a mind to know whether I can keep a secret or no?"

BEV. JUN.   And so, by showing him you could, you told him you had one?

TOM.   *(confused)* Sir—

BEV. JUN.   What mean actions does jealousy make a man stoop to! How poorly has he used art with a servant to make him betray his own master!—Well, and when did he give you this letter for me?

TOM.   Sir, he writ it before he pulled off his lawyer's gown, at his own chambers.

BEV. JUN.   Very well; and what did he say when you brought him my answer to it?

TOM.   He looked a little out of humour, Sir, and said it was very well.

BEV. JUN.   I knew he would be grave upon't. Wait without.

TOM.   Humh! 'gad, I don't like this; I am afraid we are all in the wrong box here. *(Exit* TOM)

BEV. JUN.   I put on a serenity while my fellow was present; but I have never been more thoroughly disturbed. This hot man! to write me a challenge, on supposed artificial dealing, when I professed myself his friend! I can live contented without glory, but I cannot suffer shame: What's to be done? But first let me consider Lucinda's letter again. *(reads)*

"SIR,

"I hope it is consistent with the laws a woman ought to impose upon herself, to acknowledge that your manner of declining a treaty of marriage in our family, and desiring the refusal may come from me, has something more engaging in it than the courtship of him who, I fear, will fall to my lot, except your friend exerts himself for our common safety and happiness. I have reasons for desiring Mr. Myrtle may not know of this letter till hereafter, and am your most obliged humble servant,

"Lucinda Sealand."

Well, but the postscript— *(reads)*

"I won't, upon second thoughts, hide anything from you. But my reason for concealing this is that Mr. Myrtle has a jealousy in his temper which gives me some terrors; but my esteem for him inclines me to hope that only an ill effect which sometimes accompanies a tender love, and what may be cured by a careful and unblameable conduct."

Thus has this lady made me her friend and confidant, and put herself, in a kind, under my protection. I cannot tell him immediately the purport of her letter, except I could cure him of the violent and untractable passion of jealousy, and so serve him and her, by disobeying her in the article of secrecy, more than I should by complying with her directions. But then this duelling, which custom has imposed upon every man who would live with reputation and honour in the world—how must I preserve myself from imputations there? He'll, forsooth, call it or think it fear, if I explain without fighting. But his letter—I'll read it again—

"SIR,

"You have used me basely in corresponding and carrying on a treaty where you told me you were indifferent. I have changed my sword since I saw you, which advertisement I thought proper to send you against the next meeting between you and the injured

"Charles Myrtle."

Enter TOM

TOM.   Mr. Myrtle, Sir. Would your honour please to see him?
BEV. JUN.   Why, you stupid creature! Let Mr. Myrtle wait at my lodgings? Show him up.

(Exit TOM)

Well! I am resolved upon my carriage to him. He is in love, and in every circumstance of life a little distrustful, which I must allow for—but here he is.

Enter TOM, *introducing* MYRTLE

Sir, I am extremely obliged to you for this honour.—But, Sir, you, with your very discerning face, leave the room.

(Exit TOM)

Well, Mr. Myrtle, your commands with me?

MYRT.   The time, the place, our long acquaintance, and many other circumstances which affect me on this occasion, oblige me, without farther ceremony or conference, to desire you would not only, as you already have, acknowledge the receipt of my letter, but also comply with the request in it. I must have farther notice taken of my message than these half lines—"I have yours—I shall be at home."

BEV. JUN.   Sir, I own I have received a letter from you in a very unusual style; but as I design everything in this matter shall be your own action, your own seeking, I shall understand nothing but what you are pleased to confirm face to face, and I have already forgot the contents of your epistle.

MYRT.   This cool manner is very agreeable to the abuse you have already made of my simplicity and frankness, and I see your moderation tends to your own advantage and not mine; to your own safety, not consideration of your friend.

BEV. JUN.   My own safety, Mr. Myrtle?

MYRT.   Your own safety, Mr. Bevil.

BEV. JUN.   Look you, Mr. Myrtle, there's no disguising that I understand what you would be at; but, Sir, you know I have often dared to disapprove of the decisions a tryant custom has introduced, to the breach of all laws, both divine and human.

MYRT.   Mr. Bevil, Mr. Bevil, it would be a good first principle in those who have so tender a conscience that way, to have as much abhorrence of doing injuries as—

BEV. JUN.   As what?

MYRT.   As fear of answering for 'em.

BEV. JUN.   As fear of answering for 'em! But that apprehension is just or blameable according to the object of that fear. I have often told you, in confidence of heart, I abhorred the daring to offend the Author of life, and rushing into His presence—I say, by the very same act, to commit the crime against Him, and immediately to urge on to His tribunal.

MYRT.   Mr. Bevil, I must tell you, this coolness, this gravity, this show of conscience, shall never cheat me of my mistress. You have, indeed, the best excuse for life—the hopes of possessing Lucinda. But consider, Sir, I have as much reason to be weary of it, if I am to lose her; and my first attempt to recover her shall be to let her see the dauntless man who is to be her guardian and protector.

BEV. JUN.   Sir, show me but the least glimpse of argument that I am authorized by my own hand to vindicate any lawless insult of this nature, and I will show thee, to chastise thee hardly deserves the name of courage—slight, inconsiderate man! There is, Mr. Myrtle, no such terror in quick anger; and you shall, you know not why, be cool, as you have, you know not why, been warm.

MYRT.   Is the woman one loves so little an occasion of anger? You, perhaps, who know not what it is to love, who have your ready, your commodious, your foreign trinket for your loose hours, and from your fortune, your specious outward carriage, and other lucky circumstances, as easy a way to the possession of a woman of honour—you know nothing of what it is to be alarmed, to be distracted with anxiety and terror of losing more than life. Your marriage, happy man! goes on like common business, and in the interim you have your rambling captive, your Indian princess, for your soft moments of dalliance—your convenient, your ready Indiana.

BEV. JUN.   You have touched me beyond the patience of a man, and I'm excusable, in the guard of innocence (or from the infirmity of human nature, which can bear no more), to accept your invitation and observe your letter. Sir, I'll attend you.

Enter TOM

TOM.   Did you call, Sir? I thought you did: I heard you speak aloud.

BEV. JUN.   Yes; go call a coach.

TOM.   Sir—master—Mr. Myrtle—friends-gentleman—what d'ye mean? I am but a servant, or—

BEV. JUN.   Call a coach! *(Exit* TOM)

(a long pause, walking sullenly by each other)

(aside) Shall I (though provoked to the uttermost) recover myself at the entrance of a third person, and that my servant, too, and not have respect enough to all I have ever been receiving from infancy, the obligation to the best of fathers, to an unhappy virgin too, whose life depends on mine? *(shutting the door—to* MYRTLE) I have, thank heaven, had time to recollect myself, and shall not, for fear of what such a rash man as you think of me, keep longer unexplained the false appearances under which your infirmity of temper makes you suffer, when perhaps too much regard to a false point of honour makes me prolong that suffering.

MYRT.   I am sure Mr. Bevil cannot doubt but I had rather have satisfaction from his innocence than his sword.

BEV. JUN.   Why, then, would you ask it first that way?

MYRT.   Consider, you kept your temper yourself no longer than till I spoke to the disadvantage of her you loved.

BEV. JUN.   True; but let me tell you, I have saved you from the most exquisite distress, even though you had succeeded in the dispute. I know you so well that I am sure to have found this letter about a man you had killed would have been worse than death to yourself. Read it.—*(aside)* When he is thoroughly mortified and shame has got the better of jealousy, when he has seen himself throughly, he will deserve to be assisted towards obtaining Lucinda.

MYRT.   *(aside)* With what a superiority has he turned the injury on me, as the aggressor! I begin to fear I have been too far transported. "A treaty in our family" is not that saying much? I shall relapse. But I find (on the postscript) "something like jealousy." With what face can I see my benefactor, my advocate, whom I have treated like a betrayer?—Oh! Bevil, with what words shall I—

BEV. JUN.   There needs none; to convince is much more than to conquer.

MYRT.   But can you—

BEV. JUN.   You have o'erpaid the inquietude you gave me, in the change I see in you towards me. Alas! what machines are we! Thy face is altered to that of another man—to that of my companion, my friend.

123

MYRT.   That I could be such a precipitant wretch!

BEV. JUN.   Pray, no more!

MYRT.   Let me reflect how many friends have died by the hands of friends, for want of temper; and you must give me leave to say again and again how much I am beholden to that superior spirit you have subdued me with. What had become of one of us, or perhaps both, had you been as weak as I was, and as incapable of reason?

BEV. JUN.   I congratulate to us both the escape from ourselves, and hope the memory of it will make us dearer friends than ever.

MYRT.   Dear Bevil, your friendly conduct has convinced me that there is nothing manly but what is conducted by reason and agreeable to the practice of virtue and justice. And yet how many have been sacrificed to that idol, the unreasonable opinion of men! Nay, they are so ridiculous, in it, that they often use their swords against each other with dissembled anger and real fear.

> Betray'd by honour and compell'd by shame,
> They hazard being to preserve a name:
> Nor dare enquire into the dread mistake,
> Till plung'd in sad eternity they wake.

(Exeunt)

SCENE II

SCENE: *St. James's Park*

Enter SIR JOHN BEVIL *and* MR. SEALAND

SIR J. BEV.   Give me leave, however, Mr. Sealand, as we are upon a treaty for uniting our families, to mention only the business of an ancient house. Genealogy and descent are to be of some consideration in an affair of this sort.

MR. SEAL.   Genealogy and descent! Sir, there has been in our family a very large one. There was Galfrid the father of Edward, the father of Ptolemy, the father of Crassus, the father of Earl Richard, the father of Henry the Marquis, the father of Duke John—

SIR J. BEV.   What, do you rave, Mr. Sealand?—all these great names in your family?

MR. SEAL.   These? Yes, Sir. I have heard my father name 'em all, and more.

SIR J. BEV.   Ay, Sir? and did he say they were all in your family?

MR. SEAL.   Yes, Sir, he kept 'em all. He was the greatest cocker in England. He said Duke John won him many battles, and never lost one.

SIR J. BEV.   Oh, Sir, your servant! you are laughing at my laying any stress upon descent; but I must tell you, Sir, I never knew anyone but he that wanted that advantage turn it into ridicule.

MR. SEAL.   And I never knew anyone who had many better advantages put that into his account. But, Sir John, value yourself as you please upon your ancient house, I am to talk freely of everything you are pleased to put into your bill of rates on this occasion. Yet, Sir, I have made no objections to your son's family. 'Tis his morals that I doubt.

SIR J. BEV.   Sir, I can't help saying that what might injure a citizen's credit may be no stain to a gentleman's honour.

MR. SEAL.   Sir John, the honour of a gentleman is liable to be tainted by as small a matter as the credit of a trader. We are talking of a marriage, and in such a case the father of a young woman will not think it an addition to the honour or credit of her lover that he is a keeper—

SIR J. BEV.   Mr. Sealand, don't take upon you to spoil my son's marriage with any woman else.

MR. SEAL.   Sir John, let him apply to any woman else, and have as many mistresses as he pleases.

SIR J. BEV.   My son, Sir, is a discreet and sober gentleman.

MR. SEAL.   Sir, I never saw a man that wenched soberly and discreetly that ever left it off; the decency observed in the practice hides, even from the sinner, the iniquity of it. They pursue it, not that their appetites hurry 'em away, but, I warrant you, because 'tis their opinion they may do it.

SIR J. BEV.   Were what you suspect a truth—do you design to keep your daughter a virgin till you find man unblemished that way?

MR. SEAL.   Sir, as much a cit as you take me for, I know the town and the world—and give me leave to say that we merchants are a species of gentry that have grown into the world this last century, and are as honourable, and almost as useful, as you landed folks that have always thought yourselves so much above us; for your trading, forsooth! is extended no farther than a load of hay or a fat ox. You are pleasant people, indeed, because you are generally bred up to be lazy; therefore, I warrant you, industry is dishonourable.

SIR J. BEV.   Be not offended, Sir; let us go back to our point.

MR. SEAL.   Oh, not at all offended! but I don't love to leave any part of the account unclosed; look you, Sir John, comparisons are odious, and more particularly so on occasions of this kind, when we are projecting races that are to be made out of both sides of the comparisons.

SIR J. BEV.   But my son, Sir, is, in the eye of the world, a gentleman of merit.

MR. SEAL.   I own to you, I think him so. But, Sir John, I am a man exercised and experienced in chances and disasters. I lost, in my earlier years, a very fine wife, and with her a poor little infant; this makes me, perhaps, overcautious to preserve the second bounty of Providence to me, and be as careful as I can of this child. You'll pardon me; my poor girl, Sir, is as valuable to me as your boasted son to you.

SIR J. BEV.   Why, that's one very good reason, Mr. Sealand, why I wish my son had her.

MR. SEAL.   There is nothing but this strange lady here, this *incognita*, that can be objected to him. Here and there a man falls in love with an artful creature, and gives up all the motives of life to that one passion.

SIR J. BEV.   A man of my son's understanding cannot be supposed to be one of them.

MR. SEAL.   Very wise men have been so enslaved, and when a man marries with one of them upon his hands, whether moved from the demand of the world or slighter reasons, such a husband soils with his wife for a month perhaps—then "Good b'w'ye, Madam!"—the show's over. Ah! John Dryden points out such a husband to a hair, where he says,

And while abroad so prodigal the dolt is,
Poor spouse at home as ragged as a colt is.

Now in plain terms, Sir, I shall not care to have my poor girl turned a-grazing, and that must be the case when-

SIR J. BEV.   But pray consider, Sir, my son—

MR. SEAL.   Look you, Sir, I'll make the matter short. This unknown lady, as I told you, is all the objection I have to him; but, one way or other, he is, or has been, certainly engaged to her. I am therefore resolved this very afternoon to visit her. Now, from her behaviour or appearance I shall soon be let into what I may fear or hope for.

SIR J. BEV.   Sir, I am very confident there can be nothing enquired into, relating to My son, that will not, upon being understood, turn to his advantage.

MR. SEAL.   I hope that as sincerely as you believe it. Sir John Bevil, when I am satisfied in this great point, if your son's conduct answers the character you give him, I shall wish your alliance more than that of any gentleman in Great Britain—and so, your servant!   *(Exit)*

SIR J. BEV.   He is gone in a way but barely civil; but his great wealth, and the merit of his only child, the heiress of it, are not to be lost for a little peevishness.

Enter HUMPHREY

Oh, Humphrey! you are come in a seasonable minute. I want to talk to thee, and to tell thee that my head and heart are on the rack about my son.

HUMPH.   Sir, you may trust his discretion; I am sure you may.

SIR J. BEV.   Why, I do believe I may, and yet I'm in a thousand fears when I lay this vast wealth before me. When I consider his prepossessions, either generous to a folly in an honourable love, or abandoned past redemption in a vicious one; and, from the one or the other, his insensibility to the fairest prospect towards doubling our estate: a father who knows how useful wealth is, and how necessary, even to those who despise it—I say a father, Humphrey, a father cannot bear it.

HUMPH.   Be not transported, Sir; you will grow incapable of taking any resolution in your perplexity.

SIR J. BEV.   Yet, as angry as I am with him, I would not have him surprised in anything. This mercantile rough man may go grossly into the examination of this matter, and talk to the gentlewoman so as to—

HUMPH.   No, I hope, not in an abrupt manner.

SIR J. BEV.   No, I hope not! Why, dost thou know anything of her, or of him, or of anything of it, or all of it?

HUMPH.   My dear master, I know so much that I told him this very day you had reason to be secretly out of humour about her.

SIR J. BEV.   Did you go so far? Well, what said he to that?

HUMPH.   His words were, looking upon me steadfastly: "Humphrey," says he, "that woman is a woman of honour."

SIR J. BEV.   How! Do you think he is married to her, or designs to marry her?

HUMPH.   I can say nothing to the latter, but he says he can marry no one without your consent while you are living.

SIR J. BEV.   If he said so much, I know he scorns to break his word with me.

HUMPH.   I am sure of that.

SIR J. BEV.   You are sure of that. Well! that's some comfort. Then I have nothing to do but to see the bottom of this matter during this present ruffle.—O Humphrey—

HUMPH.   You are not ill, I hope, Sir.

SIR J. BEV.   Yes, a man is very ill that's in a very ill humour. To be a father is to be in care for one whom you oftener disoblige than please by that very care. Oh, that sons could know the duty to a father before they themselves are fathers! But perhaps you'll say now that I am one of the happiest fathers in the world; but I assure you, that of the very happiest is not a condition to be envied.

HUMPH.   Sir, your pain arises, not from the thing itself, but your particular sense of it. You are overfond—nay, give me leave to say you are unjustly apprehensive from your fondness. My master Bevil never disobliged you, and he will—I know he will—do everything you ought to expect.

SIR J. BEV.   He won't take all this money with this girl. For aught I know, he will, forsooth, have so much moderation as to think he ought not to force his liking for any consideration.

HUMPH.   He is to marry her, not you; he is to live with her, not you, Sir.

SIR J. BEV.   I know not what to think. But I know nothing can be more miserable than to be in this doubt. Follow me; I must come to some resolution.   *(Exeunt)*

SCENE III

SCENE: BEVIL JUNIOR'S *lodgings*

Enter TOM *and* PHILLIS

TOM.   Well, Madam, if you must speak with Mr. Myrtle, you shall; he is now with my master in the library.

PHIL.   But you must leave me alone with him, for he can't make me a present, nor I so handsomely take anything from him, before you: it would not be decent.

TOM.   It will be very decent, indeed, for me to retire and leave my mistress with another man.

PHIL.   He is a gentleman and will treat one properly.

TOM.   I believe so; but, however, I won't be far off, and therefore will venture to trust you. I'll call him to you.

(Exit TOM)

PHIL.   What a deal of pother and sputter here is between my mistress and Mr. Myrtle from mere punctilio! I could, any hour of the day, get her to her lover, and would do it—but she, forsooth, will allow no plot to get him; but, if he can come to her, I know she would be glad of it. I must, therefore, do her an acceptable violence and surprise her into his arms. I am sure I go by the best rule imaginable. If she were my maid, I should think her the best servant in the world for doing so by me.

Enter MYRTLE *and* TOM

Oh, Sir! You and Mr. Bevil are fine gentlemen to let a lady remain under such difficulties as my poor mistress, and no attempt to set her at liberty or release her from the danger of being instantly married to Cimberton.

MYRT.   Tom has been telling—but what is to be done?

PHIL.   What is to be done—when a man can't come at his mistress! Why, can't you fire our house, or the next house to us, to make us run out, and you take us?

MYRT.   How, Mrs. Phillis!

PHIL.   Ay; let me see that rogue deny to fire a house, make a riot, or any other little thing, when there were no other way to come at me.

TOM.   I am obliged to you, Madam.

PHIL.   Why, don't we hear every day of people's hanging themselves for love, and won't they venture the hazard of being hanged for love? Oh! were I a man—

MYRT.   What manly thing would you have me undertake, according to your ladyship's notion of a man?

PHIL.   Only be at once what, one time or other, you may be, and wish to be, or must be.

MYRT.   Dear girl, talk plainly to me, and consider I, in my condition, can't be in very good humour. You say, to be at once what I must be.

PHIL.   Ay, ay—I mean no more than to be an old man; I saw you do it very well at the masquerade. In a word, old Sir Geoffry Cimberton is every hour expected in town to join in the deeds and settlements for marrying Mr. Cimberton. He is half blind, half lame, half deaf, half dumb; though as to his passions and desires he is as warm and ridiculous as when in the heat of youth.

TOM.   Come to the business, and don't keep the gentleman in suspense for the pleasure of being courted, as you serve me.

PHIL.   I saw you at the masquerade act such a one to perfection. Go and put on that very habit, and come to our house as Sir Geoffry. There is not one there but myself knows his person; I was born in the parish where he is lord of the manor. I have seen him often and often at church in the country. Do not hesitate, but come thither; they will think you bring a certain security against Mr. Myrtle, and you bring Mr. Myrtle! Leave the rest to me. I leave this with you, and expect—They don't, I told you, know you; they think you out of town, which you had as good be for ever if you lose this opportunity. I must be gone; I know I am wanted at home.

MYRT.   My dear Phillis!

(catches and kisses her, and gives her money)

PHIL.   O fie! my kisses are not my own; you have committed violence; but I'll carry 'em to the right owner. (TOM *kisses her—To* TOM) Come, see me downstairs, and leave the lover to think of his last game for the prize.

(Exeunt TOM *and* PHILLIS)

MYRT.   I think I will instantly attempt this wild expedient. The extravagance of it will make me less suspected, and it will give me opportunity to assert my own right to Lucinda, without whom I cannot live. But I am so mortified at this conduct of mine towards poor Bevil. He must think meanly of me.

128

I know not how to reassume myself and be in spirit enough for such an adventure as this. Yet I must attempt it, if it be only to be near Lucinda under her present perplexities; and sure—

The next delight to transport with the fair,

Is to relieve her in her hours of care.   (*Exit*)

ACT V

SCENE I

SCENE: SEALAND'S *house*

Enter PHILLIS, *with lights, before* MYRTLE, *disguised like old* SIR GEOFFRY, *supported by* MRS. SEALAND, LUCINDA, *and* CIMBERTON

MRS. SEAL. Now I have seen you thus far, Sir Geoffry, will you excuse me a moment while I give my necessary orders for your accommodation?   (*Exit* MRS. SEALAND)

MYRT. I have not seen you, Cousin Cimberton, since you were ten years old; and as it is incumbent on you to keep up our name and family, I shall, upon very reasonable terms, join with you in a settlement to that purpose. Though I must tell you, Cousin, this is the first merchant that has married into our house.

LUC. (*aside*) Deuce on 'em! am I a merchant because my father is?

MYRT. But is he directly a trader at this time?

CIMB. There's no hiding the disgrace, Sir; he trades to all parts of the world.

MYRT. We never had one of our family before who descended from persons that did anything.

CIMB. Sir, since it is a girl that they have, I am, for the honour of my family, willing to take it in again, and to sink her into our name, and no harm done.

MYRT. 'Tis prudently and generously resolved. Is this the young thing?

CIMB. Yes, Sir.

PHIL. (*to* LUCINDA) Good Madam, don't be out of humour, but let them run to the utmost of their extravagance. Hear them out.

MYRT. Can't I see her nearer? My eyes are but weak.

PHIL. (*to* LUCINDA) Beside, I am sure the uncle has something worth your notice. I'll take care to get off the young one, and leave you to observe what may be wrought out of the old one for your good.   (*Exit*)

CIMB. Madam, this old gentleman, your great-uncle, desires to be introduced to you and to see you nearer—Approach, Sir.

MYRT. By your leave, young lady. (*puts on spectacles*)—Cousin Cimberton! She has exactly that sort of neck and bosom for which my sister Gertrude was so much admired in the year sixty-one, before the French dresses first discovered anything in women below the chin.

LUC. (*aside*) What a very odd situation am I in!—though I cannot but be diverted at the

129

extravagance of their humours, equally unsuitable to their age.—Chin, quotha! I don't believe my passionate lover there knows whether I have one or not. Ha! Ha!

MYRT.   Madam, I would not willingly offend, but I have a better *glass—(pulls out a large one)*

Enter PHILLIS to CIMBERTON

PHIL.   Sir, my lady desires to show the apartment to you that she intends for Sir Geoffry.

CIMB.   Well, Sir, by that time you have sufficiently gazed and sunned yourself in the beauties of my spouse there, I will wait on you again.   *(Exeunt CIMBERTON and PHYLLIS)*

MYRT.   Were it not, Madam, that I might be troublesome, there is something of importance, though we are alone, which I would say more safe from being heard.

LUC.   There is something in this old fellow, methinks, that raises my curiosity.

MYRT.   To be free, Madam, I as heartily contemn this kinsman of mine as you do, and am sorry to see so much beauty and merit devoted by your parents to so insensible a possessor.

LUC.   Surprising!—I hope, then, Sir, you will not contribute to the wrong you are so generous as to pity, whatever may be the interest of your family.

MYRT.   This hand of mine shall never be employed to sign anything against your good and happiness.

LUC.   I am sorry, Sir, it is not in my power to make you proper acknowledgments, but there is a gentleman in the world whose gratitude will, I am sure, be worthy of the favour.

MYRT.   All the thanks I desire, Madam, are in your power to give.

LUC.   Name them, and command them.

MYRT.   Only, Madam, that the first time you are alone with your lover you will with open arms receive him.

LUC.   As willingly as his heart could wish it.

MYRT.   Thus, then, he claims your promise.—O Lucinda!

LUC.   Oh! a cheat! a cheat! a cheat!

MYRT.   Hush! 'tis I, 'tis I, your lover, Myrtle himself, Madam.

LUC.   Oh, bless me! what a rashness and folly to surprise me so—But hush—my mother.

Enter MRS. SEALAND, CIMBERTON, and PHILLIS

MRS. SEAL.   How now! What's the matter?

LUC.   O Madam! as soon as you left the room my uncle fell into a sudden fit, and—and—so I cried out for help to support him and conduct him to his chamber.

MRS. SEAL.   That was kindly done. Alas, Sir! how do you find yourself?

MYRT.   Never was taken in so odd a way in my life—pray, lead me! Oh! I was talking here—pray carry me—to my Cousin Cimberton's young lady—

MRS. SEAL.   *(aside)* My Cousin Cimberton's young lady! How zealous he is, even in his extremity, for the match! a right Cimberton.

(CIMBERTON and LUCINDA lead him as one in pain, etc.)

CIMB.   Pox! Uncle, you will pull my ear off.

LUC.   Pray, Uncle! you will squeeze me to death.

MRS. SEAL. No matter, no matter—he knows not what he does. Come, Sir, shall I help you out?

MYRT.   By no means! I'll trouble nobody but my young cousins here.   *(They lead him oft)*

PHIL.   But pray, Madam, does your ladyship intend that Mr. Cimberton shall really marry my young mistress at last? I don't think he likes her.

MRS. SEAL. That's not material! Men of his speculation are above desires. But be it as it may, now I have given old Sir Geoffry the trouble of coming up to sign and seal, with what countenance can I be off?

PHIL.   As well as with twenty others, Madam. It is the glory and honour of a great fortune to live in continual treaties, and still to break off: it looks great, Madam.

MRS. SEAL. True, Phillis—yet to return our blood again into the Cimbertons' is an honour not to be rejected. But were not you saying that Sir John Bevil's creature, Humphrey, has been with Mr. Sealand?

PHIL.   Yes, Madam; I overheard them agree that Mr. Sealand should go himself and visit this unknown lady that Mr. Bevil is so great with; and if he found nothing there to fright him, that Mr. Bevil should still marry my young mistress.

MRS. SEAL. How! nay, then, he shall find she is my daughter as well as his. I'll follow him this instant and take the whole family along with me. The disputed power of disposing of my own daughter shall be at an end this very night. I'll live no longer in anxiety for a little hussy that hurts my appearance wherever I carry her, and for whose sake I seem to be not at all regarded, and that in the best of my days.

PHIL.   Indeed, Madam, if she were married, your ladyship might very well be taken for Mr. Sealand's daughter.

MRS. SEAL. Nay, when the chit has not been with me, I have heard the men say as much. I'll no longer cut off the greatest pleasure of a woman's life—the shining in assemblies—by her forward anticipation of the respect that's due to her superior. She shall down to Cimberton Hall—she shall—she shall!

PHIL.   I hope, Madam, I shall stay with your ladyship.

MRS. SEAL. Thou shalt, Phillis, and I'll place thee then more about me. But order chairs immediately—
            I'll be gone this minute.   *(Exeunt)*

SCENE II

SCENE: *Charing Cross*

Enter MR. SEALAND *and* HUMPHREY

MR. SEAL.   I am very glad, Mr. Humphrey, that you agree with me that it is for our common good I should look thoroughly into this matter.

HUMPH.   I am, indeed, of that opinion; for there is no artifice, nothing concealed, in our family, which ought injustice to be known. I need not desire you, Sir, to treat the lady with care and respect.

MR. SEAL.   Master Humphrey, I shall not be rude, though I design to be a little abrupt and come into the matter at once, to see how she will bear upon a surprise.

HUMPH.   That's the door, Sir; I wish you success.—(While *HUMPHREY speaks* SEALAND *consults his table book.)* I am less concerned what happens there because I hear Mr. Myrtle is well lodged as old Sir Geoffry; so I am willing to let this gentleman employ himself here, to give them time at home: for I am sure 'tis necessary for the quiet of our family Lucinda were disposed of out of it, since Mr. Bevil's inclination is so much otherwise engaged.   *(Exit)*

MR. SEAL.   I think this is the door. *(knocks)* I'll carry this matter with an air of authority, to enquire, though I make an errand to begin discourse. *(knocks again, and enter a Foot-boy)* So, young man! is your lady within?

BOY.   Alack, Sir! I am but a country boy—I don't know whether she is or noa; but an you'll stay a bit, I'll go and ask the gentlewoman that's with her.

MR. SEAL.   Why, Sirrah, though you are a country boy, you can see, can't you? you know whether she is at home, when you see her, don't you?

BOY.   Nay, nay, I'm not such a country lad neither, master, to think she's at home because I see her. I have been in town but a month, and I lost one place already for believing my own eyes.

MR. SEAL.   Why, Sirrah! have you learnt to lie already?

BOY.   Ah, master! things that are lies in the country are not lies at London—I begin to know my business a little better than so. But an you please to walk in, I'll call a gentlewoman to you that can tell you for certain—she can make bold to ask my lady herself.

MR. SEAL.   Oh! then she is within, I find, though you dare not say so.

BOY.   Nay, nay! That's neither here nor there: what's matter whether she is within or no, if she has not a mind to see anybody?

MR. SEAL.   I can't tell, Sirrah, whether you are arch or simple; but, however, get me a direct answer, and here's a shilling for you.

BOY.   Will you please to walk in; I'll see what I can do for you.

MR. SEAL.   I see you will be fit for your business in time, child. But I expect to meet with nothing but extraordinaries in such a house.

BOY.   Such a house! Sir, you han't seen it yet. Pray walk in.

MR. SEAL.   Sir, I'll wait upon you.   *(Exeunt)*

SCENE III

SCENE: INDIANA'S *house*

Enter ISABELLA

ISAB.   What anxiety do I feel for this poor creature! What will be the end of her? Such a languishing, unreserved passion for a man that at last must certainly leave or ruin her—and perhaps both! Then the aggravation of the distress is, that she does not believe he will—not but, I must own, if they are both what they would seem, they are made for one another as much as Adam and Eve were, for there is no other of their kind but themselves.

Enter Boy

So, Daniel! what news with you?

BOY.   Madam, there's a gentleman below would speak with my lady.

ISAB.   Sirrah! don't you know Mr. Bevil yet?

BOY.   Madam, 'tis not the gentleman who comes every day, and asks for you, and won't go in till he knows whether you are with her or no.

ISAB.   Ha! That's a particular I did not know before.—Well, be it who it will, let him come up to me.

(Exit Boy, and re-enters with MR. SEALAND; ISABELLA *looks amazed)*

MR. SEAL.   Madam, I can't blame your being a little surprised to see a perfect stranger make a visit, and—

ISAB.   I am indeed surprised!—(aside) I see he does not know me.

MR. SEAL.   You are very prettily lodged here, Madam; in troth, you seem to have everything in plenty.—(aside, *and looking about*) A thousand a year, I warrant you, upon this pretty nest of rooms and the dainty one within them.

ISAB.   *(apart)* Twenty years, it seems, have less effect in the alteration of a man of thirty than of a girl of fourteen—he's almost still the same. But alas! I find by other men, as well as himself, I am not what I was. As soon as he spoke I was convinced 'twas he. How shall I contain my surprise and satisfaction! he must not know me yet.

MR. SEAL.   Madam, I hope I don't give you any disturbance, but there is a young lady here with whom I have a particular business to discourse, and I hope she will admit me to that favour.

ISAB.   Why, Sir, have you had any notice concerning her? I wonder who could give it you.

MR. SEAL.   That, Madam, is fit only to be communicated to herself.

ISAB.   Well, Sir! you shall see *her.—(aside)* I find he knows nothing yet, nor shall from me. I am resolved I will observe this interlude, this sport of nature and of fortune.—You shall see her presently, Sir, for now I am as a mother, and will trust her with you.   *(Exit)*

MR. SEAL.   As a mother! right; that's the old phrase for one of those commode ladies, who lend out beauty for hire to young gentlemen that have pressing occasions. But here comes the precious lady herself. In troth, a very sightly woman!

Enter INDIANA

IND.   I am told, Sir, you have some affair that requires your speaking with me.

MR. SEAL.   Yes, Madam: there came to my hands a bill drawn by Mr. Bevil, which is payable to-morrow, and he, in the intercourse of business, sent it to me, who have cash of his, and desired me to send a servant with it; but I have made bold to bring you the money myself.

IND.   Sir! was that necessary?

MRS. SEAL. No, Madam; but, to be free with you, the fame of your beauty and the regard which Mr. Bevil is a little too well known to have for you, excited my curiosity.

IND.   Too well known to have for me! Your sober appearance, Sir, which my friend described, made me expect no rudeness, or absurdity, at least.—Who's there?—Sir, if you pay the money to a servant 'twill be as well.

MR. SEAL.   Pray, Madam, be not offended. I came hither on an innocent, nay, a virtuous design; and if you will have patience to hear me it may be as useful to you, as you are in a friendship with Mr. Bevil, as to my only daughter, whom I was this day disposing of.

IND.   You make me hope, Sir, I have mistaken you. I am composed again; be free, say on— (aside) what I am afraid to hear.

MR. SEAL.   I feared, indeed, an unwarranted passion here, but I did not think it was in abuse of so worthy an object, so accomplished a lady as your sense and mien bespeak. But the youth of our age care not what merit and virtue they bring to shame, so they gratify—

IND.   Sir, you are going into very great errors; but as you are pleased to say you see something in me that has changed at least the colour of your suspicions, so has your appearance altered mine, and made me earnestly attentive to what has any way concerned you to enquire into my affairs and character.

MR. SEAL.   (aside) How sensibly, with what an air she talks!

IND.   Good Sir, be seated, and tell me tenderly—keep all your suspicions concerning me alive, that you may in a proper and prepared way acquaint me why the care of your daughter obliges a person of your seeming worth and fortune to be thus inquisitive about a wretched, helpless, friendless— (weeping). But I beg your pardon: though I am an orphan, your child is not; and your concern for her, it seems, has brought you hither. I'll be composed; pray go on, Sir.

MR. SEAL.   How could Mr. Bevil be such a monster, to injure such a woman?

IND.   No, Sir, you wrong him; he has not injured me; my support is from his bounty.

MR. SEAL.   Bounty! when gluttons give high prices for delicates, they are prodigious bountiful!

IND.   Still, still you will persist in that error. But my own fears tell me all. You are the gentleman, I suppose, for whose happy daughter he is designed a husband by his good father, and he has, perhaps, consented to the overture. He was here this morning, dressed beyond his usual plainness—nay, most sumptuously—and he is to be, perhaps, this night a bridegroom.

MR. SEAL.   I own he was intended such; but, Madam, on your account, I have determined to defer my daughter's marriage till I am satisfied from your own mouth of what nature are the obligations you are under to him.

IND.   His actions, Sir, his eyes, have only made me think he designed to make me the partner of his heart. The goodness and gentleness of his demeanour made me misinterpret all. 'Twas my own hope, my own passion, that deluded me, he never made one amorous advance to me. His large heart and bestowing hand have only helped the miserable. Nor know I why, but from his mere delight in virtue, that I have been his care, the object on which to indulge and please himself with pouring favours.

MR. SEAL.   Madam, I know not why it is, but I, as well as you, am methinks afraid of entering into the matter I came about; but 'tis the same thing as if we had talked never so distinctly: he ne'er shall have a daughter of mine.

IND.   If you say this from what you think of me, you wrong yourself and him. Let not me, miserable though I may be, do injury to my benefactor. No, Sir, my treatment ought rather to reconcile you to his virtues. If to bestow without a prospect of return; if to delight in supporting what might, perhaps, be thought an object of desire, with no other view than to be her guard against those who would not be so disinterested—if these actions, Sir, can in a careful parent's eye commend him to a daughter, give yours, Sir, give her to my honest, generous Bevil. What have I to do but sigh and weep, to rave, run wild, a lunatic in chains, or, hid in darkness, mutter in distracted starts and broken accents my strange, strange story!

MR. SEAL.   Take comfort, Madam.

IND.   All my comfort must be to expostulate in madness, to relieve with frenzy my despair, and shrieking to demand of fate, "Why—why was I born to such variety of sorrows?"

MR. SEAL.   If I have been the least occasion—

IND.   No, 'twas heaven's high will I should be such—to be plundered in my cradle! tossed on the seas! and even there an infant captive! to lose my mother, hear but of my father! to be adopted! lose my adopter! then plunged again in worse calamities!

MR. SEAL.   An infant captive!

IND.   Yet then to find the most charming of mankind, once more to set me free from what I thought the last distress; to load me with his services, his bounties and his favours; to support my very life in a way that stole, at the same time, my very soul itself from me!

MR. SEAL.   And has young Bevil been this worthy man?

IND.   Yet then, again, this very man to take another! without leaving me the right, the pretence, of easing my fond heart with tears! For, oh! I can't reproach him, though the same hand that raised me to this height now throws me down the precipice.

MR. SEAL.   Dear lady! Oh, yet one moment's patience: my heart grows full with your affliction. But yet there's something in your story that—

IND.   My portion here is bitterness and sorrow.

MR. SEAL.   Do not think so. Pray answer me: does Bevil know your name and family?

IND.   Alas, too well! Oh, could I be any other thing than what I am! I'll tear away all traces of my former self, my little ornaments, the remains of my first state, the hints of what I ought to have been—

(In her disorder she throws away a bracelet, which SEALAND takes up, and looks earnestly on it.)

MR. SEAL.   Ha! what's this? My eyes are not deceived? It is, it is the same! the very bracelet which I bequeathed my wife at our last mournful parting!

IND.   What said you, Sir! Your wife! Whither does my fancy carry me? What means this unfelt motion at my heart? And yet again my fortune but deludes me; for if I err not, Sir, your name is Sealand, but my lost father's name was—

MR. SEAL.   Danvers! was it not?

IND.   What new amazement! That is, indeed, my family.

MR. SEAL.   Know, then, when my misfortunes drove me to the Indies, for reasons too tedious now to mention, I changed my name of Danvers into Sealand.

Enter ISABELLA

ISAB.   If yet there wants an explanation of your wonder, examine well this face: yours, Sir, I well remember. Gaze on, and read in me your sister, Isabella.

MR. SEAL.   My sister!

ISAB.   But here's a claim more tender yet—your Indiana, Sir, your long-lost daughter.

MR. SEAL.   O my child! my child!

IND.   All-gracious heaven! is it possible! do I embrace my father!

MR. SEAL.   And do I hold thee? These passions are too strong for utterance. Rise, rise, my child, and give my tears their way.—O my Sister!   *(embracing her)*

ISAB.   Now, dearest Niece, my groundless fears, my painful cares no more shall vex thee. If I have wronged thy noble lover with too hard suspicions, my just concern for thee, I hope, will plead my pardon.

MR. SEAL.   Oh! make him, then, the full amends, and be yourself the messenger of joy. Fly this instant! tell him all these wondrous turns of Providence in his favour! Tell him I have now a daughter to bestow which he no longer will decline; that this day he still shall be a bridegroom; nor shall a fortune, the merit which his father seeks, be wanting; tell him the reward of all his virtues waits on his acceptance.

(Exit ISABELLA*)*

My dearest Indiana! *(turns and embraces her)*

IND.   Have I then, at last, a father's sanction on my love? his bounteous hand to give, and make my heart a present worthy of Bevil's generosity?

MR. SEAL.   O my child! how are our sorrows past o'erpaid by such a meeting! Though I have lost so many years of soft paternal dalliance with thee, yet, in one day to find thee thus, and thus bestow thee in such perfect happiness, is ample, ample reparation! And yet again, the merit of thy lover—

IND.   Oh, had I spirits left to tell you of his actions! how strongly filial duty has suppressed his love, and how concealment still has doubled all his obligations; the pride, the joy of his alliance, Sir, would warm your heart, as he has conquered mine.

MR. SEAL.   How laudable is love when born of virtue! I burn to embrace him—

IND.   See, Sir, my aunt already has succeeded, and brought him to your wishes.

Enter ISABELLA, *with* SIR JOHN BEVIL, BEVIL JUNIOR, MRS. SEALAND,
CIMBERTON, MYRTLE *and* LUCINDA

SIR J. BEV.   *(entering)* Where, where's this scene of wonder? Mr. Sealand, I congratulate, on this occasion, our mutual happiness. Your good sister, Sir, has, with the story of your daughter's fortune, filled us with surprise and joy. Now all exceptions are removed; my son has now avowed his love, and turned all former jealousies and doubts to approbation; and, I am told, your goodness has consented to reward him.

MR. SEAL.   If, Sir, a fortune equal to his father's hopes can make this object worthy his acceptance.

BEV. JUN.   I hear your mention, Sir, of fortune, with pleasure only as it may prove the means to reconcile the best of fathers to my love. Let him be provident, but let me be happy.—
(embracing INDIANA*)* My ever-destined, my acknowledged wife!

IND.   Wife! Oh, my ever loved! my lord! my master!

SIR J. BEV.   I congratulate myself, as well as you, that I had a son who could, under such disadvantages, discover your great merit.

MR. SEAL.   O Sir John! how vain, how weak is human prudence! What care, what foresight, what imagination could contrive such blest events to make our children happy as Providence in one short hour has laid before us?

CIMB.   (*to* MRS. SEALAND) I am afraid, Madam, Mr. Sealand is a little too busy for our affair: if you please, we'll take another opportunity.

MRS. SEAL.   Let us have patience, Sir.

CIMB.   But we make Sir Geoffry wait, Madam.

MYRT.   O Sir! I am not in haste.

(During this BEVIL JUNIOR *presents* LUCINDA *to* INDIANA.)

MR. SEAL.   But here—here's our general benefactor! Excellent young man, that could be at once a lover to her beauty and a parent to her virtue.

BEV. JUN.   If you think that an obligation, Sir, give me leave to overpay myself, in the only instance that can now add to my felicity, by begging you to bestow this lady on Mr. Myrtle.

MR. SEAL.   She is his without reserve; I beg he may be sent for.—Mr. Cimberton, notwithstanding you never had my consent, yet there is, since I last saw you, another objection to your marriage with my daughter.

CIMB.   I hope, Sir, your lady has concealed nothing from me?

MR. SEAL.   Troth, Sir! nothing but what was concealed from myself—another daughter, who has an undoubted title to half my estate.

CIMB.   How, Mr. Sealand! Why then, if half Mrs. Lucinda's fortune is gone, you can't say that any of my estate is settled upon her. I was in treaty for the whole, but if that is not to be come at, to be sure there can be no bargain. Sir, I have nothing to do but to take my leave of your good lady, my cousin, and beg pardon for the trouble I have given this old gentleman.

MYRT.   That you have, Mr. Cimberton, with all my heart.

(discovers himself)

OMN.   Mr. Myrtle!

MYRT.   And I beg pardon of the whole company that I assumed the person of Sir Geoffry, only to be present at the danger of this lady's being disposed of, and in her utmost exigence to assert my right to her; which, if her parents will ratify, as they once favoured my pretensions, no abatement of fortune shall lessen her value to me.

LUC.   Generous man!

MR. SEAL.   If, Sir, you can overlook the injury of being in treaty with one who as meanly left her as you have generously asserted your right in her, she is yours.

LUC.   Mr. Myrtle, though you have ever had my heart, yet now I find I love you more because I bring you less.

MYRT.   We have much more than we want, and I am glad any event has contributed to the discovery of our real inclinations to each other.

MRS. SEAL.   *(aside)* Well! However, I'm glad the girl's disposed of, anyway.

BEV. JUN.   Myrtle, no longer rivals now, but brothers!

MYRT.   Dear Bevil, you are born to triumph over me. But now our competition ceases; I rejoice in the pre-eminence of your virtue, and your alliance adds charms to Lucinda.

SIR J. BEV.   Now, ladies and gentlemen, you have set the world a fair example. Your happiness is owing to your constancy and merit, and the several difficulties you have struggled with evidently show

>Whate'er the generous mind itself denies,
>
>The secret care of Providence supplies.

(Exeunt)

EPILOGUE

BY MR. WELSTED

INTENDED TO BE SPOKEN BY INDIANA

Our author, whom intreaties cannot move,

Spite of the dear coquetry that you love,

Swears he'll not frustrate (so he plainly means),

By a loose epilogue, his decent scenes.

Is it not, Sirs, hard fate I meet to-day,

To keep me rigid still beyond the play?

And yet I'm sav'd a world of pains that way.

I now can look, I now can move at ease,

Nor need I torture these poor limbs to please,

Nor with the hand or foot attempt surprise,

Nor wrest my features, nor fatigue my eyes.

Bless me! what freakish gambols have I play'd!

What motions tried, and wanton looks betray'd!

Out of pure kindness all, to overrule

The threaten'd hiss, and screen some scribbling fool.

With more respect I'm entertain'd to-night:

Our author thinks I can with ease delight.

My artless looks while modest graces arm,

He says I need but to appear and charm.

A wife so form'd, by these examples bred,

Pours joy and gladness round the marriage bed,

Soft source of comfort, kind relief from care,

And 'tis her least perfection to be fair.

The nymph with Indiana's worth who vies,

A nation will behold with Bevil's eyes.

Endnote

1. The kind of story told on the stage should have gay speech, diversity of personages, seriousness, ease, hope, fear, suspicion, desire, make-believe, pity, variety of matter, change of fortune, unexpected trouble, sudden joy and a happy outcome.

Jonathan Swift

A Modest Proposal

For Preventing the Children of poor People in Ireland, *from being a Burden to their Parents or Country; and for making them beneficial to the Publick.*

Written in the Year 1729

It is a melancholly Object to those, who walk through this great Town, or travel in the Country; when they see the *Streets*, the *Roads*, and *Cabbin-doors* crowded with *Beggars* of the Female Sex, followed by three, four, or six Children, *all in Rags*, and importuning every Passenger for an Alms. These *Mothers*, instead of being able to work for their honest Livelyhood, are forced to employ all their Time in stroling to beg Sustenance for their *helpless Infants*; who, as they grow up, either turn *Thieves* for want of Work; or leave their *dear Native Country, to fight for the Pretender* in Spain, or sell themselves to the *Barbadoes*.

I THINK it is agreed by all Parties, that this prodigious Number of Children in the Arms, or on the Backs, or at the *Heels* of their *Mothers*, and frequently of their *Fathers*, is *in the present deplorable State of the Kingdom*, a very great additional Grievance; and therefore, whoever could find out a fair, cheap, and easy Method of making these Children sound and useful Members of the Commonwealth, would deserve so well of the Publick, as to have his Statue set up for a Preserver of the Nation.

But my Intention is very far from being confined to provide only for the Children of *professed Beggars:* It is of a much greater Extent, and shall take in the whole Number of Infants at a certain Age, who are born of Parents, in effect as little able to support them, as those who demand our Charity in the Streets.

As to my own Part, having turned my Thoughts for many Years, upon this important Subject, and maturely weighed the several *Schemes of other Projectors*, I have always found them grosly mistaken in their Computation. It is true a Child, *just dropt from its Dam*, may be supported by her Milk, for a Solar Year with little other Nourishment: at most not above the Value of two Shillings; which the Mother may certainly get, or the Value in *Scraps*, by her lawful Occupation of *Begging*: And, it is exactly at one Year old, that I propose to provide for them in such a Manner, as, instead of being a Charge upon their *Parents*, or the *Parish*, or *wanting Food and Raiment* for the rest of their Lives; they shall, on the contrary, contribute to the Feeding, and partly to the Cloathing, of many Thousands.

THERE is likewise another great Advantage in my *Scheme*, that it will prevent those *voluntary Abortions*, and that horrid Practice of *Women murdering their Bastard Children*; alas! too frequent among us; sacrificing the *poor innocent Babes*, I doubt, more to avoid the Expence than the Shame; which would move Tears and Pity in the most Savage and inhuman Breast.

THE Number of Souls in *Ireland* being usually reckoned one Million and a half; of these I calculate there may be about Two hundred Thousand Couple whose Wives are Breeders; from which Number I

From *The Prose Works of Jonathan Swift, Irish Tracts 1728-1733.*

subtract thirty thousand Couples, who are able to maintain their own Children; although I apprehend there cannot be so many, under *the present Distresses of the Kingdom*; but this being granted, there will remain an Hundred and Seventy Thousand Breeders. I again subtract Fifty Thousand, for those Women who miscarry, or whose Children die by Accident, or Disease, within the Year. There only remain an Hundred and Twenty Thousand Children of poor Parents, annually born: The Question therefore is, How this Number shall be reared, and provided for? Which, as I have already said, under the present Situation of Affairs, is utterly impossible, by all the Methods hitherto proposed: For we can *neither employ them in Handicraft* or *Agriculture*; we neither build Houses, (I mean in the Country) nor cultivate Land: They can very seldom pick up a Livelyhood *by Stealing* until they arrive at six Years old; except where they are of towardly Parts; although, I confess, they learn the Rudiments much earlier; during which Time, they can, however, be properly looked upon only as *Probationers*; as I have been informed by a principal Gentleman in the County of *Cavan*, who protested to me, that he never knew above one or two Instances under the Age of six, even in a Part of the Kingdom *so renowned for the quickest Proficiency in that Art*.

I Am assured by our Merchants, that a Boy or a Girl before twelve Years old, is no saleable Commodity; and even when they come to this Age, they will not yield above Three Pounds, or Three Pounds and half a Crown at most, on the Exchange; which cannot turn to Account either to the Parents or the Kingdom; the Charge of Nutriment and Rags, having been at least four Times that Value.

I Shall now therefore humbly propose my own Thoughts; which I hope will not be liable to the least Objection.

I Have been assured by a very knowing *American* of my Acquaintance in *London*; that a young healthy Child, well nursed, is, at a Year old, a most delicious, nourishing, and wholesome Food; whether *Stewed, Roasted, Baked*, or *Boiled;* and, I make no doubt, that it will equally serve in a *Fricasie*, or *Ragoust*.

I Do therefore humbly offer it to *publick Consideration*, that of the Hundred and Twenty Thousand Children, already computed, Twenty thousand may be reserved for Breed; whereof only one Fourth Part to be Males; which is more than we allow to *Sheep, black Cattle*, or *Swine;* and my Reason is, that these Children are seldom the Fruits of Marriage, a *Circumstance not much regarded by our Savages;* therefore, *one Male* will be sufficient to serve *four Females*. That the remaining Hundred thousand, may, at a Year old, be offered in Sale to the *Persons of Quality* and *Fortune*, through the Kingdom; always advising the Mother to let them suck plentifully in the last Month, so as to render them plump, and fat for a good Table. A Child will make two Dishes at an Entertainment for Friends; and when the Family dines alone, the fore or hind Quarter will make a reasonable Dish; and seasoned with a little Pepper or Salt, will be very good Boiled on the fourth Day, especially in *Winter*.

I Have reckoned upon a Medium, that a Child just born will weigh Twelve Pounds; and in a solar Year, if tolerably nursed, encreaseth to twenty eight Pounds.

I Grant this Food will be somewhat dear, and therefore very *proper for Landlords*; who, as they have already devoured most of the Parents, seem to have the best Title to the Children.

Infants Flesh will be in Season throughout the Year; but more plentiful in *March*, and a little before and after: For we are told by a grave * Author, an eminent *French* Physician, that *Fish being a prolifick Dyet*, there are more Children born in *Roman Catholick Countries* about Nine Months after *Lent*, than

* Rabelais.

at any other Season: Therefore reckoning a Year after *Lent*, the Markets will be more glutted than usual; because the Number of *Popish Infants*, is, at least, three to one in this Kingdom; and therefore it will have one other Collateral Advantage, by lessening the Number of *Papists* among us.

I HAVE already computed the Charge of nursing a Beggar's Child (in which List I reckon all *Cottagers, Labourers*, and Four fifths of the *Farmers*) to be about two Shillings *per Annum*, Rags included; and I believe, no Gentleman would repine to give Ten Shillings for the *Carcase of a good fat Child;* which, as I have said, will make four Dishes of excellent nutritive Meat, when he hath only some particular Friend, or his own Family, to dine with him. Thus the Squire will learn to be a good Landlord, and grow popular among his Tenants; the Mother will have Eight Shillings net Profit, and be fit for Work until she produceth another Child.

THOSE who are more thrifty *(as I must confess the Times require)* may flay the Carcase; the Skin of which, artificially dressed, will make admirable *Gloves for Ladies*, and *Summer Boots for fine Gentlemen*.

As to our City of *Dublin*; Shambles may be appointed for this Purpose, in the most convenient Parts of it; and Butchers we may be assured will not be wanting; although I rather recommend buying the Children alive, and dressing them hot from the Knife, as we do *roasting Pigs*.

A VERY worthy Person, *a true Lover of his Country,* and whose Virtues I highly esteem, was lately pleased, in discoursing on this Matter, to offer a Refinement upon my Scheme. He said, that many Gentlemen of this Kingdom, having of late destroyed their Deer; he conceived, that the Want of Venison might be well supplied by the Bodies of young Lads and Maidens, not exceeding fourteen Years of Age, nor under twelve; so great a Number of both Sexes in every County being now ready to starve, for Want of Work and Service: And these to be disposed of by their Parents, if alive, or otherwise by their nearest Relations. But with due Deference to so excellent a Friend, and so deserving a Patriot, I cannot be altogether in his Sentiments. For as to the Males, my *American* Acquaintance assured me from frequent Experience, that their Flesh was generally tough and lean, like that of our School-boys, by continual Exercise, and their Taste disagreeable; and to fatten them would not answer the Charge. Then, as to the Females, it would, I think, with humble Submission, *be a Loss to the Publick*, because they soon would become Breeders themselves: And besides it is not improbable, that some scrupulous People might be apt to censure such a Practice (although indeed very unjustly) as a little bordering upon Cruelty; which, I confess, hath always been with me the strongest Objection against any Project, how well soever intended.

BUT in order to justify my Friend; he confessed, that this Expedient was put into his Head by the famous *Salmanaazor*, a Native of the Island *Formosa*, who came from thence to *London*, above twenty years ago, and in Conversation told my Friend, that in his Country, when any young Person happened to be put to Death, the Executioner sold the Carcase to *Persons of Quality*, as a prime Dainty; and that, in his Time, the Body of a plump Girl of fifteen, who was crucified for an Attempt to poison the Emperor, was sold to his Imperial *Majesty's prime Minister of State*, and other great *Mandarins* of the Court, *in Joints from the Gibbet*, at Four hundred Crowns. Neither indeed can I deny, that if the same Use were made of several plump young girls in this Town, who, without one single Groat to their Fortunes, cannot stir Abroad without a Chair, and appear at the *Play-house*, and *Assemblies* in foreign Fineries, which they never will pay for; the Kingdom would not be the worse.

SOME Persons of a desponding Spirit are in great Concern about that vast Number of poor People, who are Aged, Diseased, or Maimed; and I have been desired to employ my Thoughts what Course may be taken, to ease the Nation of so grievous an Incumbrance. But I am not in the least Pain upon that Matter; because it is very well known, that they are every Day *dying*, and *rotting*, by *Cold* and *Famine*, and *Filth*, and *Vermin*, as fast as can be reasonably expected. And as to the younger Labourers, they are now in almost as hopeful a Condition: They can not get Work, and consequently pine away for Want of Nourishment, to a Degree, that if at any Time they are accidentally hired to common Labour, they have not Strength to perform it; and thus the Country, and themselves, are in a fair Way of being soon delivered from the Evils to come.

I HAVE too long digressed; and therefore shall return to my Subject. I think the Advantages by the Proposal which I have made, are obvious, and many, as well as of the highest Importance.

FOR, *First*, as I have already observed, it would greatly lessen the *Number of Papists*, with whom we are yearly overrun; being the principal Breeders of the Nation, as well as our most dangerous Enemies; and who stay at home on Purpose, with a Design to *deliver the Kingdom to the Pretender*; hoping to take their Advantage by the Absence *of so many good Protestants*, who have chosen rather to leave their Country, than stay at home, and pay Tithes against their Conscience, to an idolatrous *Episcopal Curate*.

SECONDLY, The poorer Tenants will have something valuable of their own, which, by Law, may be made liable to Distress, and help to pay their Landlord's Rent; their Corn and Cattle being already seized, and *Money a Thing unknown*.

THIRDLY, Whereas the Maintenance of an Hundred Thousand Children, from two Years old, and upwards, cannot be computed at less than ten Shillings a Piece *per Annum*, the Nation's Stock will be thereby encreased Fifty Thousand Pounds *per Annum;* besides the Profit of a new Dish, introduced to the Tables of all *Gentlemen of Fortune* in the Kingdom, who have any Refinement in Taste; and the Money will circulate among ourselves, the Goods being entirely of our own Growth and Manufacture.

FOURTHLY, The constant Breeders, besides the Gain of Eight Shillings *Sterling per Annum*, by the Sale of their Children, will be rid of the Charge of maintaining them after the first Year.

FIFTHLY, This Food would likewise bring great *Custom to Taverns*, where the Vintners will certainly be so prudent, as to procure the best Receipts for dressing it to Perfection; and consequently, have their Houses frequented by all the *fine Gentlemen*, who justly value themselves upon their Knowledge in good Eating; and a skilful Cook, who understands how to oblige his Guests, will contrive to make it as expensive as they please.

SIXTHLY, This would be a great Inducement to Marriage, which all wise Nations have either encouraged by Rewards, or enforced by Laws and Penalties. It would encrease the Care and Tenderness of Mothers towards their Children, when they were sure of a Settlement for Life, to the poor Babes, provided in some Sort by the Publick, to their annual Profit instead of Expence. We should soon see an honest Emulation among the married Women, *which of them could bring the fattest Child to the Market*. Men would become as *fond* of their Wives, during the Time of their Pregnancy, as they are now of their *Mares* in Foal, their *Cows* in Calf, or *Sows* when they are ready to farrow; nor offer to beat or kick them, (as it is too *frequent* a Practice) for fear of a Miscarriage.

MANY other Advantages might be enumerated. For instance, the Addition of some Thousand Carcasses in our Exportation of barrelled Beef: The Propagation of *Swines Flesh*, and Improvement in the Art of making good *Bacon*; so much wanted among us by the great Destruction of *Pigs*, too frequent at our Tables, and are no way comparable in Taste, or Magnificence, to a well-grown fat yearling Child; which, roasted whole, will make a considerable Figure at a *Lord Mayor's Feast*, or any other publick Entertainment. But this, and many others, I omit; being studious of Brevity.

SUPPOSING that one Thousand Families in this City, would be constant Customers for Infants Flesh; besides others who might have it at *merry Meetings*, particularly *Weddings* and *Christenings*; I compute that *Dublin* would take off, annually, about Twenty Thousand Carcasses; and the rest of the Kingdom (where probably they will be sold somewhat cheaper) the remaining Eighty Thousand.

I CAN think of no one Objection, that will possibly be raised against this Proposal; unless it should be urged, that the Number of People will be thereby much lessened in the Kingdom. This I freely own; and it was indeed one principal Design in offering it to the World. I desire the Reader will observe, that I calculate my Remedy *for this one individual Kingdom* of IRELAND, *and for no other that ever was, is, or I think ever can be upon Earth*. Therefore, let no man talk to me of other Expedients: *Of taxing our Absentees at five Shillings a Pound: Of using neither Cloaths, nor Houshold Furniture except what is of our own Growth and Manufacture: Of utterly rejecting the Materials and Instruments that promote foreign Luxury: Of curing the Expensiveness of Pride, Vanity, Idleness, and Gaming in our Women: Of introducing a Vein of Parsimony, Prudence and Temperance: Of learning to love our Country, wherein we differ even from* LAPLANDERS, *and the Inhabitants of* TOPINAMBOO: *Of quitting our Animosities, and Factions; nor act any longer like the Jews, who were murdering one another at the very Moment their City was taken: Of being a little cautious not to sell our Country and Consciences for nothing: Of teaching Landlords to have, at least, one Degree of Mercy towards their Tenants. Lastly, Of putting a Spirit of Honesty, Industry, and Skill into our Shopkeepers; who, if a Resolution could now be taken to buy only our native Goods, would immediately unite to cheat and exact upon us in the Price, the Measure, and the Goodness; nor could ever yet be brought to make one fair Proposal of just Dealing, though often and earnestly invited to it.*

THEREFORE I repeat, let no Man talk to me of these and the like Expedients; till he hath, at least, a Glimpse of Hope, that there will ever be some hearty and sincere Attempt to put *them in Practice*.

BUT, as to my self; having been wearied out for many Years with offering vain, idle, visionary Thoughts; and at length utterly despairing of Success, I fortunately fell upon this Proposal; which, as it is wholly new, so it hath something *solid* and *real*, of no Expence, and little Trouble, full in our own Power; and whereby we can incur no Danger in *disobliging* ENGLAND: For, this Kind of Commodity will not bear Exportation; the Flesh being of too tender a Consistence, to admit a long Continuance in Salt; *although, perhaps, I could name a Country, which would be glad to eat up our whole Nation without it.*

AFTER all, I am not so violently bent upon my own Opinion, as to reject any Offer proposed by wise Men, which shall be found equally innocent, cheap, easy, and effectual. But before something of that Kind shall be advanced, in Contradiction to my Scheme, and offering a better; I desire the Author, or Authors, will be pleased maturely to consider two Points. *First*, As Things now stand, how they will be able to find Food and Raiment, for a Hundred Thousand useless Mouths and Backs? And *secondly*, There being a round Million of Creatures in human Figure, throughout this Kingdom; whose whole Subsistence, put into a common Stock, would leave them in Debt two Millions of Pounds *Sterling;* adding those, who are Beggars by Profession, to the Bulk of Farmers, Cottagers, and Labourers, with their Wives and Children, who are Beggars in Effect; I desire those Politicians, who dislike my Overture, and may perhaps be so bold to attempt an Answer, that they will first ask the Parents of these Mortals, Whether they would not, at this Day, think it a great Happiness to have been sold for Food at a Year old, in the Manner I prescribe; and thereby have avoided such a perpetual Scene of Misfortunes, as they have since gone through; by the *Oppression of Landlords;* the Impossibility of paying Rent, without Money or Trade; the Want of common Sustenance, with neither House nor Cloaths, to cover them from the Inclemencies of Weather; and the most inevitable Prospect of intailing the like, or greater Miseries upon their Breed for ever.

I PROFESS, in the Sincerity of my Heart, that I have not the least personal Interest, in endeavouring to promote this necessary Work; having no other Motive than the *publick Good of my Country, by advancing our Trade, providing for Infants, relieving the Poor, and giving some Pleasure to the Rich.* I have no Children, by which I can propose to get a single Penny; the youngest being nine Years old, and my Wife past Child-bearing.

Samuel Johnson

The Rambler

NO. 60. SATURDAY, 13 OCTOBER 1750.

—Quid sit pulchrum, quid turpe, quid utile, quid non, Plenius et melius
Chrysippo et Crantore dicit.

Horace, EPISTLES, 1.2.3–4

Whose works the beautiful and base contain;
Of vice and virtue more instructive rules,
Than all the sober sages of the schools.

Francis.

All joy or sorrow for the happiness or calamities of others is produced by an act of the imagination, that realises the event however fictitious, or approximates it however remote, by placing us, for a time, in the condition of him whose fortune we contemplate; so that we feel, while the deception lasts, whatever motions would be excited by the same good or evil happening to ourselves.

Our passions are therefore more strongly moved, in proportion as we can more readily adopt the pains or pleasures proposed to our minds, by recognising them as once our own, or considering them as naturally incident to our state of life. It is not easy for the most artful writer to give us an interest in happiness or misery, which we think ourselves never likely to feel, and with which we have never yet been made acquainted. Histories of the downfal of kingdoms, and revolutions of empires, are read with great tranquillity; the imperial tragedy pleases common auditors only by its pomp of ornament, and grandeur of ideas; and the man whose faculties have been engrossed by business, and whose heart never fluttered but at the rise or fall of stocks, wonders how the attention can be seized, or the affections agitated by a tale of love.

Those parallel circumstances, and kindred images, to which we readily conform our minds, are, above all other writings, to be found in narratives of the lives of particular persons; and therefore no species of writing seems more worthy of cultivation than biography, since none can be more delightful or more useful, none can more certainly enchain the heart by irresistible interest, or more widely diffuse instruction to every diversity of condition.

The general and rapid narratives of history, which involve a thousand fortunes in the business of a day, and complicate innumerable incidents in one great transaction, afford few lessons applicable to private life, which derives its comforts and its wretchedness from the right or wrong management of things which nothing but their frequency makes considerable, *Parva, si non fiant quotidie*, says Pliny, and which can

From *The Rambler*, Volume 1 by Samuel Johnson, Pafraets Books Company, Troy, NY 1903.

145

have no place in those relations which never descend below the consultation of senates, the motions of armies, and the schemes of conspirators.

I have often thought that there has rarely passed a life of which a judicious and faithful narrative would not be useful. For, not only every man has, in the mighty mass of the world, great numbers in the same condition with himself, to whom his mistakes and miscarriages, escapes and expedients, would be of immediate and apparent use; but there is such an uniformity in the state of man, considered apart from adventitious and separable decorations and disguises, that there is scarce any possibility of good or ill, but is common to human kind. A great part of the time of those who are placed at the greatest distance by fortune, or by temper, must unavoidably pass in the same manner; and though, when the claims of nature are satisfied, caprice, and vanity, and accident, begin to produce discriminations and peculiarities, yet the eye is not very heedful, or quick, which cannot discover the same causes still terminating their influence in the same effects, though sometimes accelerated, sometimes retarded, or perplexed by multiplied combinations. We are all prompted by the same motives, all deceived by the same fallacies, all animated by hope, obstructed by danger, entangled by desire and seduced by pleasure.

It is frequently objected to relations of particular lives, that they are not distinguished by any striking or wonderful vicissitudes. The scholar who passed his life among his books, the merchant who conducted only his own affairs, the priest, whose sphere of action was not extended beyond that of his duty, are considered as no proper objects of publick regard, however they might have excelled in their several stations, whatever might have been their learning, integrity, and piety. But this notion arises from false measures of excellence and dignity, and must be eradicated by considering, that, in the esteem of uncorrupted reason, what is of most use is of most value.

It is, indeed, not improper to take honest advantages of prejudice, and to gain attention by a celebrated name; but the business of the biographer is often to pass slightly over those performances and incidents, which produce vulgar greatness, to lead the thoughts into domestick privacies, and display the minute details of daily life, where exterior appendages are cast aside, and men excel each other only by prudence and by virtue. The account of Thuanus is, with great propriety, said by its author to have been written, that it might lay open to posterity the private and familiar character of that man, *cujus ingenium et canclorem ex ipsius scriptis sunt ohm semper miraturi*, whose candour and genius will to the end of time be by his writings preserved in admiration.

There are many invisible circumstances which, whether we read as enquirers after natural or moral knowledge, whether we intend to enlarge our science, or increase our virtue, are more important than publick occurrences. Thus Salust, the great master of nature, has not forgot, in his account of Catiline, to remark that "his walk was now quick, and again slow," as an indication of a mind revolving something with violent commotion. Thus the story of Melancthon affords a striking lecture on the value of time, by informing us, that when he made an appointment, he expected not only the hour, but the minute to be fixed, that the days might not run out in the idleness of suspense; and all the plans and enterprizes of De Wit are now of less importance to the world, than that part of his personal character which represents him as "careful of his health, and negligent of his life."

But biography has often been allotted to writers who seem very little acquainted with the nature of their task, or very negligent about the performance. They rarely afford any other account than might be collected from publick papers, but imagine themselves writing a life when they exhibit a chronological series of actions or preferments; and so little regard the manners or behaviour of their heroes, that more knowledge may be gained of a man's real character, by a short conversation with one of his servants, than from a formal and studied narrative, begun with his pedigree, and ended with his funeral.

If now and then they condescend to inform the world of particular facts, they are not always so happy as to select the most important. I know not well what advantage posterity can receive from the only circumstance by which Tickell has distinguished Addison from the rest of mankind, "the irregularity of his pulse": nor can I think myself overpaid for the time spent in reading the life of Malherb, by being enabled to relate, after the learned biographer, that Malherb had two predominant opinions; one, that the looseness of a single woman might destroy all her boast of ancient descent; the other, that the French beggars made use very improperly and barbarously of the phrase "noble Gentleman," because either word included the sense of both.

There are, indeed, some natural reasons why these narratives are often written by such as were not likely to give much instruction or delight, and why most accounts of particular persons are barren and useless. If a life be delayed till interest and envy are at an end, we may hope for impartiality, but must expect little intelligence; for the incidents which give excellence to biography are of a volatile and evanescent kind, such as soon escape the memory, and are rarely transmitted by tradition. We know how few can portray a living acquaintance, except by his most prominent and observable particularities, and the grosser features of his mind; and it may be easily imagined how much of this little knowledge may be lost in imparting it and how soon a succession of copies will lose all resemblance of the original.

If the biographer writes from personal knowledge, and makes haste to gratify the publick curiosity, there is danger lest his interest, his fear, his gratitude, or his tenderness, overpower his fidelity, and tempt him to conceal, if not to invent. There are many who think it an act of piety to hide the faults or failings of their friends, even when they can no longer suffer by their detection; we therefore see whole ranks of characters adorned with uniform panegyrick, and not to be known from one another, but by extrinsick and casual circumstances. "Let me remember," says Hale, "when I find myself inclined to pity a criminal, that there is likewise a pity due to the country." If we owe regard to the memory of the dead, there is yet more respect to be paid to knowledge, to virtue, and to truth.

NO. 149. TUESDAY, 20 AUGUST 1751.

Quod non sit Pylades hoc tempore, non sit Orestes
Miraris? Pylades, Marce, bibebat idem.
Nec melior panis, turdusve dabatur Oresti:
Sed par, atque eadem coena duobus erat.—
Te Cadmaea Tyros, me pinguis Gallia vestit:
Vis te purpureum, Marce, saga tus amem?
Ut praestem Pyladen, aliquis mihi praestet Orestem:
Hoc non fit verbis, Marce: ut ameris, ama.

Martial, VI.1 1. 1—4, 7—10.

You wonder now that no man sees
Such friends as those of ancient Greece.
Here lay the point—Orestes' meat
Was just the same his friend did eat.
Nor can it yet be found, his wine
Was better, Pylades, than thine.
In home-spun russet I am drest,
Your cloth is always of the best.
But honest Marcus, if you please
To choose me for your Pylades,
Remember, words alone are vain;
Love—if you wou'd be lov'd again.

F. Lewis.

Sɪʀ,

No depravity of the mind has been more frequently or justly censured than ingratitude. There is indeed sufficient reason for looking on those that can return evil for good, and repay kindness and assistance with hatred or neglect, as corrupted beyond the common degrees of wickedness; nor will he who has once been clearly detected in acts of injury to his benefactor, deserve to be numbered among social beings; he has endeavoured to destroy confidence, to intercept sympathy, and to turn every man's attention wholly on himself.

There is always danger lest the honest abhorrence of a crime should raise the passions with too much violence against the man to whom it is imputed. In proportion as guilt is more enormous, it ought to be ascertained by stronger evidence. The charge against ingratitude is very general; almost every man can tell what favours he has conferred upon insensibility, and how much happiness he has bestowed without return; but perhaps if these patrons and protectors were confronted with any whom they boast of having befriended, it would often appear that they consulted only their pleasure or vanity, and repaid themselves their petty donatives by gratifications of insolence and indulgence of contempt.

It has happened that much of my time has been passed in a dependant state, and consequently I have received many favours in the opinion of those at whose expence I have been maintained; yet I do not feel in my heart any burning gratitude or tumultuous affection; and as I would not willingly suppose myself less susceptible of virtuous passions than the rest of mankind, I shall lay the history of my life before you, that you may, by your judgment of my conduct, either reform or confirm my present sentiments.

My father was the second son of a very antient and wealthy family. He married a lady of equal birth, whose fortune, joined to his own, might have supported his posterity in honour; but being gay and ambitious, he prevailed on his friends to procure him a post, which gave him an opportunity of displaying his elegance and politeness. My mother was equally pleased with splendor, and equally careless of expence; they both justified their profusion to themselves, by endeavouring to believe it necessary to the extension of their acquaintance and improvement of their interest; and whenever any place became vacant, they expected to be repaid. In the midst of these hopes my father was snatched away by an apoplexy; and my mother, who had no pleasure but in dress, equipage, assemblies and compliments, finding that she could live no longer in her accustomed rank, sunk into dejection, and in two years wore out her life with envy and discontent.

I was sent with a sister, one year younger than myself, to the elder brother of my father. We were not yet capable of observing how much fortune influences affection, but flattered ourselves on the road with the tenderness and regard with which we should be treated by our uncle. Our reception was rather frigid than malignant; we were introduced to our young cousins, and for the first month more frequently consoled than upbraided; but in a short time we found our prattle repressed, our dress neglected, our endearments unregarded, and our requests referred to the housekeeper.

The forms of decency were now violated, and every day produced new insults. We were soon brought to the necessity of receding from our imagined equality with our cousins, to whom we sunk into humble companions without choice or influence, expected only to echo their opinions, facilitate their desires, and accompany their rambles. It was unfortunate that our early introduction into polite company and habitual knowledge of the arts of civility, had given us such an appearance of superiority to the awkward bashfulness of our relations, as naturally drew respect and preference from every stranger; and my aunt was forced to assert the dignity of her own children, while they were sculking in corners for fear of notice, and hanging down their heads in silent confusion, by relating the indiscretion of our father, displaying her own kindness, lamenting the misery of birth without estate, and declaring her anxiety for our future provision, and the expedients which she had formed to secure us from those follies or crimes, to which the conjunction of pride and want often gives occasion. In a short time care was taken to prevent such vexatious mistakes; we were told, that fine cloaths would only fill our heads with false expectations, and our dress was therefore accommodated to our fortune.

Childhood is not easily dejected or mortified. We felt no lasting pain from insolence or neglect; but finding that we were favoured and commended by all whose interest did not prompt them to discountenance us, preserved our vivacity and spirit to years of greater sensibility. It then became irksome and disgusting to live without any principle of action but the will of another, and we often met privately in the garden to lament our condition, and to ease our hearts with mutual narratives of caprice, peevishness, and affront.

There are innumerable modes of insult and tokens of contempt, for which it is not easy to find a name, which vanish to nothing in an attempt to describe them, and yet may, by continual repetition, make day pass after day in sorrow and in terror. Phrases of cursory compliment and established salutation may by a different modulation of the voice or cast of the countenance convey contrary meanings, and be changed from indications of respect to expressions of scorn. The dependant who cultivates delicacy in himself very little consults his own tranquillity. My unhappy vigilance is every moment discovering some petulance of accent, or arrogance of mien, some vehemence of interrogation, or quickness of reply, that recalls my poverty to my mind, and which I feel more acutely as I know not how to resent it.

You are not however to imagine, that I think myself discharged from the duties of gratitude, only because my relations do not adjust their looks or tune their voices to my expectation. The insolence of benefaction terminates not in negative rudeness or obliquities of insult. I am often told in express terms of the miseries from which charity has snatched me, while multitudes are suffered by relations equally near to devolve upon the parish; and have more than once heard it numbered among other favours that I am admitted to the same table with my cousins.

That I sit at the first table I must acknowledge, but I sit there only that I may feel the stings of inferiority. My enquiries are neglected, my opinion is overborn, my assertions are controverted; and as insolence always propagates itself, the servants overlook me, in imitation of their master; if I call modestly, I am not heard; if loudly, my usurpation of authority is checked by a general frown. I am often obliged to look uninvited upon delicacies, and sometimes desired to rise upon very slight pretences.

The incivilities to which I am exposed would give me less pain were they not aggravated by the tears of my sister, whom the young ladies are hourly tormenting with every art of feminine persecution. As it is said of the supreme magistrate of Venice, that he is a prince in one place and a slave in another, my sister is a servant to her cousins in their apartments, and a companion only at the table. Her wit and beauty draw so much regard away from them, that they never suffer her to appear with them in any place where they solicit notice, or expect admiration, and when they are visited by neighbouring ladies, and pass their hours in domestic amusements, she is sometimes called to fill a vacancy, insulted with contemptuous freedoms, and dismissed to her needle when her place is supplied. The heir has of late, by the instigation of his sisters, begun to harass her with clownish jocularity; he seems inclined to make his first rude essays of waggery upon her; and by the connivance, if not encouragement of his father, treats her with such licentious brutality, as I cannot bear, though I cannot punish it.

I beg to be informed, Mr. Rambler, how much we can be supposed to owe to beneficence, exerted on terms like these? to beneficence which pollutes its gifts with contumely, and may be truly said to pander to pride? I would willingly be told, whether insolence does not reward its own liberalities, and whether he that exacts servility, can with justice at the same time expect affection?

I am, Sir, &c.
HYPERDULUS.

Samuel Johnson

The Life of Savage

It has been observed in all ages, that the advantages of nature or of fortune have contributed very little to the promotion of happiness; and that those whom the splendour of their rank, or the extent of their capacity, have placed upon the summits of human life, have not often given any just occasion to envy in those who look up to them from a lower station: whether it be that apparent superiority incites great designs, and great designs are naturally liable to fatal miscarriages; or that the general lot of mankind is misery, and the misfortunes of those whose eminence drew upon them an universal attention, have been more carefully recorded, because they were more generally observed, and have in reality been only more conspicuous than those of others, not more frequent, or more severe.

That affluence and power, advantages extrinsic and adventitious, and therefore easily separable from those by whom they are possessed, should very often flatter the mind with expectations of felicity which they cannot give, raises no astonishment; but it seems rational to hope, that intellectual greatness should produce better effects: that minds qualified for great attainments should first endeavor their own benefit; and that they who are most able to teach others the way to happiness, should with most certainty follow it themselves.

But this expectation, however plausible, has been very frequently disappointed. The heroes of literary as well as civil history have been very often no less remarkable for what they have atchieved; and volumes have been written only to enumerate the miseries of the learned, and relate their unhappy lives, and untimely deaths.

To these mournful narratives, I am about to add the Life of Richard Savage, a man whose writings entitle him to an eminent rank in the classes of learning, and whose misfortunes claim a degree of compassion, not always due to the unhappy, as they were often the consequences of the crimes of others, rather than his own.

In the year 1697, Anne Countess of Macclesfield, having lived for some time upon very uneasy terms with her husband, thought a public confession of adultery the most obvious and expeditious method of obtaining her liberty; and therefore declared, that the child, with which she was then great, was begotten by the Earl Rivers. This, as may be imagined, made her husband no less desirous of a separation than herself, and he prosecuted his design in the most effectual manner; for he applied not to the ecclesiastical courts for a divorce, but to the parliament for an act, by which his marriage might be dissolved, the nuptial contract totally annulled, and the children of his wife illegitimated. This act, after the usual deliberation, he obtained, though without the approbation of some, who considered marriage as an affair only cognizable by ecclesiastical judges; and on March 3d was separated from his wife, whose fortune, which was very great, was repaid her, and who having, as well as her husband, the liberty of making another choice, was in a short time married to Colonel Brett.

While the Earl of Macclesfield was prosecuting this affair, his wife was, on the 10th of January 1697–8,

Published by Johnson, released 1744.

delivered of a son, and the Earl Rivers, by appearing to consider him as his own, left none any reason to doubt of the sincerity of her declaration; for he was his godfather, and gave him his own name, which was by his direction inserted in the register of St. Andrew's parish in Holborn, but unfortunately left him to the care of his mother, whom, as she was now set free from her husband, he probably imagined likely to treat with great tenderness the child that had contributed to so pleasing an event. It is not indeed easy to discover what motives could be found to over-balance that natural affection of a parent, or what interest could be promoted by neglect or cruelty. The dread of shame or of poverty, by which some wretches have been incited to abandon or to murder their children, cannot be supposed to have affected a woman who had proclaimed her crimes and solicited reproach, and on whom the clemency of the legislature had undeservedly bestowed a fortune, which would have been very little diminished by the expences which the care of her child could have brought upon her. It was therefore not likely that she would be wicked without temptation, that she would look upon her son from his birth with a kind of resentment and abhorrence; and, instead of supporting, assisting, and defending him, delight to see him struggling with misery, or that she would take every opportunity of aggravating his misfortunes, and obstructing his resources, and with an implacable and restless cruelty continue her persecution from the first hour of his life to the last.

But whatever were her motives, no sooner was her son born, than she discovered a resolution of disowning him; and in a very short time removed him from her sight, by committing him to the care of a poor woman, whom she directed to educate him as her own, and injoined never to inform him of his true parents.

Such was the beginning of the life of Richard Savage. Born with a legal claim to honour and to affluence, he was in two months illegitimated by the parliament, and disowned by his mother, doomed to poverty and obscurity, and launched upon the ocean of life, only that he might be swallowed by its quicksands or dashed upon its rocks.

His mother could not indeed infect others with the same cruelty. As it was impossible to avoid the inquiries which the curiosity or tenderness of her relations made after her child, she was obliged to give some account of the measures that she had taken; and her mother, the Lady Mason, whether in approbation of her design, or to prevent more criminal contrivances, engaged to transact with the nurse, to pay her for her care, and to superintend the education of the child.

In this charitable office she was assisted by his godmother, Mrs. Lloyd, who, while she lived, always looked upon him with that tenderness, which the barbarity of his mother made peculiarly necessary; but her death, which happened in his tenth year, was another of the misfortunes of his childhood; for though she kindly endeavoured to alleviate his loss by a legacy of three hundred pounds; yet, as he had none to prosecute his claim, to shelter him from oppression, or call-in law to the assistance of justice, her will was eluded by the executors, and no part of the money was ever paid.

He was, however, not yet wholly abandoned. The Lady Mason still continued her care, and directed him to be placed at a small grammar-school near St. Alban's, where he was called by the name of his nurse, without the least intimation that he had a claim to any other.

Here he was initiated in literature, and passed through several of the classes, with what rapidity or what applause cannot now be known. As he always spoke with respect of his master, it is probable that the mean rank, in which he then appeared, did not hinder his genius from being distinguished, or his industry from being rewarded; and if in so low a state he obtained distinction and rewards, it is not likely that they were gained but by genius and industry.

It is very reasonable to conjecture, that his application was equal to his abilities, because his improvement was more than proportioned to the opportunities which he enjoyed; nor can it be doubted, that if his earliest productions had been preserved, like those of happier students, we might in some have found vigorous sallies of that sprightly humour which distinguishes *The Author to be let*, and in others strong touches of that ardent imagination which painted the solemn scenes of *The Wanderer*.

While he was thus cultivating his genius, his father the Earl Rivers was seized with a distemper, which in a short time put an end to his life. He had frequently inquired after his son, and had always been amused[1] with fallacious and evasive answers; but, being now in his own opinion on his death-bed, he thought it his duty to provide for him among his other natural children, and therefore demanded a positive account of him, with an importunity not to be diverted or denied. His mother, who could no longer refuse an answer, determined at least to give such as should cut him off for ever from that happiness which competence affords, and therefore declared that he was dead; which is perhaps the first instance of a lye invented by a mother to deprive her son of a provision which was designed him by another, and which she could not expect herself, though he should lose it.

This was therefore an act of wickedness which could not be defeated, because it could not be suspected; the Earl did not imagine there could exist in a human form a mother that would ruin her son without enriching herself, and therefore bestowed upon some other person six thousand pounds, which he had in his will bequeathed to Savage.

The same cruelty which incited his mother to intercept this provision which had been intended him, prompted her in a short time to another project, a project worthy of such a disposition. She endeavoured to rid herself from the danger of being at any time made known to him, by sending him secretly to the American plantations.

By whose kindness this scheme was counteracted, or by what interposition she was induced to lay aside her design, I know not; it is not improbable that the Lady Mason might persuade or compel her to desist, or perhaps she could not easily find accomplices wicked enough to concur in so cruel an action; for it may be conceived, that those who had by a long gradation of guilt hardened their hearts against the sense of common wickedness, would yet be shocked at the design of a mother to expose her son to slavery and want, to expose him without interest, and without provocation; and Savage might on this occasion find protectors and advocates among those who had long traded in crimes, and whom compassion had never touched before.

Being hindered, by whatever means, from banishing him into another country, she formed soon after a scheme for burying him in poverty and obscurity in his own; and, that his station of life, if not the place of his residence, might keep him for ever at a distance from her, she ordered him to be placed with a shoemaker in Holborn, that, after the usual time of trial, he might become his apprentice.

It is generally reported, that this project was for some time successful, and that Savage was employed at the awl longer than he was willing to confess; nor was it perhaps any great advantage to him, that an unexpected discovery determined him to quit his occupation.

About this time his nurse, who had always treated him as her own son, died; and it was natural for him to take care of those effects, which by her death were, as he imagined, become his own; he therefore went to her house, opened her boxes, and examined her papers, among which he found some letters written to her by the Lady Mason, which informed him of his birth and the reasons for which it was concealed.

He was no longer satisfied with the employment which had been allotted him, but thought he had a right to share the affluence of his mother; and therefore without scruple applied to her as her son, and made use of every art to awaken her tenderness, and attract her regard. But neither his letters, nor the interposition of those friends which his merit or his distress procured him, made any impression upon her mind. She still resolved to neglect, though she could no longer disown him.

It was to no purpose that he frequently solicited her to admit him to see her; she avoided him with the most vigilant precaution, and ordered him to be excluded from her house, by whomsoever he might be introduced, and what reason soever he might give for entering it.

Savage was at the same time so touched with the discovery of his real mother, that it was his frequent practice to walk in the dark evenings for several hours before her door, in hopes of seeing her as she might come by accident to the window, or cross her apartment with a candle in her hand.

But all his assiduity and tenderness were without effect, for he could neither soften her heart, nor open her hand, and was reduced to the utmost miseries of want, while he was endeavouring to awaken the affection of a mother: He was therefore obliged to seek some other means of support; and, having no profession, became by necessity an author.

At this time the attention of all the literary world was engrossed by the Bangorian controversy, which filled the press with pamphlets, and the coffee-houses with disputants. Of this subject, as most popular, he made choice for his first attempt, and without any other knowledge of the question than he had casually collected from conversation, published a poem against the Bishop.[2]

What was the success or merit of this performance, I know not; it was probably lost among the innumerable pamphlets to which that dispute gave occasion. Mr. Savage was himself in a little time ashamed of it, and endeavoured to suppress it, by destroying all the copies that he could collect.

He then attempted a more gainful kind of writing, and in his eighteenth year offered to the stage a comedy borrowed from a Spanish plot, which was refused by the players, and was therefore given by him to Mr. Bullock, who, having more interest, made some slight alterations, and brought it upon the stage,[3] under the title of WOMAN'S A RIDDLE, but allowed the unhappy author no part of the profit.

Not discouraged, however, at his repulse, he wrote two years afterwards LOVE IN A VEIL, another comedy, borrowed likewise from the Spanish, but with little better success than before; for though it was received and acted,[4] yet it appeared so late in the year, that the author obtained no other advantage from it, than the acquaintance of Sir Richard Steele, and Mr. Wilks, by whom he was pitied, caressed, and relieved.

Sir Richard Steele, having declared in his favour with all the ardour of benevolence which constituted his character, promoted his interest with the utmost zeal, related his misfortunes, applauded his merit, took all the opportunities of recommending him, and asserted, that "the inhumanity of his mother had given him a right to find every good man his father."

Nor was Mr. Savage admitted to his acquaintance only, but to his confidence, of which he sometimes related an instance too extraordinary to be omitted, as it affords a very just idea of his patron's character.

He was once desired by Sir Richard, with an air of the utmost importance, to come very early to his house the next morning. Mr. Savage came as he had promised, found the chariot at the door, and Sir Richard waiting for him, and ready to go out. What was intended, and whither they were to go, Savage could not conjecture, and was not willing to enquire; but immediately seated himself with Sir Richard; the coachman was ordered to drive, and they hurried with the utmost expedition to Hyde-Park Corner, where they stopped at a petty tavern, and retired to a private room. Sir Richard than informed him, that he intended to publish a pamphlet, and that he had desired him to come thither that he might write for him. They soon sat down to the work. Sir Richard dictated, and Savage wrote, till the dinner that had been ordered was put upon the table. Savage was surprized at the meanness of the entertainment, and after some hesitation ventured to ask for wine, which Sir Richard, not without reluctance, ordered to be brought. They then finished their dinner, and proceeded in their pamphlet, which they concluded in the afternoon.

Mr. Savage then imagined his task over, and expected that Sir Richard would call for the reckoning, and return home; but his expectations deceived him, for Sir Richard told him, that he was without money, and that the pamphlet must be sold before the dinner could be paid for; and Savage was therefore obliged to go and offer their new production to sale for two guineas, which with some difficulty he obtained. Sir Richard then returned home, having retired that day only to avoid his creditors, and composed the pamphlet only to discharge his reckoning.

Mr. Savage related another fact equally uncommon, which, though it has no relation to his life, ought to be preserved. Sir Richard Steele having one day invited to his house a great number of persons of the first quality, they were surprized at the number of liveries which surrounded the table; and after dinner, when wine and mirth had set them free from the observation of rigid ceremony, one of them enquired of Sir Richard, how such an expensive train of domestics could be consistent with his fortune. Sir Richard very frankly confessed, that they were fellows of whom he would very willingly be rid. And being then asked, why he did not discharge them, declared that they were bailiffs who had introduced themselves with an execution, and whom, since he could not send them away, he had thought it convenient to embellish with liveries, that they might do him credit while they staid.

His friends were diverted with the expedient, and, by paying the debt, discharged their attendance, having obliged Sir Richard to promise that they should never again find him graced with a retinue of the same kind.

Under such a tutor, Mr. Savage was not likely to learn prudence or frugality; and perhaps many of the misfortunes, which the want of those virtues brought upon him in the following parts of his life, might be justly imputed to so unimproving an example.

Nor did the kindness of Sir Richard end in common favours. He proposed to have established him in some settled scheme of life, and to have contracted a kind of alliance with him, by marrying him to a natural daughter, on whom he intended to bestow a thousand pounds. But though he was always lavish of future bounties, he conducted his affairs in such a manner, that he was very seldom able to keep his promises, or execute his own intentions; and, as he was never able to raise the sum which he had offered, the marriage was delayed. In the mean time he was officiously informed, that Mr. Savage had ridiculed him; by which he was so much exasperated, that he withdrew the allowance which he had paid him, and never afterwards admitted him to his house.

It is not indeed unlikely that Savage might by his imprudence, expose himself to the malice of a talebearer; for his patron had many follies, which, as his discernment easily discovered, his imagination might sometimes incite him to mention too ludicrously. A little knowledge of the world is sufficient to discover that such weakness is very common, and that there are few who do not sometimes, in the wantonness of thoughtless mirth, or the heat of transient resentment, speak of their friends and benefactors with levity and contempt, though in their cooler moments they want neither sense of their kindness, nor reverence for their virtue. The fault therefore of Mr. Savage was rather negligence than ingratitude; but Sir Richard must likewise be acquitted of severity, for who is there that can patiently bear contempt from one whom he has relieved and supported, whose establishment he has laboured, and whose interest he has promoted?

He was now again abandoned to fortune, without any other friend than Mr. Wilks; a man, who, whatever were his abilities or skill as an actor, deserves at least to be remembered for his virtues, which are not often to be found in the world, and perhaps less often in his profession than in others. To be humane, generous, and candid, is a very high degree of merit in any case; but those qualities deserve still greater praise, when they are found in that condition, which makes almost every other man, for whatever reason, contemptuous, insolent, petulant, selfish, and brutal.[5]

As Mr. Wilks was one of those to whom calamity seldom complained without relief, he naturally took an unfortunate wit into his protection, and not only assisted him in any casual distresses, but continued an equal and steady kindness to the time of his death.

By his interposition Mr. Savage once obtained from his mother fifty pounds,[6] and a promise of one hundred and fifty more; but it was the fate of this unhappy man, that few promises of any advantage to him were performed. His mother was infected among others with the general madness of the South Sea traffic; and, having been disappointed in her expectations, refused to pay what perhaps nothing but the prospect of sudden affluence prompted her to promise.

Being thus obliged to depend upon the friendship of Mr. Wilks, he was consequently an assiduous frequenter of the theatres; and in a short time the amusements of the stage took such possession of his mind, that he never was absent from a play in several years.

This constant attendance naturally procured for him the acquaintance of the players, and, among others, of Mrs. Oldfield,[7] who was so much pleased with his conversation, and touched with his misfortunes, that she allowed him a settled pension of fifty pounds a year, which was during her life regularly paid.

That this act of generosity may receive its due praise, and that the good actions of Mrs. Oldfield may not be sullied by her general character, it is proper to mention what Mr. Savage often declared in the strongest terms, that he never saw her alone, or in any other place than behind the scenes.

At her death he endeavoured to show his gratitude in the most decent manner, by wearing mourning as for a mother; but did not celebrate her in elegies, because he knew that too great profusion of praise would only have revived those faults which his natural equity did not allow him to think less, because they were committed by one who favoured him; but of which, though his virtue would not endeavour to palliate them, his gratitude would not suffer him to prolong the memory, or diffuse the censure.

In his *Wanderer*, he has indeed taken an opportunity of mentioning her, but celebrates her not for her virtue, but her beauty, an excellence which none ever denied her: this is the only encomium with which he has rewarded her liberality, and perhaps he has even in this been too lavish of his praise. He seems to have thought, that never to mention his benefactress would have an appearance of ingratitude, though to have dedicated any particular performance to her memory would have only betrayed an officious partiality, that, without exalting her character, would have depressed his own.

He had sometimes, by the kindness of Mr. Wilks, the advantage of a benefit,[8] on which occasions he often received uncommon marks of regard and compassion; and was once told by the Duke of Dorset, that it was just to consider him as an injured nobleman, and that in his opinion the nobility ought to think themselves obliged, without solicitation, to take every opportunity of supporting him by their countenance and patronage. But he had generally the mortification to hear that the whole interest of his mother was employed to frustrate his applications, and that she never left any expedient untried, by which he might be cut off from the possibility of supporting life. The same disposition she endeavoured to diffuse among all those over whom nature or fortune gave her any influence, and indeed succeeded too well in her design; but could not always propagate her effrontery with her cruelty, for some of those, whom she incited against him, were ashamed of their own conduct, and boasted of that relief which they never gave him.

In this censure I do not indiscriminately involve all his relations; for he has mentioned with gratitude the humanity of one Lady, whose name I am now unable to recollect, and to whom therefore I cannot pay the praises which she deserves for having acted well in opposition to influence, precept, and example.

The punishment which our laws inflict upon those parents who murder their infants is well known, nor has its justice ever been contested; but if they deserve death who destroy a child in its birth, what pains can be severe enough for her who forbears to destroy him only to inflict sharper miseries upon him; who prolongs his life only to make him miserable; and who exposes him, without care and without pity, to the malice of oppression, the caprices of chance, and the temptations of poverty; who rejoices to see him overwhelmed with calamities; and, when his own industry, or the charity of others, has enabled him to rise for a short time above his miseries, plunges him again into his former distress?

The kindness of his friends not affording him any constant supply, and the prospect of improving his fortune by enlarging his acquaintance necessarily leading him to places of expence, he found it necessary to endeavour once more at dramatic poetry,[9] for which he was now better qualified by a more extensive knowledge, and longer observation. But having been unsuccessful in comedy, though rather for want of opportunities than genius, he resolved now to try whether he should not be more fortunate in exhibiting a tragedy.

The story which he chose for the subject, was that of Sir Thomas Overbury, a story well adapted to the stage, though perhaps not far enough removed from the present age, to admit properly the fictions necessary to complete the plan: for the mind, which naturally loves truth, is always most offended with the violation of those truths of which we are most certain; and we of course conceive those facts most certain, which approach nearest to our own time.

Out of this story he formed a tragedy, which, if the circumstances in which he wrote it be considered, will afford at once an uncommon proof of strength of genius, and evenness of mind, of a serenity not to be ruffled, and an imagination not to be suppressed.

During a considerable part of the time in which he was employed upon this performance, he was without lodging, and often without meat nor had he any other conveniences for study than the fields or the street allowed him; there he used to walk and form his speeches, and afterwards step into a shop, beg for a few moments the use of the pen and ink, and write down what he had composed, upon paper which he had picked up by accident.

If the performance of a writer thus distressed is not perfect, its faults ought surely to be imputed to a cause very different from want of genius, and must rather excite pity than provoke censure.

But when under these discouragements the tragedy was finished, there yet remained the labour of introducing it on the stage, an undertaking, which, to an ingenuous mind, was in a very high degree vexatious and disgusting; for, having little interest or reputation, he was obliged to submit himself wholly to the players, and admit, with whatever reluctance, the emendations of Mr. Gibber, which he always considered as the disgrace of his performance.

He had indeed in Mr. Hill[10] another critic of a very different class, from whose friendship he received great assistance on many occasions, and whom he never mentioned but with the utmost tenderness and regard. He had been for some time distinguished by him with very particular kindness, and on this occasion it was natural to apply to him as an author of an established character. He therefore sent this tragedy to him, with a short copy of verses, in which he desired his correction. Mr. Hill, whose humanity and politeness are generally known, readily complied with his request; but as he is remarkable for singularity of sentiment, and bold experiments in language, Mr. Savage did not think his play much improved by his innovation, and had even at that time the courage to reject several passages which he could not approve; and, what is still more laudable, Mr. Hill had the generosity not to resent the neglect of his alterations, but wrote the prologue and epilogue, in which he touches on the circumstances of the author with great tenderness.

After all these obstructions and compliances, he was only able to bring his play upon the stage in the summer, when the chief actors had retired, and the rest were in possession of the house for their own advantage. Among these, Mr. Savage was admitted to play the part of Sir Thomas Overbury, by which he gained no great reputation, the theatre being a province for which nature seemed not to have designed him; for neither his voice, look, nor gesture, were such as were expected on the stage; and he was so much ashamed of having been reduced to appear as a player, that he always blotted out his name from the list, when a copy of his tragedy was to be shown to his friends.

In the publication of his performance he was more successful, for the rays of genius that glimmered in it, that glimmered through all the mists which poverty and Gibber had been able to spread over it, procured him the notice and esteem of many persons eminent for their rank, their virtue, and their wit.

Of this play, acted, printed, and dedicated, the accumulated profits arose to an hundred pounds, which he thought at that time a very large sum, having been never master of so much before.

In the Dedication, for which he received ten guineas, there is nothing remarkable. The Preface contains a very liberal encomium on the blooming excellences of Mr. Theophilus Gibber, which Mr. Savage could not in the latter part of his life see his friends about to read without snatching the play out of their hands. The generosity of Mr. Hill did not end on this occasion; for afterwards, when Mr. Savage's necessities returned, he encouraged a subscription to a Miscellany of Poems in a very extraordinary manner, by publishing his story in the *Plain Dealer,*[11] with some affecting lines, which he asserts to have been written by Mr. Savage upon the treatment received by him from his mother, but of which he was himself the author, as Mr. Savage afterwards declared. These lines, and the paper in which they were inserted, had a very powerful effect upon all but his mother, whom, by making her cruelty more public, they only hardened in her aversion.

Mr. Hill not only promoted the subscription to the Miscellany, but furnished likewise the greatest part of the Poems of which it is composed, and particularly *The Happy Man*, which he published as a specimen.

The subscriptions of those whom these papers should influence to patronize merit in distress, without any other solicitation, were directed to be left at Button's coffee-house; and Mr. Savage going thither a few days afterwards, without expectation of any effect from his proposal, found to his surprise seventy guineas, which had been sent him in consequence of the compassion excited by Mr. Hill's pathetic representation.

To this Miscellany he wrote a Preface, in which he gives an account of his mother's cruelty in a very uncommon strain of humour, and with a gaiety of imagination, which the success of his subscript ion probably produced.

The Dedication is addressed to the Lady Mary Wortley Montagu, whom he flatters without reserve, and, to confess the truth, with very little art. The same observation may be extended to all his Dedications: his compliments are constrained and violent, heaped together without the grace of order, or the decency of introduction; he seems to have written his panegyrics for the perusal only of his patrons, and to have imagined that he had no other task than to pamper them with praises however gross, and that flattery would make its way to the heart, without the assistance of elegance or invention.

Soon afterwards, the death of the king furnished a general subject for a poetical contest, in which Mr. Savage engaged, and is allowed to have carried the prize of honour from his competitors; but I know not whether he gained by his performance any other advantage than the increase of his reputation; though it must certainly have been with farther views that he prevailed upon himself to attempt a species of writing, of which all the topics had been long before exhausted, and which was made at once difficult by the multitudes that failed in it, and those that had succeeded.

He was now advancing in reputation, and though frequently involved in very distressful perplexities, appeared however to be gaining upon mankind, when both his fame and his life were endangered by an event, of which it is not yet determined, whether it ought to be mentioned as a crime or a calamity.

On the 20th of November 1727, Mr. Savage came from Richmond, where he then lodged, that he might pursue his studies with less interruption, with an intent to discharge another lodging which he had in Westminster; and accidentally meeting two gentlemen his acquaintances, whose names were Merchant and Gregory, he went in with them to a neighbouring coffee-house, and sat drinking till it was late, it being in no time of Mr. Savage's life any part of his character to be the first of the company that desired to separate. He would willingly have gone to bed in the same house; but there was not room for the whole company, and therefore they agreed to ramble about the streets, and divert themselves with such amusements as should offer themselves till morning.

In this walk they happened unluckily to discover a light in Robinson's coffee-house, near Charing–cross, and therefore went in. Merchant, with some rudeness, demanded a room, and was told that there was a good fire in the next parlour, which the company were about to leave, being then paying their reckoning. Merchant, not satisfied with this answer, rushed into the room, and was followed by his companions. He then petulantly placed himself between the company and the fire, and soon after kicked down the table. This produced a quarrel, swords were drawn on both sides, and one Mr. James Sinclair was killed. Savage, having wounded likewise a maid that held him, forced his way with Merchant out of the house; but being intimidated and confused, without resolution either to fly or stay, they were taken in a back-court by one of the company and some soldiers, whom he had called to his assistance.

Being secured and guarded that night, they were in the morning carried before three justices, who committed them to the Gatehouse, from whence, upon the death of Mr. Sinclair, which happened the same day, they were removed in the night to Newgate, where they were however treated with some distinction, exempted from the ignominy of chains, and confined, not among the common criminals, but in the Press-yard.

When the day of trial came, the court was crowded in a very unusual manner, and the public appeared to interest itself as in a cause of general concern. The witnesses against Mr. Savage and his friends were, the woman who kept the house, which was a house of illfame, and her maid, the men who were in the room with Mr. Sinclair, and a woman of the town, who had been drinking with them, and with whom one of them had been seen in bed. They swore in general, that Merchant gave the provocation, which Savage and Gregory drew their swords to justify; that Savage drew first, and that he stabbed Sinclair when he was not in a posture of defence, or while Gregory commanded his sword; that after he had given the thrust he turned pale, and would have retired, but that the maid clung round him, and one of the company endeavoured to detain him, from whom he broke, by cutting the maid on the head, but was afterwards taken in a court.

There was some difference in their depositions; one did not see Savage give the wound, another saw it given when Sinclair held his point towards the ground; and the woman of the town asserted, that she did not see Sinclair's sword at all: this difference however was very far from amounting to inconsistency; but it was sufficient to shew, that the hurry of the dispute was such, that it was not easy to discover the truth with relation to particular circumstances, and that therefore some deductions were to be made from the credibility of the testimonies.

Sinclair had declared several times before his death, that he received his wound from Savage, nor did Savage at his trial deny the fact, but endeavoured partly to extenuate it, by urging the suddenness of the whole action, and the impossibility of any ill design, or premeditated malice, and partly to justify it by the necessity of self-defence, and the hazard of his own life, if he had lost that opportunity of giving the thrust: he observed, that neither reason nor law obliged a man to wait for the blow which was threatened, and which, if he should suffer it, he might never be able to return; that it was always allowable to prevent an assault, and to preserve life, by taking away that of the adversary, by whom it was endangered.

With regard to the violence with which he endeavoured to escape, he declared, that it was not his design to fly from justice, or decline a trial, but to avoid the expences and severities of a prison; and that he intended to have appeared at the bar without compulsion.

This defence, which took up more than an hour, was heard by the multitude that thronged the court with the most attentive and respectful silence: those who thought he ought not to be acquitted, owned that applause could not be refused him; and those who before pitied his misfortunes, now reverenced his abilities.

The witnesses which appeared against him were proved to be persons of characters which did not entitle them to much credit; a common strumpet, a woman by whom strumpets were entertained, and a man by whom they were supported; and the character of Savage was by several persons of distinction asserted to be that of a modest inoffensive man, not inclined to broils, or to insolence, and who had, to that time, been only known for his misfortunes and his wit.

Had his audience been his judges, he had undoubtedly been acquitted; but Mr. Page, who was then upon the bench, treated him with his usual insolence and severity, and when he had summed up the evidence, endeavoured to exasperate the jury, as Mr. Savage used to relate it, with this eloquent harangue:

'Gentlemen of the jury, you are to consider that Mr. Savage is a very great man, a much greater man than you or I, gentlemen of the jury; that he wears very fine clothes, much finer clothes than you or I, gentlemen of the jury; that he has abundance of money in his pocket, much more money than you or I, gentlemen of the jury; but, gentlemen of the jury, is it not a very hard case, gentlemen of the jury, that Mr. Savage should therefore kill you or me, gentlemen of the jury?'

Mr. Savage, hearing his defence thus misrepresented, and the men who were to decide his fate incited against him by invidious comparisons, resolutely asserted, that his cause was not candidly explained, and began to recapitulate what he had before said with regard to his condition, and the necessity of endeavouring to escape the expences of imprisonment; but the judge having ordered him to be silent, and repeated his orders without effect, commanded that he should be taken from the bar by force.

The jury then heard the opinion of the judge, that good characters were of no weight against positive evidence, though they might turn the scale where it was doubtful; and that though, when two men attack each other, the death of either is only manslaughter; but where one is the aggressor, as in the case before them, and, in pursuance of his first attack, kills the other, the law supposes action, however sudden, to be malicious. They then deliberated upon their verdict, and determined that Mr. Savage and Mr. Gregory were guilty of murder, and Mr. Merchant, who had no sword, only of manslaughter.

Thus ended this memorable trial, which lasted eight hours. Mr. Savage and Mr. Gregory were conducted back to prison, where they were more closely confined, and loaded with irons of fifty pounds weight: four days afterwards they were sent back to the court to receive sentence; on which occasion Mr. Savage made, as far as it could be retained in memory, the following speech.

'It is now, my Lord, too late to offer any thing by way of defence or vindication; nor can we expect from your Lordships, in this court, but the sentence which the law requires you, as judges, to pronounce against men of our calamitous condition.—But we are also persuaded, that as mere men, and out of this seat of rigorous justice, you are susceptive of the tender possessions, and too humane, not to commiserate the unhappy situation of those, whom the law sometimes perhaps—exacts—from you to pronounce upon. No doubt you distinguish between offences, which arise out of premeditation, and a disposition habituated to vice or immorality, and transgressions, which are the unhappy and unforeseen effects of casual absence of reason, and sudden impulse of passion: we therefore hope you will contribute all you can to an extension of that mercy, which the gentlemen of the jury have been pleased to shew Mr. Merchant, who (allowing facts as sworn against us by the evidence) has led us into this our calamity. I hope this will not be construed, as if we meant to reflect upon that gentleman, or remove any thing from us upon him, or that we repine the more at our fate, because he has no participation of it: No, my Lord! For my part, I declare nothing could more soften my grief, than to be without any companion in so great a misfortune.[12]

Mr. Savage had now no hopes of life, but from the mercy of the crown, which was very earnestly solicited by his friends, and which, with whatever difficulty the story may obtain belief, was obstructed only by his mother.

To prejudice the Queen against him, she made use of an incident, which was omitted in the order of time, that it might be mentioned together with the purpose which it was made to serve. Mr. Savage, when he had discovered his birth, had an incessant desire to speak to his mother, who always avoided him in publick, and refused him admission into her house. One evening walking, as it was his custom, in the street that she inhabited, he saw the door of her house by accident open; he entered it, and finding no person in the passage to hinder him, went up stairs to salute her. She discovered him before he could enter her chamber, alarmed the family with the most distressful outcries, and when she had by her screams gathered them about her, ordered them to drive out of the house that villain, who had forced himself in upon her, and endeavoured to murder her. Savage, who had attempted with the most submissive tenderness to soften her rage, hearing her utter so detestable an accusation, thought it prudent to retire; and, I believe, never attempted afterwards to speak to her.

But, shocked as he was with her falsehood and her cruelty, he imagined that she intended no other use of her lye, than to set herself free from his embraces and solicitations, and was very far from suspecting that she would treasure it in her memory, as an instrument of future wickedness, or that she would endeavour for this fictitious assault to deprive him of his life.

But when the Queen was solicited for his pardon, and informed of the severe treatment which he had suffered from his judge, she answered, that, however unjustifiable might be the manner of his trial, or whatever extenuation the action for which he was condemned might admit, she could not think that man a proper object of the King's mercy, who had been capable of entering his mother's house in the night, with an intent to murder her.

By whom this atrocious calumny had been transmitted to the Queen; whether she that invented had the front to relate it; whether she found any one weak enough to credit it, or corrupt enough to concur with her in her hateful design, I know not: but methods had been taken to persuade the Queen so strongly of the truth of it, that she for a long time refused to hear any of those who petitioned for his life.

Thus had Savage perished by the evidence of a bawd, a strumpet, and his mother, had not justice and compassion procured him an advocate of rank too great to be rejected unheard, and of virtue too eminent to be heard without being believed. His merit and his calamities happened to reach the ear of the Countess of Hertford, who engaged in his support with all the tenderness that is excited by pity, and all the zeal which is kindled by generosity; and, demanding an audience of the Queen, laid before her the whole series of his mother's cruelty, exposed the improbability of an accusation by which he was charged with an intent to commit a murder that could produce no advantage, and soon convinced her how little his former conduct could deserve to be mentioned as a reason for extraordinary severity.

The interposition of this lady was so successful, that he was soon after admitted to bail, and, on the 9th of March 1728, pleaded the King's pardon.

It is natural to enquire upon what motives his mother could prosecute him in a manner so outrageous and implacable; for what reason she could employ all the arts of malice, and all the snares of calumny, to take away the life of her own son, of a son who never injured her, who was never supported by her expence, nor obstructed any prospect of pleasure or advantage; why she should endeavour to destroy him by a lye—a lye which could not gain credit, but must vanish of itself at the first moment of examination, and of which only this can be said to make it probable, that it may be observed from her conduct, that the most execrable crimes are sometimes committed without apparent temptation.

This mother is still alive, and may perhaps even yet, though her malice was so often defeated, enjoy the pleasure of reflecting, that the life, which she often endeavoured to destroy, was at least shortened by her maternal offices; that though she could not transport her son to the plantations, bury him in the shop of a mechanic, or hasten the hand of the public executioner, she has yet had the satisfaction of imbittering all his hours, and forcing him into exigences that hurried on his death.

It is by no means necessary to aggravate the enormity of this woman's conduct, by placing it in opposition to that of the Countess of Hertford; no one can fail to observe how much more amiable it is to relieve, than to oppress, and to rescue innocence from destruction, than to destroy without an injury.

Mr. Savage, during his imprisonment, his trial, and the time in which he lay under sentence of death, behaved with great firmness and equality of mind, and confirmed by his fortitude the esteem of those who before admired him for his abilities. The peculiar circumstances of his life were made more generally known by a short account,[13] which was then published, and of which several thousands were in a few weeks dispersed over the nation: and the compassion of mankind operated so powerfully in his favour, that he was enabled, by frequent presents, not only to support himself, but to assist Mr. Gregory in prison; and, when he was pardoned and released, he found the number of his friends not lessened.

The nature of the act for which he had been tried was in itself doubtful; of the evidences which appeared against him, the character of the man was not unexceptionable, that of the woman notoriously infamous: she, whose testimony chiefly influenced the jury to condemn him, afterwards retracted her assertions. He always himself denied that he was drunk, as had been generally reported. Mr. Gregory, who is now Collector of Antigua, is said to declare him far less criminal than he was imagined, even by some who favoured him: and Page himself afterwards confessed, that he had treated him with uncommon rigour. When all these particulars are rated together, perhaps the memory of Savage may not be much sullied by his trial.

Some time after he had obtained his liberty, he met in the street the woman that had sworn with so much malignity against him. She informed him, that she was in distress, and, with a degree of confidence not easily attainable, desired him to relieve her. He, instead of insulting her misery, and taking pleasure in the calamities of one who had brought his life into danger, reproved her gently for her perjury; and changing the only guinea that he had, divided it equally between her and himself.

This is an action which in some ages would have made a saint, and perhaps in others a hero, and which, without any hyperbolical encomiums, must be allowed to be an instance of uncommon generosity, an act of complicated virtue; by which he at once relieved the poor, corrected the vicious, and forgave an enemy; by which he at once remitted the strongest provocations, and exercised the most ardent charity.

Compassion was indeed the distinguishing quality of Savage; he never appeared inclined to take advantage of weakness, to attack the defenceless, or to press upon the falling: whoever was distressed was certain at least of his good wishes; and when he could give no assistance to extricate them from misfortunes, he endeavoured to sooth them by sympathy and tenderness.

But when his heart was not softened by the sight of misery, he was sometimes obstinate in his resentment, and did not quickly lose the remembrance of an injury. He always continued to speak with anger of the insolence and partiality of Page, and a short time before his death revenged it by a satire.[14]

It is natural to enquire in what terms Mr. Savage spoke of this fatal action, when the danger was over, and he was under no necessity of using any art to set his conduct in the fairest light. He was not willing to dwell upon it; and, if he transiently mentioned it, appeared neither to consider himself as a murderer, nor as a man wholly free from the guilt of blood. How much and how long he regretted it, appeared in a poem which he published many years afterwards. On occasion of a copy of verses, in which the failings of good men were recounted, and in which the author had endeavoured to illustrate his position, that "the best may sometimes deviate from virtue," by an instance of murder committed by Savage in the heat of wine, Savage remarked, that it was no very just representation of a good man, to suppose him liable to drunkenness, and disposed in his riots to cut throats.

He was now indeed at liberty, but was, as before, without any other support that accidental favours and uncertain patronage afforded him; sources by which he was sometimes very liberally supplied, and which at other times were suddenly stopped; so that he spent his life between want and plenty; or, what was yet worse, between beggary and extravagance; for as whatever he received was the gift of chance, which might as well favour him at one time as another, he was tempted to squander what he had, because he always hoped to be immediately supplied.

Another cause of his profusion was the absurd kindness of his friends, who at once rewarded and enjoyed his abilities, by treating him at taverns, and habituating him to pleasures which he could not afford to enjoy, and which he was not able to deny himself, though he purchased the luxury of a single night by the anguish of cold and hunger for a week.

The experience of these inconveniences determined him to endeavour after some settled income, which, having long found submission and intreaties fruitless, he attempted to extort from his mother by rougher methods. He had now, as he acknowledged, lost that tenderness for her, which the whole series of her cruelty had not been able wholly to repress, till he found, by the efforts which she made for his destruction, that she was not content with refusing to assist him, and being neutral in his struggles with poverty, but was as ready to snatch every opportunity of adding to his misfortunes, and that she was to be considered as an enemy implacably malicious, whom nothing but his blood could satisfy. He therefore threatened to harass her with lampoons, and to publish a copious narrative of her conduct, unless she consented to purchase an exemption from infamy, by allowing him a pension.

This expedient proved successful. Whether shame still survived, though virtue was extinct, or whether her relations had more delicacy than herself, and imagined that some of the darts which satire might point at her would glance upon them; Lord Tyrconnel, whatever were his motives, upon his promise to lay aside his design of exposing the cruelty of his mother, received him into his family, treated him as his equal, and engaged to allow him a pension of two hundred pounds a year.[15]

This was the golden part of Mr. Savage's life; and for some time he had no reason to complain of fortune; his appearance was splendid, his expences large, and his acquaintance extensive. He was courted by all who endeavoured to be thought men of genius, and caressed by all who valued themselves upon a refined taste. To admire Mr. Savage, was a proof of discernment; and to be acquainted with him, was a title to poetical reputation. His presence was sufficient to make any place of publick entertainment popular: and his approbation and example constituted the fashion. So powerful is genius, when it is invested with the glitter of affluence! Men willingly pay to fortune that regard which they owe to merit, and are pleased when they have an opportunity at once of gratifying their vanity, and practising their duty.

This interval of prosperity furnished him with opportunities of enlarging his knowledge of human nature, by contemplating life from its highest gradations to its lowest; and, had he afterwards applied to dramatic poetry, he would perhaps not have had many superiors; for as he never suffered any scene to pass before his eyes without notice, he had treasured in his mind all the different combinations of passions, and the innumerable mixtures of vice and virtue, which distinguish one character from another; and, as his conception was strong, his expressions were clear, he easily received impressions from objects, and very forcibly transmitted them to others.

Of his exact observations on human life he has left a proof, which would do honour to the greatest names, in a small pamphlet, called *The Author to be let*, where he introduces Iscariot Hackney, a prostitute scribbler, giving an account of his birth, his education, his disposition and morals, habits of life, and maxims of conduct. In the introduction are related many secret histories of the petty writers of that time, but sometimes mixed with ungenerous reflections on their birth, their circumstances, or those of their relations; nor can it be denied, that some passages are such as Iscariot Hackney might himself have produced.

He was accused likewise of living in an appearance of friendship with some whom he satirised, and of making use of the confidence which he gained by a seeming kindness to discover failings and expose them: it must be confessed, that Mr. Savage's esteem was no very certain possession, and that he would lampoon at one time those whom he had praised at another.

It may be alleged, that the same man may change his principles, and that he, who was once deservedly commended, may be afterwards satirised with equal justice, or that the poet was dazzled with the appearance of virtue, and found the man whom he had celebrated, when he had an opportunity of examining him more narrowly, unworthy of the panegyrick which he had too hastily bestowed; and that, as a false satire ought to be recanted, for the sake of him whose reputation may be injured, false praise ought likewise to be obviated, lest the distinction between vice and virtue should be lost, lest a bad man should be trusted upon the credit of his encomiast, or lest others should endeavour to obtain the like praises by the same means.

But though these excuses may be often plausible, and sometimes just, they are very seldom satisfactory to mankind; and the writer, who is not constant to his subject, quickly sinks into contempt, his satire loses its force, and his panegyrick, its value, and he is only considered at one time as a flatterer, and as a calumniator at another.

To avoid these imputations, it is only necessary to follow the rules of virtue, and to preserve an unvaried regard to truth. For though it is undoubtedly possible that a man, however cautious, may be sometimes deceived by an artful appearance of virtue, or by false evidences of guilt, such errors will not be frequent; and it will be allowed, that the name of an author would never have been made contemptible, had no man ever said what he did not think, or misled others but when he was himself deceived.

If[16] *The Author to be let* was first published in a single pamphlet, and afterwards inserted in a collection of pieces relating to the *Dunciad*, which were addressed by Mr. Savage to the Earl of Middlesex, in a dedication which he was prevailed upon to sign, though he did not write it, and in which there are some positions, that the true author would perhaps not have published under his own name, and on which Mr. Savage afterwards reflected with no great satisfaction; the enumeration of the bad effects of the uncontroled freedom of the press, and the assertion that the "liberties taken by the writers of Journals with their superiors were exorbitant and unjustifiable," very ill became men, who have themselves not always shewn the exactest regard to the laws of subordination in their writings, and who have often satirised those that at least thought themselves their superiors, as they were eminent for their hereditary rank, and employed in the highest offices of the kingdom. But this is only an instance of that partiality which almost every man indulges with regard to himself; the liberty of the press is a blessing when we are inclined to write against others, and a calamity when we find ourselves overborne by the multitude of our assailants; as the power of the crown is always thought too great by those who suffer by its influence and too little by those in whose favour it is exerted; and a standing army is generally accounted necessary by those who command, and dangerous and oppressive by those who support it.

Mr. Savage was likewise very far from believing, that the letters[17] annexed to each species of bad poets in the *Bathos*, were, as he was directed to assert, "set down at random;" for when he was charged by one of his friends with putting his name to such an improbability, he had no answer to make, than that "he did not think of it;" and his friends had too much tenderness to reply, that next to the crime of writing contrary to what he thought, was that of writing without thinking.

After having remarked what is false in this dedication, it is proper that I observe the impartiality which I recommend, by declaring what Savage asserted, that the account of the circumstances which attended the publication of the Dunciad, however strange and improbable, was exactly true.

The publication of this piece at this time raised Mr. Savage a great number of enemies among those that were attacked by Mr. Pope, with whom he was considered as a kind of confederate, and whom he was suspected of supplying with private intelligence and secret incidents: so that the ignominy of an informer was added to the terror of a satirist.

That he was not altogether free from literary hypocrisy, and that he sometimes spoke one thing, and wrote another, cannot be denied; because he himself confessed, that, when he lived in great familiarity with Dennis, he wrote an epigram against him.[18]

Mr. Savage however set all the malice of all the pigmy writers at defiance, and thought the friendship of Mr. Pope cheaply purchased by being exposed to their censure and their hatred; nor had he any reason to repent of the preference, for he found Mr. Pope a steady and unalienable friend almost to the end of his life.

About this time, notwithstanding his avowed neutrality with regard to party, he published a panegyrick on Sir Robert Walpole, for which he was rewarded by him with twenty guineas, a sum not very large, if either the excellence of the performance, or the affluence of the patron be considered; but greater than he afterwards obtained from a person of yet higher rank, and more desirous in appearance of being distinguished as a patron of literature.

As he was very far from approving the conduct of Sir Robert Walpole, and in conversation mentioned him sometimes with acrimony, and generally with contempt; as he was one of those who were always zealous in their assertions of the justice of the late opposition, jealous of the rights of the people, and alarmed by the long-continued triumph of the court; it was natural to ask him what could induce him to employ his poetry in praise of that man who was, in his opinion, an enemy to liberty, and an oppressor of his country? He alleged, that he was then dependent upon the Lord Tyrconnel, who was an implicit follower of the ministry; and that being enjoined by him, not without menaces, to write in praise of his leader, he had not resolution sufficient to sacrifice the pleasure of affluence to that of integrity.

On this, and on many other occasions, he was ready to lament the misery of living at the tables of other men, which was his fate from the beginning to the end of his life; for I know not whether he ever had, for three months together, a settled habitation, in which he could claim a right of residence.

To this unhappy state it is just to impute much of the inconsistancy of his conduct; for though a readiness to comply with the inclination of others was no part of his natural character, yet he was sometimes obliged to relax his obstinacy, and submit his own judgement, and even his virtue, to the government of those by whom he was supported: so that, if his miseries were sometimes the consequences of his faults, he ought not yet to be wholly excluded from compassion, because his faults were very often the effects of his misfortunes.

In this gay period of his life, while he was surrounded by affluence and pleasure, he published *The Wanderer*, a moral poem, of which the design is comprised in these lines:

> I fly all public care, all venal strife,
> To try the still compar'd with active life;
> To prove, by these the sons of men may owe
> The fruits of bliss to bursting clouds of woe;
> That ev'n calamity, by thought refin'd,
> Inspirits and adorns the thinking mind.

And more distinctly in the following passage:

> By woe, the soul to daring action swells;
> By woe, in plaintless patience it excels;
> From patience, prudent clear experience springs,
> And traces knowledge thro' the course of things!
> Thence hope is form'd, thence fortitude, success,
> Renown:—whate'er men covet and caress.

This performance was always considered by himself as his master-piece; and Mr. Pope, when he asked his opinion of it, told him, that he read it once over, and was not displeased with it, that it gave him more pleasure at the second perusal, and delighted him still more at the third.

It has been generally objected to *The Wanderer*, that the disposition of the parts is irregular; that the design is obscure, and the plan perplexed; that the images, however beautiful, succeed each other without order; and that the whole performance is not so much a regular fabrick, as a heap of shining materials thrown together by accident, which strikes rather with the solemn magnificence of a stupendous ruin, than the elegant grandeur of a finished pile.

This criticism is universal, and therefore it is reasonable to believe it at least in a great degree just; but Mr. Savage was always of a contrary opinion, and thought his drift could only be missed by negligence or stupidity, and that the whole plan was regular, and the parts distinct.

It was never denied to abound with strong representations of nature, and just observations upon life; and it may easily be observed, that most of his pictures have an evident tendency to illustrate his first great position, "that good is the consequence of evil." The sun that burns up the mountains, fructifies the vales;

the deluge that rushes down the broken rocks with dreadful impetuosity, is separated into purling brooks; and the rage of the hurricane purifies the air.

Even in this poem he has not been able to forbear one touch upon the cruelty of his mother, which, though remarkably delicate and tender, is a proof how deep an impression it had upon his mind.

This must be at least acknowledged, which ought to be thought equivalent to many other excellences, that this poem can promote no other purposes than those of virtue, and that it is written with a very strong sense of the efficacy of religion.

But my province is rather to give the history of Mr. Savage's performances, than to display their beauties, or to obviate the criticisms which they have occasioned; and therefore I shall not dwell upon the particular passages which deserve applause: I shall neither shew the excellence of his descriptions, nor expatiate on the terrifick portrait of suicide, nor point out the artful touches, by which he has distinguished the intellectual features of the rebels, who suffered death in his last canto. It is, however, proper to observe, that Mr. Savage always declared the characters wholly fictitious, and without the least allusion to any real persons or actions.

From a poem so diligently laboured, and so successfully finished, it might be reasonably expected that he should have gained considerable advantage; nor can it, without some degree of indignation and concern, be told, that he sold the copy for ten guineas, of which he afterwards returned two, that the two last sheets of the work might be reprinted, of which he had in his absence intrusted the correction to a friend, who was too indolent to perform it with accuracy.

A superstitious regard to the correction of his sheets was one of Mr. Savage's peculiarities: he often altered, revised, recurred to his first reading or punctuation, and again adopted the alteration; he was dubious and irresolute without end, as on a question of the last importance, and at last was seldom satisfied: the intrusion or omission of a comma was sufficient to discompose him, and he would lament an error of a single letter as a heavy calamity. In one of his letters relating to an impression of some verses, he remarks, that he had, with regard to the correction of the proof, "a spell upon him;" and indeed the anxiety with which he dwelt upon the minutest and most trifling niceties, deserved no other name than that of fascination.

That he sold so valuable a performance for so small a price, was not to be imputed either to necessity, by which the learned and ingenious are often obliged to submit to very hard conditions; or to avarice, by which the book-sellers are frequently incited to oppress that genius by which they are supported; but to that intemperate desire of pleasure, and habitual slavery to his passions, which involved him in many perplexities. He happened at that time to be engaged in the pursuit of some trifling gratification, and, being without money for the present occasion, sold his poem to the first bidder, and perhaps for the first price that was proposed, and would probably have been content with less, if less had been offered him.

This poem was addressed to the Lord Tyrconnel, not only in the first lines, but in a formal dedication filled with the highest strains of panegyrick, and the warmest professions of gratitude, but by no means remarkable for delicacy of connection or elegance of style.

These praises in a short time he found himself inclined to retract, being discarded by the man on whom he had bestowed them, and whom he then immediately discovered not to have deserved them. Of this quarrel, which every day made more bitter, Lord Tyrconnel and Mr. Savage assigned very different reasons, which might perhaps all in reality concur, though they were not all convenient to be alleged by either party. Lord Tyrconnel affirmed, that it was the constant practice of Mr. Savage to enter a tavern with any company that proposed it, drink the most expensive wines with great profusion, and when the reckoning was demanded, to be without money: If, as it often happened, his company were willing to defray his part, the affair ended, without any ill consequences; but, if they were refractory, and expected that the wine should be paid for by him that drank it, his method of composition was, to take them with him to his own apartment, assume the government of the house, and order the butler in an imperious manner to set the best wine in the cellar before his company, who often drank till they forgot the respect due to the house in which they were entertained, indulged themselves in the utmost extravagance of merriment, practised the most licentious frolicks, and committed all the outrages of drunkenness.

Nor was this the only charge which Lord Tyrconnel brought against him: Having given him a collection of valuable books, stamped with his own arms, he had the mortification to see them in a short time exposed to sale upon the stalls, it being usual with Mr. Savage, when he wanted a small sum, to take his books to the pawnbroker.

Whoever was acquainted with Mr. Savage easily credited both these accusations: for, having been obliged, from his first entrance into the world, to subsist upon expedients, affluence was not able to exalt him above them; and so much was he delighted with wine and conversation, and so long had he been accustomed to live by chance, that he would at any time to go to the tavern without scruple, and trust for the reckoning to the liberality of his company, and frequently of company to whom he was very little known. This conduct indeed very seldom drew upon him those inconveniences that might be feared by any other person; for his conversation was so entertaining, and his address so pleasing, that few thought the pleasure which they received from him dearly purchased, by paying for his wine. It was his peculiar happiness, that he scarcely ever found a stranger, whom he did not leave a friend; but it must likewise be added, that he had not often a friend long, without obliging him to become a stranger.

Mr. Savage, on the other hand, declared, that Lord Tyrconnel quarreled with him, because he would subtract from his own luxury and extravagance what he had promised to allow him, and that his resentment was only a plea for the violation of his promise: He asserted, that he had done nothing that ought to exclude him from that subsistence which he thought not so much a favour, as a debt, since it was offered him upon conditions, which he had never broken; and that his only fault was, that he could not be supported with nothing.

He acknowledged, that Lord Tyrconnel often exhorted him to regulate his method of life, and not to spend all his nights in taverns, and that he appeared very desirous, that he would pass those hours with him, which he so freely bestowed upon others. This demand Mr. Savage considered as a censure of his conduct, which he could never patiently bear; and which, in the latter and cooler part of his life, was so offensive to him, that he declared it as his resolution, "to spurn that friend who should presume to dictate to him;" and it is not likely, that in his earlier years he received admonitions with more calmness.

He was likewise inclined to resent such expectations, as tending to infringe his liberty, of which he was very jealous, when it was necessary to the gratification of his passions; and declared, that the request was still more unreasonable, as the company to which he was to have been confined was insupportably disagreeable. This assertion affords another instance of that inconsistency of his writings with his conversation, which was so often to be observed. He forgot how lavishly he had, in his Dedication to *The Wanderer*, extolled the delicacy and penetration, the humanity and generosity, the candour and politeness, of the man, whom, when he no longer loved him, he declared to be a wretch without understanding, without good-nature, and without justice; of whose name he thought himself obliged to leave no trace in any future edition of his writings; and accordingly blotted it out of that copy of *The Wanderer* which was in his hands.

During his continuance with the Lord Tyrconnel, he wrote *The Triumph of Health and Mirth*, on the recovery of Lady Tyrconnel from a languishing illness. This performance is remarkable, not only for the gaiety of the ideas, and the melody of the numbers, but for the agreeable fiction upon which it is formed. Mirth, overwhelmed with sorrow for the sickness of her favourite, takes a flight in quest of her sister Health, whom she finds reclined upon the brow of a lofty mountain, amidst the fragrance of perpetual spring, with the breezes of the morning sporting about her. Being solicited by her sister Mirth, she readily promises her assistance, flies away in a cloud, and impregnates the waters of Bath with new virtues, by which the sickness of Belinda is relieved.

As the reputation of his abilities, the particular circumstances of his birth and life, the splendour of his appearance, and the distinction which was for some time paid him by Lord Tyrconnel, intitled him to familiarity with persons of higher rank than those to whose conversation he had been before admitted, he did not fail to gratify that curiosity, which induced him to take a nearer view of those whom their birth, their employments, or their fortunes, necessarily place at a distance from the greatest part of mankind, and to examine whether their merit was magnified or diminished by the medium through which it was contemplated; whether the splendour with which they dazzled their admirers was inherent in themselves, or only reflected on them by the objects that surrounded them; and whether great men were selected for high stations, or high stations made great men.

For this purpose he took all opportunities of conversing familiarly with those who were most conspicuous at that time for their power or their influence; he watched their looser moments, and examined their domestick behaviour, with that acuteness which nature had given him, and which the uncommon variety of his life had contributed to increase, and that inquisitiveness which must always be produced in a vigorous mind, by an absolute freedom from all pressing or domestick engagements. His discernment was quick, and therefore he soon found in every person, and in every affair, something that deserved attention; he was supported by others, without any care for himself, and was therefore at leisure to pursue his observations.

More circumstances to constitute a critick on human life could not easily concur; nor indeed could any man, who assumed from accidental advantages more praise than he could justly claim from his real merit, admit an acquaintance more dangerous than that of Savage; of whom likewise it must be confessed, that abilities really exalted above the common level, or virtue refined from passion, or proof against corruption, could not easily find an abler judge, or a warmer advocate.

What was the result of Mr. Savage's enquiry, though he was not much accustomed to conceal his discoveries, it may not be entirely safe to relate, because the persons whose characters he criticised are powerful; and power and resentment are seldom strangers; nor would it perhaps be wholly just, because what he asserted in conversation might, though true in general, be heightened by some momentary ardour of imagination, and, as it can be delivered only from memory, may be imperfectly represented; so that the picture at first aggravated, and then unskillfully copied, may be justly suspected to retain no great resemblance of the original.

It may however be observed, that he did not appear to have formed very elevated ideas of those to whom the administration of affairs, or the conduct of parties, has been intrusted; who have been considered as the advocates of the crown, or the guardians of the people; and who have obtained the most implicit confidence, and the loudest applauses. Of one particular person, who has been at one time so popular as to be generally esteemed, and at another so formidable as to be universally detested, he observed, that his acquisitions had been small, or that his capacity was narrow, and that the whole range of his mind was from obscenity to politicks, and from politicks to obscenity.[19]

But the opportunity of indulging his speculations on great characters was now at an end. He was banished from the table of Lord Tyrconnel, and turned again adrift upon the world, without prospect of finding quickly any other harbour. As prudence was not one of the virtues by which he was distinguished, he had made no provision against a misfortune like this. And though it is not to be imagined but that the separation must for some time have been preceded by coldness, peevishness, or neglect, though it was undoubtedly the consequence of accumulated provocations on both sides; yet every one that knew Savage will readily believe, that to him it was sudden as a stroke of thunder; that, though he might have transiently suspected it, he had never suffered any thought so unpleasing to sink into his mind, but that he had driven it away by amusements, or dreams of future felicity and affluence, and had never taken any measures by which he might prevent a precipitation from plenty to indigence.

This quarrel and separation, and the difficulties to which Mr. Savage was exposed by them, were soon known both to his friends and enemies; nor was it long before he perceived, from the behavior of both, how much is added to the lustre of genius by the ornaments of wealth.

His condition did not appear to excite much compassion; for he had not always been careful to use the advantages he enjoyed with that moderation which ought to have been with more than usual caution preserved by him, who knew, if he had reflected, that he was only a dependant on the bounty of another, whom he could expect to support him no longer than he endeavoured to preserve his favour by complying with his inclinations, and whom he nevertheless set at defiance, and was continually irritating by negligence or encroachments.

Examples need not be sought at any great distance to prove, that superiority of fortune has a natural tendency to kindle pride, and that pride seldom fails to exert itself in contempt and insult; and if this is often the effect of hereditary wealth, and of honours enjoyed only by the merit of others, it is some extenuation of any indecent triumphs to which this unhappy man may have been betrayed, that his prosperity was heightened by the force of novelty, and made more intoxicating by a sense of the misery in which he had so long languished, and perhaps of the insults which he had formerly borne, and which he might now think himself entitled to revenge. It is too common for those who have unjustly suffered pain, to inflict it likewise in their turn with the same injustice, and to imagine that they have a right to treat others as they have themselves been treated.

That Mr. Savage was too much elevated by any good fortune, is generally known; and some passages of his Introduction to *The Author to be let* sufficiently shew, that he did not wholly refrain from such satire as he afterwards thought very unjust, when he was exposed to it himself; for when he was afterwards ridiculed in the character of a distressed poet, he very easily discovered that distress was not a proper subject for merriment, or topick of invective. He was then able to discern, that, if misery be the effect of virtue, it ought to be reverenced; if of ill-fortune, to be pitied; and if of vice, not to be insulted, because it is perhaps itself a punishment adequate to the crime by which it was produced. And the humanity of that man can deserve no panegyrick, who is capable of reproaching a criminal in the hands of the executioner.

But these reflections, though they readily occurred to him in the first and last parts of his life, were, I am afraid, for a long time forgotten; at least they were, like many other maxims, treasured up in his mind, rather for shew than use, and operated very little upon his conduct, however elegantly he might sometimes explain, or however forcibly he might inculcate, them.

His degradation therefore from the condition which he had enjoyed with such wanton thoughtlessness, was considered by many as an occasion of triumph. Those who had before paid their court to him without success, soon returned the contempt which they had suffered; and they who had received favours from him, for of such favours as he could bestow he was very liberal, did not always remember them. So much more certain are the effects of resentment than of gratitude; it is not only to many more pleasing to recollect those faults which place others below them, than those virtues by which they are themselves comparatively depressed; but it is likewise more easy to neglect, than to recompense; and though there are few who will practise a laborious virtue, there will never be wanting multitudes that will indulge an easy vice.

Savage, however, was very little disturbed at the marks of contempt which his ill-fortune brought upon him, from those whom he never esteemed, and with whom he never considered himself as levelled by any calamities: and though it was not without some uneasiness that he saw some, whose friendship he valued, change their behaviour; he yet observed their coldness without much emotion, considered them as the slaves of fortune and the worshippers of prosperity, and was more inclined to despise them, than to lament himself.

It does not appear that, after this return of his wants, he found mankind equally favourable to him, as at his first appearance in the world. His story, though in reality not less melancholy, was less affecting, because it was no longer new; it therefore procured him no new friends; and those that had formerly relieved him, thought they might now consign him to others. He was now likewise considered by many rather as criminal, than as unhappy; for the friends of Lord Tyrconnel, and of his mother, were sufficiently industrious to publish his weaknesses, which were indeed very numerous; and nothing was forgotten, that might make him either hateful or ridiculous.

It cannot but be imagined, that such representations of his faults must make great numbers less sensible of his distress; many, who had only an opportunity to hear one part, made no scruple to propagate the account which they received; many assisted their circulation from malice or revenge; and perhaps many pretended to credit them, that they might with a better grace withdraw their regard, or withhold their assistance.

Savage however was not one of those, who suffered himself to be injured without resistance, nor was less diligent in exposing the faults of Lord Tyrconnel, over whom he obtained at least this advantage, that he drove him first to the practice of outrage and violence; for he was so much provoked by the wit and virulence of Savage, that he came with a number of attendants, that did no honour to his courage, to beat him at a coffee-house. But it happened that he had left the place a few minutes, and his lordship had, without danger, the pleasure of boasting how he would have treated him. Mr. Savage went next day to repay his visit at his own house; but was prevailed on, by his domesticks, to retire without insisting upon seeing him.

Lord Tyrconnel was accused by Mr. Savage of some actions, which scarcely any provocations will be thought sufficient to justify; such as seizing what he had in his lodgings, and other instances of wanton cruelty, by which he increased the distress of Savage, without any advantage to himself.

These mutual accusations were retorted on both sides, for many years, with the utmost degree of virulence and rage; and time seemed rather to augment than diminish their resentment. That the anger of Mr. Savage should be kept alive, is not strange, because he felt every day the consequences of the quarrel; but it might reasonably have been hoped, that Lord Tyrconnel might have relented, and at length have forgot those provocations, which, however they might have once inflamed him, had not in reality much hurt him.

The spirit of Mr. Savage indeed never suffered him to solicit a reconciliation; he returned reproach for reproach, and insult for insult; his superiority of wit supplied the disadvantages of his fortune, and enabled him to form a party, and prejudice great numbers in his favour.

But though this might be some gratification of his vanity, it afforded very little relief to his necessities; and he was very frequently reduced to uncommon hardships, of which, however, he never made any mean or importunate complaints, being formed rather to bear misery with fortitude, than enjoy prosperity with moderation.

He now thought himself again at liberty to expose the cruelty of his mother, and therefore, I believe, about this time, published *The Bastard*, a poem remarkable for the vivacious sallies of thought in the beginning, where he makes a pompous enumeration of the imaginary advantages of base birth; and the pathetick sentiments at the end, where he recounts the real calamities which he suffered by the crime of his parents.

The vigour and spirit of the verses, the peculiar circumstances of the author, the novelty of the subject, and the notoriety of the story to which the allusions are made, procured this performance a very favourable reception; great numbers were immediately dispersed, and editions were multiplied with unusual rapidity.

One circumstance attended the publication, which Savage used to relate with great satisfaction. His mother, to whom the poem was with "due reverence" inscribed, happened then to be at Bath, where she could not conveniently retire from censure, or conceal herself from observation; and no sooner did the reputation of the poem begin to spread, than she heard it repeated in all places of concourse, nor could she enter the assembly-rooms, or cross the walks, without being saluted with some lines from *The Bastard*.

This was perhaps the first time that ever she discovered a sense of shame, and on this occasion the power of wit was very conspicuous; the wretch who had, without scruple, proclaimed herself an adulteress, and who had first endeavoured to starve her son, then to transport him, and afterwards to hang him, was not able to bear the representation of her own conduct; but fled from reproach, though she felt no pain from guilt, and left Bath with the utmost haste, to shelter herself among the crowds of London.

Thus Savage had the satisfaction of finding, that, though he could not reform his mother, he could punish her, and that he did not always suffer alone.

The pleasure which he received from this increase of his poetical reputation, was sufficient for some time to overbalance the miseries of want, which this performance did not much alleviate; for it was sold for a very trivial sum to a bookseller, who, though the success was so uncommon that five impressions were sold, of which many were undoubtedly very numerous, had not generosity sufficient to admit the unhappy writer to any part of the profit.

The sale of this poem was always mentioned by Savage with the utmost elevation of heart, and deferred to by him as an incontestable proof of a general acknowledgement of his abilities. It was indeed the only production of which he could justly boast a general reception.

But though he did not lose the opportunity which success gave him, of setting a high rate on his abilities, but paid due deference to the suffrages of mankind when they were given in his favour, he did not suffer his esteem of himself to depend upon others, nor found any thing sacred in the voice of the people when they were inclined to censure him; he then readily shewed the folly of expecting that the publick should judge right, observed how slowly poetical merit had often forced its way into the world; he contented himself with the applause of men of judgement, and was somewhat disposed to exclude all those from the character of men of judgement who did not applaud him.

But he was at other times more favourable to mankind than to think them blind to the beauties of his works, and imputed the slowness of their sale to other causes; either they were published at a time when the town was empty, or when the attention of the publick was engrossed by some struggle in the parliament, or some other object of general concern; or they were by the neglect of the publisher not diligently dispersed, or by his avarice not advertised with sufficient frequency. Address, or industry, or liberality, was always wanting; and the blame was laid rather on any person than the author.

By arts like these, arts which every man practises in some degree, and to which too much of the little tranquillity of life is to be ascribed, Savage was always able to live at peace with himself. Had he indeed only made use of these expedients to alleviate the loss or want of fortune or reputation, or any other advantages, which it is not in man's power to bestow upon himself, they might have been justly mentioned as instances of a philosophical mind, and very properly proposed to the imitation of multitudes, who, for want of diverting their imaginations with the same dexterity, languish under afflictions which might be easily removed.

It were doubtless to be wished, that truth and reason were universally prevalent; that every thing were esteemed according to its real value; and that men would secure themselves from being disappointed in their endeavours after happiness, by placing it only in virtue, which is always to be obtained; but if adventitious and foreign pleasures must be pursued, it would be perhaps of some benefit, since that pursuit must frequently be fruitless, if the practice of Savage could be taught, that folly might be an antidote to folly, and one fallacy be obviated by another.

But the danger of this pleasing intoxication must not be concealed; nor indeed can any one, after having observed the life of Savage, need to be cautioned against it. "By imputing none of his miseries to himself, he continued to act upon the same principles, and to follow the same path; was never made wiser by his sufferings, nor preserved by one misfortune from falling into another. He proceeded throughout his life to tread the same steps on the same circle; always applauding his past conduct, or at least forgetting it, to amuse himself with phantoms of happiness, which were dancing before him; and willingly turned his eyes from the light of reason, when it would have discovered the illusion, and shewn him, what he never wished to see, his real state.

He is even accused, after having lulled his imagination with those ideal opiates, of having tried the same experiment upon his conscience; and, having accustomed himself to impute all deviations from the right to foreign causes, it is certain that he was upon every occasion too easily reconciled to himself, and that he appeared very little to regret those practices which had impaired his reputation. The reigning error of his life was, that he mistook the love for the practice of virtue, and was indeed not so much a good man, as the friend of goodness.

This at least must be allowed him, that he always preserved a strong sense of the dignity, the beauty, and the necessity of virtue, and that he never contributed deliberately to spread corruption amongst mankind. His actions, which were generally precipitate, were often blameable; but his writings, being the productions of study, tended to the exaltation of the mind, and the propagation of morality and piety.

These writings may improve mankind, when his failings shall be forgotten; and therefore he must be considered, upon the whole, as a benefactor to the world; nor can his personal example do any hurt, since, whoever hears of his faults, will hear of the miseries which they brought upon him, and which would deserve less pity, had not his condition been such as made his faults pardonable. He may be considered as a child exposed to all the temptations of indigence, at an age when resolution was not yet strengthened by conviction, nor virtue confirmed by habit; a circumstance which in his *Bastard* he laments in a very affecting manner:

—No Mother's care
Shielded my infant innocence with prayer:
No Father's guardian-hand my youth maintain'd,
Call'd forth my virtues, or from vice restrain'd.

The Bastard, however it might provoke or mortify his mother, could not be expected to melt her to compassion, so that he was still under the same want of the necessities of life; and he therefore exerted all the interest which his wit, or his birth, or his misfortunes, could procure, to obtain, upon the death of Eusden,[20] the place of Poet Laureat, and prosecuted his application with so much diligence, that the King publickly declared it his intention to bestow it upon him; but such was the fate of Savage, that even the King, when he intended his advantage, was disappointed in his schemes; for the Lord Chamberlain, who has the disposal of the laurel, as one of the appendages of his office, either did not know the King's design, or did not approve it, or thought the nomination of the Laureat an encroachment upon his rights, and therefore bestowed the laurel upon Colley Gibber.

Mr. Savage, thus disappointed, took a resolution of applying to the queen, that, having once given him life, she would enable him to support it, and therefore published a short poem on her birthday, to which he gave the odd title of Volunteer Laureat. The event of this essay he has himself related in the following letter, which he prefixed to the poem, when he afterwards reprinted it in *The Gentleman's Magazine*, from whence I have copied it intire, as this was one of the few attempts in which Mr. Savage succeeded.

"Mr. Urban, In your Magazine for February you published the last Volunteer Laureat, written on a very melancholy occasion, the death of the royal patroness of arts and literature in general, and of the author of that poem in particular; I now send you the first that Mr. Savage wrote under that title.—This gentleman, notwithstanding a very considerable interest, being, on the death of Mr. Eusden, disappointed of the Laureat's place, wrote the before-mentioned poem; which was no sooner published, but the late

Queen sent to a bookseller for it: the author had not at that time a friend either to get him introduced, or his poem presented at court; yet such was the unspeakable goodness of that Princess, that notwithstanding this act of ceremony was wanting, in a few days after publication, Mr. Savage received a Bank-bill of fifty pounds, and a gracious message from her Majesty, by the Lord North and Guilford, to this effect; 'That her Majesty was highly pleased with the verses; that she took particularly kind his lines there relating to the King; that he had permission to write annually on the same subject; and that he should yearly receive the like present, till something better (which was her Majesty's intention) could be done for him.' After this, he was permitted to present one of his annual poems to her Majesty, had the honour of kissing her hand, and met with the most gracious reception. Yours, &c."

Such was the performance, and such its reception; a reception which, though by no means unkind, was not yet in the highest degree generous: to chain down the genius of a writer to an annual panegyric, shewed in the Queen too much desire of hearing her own praises, and a greater regard to herself than to him on whom her bounty was conferred. It was a kind of avaricious generosity, by which flattery was rather purchased, than genius rewarded.

Mrs. Oldfield had formerly given him the same allowance with much more heroic intention; she had no other view than to enable him to prosecute his studies, and to set himself above the want of assistance, and was contented with doing good without stipulating for encomiums.

Mr. Savage however was not at liberty to make exceptions, but was ravished with the favours which he had received, and probably yet more with those which he was promised; he considered himself now as a favourite of the Queen, and did not doubt but a few annual poems would establish him in some profitable employment.

He therefore assumed the title of *Volunteer Laureat*, not without some reprehensions from Gibber, who informed him, that the title of Laureat was a mark of honour conferred by the King, from whom all honour is derived, and which therefore no man has a right to bestow upon himself; and added, that he might, with equal propriety, style himself a Volunteer Lord, or Volunteer Baronet. It cannot be denied that the remark was just; but Savage did not think any title, which was conferred upon Mr. Cibber, so honourable as that the usurpation of it could be imputed to him as an instance of very exorbitant vanity, and therefore continued to write under the same title, and received every year the same reward.

He did not appear to consider these encomiums as tests of his abilities, or as any thing more than annual hints to the Queen of her promise, or acts of ceremony, by the performance of which he was intitled to his pension, and therefore did not labour them with great diligence, or print more than fifty each year, except that for some of the last years he regularly inserted them in *The Gentleman's Magazine*, by which they were dispersed over the kingdom.

Of some of them he had himself so low an opinion, that he intended to omit them in the collection of poems, for which he printed proposals, and solicited subscriptions; nor can it seem strange, that, being confined to the same subject, he should be at some times indolent, and at others unsuccessful; that he should sometimes delay a disagreeable task, till it was too late to perform it well; or that he should sometimes repeat the same sentiment on the same occasion, or at others be misled by an attempt after novelty to forced conceptions and farfetched images.

He wrote indeed with a double intention, which supplied him with some variety; for his business was to praise the Queen for the favours which he had received, and to complain to her of the delay of those which she had promised: in some of his pieces, therefore, gratitude is predominant, and in some discontent; in some he represents himself as happy in her patronage, and in others as disconsolate to find himself neglected.

Her promise, like other promises made to this unfortunate man, was never performed, though he took sufficient care that it should not be forgotten. The publication of his *Volunteer Laureat* procured him no other reward than a regular remittance of fifty pounds.

He was not so depressed by his disappointments as to neglect any opportunity that was offered of advancing his interest. When the Princess Anne was married,[21] he wrote a poem upon her departure, only, as he declared, "because it was expected from him," and he was not willing to bar his own prospects by any appearance of neglect.

He never mentioned any advantage gained by this poem, or any regard that was paid to it; and therefore it is likely that it was considered at court as an act of duty to which he was obliged by his dependence, and which it was therefore not necessary to reward by any new favour: or perhaps the Queen really intended his advancement, and therefore thought it superfluous to lavish presents upon a man whom she intended to establish for life.

About this time not only his hopes were in danger of being frustrated, but his pension likewise of being obstructed, by an accidental calumny. The writer of *The Daily Courant*, a paper then published under the direction of the ministry, charged him with a crime, which, though not very great in itself, would have been remarkably invidious in him, and might very justly have incensed the Queen against him. He was accused by name of influencing elections against the court, by appearing at the head of a tory mob; nor did the accuser fail to aggravate his crime, by representing it as the effect of the most atrocious ingratitude, and a kind of rebellion against the Queen, who had first preserved him from an infamous death, and afterwards distinguished him by her favour, and supported him by her charity. The charge, as it was open and confident, was likewise by good fortune very particular. The place of the transaction was mentioned, and the whole series of the rioter's conduct related. This exactness made Mr. Savage's vindication easy; for he never had in his life seen the place which was declared to be the scene of his wickedness, nor ever had been present in any town when its representatives were chosen. This answer he therefore made haste to publish, with all the circumstances necessary to make it credible; and very reasonably demanded, that the accusation should be retracted in the same paper, that he might no longer suffer the imputation of sedition and ingratitude. This demand was likewise pressed by him in a private letter to the author of the paper, who, either trusting to the protection of those whose defence he had undertaken, or having entertained some personal malice against Mr. Savage, or fearing, lest, by retracting so confident an assertion, he should impair the credit of his paper, refused to give him that satisfaction.

Mr. Savage therefore thought it necessary, to his own vindication, to prosecute him in the King's Bench; but as he did not find any ill effects from the accusation, having sufficiently cleared his innocence, he thought any further procedure would have the appearance of revenge; and therefore willingly dropped it.

He saw soon afterwards a process commenced in the same court against himself, on an information in which he was accused of writing and publishing an obscene pamphlet.

It was always Mr. Savage's desire to be distinguished; and, when any controversy became popular, he never wanted some reason for engaging in it with great ardour, and appearing at the head of the party which he had chosen. As he was never celebrated for his prudence, he had no sooner taken his side, and informed himself of the chief topicks of the dispute, than he took all opportunities of asserting and propagating his principles, without much regard to his own interest, or any other visible design than that of drawing upon himself the attention of mankind.

The dispute between the bishop of London and the chancellor[22] is well known to have been for some time the chief topick of political conversation; and therefore Mr. Savage, in pursuance of his character, endeavoured to become conspicuous among the controvertists with which every coffee-house was filled on that occasion. He was an indefatigable opposer of all the claims of ecclesiastical power, though he did not know on what they were founded; and was therefore no friend to the Bishop of London. But he had another reason for appearing as a warm advocate for Dr. Rundle; for he was the friend of Mr. Foster and Mr. Thomson,[23] who were the friends of Mr. Savage.

Thus remote was his interest in the question, which, however, as he imagined, concerned him so nearly, that it was not sufficient to harangue and dispute, but necessary likewise to write upon it.

He therefore engaged with great ardour in a new Poem, called by him, *The Progress of a Divine*; in which he conducts a profligate priest by all the gradations of wickedness from a poor curacy in the country, to the highest preferments of the Church, and describes with that humour which was natural to him, and that knowledge which was extended to all the diversities of human life, his behaviour in every station; and insinuates that this priest, thus accomplished, found at last a patron in the Bishop of London.

When he was asked by one of his friends, on what pretence he could charge the bishop with such an action? he had no more to say than that he had only inverted the accusation, and that he thought it reasonable to believe, that he who obstructed the rise of a good man without reason, would for bad reasons promote the exaltation of a villain.

The clergy were universally provoked by this satire; and Savage, who, as was his constant practice, had set his name to his performance, was censured in *The Weekly Miscellany* with severity which he did not seem inclined to forget.

But a return of invective was not thought a sufficient punishment. The Court of King's Bench was therefore moved against him, and he was obliged to return an answer to a charge of obscenity. It was urged, in his defence, that obscenity was criminal when it was intended to promote the practice of vice; but that Mr. Savage had only introduced obscene ideas with the view of exposing them to detestation, and of amending the age by showing the deformity of wickedness. This plea was admitted; and Sir Philip Yorke, who then presided in that court, dismissed the information with encomiums upon the purity and excellence of Mr. Savage's writings.

The prosecution, however, answered in some measure the purpose of those by whom it was set on foot; for Mr. Savage was so far intimidated by it, that, when the edition of his poem was sold, he did not venture to reprint it; so that it was in a short time forgotten, or forgotten by all but those whom it offended.

It is said that some endeavours were used to incense the Queen against him: but he found advocates to obviate at least part of their effect; for though he was never advanced, he still continued to receive his pension.

This poem drew more infamy upon him than any incident of his life; and, as his conduct cannot be vindicated, it is proper to secure his memory from reproach, by informing those whom he made his enemies, that he never intended to repeat the provocation; and that, though, whenever he thought he had any reason to complain of the clergy, he used to threaten them with a new edition of *The Progress of a Divine*, it was his calm and settled resolution to suppress it for ever.

He once intended to have made a better reparation for the folly or injustice with which he might be charged, by writing another poem, called *The Progress of a Freethinker*, whom he intended to lead through all the stages of vice and folly, to convert him from virtue to wickedness, and from religion to infidelity, by all the modish sophistry used for that purpose; and at last to dismiss him by his own hand into the other world.

That he did not execute this design is a real loss to mankind, for he was too well acquainted with all the scenes of debauchery to have failed in his representations of them, and too zealous for virtue not to have represented them in such a manner as should expose them either to ridicule or detestation.

But this plan was, like others, formed and laid aside till the vigour of his imagination was spent, and the effervescence of invention had subsided; but soon gave way to some other design, which pleased by its novelty for a while, and then was neglected like the former.

He was still in his usual exigences, having no certain support but the pension allowed him by the Queen, which, though it might have kept an exact economist from want, was very far from being sufficient for Mr. Savage, who had never been accustomed to dismiss any of his appetites without the gratification which they solicited, and whom nothing but want of money withheld from partaking of every pleasure that fell within his view.

His conduct with regard to his pension was very particular. No sooner had he changed the bill, than he vanished from the sight of all his acquaintances, and lay for some time out of the reach of all the enquiries that friendship or curiosity could make after him; at length he appeared again pennyless as before, but never informed even those whom he seemed to regard most, where he had been, nor was his retreat ever discovered.

This was his constant practice during the whole time that he received the pension from the Queen: He regularly disappeared and returned. He indeed affirmed that he retired to study, and that the money supported him in solitude for many months; but his friends declared, that the short time in which it was spent sufficiently confuted his own account of his conduct.

His politeness and his wit still raised him friends, who were desirous of setting him at length free from that indigence by which he had been hitherto oppressed; and therefore solicited Sir Robert Walpole in his favour with so much earnestness, that they obtained a promise of the next place that should become vacant, not exceeding two hundred pounds a year. This promise was made with an uncommon declaration, "that it was not the promise of a minister to a petitioner, but of a friend to his friend."

Mr. Savage now concluded himself set at ease for ever, and, as he observes in a poem written on that incident of his life, trusted and was trusted; but soon found that his confidence was ill-grounded, and this friendly promise was not inviolable. He spent a long time in solicitations, and at last despaired and desisted.

He did not indeed deny that he had given the minister some reason to believe that he should not strengthen his own interest by advancing him, for he had taken care to distinguish himself in coffee-houses as an advocate for the ministry of the last years of Queen Anne, and was always ready to justify the conduct, and exalt the character of Lord Bolingbroke, whom he mentions with great regard in an epistle upon authors, which he wrote about that time, but was too wise to publish, and of which only some fragments have appeared, inserted by him in the *Magazine* after his retiremen.[24]

To despair was not, however, the character of Savage; when one patronage failed, he had recourse to another. The prince was now extremely popular, and had very liberally rewarded the merit of some writers whom Mr. Savage did not think superior to himself, and therefore he resolved to address a poem to him.

For this purpose he made choice of a subject, which could regard only persons of the highest rank and highest affluence, and which was therefore proper for a poem intended to procure the patronage of a prince; and having retired for some time to Richmond, that he might prosecute his design in full tranquillity, without the temptations of pleasure, or the solicitations of creditors, by which his meditations were in equal danger of being disconcerted, he produced a poem *On Public Spirit, with regard to Publick Works*.

The plan of this poem is very extensive, and comprises a multitude of topicks, each of which might furnish matter sufficient for a long performance, and of which some have already employed more eminent writers; but as he was perhaps not fully acquainted with the whole extent of his own design, and was writing to obtain a supply of wants too pressing to admit of long or accurate enquiries, he passes negligently over many publick works, which, even in his own opinion, deserved to be more elaborately treated.

But though he may sometimes disappoint his reader by transient touches upon these subjects, which have often been considered, and therefore naturally raise expectations, he must be allowed amply to compensate his omissions, by expatiating, in the conclusion of his work, upon a kind of beneficence not yet celebrated by any eminent poet, though it now appears more susceptible of embellishments, more capable to exalt the ideas, and affect the passions, than many of those which have hitherto been thought worthy of the ornaments of verse. The settlement of colonies in uninhabited countries, the establishment of those in security, whose misfortunes have made their own country no longer pleasing or safe, the acquisition of property without injury to any, the appropriation of the waste and luxuriant bounties of nature, and the enjoyment of those gifts which heaven has scattered upon regions uncultivated and unoccupied, cannot be considered without giving rise to a great number of pleasing ideas, and bewildering the imagination in delightful prospects; and, therefore, whatever speculations they may produce in those who have confined themselves to political studies, naturally fixed the attention, and excited the applause, of a poet. The politician, when he considers men driven into other countries for shelter, and obliged to retire to forest and deserts, and pass their lives and fix their posterity in the remotest corners of the world, to avoid those hardships which they suffer or fear in their native place, may very properly enquire, why the legislature does not provide a remedy for these miseries, rather than encourage an escape from them. He may conclude, that the flight of every honest man is a loss to the community; that those who are unhappy without guilt ought to be relieved; and the life, which is overburthened by accidental calamities, set at ease by the care of the publick; and that those, who have by misconduct forfeited their claim to favour, ought rather to be made useful to the society which they have injured than driven from it.[25] But the poet is employed in a more pleasing undertaking than that of proposing laws, which, however just or expedient, will never be made; or endeavouring to reduce to rational schemes of government societies which were formed by chance, and are conducted by the private passions of those who preside in them. He guides the unhappy fugitive from want and persecution, to plenty, quiet, and security, and seats him in scenes of peaceful solitude, and undisturbed repose.

Savage has not forgotten, amidst the pleasing sentiments which this prospect of retirement suggested to him, to censure those crimes which have been generally committed by the discoverers of new regions, and to expose the enormous wickedness of making war upon barbarous nations because they cannot resist, and of invading countries because they are fruitful; of extending navigation only to propagate vice, and of visiting distant lands only to lay them waste. He has asserted the natural equality of mankind, and endeavoured to suppress that pride which inclines men to imagine that right is the consequence of power.

His description of the various miseries which force men to seek for refuge in distant countries, affords another instance of his proficiency in the important and extensive study of human life; and the tenderness with which he recounts them, another proof of his humanity and benevolence.

It is observable, that the close of this poem discovers a change which experience had made in Mr. Savage's opinions. In a poem written by him in his youth, and published in his Miscellanies, he declares his contempt of the contracted views and narrow prospects of the middle state of life, and declares his resolution either to tower like the cedar, or be trampled like the shrub; but in this poem, though addressed to a prince, he mentions this state of life as comprising those who ought most to attract reward, those who merit most the confidence of power, and the familiarity of greatness; and, accidentally mentioning this passage to one of his friends, declared, that in his opinion all the virtue of mankind was comprehended in that state.

In describing villas and gardens, he did not omit to condemn that absurd custom which prevails among the English, of permitting servants to receive money from strangers for the entertainment that they receive, and therefore inserted in his poem these lines;

> But what the flowering pride of gardens rare,
> However royal, or however fair,
> If gates, which to access should still give way,
> Ope but, like Peter's paradise, for pay
> If perquisited varlets frequent stand,
> And each new walk must a new tax demand?
> What foreign eye but with contempt surveys?
> What Muse shall from oblivion snatch their praise?

But before the publication of his performance he recollected that the Queen allowed her garden and cave at Richmond to be shewn for money, and that she so openly countenanced the practice, that she had bestowed the privilege of shewing them as a place of profit on a man, whose merit she valued herself upon rewarding, though she gave him only the liberty of disgracing his country.

He therefore thought, with more prudence than was often exerted by him, that the publication of these lines might be officiously represented as an insult upon the Queen, to whom he owed his life and his subsistence; and that the propriety of his observation would be no security against the censures which the unseasonableness of it might draw upon him; he therefore suppressed the passage in the first edition, but after the Queen's death thought the same caution no longer necessary, and restored it to the proper place.

The poem was therefore published without any political faults, and inscribed to the prince; but Mr.

Savage, having no friend upon whom he could prevail to present it to him, had no other method of attracting his observation than the publication of frequent advertisements, and therefore received no reward from his patron, however generous on other occasions.

This disappointment he never mentioned without indignation being by some means or other confident that the Prince was not ignorant of his address to him; and insinuated, that, if any advances in popularity could have been made by distinguishing him, he had not written without notice, or without reward.

He was once inclined to have presented his poem in person, and sent to the printer for a copy with that design; but either his opinion changed, or his resolution deserted him, and he continued to resent neglect without attempting to force himself into regard.

Nor was the publick much more favorable than his patron, for only seventy-two were sold, though the performance was much commended by some whose judgement in that kind of writing is generally allowed. But Savage easily reconciled himself to mankind without imputing any defect to his work, by observing that his poem was unluckily published two days after the prorogation of the parliament, and by consequence at a time when all those who could be expected to regard it were in the hurry of preparing for their departure, or engaged in taking leave of others upon their dismission from publick affairs.

It must be however allowed, in justification of the publick, that this performance is not the most excellent of Mr. Savage's works; and that, though it cannot be denied to contain many striking sentiments, majestic lines, and just observations, it is in general not sufficiently polished in the language, or enlivened in the imagery, or digested in the plan.

Thus his poem contributed nothing to the alleviation of his poverty, which was such as very few could have supported with equal patience; but to which it must likewise be confessed, that few would have been exposed who received punctually fifty pounds a year; a salary which, though by no means equal to the demands of vanity and luxury, is yet found sufficient to support families above want, and was undoubtedly more than the necessities of life require.

But no sooner had he received his pension, than he withdrew to his darling privacy, from which he returned in a short time to his former distress, and for some part of the year generally lived by chance, eating only when he was invited to the tables of his acquaintances, from which the meanness of his dress often excluded him, when the politeness and variety of his conversation would have been thought a sufficient recompense for his entertainment.

He lodged as much by accident as he dined, and passed the night sometimes in mean houses, which are set open at night to any casual wanderers, sometimes in cellars, among the riot and filth of the meanest and most profligate of the rabble; and sometimes, when he had not money to support even the expences of these receptacles, walked about the streets till he was weary, and lay down in the summer upon a bulk, or in the winter, with his associates in poverty, among the ashes of a glass-house.

In this manner were passed those days and those nights which nature had enabled him to have employed in elevated speculations, useful studies, or pleasing conversation. On a bulk, in a cellar, or in a glass-house among thieves and beggars, was to be found the Author of *The Wanderer*, the man of exalted sentiments, extensive views, and curious observations; the man whose remarks on life might have assisted the statesman, whose ideas of virtue might have enlightened the moralist, whose eloquence might have influenced senates, and whose delicacy might have polished courts.

It cannot but be imagined that such necessities might sometimes force him upon disreputable practices: and it is probable that these lines in The Wanderer were occasioned by his reflections on his own conduct:

> Though misery leads to happiness and truth,
> Unequal to the load, this languid youth,
> (Oh, let none censure, if, untried by grief,
> If, amidst woe, untempted by relief,)
> He stoop'd reluctant to low arts of shame,
> Which then, ev'n then he scorn'd, and blush'd to name.

Whoever was acquainted with him was certain to be solicited for small sums, which the frequency of the request made in time considerable, and he was therefore quickly shunned by those who were become familiar enough to be trusted with his necessities; but his rambling manner of life, and constant appearance at houses of public resort, always procured him a new succession of friends, whose kindness had not been exhausted by repeated requests; so that he was seldom absolutely without resources, but had in his utmost exigences this comfort, that he always imagined himself sure of speedy relief.

It was observed, that he always asked favours of this kind without the least submission or apparent consciousness of dependence, and that he did not seem to look upon a compliance with his request as an obligation that deserved any extraordinary acknowledgements; but a refusal was resented by him as an affront, or complained of as an injury; nor did he readily reconcile himself to those who either denied to lend, or gave him afterwards any intimation that they expected to be repaid.

He was sometimes so far compassionated by those who knew both his merits and distresses, that they received him into their families, but they soon discovered him to be a very incommodious inmate; for, being always accustomed to an irregular manner of life, he could not confine himself to any stated hours, or pay any regard to the rules of a family, but would prolong his conversation till midnight, without considering that business might require his friend's application in the morning: and, when he had persuaded himself to retire to bed, was not, without equal difficulty, called up to dinner; it was therefore impossible to pay him any distinction without the entire subversion of all economy, a kind of establishment which, wherever he went, he always appeared ambitious to overthrow.

It must therefore be acknowledged, in justification of mankind, that it was not always by the negligence or coldness of his friends that Savage was distressed, but because it was in reality very difficult to preserve him long in a state of ease. To supply him with money was a hopeless attempt; for no sooner did he see himself master of a sum sufficient to set him free from care for a day, than he became profuse and luxurious. When once he had entered a tavern, or engaged in a scheme of pleasure, he never retired till want of money obliged him to some new expedient. If he was entertained in a family, nothing was any longer to be regarded there but amusements and jollity; wherever Savage entered, he immediately expected that order and business should fly before him, that all should thenceforward be left to hazard, and that no dull principle of domestic management should be opposed to his inclination, or intrude upon his gaiety.

His distresses, however afflictive, never dejected him; in his lowest state he wanted not spirit to assert the natural dignity of wit, and was always ready to repress that insolence which superiority of fortune incited, and to trample on that reputation which rose upon any other basis than that of merit: he never admitted any gross familiarities, or submitted to be treated otherwise than as an equal. Once, when he was without lodging, meat, or clothes, one of his friends, a man not indeed remarkable for moderation in his prosperity, left a message, that he desired to see him about nine in the morning. Savage knew that his intention was to assist him; but was very much disgusted that he should presume to prescribe the hour of his attendance, and, I believe, refused to visit him, and rejected his kindness.

The same invincible temper, whether firmness or obstinacy, appeared in his conduct to the Lord Tyrconnel, from whom he very frequently demanded that the allowance which was once paid him should be restored; but with whom he never appeared to entertain for a moment the thought of soliciting a reconciliation, and whom he treated at once with all the haughtiness of superiority, and all the bitterness of resentment. He wrote to him, not in a style of supplication or respect, but of reproach, menace, and contempt; and appeared determined, if he ever regained his allowance, to hold it only by the right of conquest.

As many more can discover, that a man is richer than that he is wiser than themselves, superiority of understanding is not so readily acknowledged as that of fortune; nor is that haughtiness, which the consciousness of great abilities incites, born with the same submission as the tyranny of affluence; and therefore Savage, by asserting his claim to deference and regard, and by treating those with contempt whom better fortune animated to rebel against him, did not fail to raise a great number of enemies in the different classes of mankind. Those who thought themselves raised above him by the advantages of riches, hated him because they found no protection from the petulance of his wit. Those who were esteemed for their writings feared him as a critic, and maligned him as a rival, and almost all the smaller wits were his professed enemies.

Among these Mr. Miller so far indulged his resentment as to introduce him in a farce,[26] and direct him to be personated on the stage, in a dress like that which he then wore; a mean insult, which only insinuated that Savage had but one coat, and which was therefore despised by him rather than resented; for though he wrote a lampoon against Miller, he never printed it: and as no other person ought to prosecute that revenge from which the person who was injured desisted, I shall not preserve what Mr. Savage suppressed: of which the publication would indeed have been a punishment too severe for so impotent an assault.

The great hardships of poverty were to Savage not the want of lodging or of food, but the neglect and contempt which it drew upon him. He complained, that as his affairs grew desperate, he found his reputation for capacity visibly decline; that his opinion in questions of criticism was no longer regarded, when his coat was out of fashion; and that those who, in the interval of his prosperity, were always encouraging him to great undertakings by encomiums on his genius and assurances of success, now received any mention of his designs with coldness, thought that the subjects on which he proposed to write were very difficult, and were ready to inform him, that the event of a poem was uncertain, that an author ought to employ much time in the consideration of his plan, and not presume to sit down to write in confidence of a few cursory ideas, and a superficial knowledge; difficulties were started on all sides, and he was no longer qualified for any performance but The Volunteer Laureat.

Yet even this kind of contempt never depressed him; for he always preserved a steady confidence in his own capacity, and believed nothing above his reach which he should at any time earnestly endeavour to attain. He formed schemes of the same kind with regard to knowledge and to fortune, and flattered himself with advances to be made in science, as with riches, to be enjoyed in some distant period of his life. For the acquisition of knowledge he was indeed far better qualified than for that of riches; for he was naturally inquisitive and desirous of the conversation of those from whom any information was to be obtained, but by no means solicitous to improve those opportunities that were sometimes offered of raising his fortune; and he was remarkably retentive of his ideas, which, when once he was in possession of them, rarely forsook him; a quality which could never be communicated to his money.

While he was thus wearing out his life in expectation that the Queen would some time recollect her promise, he had recourse to the usual practice of writers, and published proposals for printing his works by subscription, to which he was encouraged by the success of many who had not a better right to the favour of the publick; but, whatever was the reason, he did not find the world equally inclined to favour him; and he observed with some discontent, that, though he offered his works at half a guinea, he was able to procure but a small number in comparison with those who subscribed twice as much to Duck.

Nor was it without indignation that he saw his proposals neglected by the Queen, who patronised Mr. Duck's with uncommon ardour, and incited a competition among those who attended the court, who should most promote his interest, and who should first offer a subscription.[27] This was a distinction to which Mr. Savage made no scruple of asserting that his birth, his misfortunes, and his genius, gave him a fairer title, than could be pleaded by him on whom it was conferred.

Savage's applications were however not universally unsuccessful; for some of the nobility countenanced his design, encouraged his proposals, and subscribed with great liberality. He related of the Duke of Chandos particularly, that, upon receiving his proposals, he sent him ten guineas.

But the money which his subscriptions afforded him was not less volatile than that which he received from his other schemes; whenever a subscription was paid him, he went to a tavern; and, as money so collected is necessarily received in small sums, he never was able to send his poems to the press, but for many years continued his solicitation, and squandered whatever he obtained.

This project of printing his works was frequently revived; and, as his proposals grew obsolete, new ones were printed with fresher dates. To form schemes for the publication was one of his favourite amusements; nor was he ever more at ease than when, with any friend who readily fell in with his schemes, he was adjusting the print, forming the advertisements, and regulating the dispersion of his new edition, which he really intended some time to publish, and which, as long as experience had shewn him the impossibility of printing the volume together, he at last determined to divide into weekly or monthly numbers, that the profits of the first might supply the expences of the next.

Thus he spent his time in mean expedients and tormenting suspense, living for the greatest part in the fear of prosecutions from his creditors, and consequently skulking in obscure parts of the town, of which he was no stranger to the remotest corners. But wherever he came, his address secured him friends, whom his necessities soon alienated; so that he had perhaps a more numerous acquaintance than any man ever before attained, there being scarcely any person eminent on any account to whom he was not known, or whose character he was not in some degree able to delineate.

To the acquisition of this extensive acquaintance every circumstance of his life contributed. He excelled in the arts of conversation, and therefore willingly practised them. He had seldom any home, or even a lodging in which he could be private; and therefore was driven into public-houses for the common conveniences of life and supports of nature. He was always ready to comply with every invitation, having no employment to withhold him, and often no money to provide for himself; and by dining with one company, he never failed of obtaining an introduction into another.

Thus dissipated was his life, and thus casual his subsistence; yet did not the distraction of his views hinder him from reflection, nor the uncertainty of his condition depress his gaiety. When he had wandered about without any fortunate adventure by which he was led into a tavern, he sometimes retired into the fields, and was able to employ his mind in study, or amuse it with pleasing imaginations; and seldom appeared to be melancholy, but when some sudden misfortune had just fallen upon him, and even then in a few moments he would disentangle himself from his perplexity, adopt the subject of conversation, and apply his mind wholly to the objects that others presented to it.

This life, unhappy as it may be already imagined, was yet imbittered, in 1738, with new calamities. The death of the Queen deprived him of all the prospects of preferment with which he so long entertained his imagination; and, as Sir Robert Walpole had before given him reason to believe that he never intended the performance of his promise, he was now abandoned again to fortune.

He was however, at that time, supported by a friend; and as it was not his custom to look out for distant calamities, or to feel any other pain than that which forced itself upon his senses, he was not much afflicted at his loss, and perhaps comforted himself that his pension would be now continued without the annual tribute of a panegyric.

Another expectation contributed likewise to support him: he had taken a resolution to write a second tragedy upon the story of Sir Thomas Overbury, in which he preserved a few lines of his former play, but made a total alteration of the plan, added new incidents, and introduced new characters; so that it was a new tragedy, not a revival of the former.

Many of his friends blamed him for not making choice of another subject; but, in vindication of himself, he asserted, that it was not easy to find a better; and that he thought it his interest to extinguish the memory of the first tragedy, which he could only do by writing one less defective upon the same story; by which he should entirely defeat the artifice of the booksellers, who, after the death of any author of reputation, are always industrious to swell his works, by uniting his worst productions with his best.

In the execution of this scheme, however, he proceeded but slowly, and probably only employed himself upon it when he could find no other amusement; but he pleased himself with counting the profits, and perhaps imagined, that the theatrical reputation which he was about to acquire, would be equivalent to all that he had lost by the death of his patroness.

He did not, in confidence of his approaching riches, neglect the measures proper to secure the continuance of his pension, though some of his favourers thought him culpable for omitting to write on her death; but on her birthday next year, he gave a proof of the solidity of his judgement, and the power of his genius. He knew that the track of elegy had been so long beaten, that it was impossible to travel in it without treading in the footsteps of those who had gone before him; and that therefore it was necessary, that he might distinguish himself from the herd of encomiasts, to find out some new walk of funeral panegyrick.

This difficult task he performed in such a manner, that his poem may be justly ranked among the best pieces that the death of princes has produced. By transferring the mention of her death to her birth-day, he has formed a happy combination of topicks, which any other man would have thought it very difficult to connect in one view, but which he has united in such a manner, that the relation between them appears natural; and it may be justly said, that what no other man would have thought on, it now appears scarcely possible for any man to miss.

The beauty of this peculiar combination of images is so masterly, that it is sufficient to set this poem above censure, and therefore it is not necessary to mention many other delicate touches which may be found in it, and which would deservedly be admired in any other performance.

To these proofs of his genius may be added, from the same poem, an instance of his prudence, an excellence for which he was not so often distinguished; he does not forget to remind the King, in the most delicate and artful manner, of continuing his pension.

With regard to the success of this address, he was for some time in suspence, but was in no great degree solicitous about it; and continued his labour upon his new tragedy with great tranquillity, till the friend who had for a considerable time supported him, removing his family to another place, took occasion to dismiss him. It then became necessary to enquire more diligently what was determined in his affair, having reason to suspect that no great favour was intnded him, because he had not received his pension at the usual time.

It is said, that he did not take those methods of retrieving his interest, which were most likely to succeed; and some of those who were employed in the Exchequer, cautioned him against too much violence in his proceedings; but Mr. Savage, who seldom regulated his conduct by the advice of others, gave way to his passion, and demanded of Sir Robert Walpole, at his levee, the reason of the distinction that was made between him and the other pensioners of the Queen, with a degree of roughness which perhaps determined him to withdraw what had been only delayed.

Whatever was the crime of which he was accused or suspected, and whatever influence was employed against him, he received soon after an account that took from him all hopes of regaining his pension; and he had now no prospect of subsistence but from his play, and he knew no way of living for the time required to finish it.

So peculiar were the misfortunes of this man, deprived of an estate and title by a particular law, exposed and abandoned by a mother, defrauded by a mother of a fortune which his father had allotted him, he entered the world without a friend; and though his abilities forced themselves into esteem and reputation, he was never able to obtain any real advantage, and whatever prospects arose were always intercepted as he began to approach them. The king's intentions in his favour were frustrated; his dedication to the Prince, whose generosity on every other occasion was eminent, procured him no reward; Sir Robert Walpole, who valued himself upon keeping his promise to others, broke it to him without regret; and the bounty of the Queen was, after her death, withdrawn from him, and from him only.

Such were his misfortunes, which yet he bore, not only with decency, but with cheerfulness; nor was his gaiety clouded even by his last disappointments, though he was in a short time reduced to the lowest degree of distress, and often wanted both lodging and food. At this time he gave another instance of the insurmountable obstinacy of his spirit: his clothes were worn out; and he received notice, that at a coffee-house some clothes and linen were left for him: the person who sent them did not, I believe, inform him to whom he was to be obliged, that he might spare the perplexity of acknowledging the benefit; but though the offer was so far generous, it was made with some neglect of ceremonies, which Mr. Savage so much resented, that he refused the present, and declined to enter the house till the clothes that had been designed for him were taken away.

His distress was now publickly known, and his friends, therefore, thought it proper to concert some measures for his relief; and one of them wrote a letter to him, in which he expressed his concern "for the miserable withdrawing of his pension;" and gave him hopes, that in a short time he should find himself supplied with a competence, "without any dependence on those little creatures whom we are pleased to call the Great."[28]

The scheme proposed for this happy and independent subsistence, was, that he should retire into Wales and receive an allowance of fifty pounds a year, to be raised by a subscription, on which he was to live privately in a cheap place, without aspiring any more to affluence, or having any farther care of reputation.

This offer Mr. Savage gladly accepted, though with intentions very different from those of his friends; for they proposed that he should continue an exile from London for ever, and spend all the remaining part of his life at Swansea; but he designed only to take the opportunity, which their scheme offered him, of retreating for a short time, that he might prepare his play for the stage, and his other works for the press, and then to return to London to exhibit his tragedy, and live upon the profits of his own labour.

With regard to his works, he proposed very great improvements, which would have required much time, or great application; and when he had finished them, he designed to do justice to his subscribers, by publishing them according to his proposals.

As he was ready to entertain himself with future pleasures, he had planned out a scheme of life for the country, of which he had no knowledge but from pastorals and songs. He imagined that he should be transported to scenes of flowery felicity, like those which one poet has reflected to another; and had projected a perpetual round of innocent pleasures, of which he suspected no interruption from pride, or ignorance, or brutality.

With these expectations he was so enchanted, that when he was once gently reproached by a friend for submitting to live upon a subscription, and advised rather by a resolute exertion of his abilities to support himself, he could not bear to debar himself from the happiness which was to be found in the calm of a cottage, or lose the opportunity of listening, without intermission, to the melody of the nightingale, which he believed was to be heard from every bramble, and which he did not fail to mention as a very important part of the happiness of a country life.

While this scheme was ripening, his friends directed him to take a lodging in the liberties of the Fleet,[29] that he might be secure from his creditors, and sent him every Monday a guinea, which he commonly spent before the next morning, and trusted, after his usual manner, the remaining part of the week to the bounty of fortune.

He now began very sensibly to feel the miseries of dependence. Those by whom he was to be supported, began to prescribe to him with an air of authority, which he knew not how decently to resent, nor patiently to bear; and he soon discovered, from the conduct of most of his subscribers, that he was yet in the hands of "little creatures."

Of the insolence that he was obliged to suffer, he gave many instances, of which none appeared to raise his indignation to a greater height, than the method which was taken of furnishing him with clothes. Instead of consulting him, and allowing him to send a taylor his orders for what they thought proper to allow him, they proposed to send for a taylor to take his measure, and then to consult how they should equip him.

This treatment was not very delicate, nor was it such as Savage's humanity would have suggested to him on a like occasion; but it had scarcely deserved mention, had it not, by affecting him in an uncommon degree, shewn the peculiarity of his character. Upon hearing the design that was formed, he came to the lodging of a friend with the most violent agonies of rage; and, being asked what it could be that gave him such disturbance, he replied with the utmost vehemence of indignation, "That they had sent for a taylor to measure him."

How the affair ended was never enquired, for fear of renewing his uneasiness. It is probable, that, upon recollection, he submitted with a good grace to what he could not avoid, and that he discovered no resentment where he had no power.

He was, however, not humbled to implicit and universal compliance; for when the gentleman, who had first informed him of the design to support him by a subscription, attempted to procure a reconciliation with the Lord Tyrconnel, he could by no means be prevailed upon to comply with the measures that were proposed.

A letter was written for him[30] to Sir William Lemon,[31] to prevail upon him to interpose his good offices with Lord Tyrconnel, in which he solicited Sir William's assistance, "for a man who really needed it as much as any man could well do;" and informed him, that he was retiring "for ever to a place where he should no more trouble his relations, friends, or enemies;" he confessed, that his passion had betrayed him to some conduct with regard to Lord Tyrconnel, for which he could not but heartily ask his pardon; and as he imagined Lord Tyrconnel's passion might be yet so high, that he would not "receive a letter from him," begged that Sir William would endeavour to soften him; and expressed his hopes that he would comply with his request, and that "so small a relation would not harden his heart against him."

That any man should presume to dictate a letter to him, was not very agreeable to Mr. Savage; and therefore he was, before he had opened it, not much inclined to approve it. But when he read it, he found it contained sentiments entirely opposite to his own, and, as he asserted, to the truth; and therefore, instead of copying it, wrote his friend a letter full of masculine resentment and warm expostulations. He very justly observed, that the style was too supplicatory, and the representation too abject, and that he ought at least to have made him complain with "the dignity of a gentleman in distress." He declared that he would not write the paragraph in which he was to ask Lord Tyrconnel's pardon; for, "he despised his pardon, and therefore could not heartily, and would not hypocritically, ask it." He remarked, that his friend made a very unreasonable distinction between himself and him; for, says he, when you mention men of high rank "in your own character," they are "those little creatures whom we are pleased to call the great"; but when you address them "in mine," no servility is sufficiently humble. He then with great propriety explained the ill consequences which might be expected from such a letter, which his relations would print in their own defence, and which would for ever be produced as a full answer to all that he should allege against them; for he always intended to publish a minute account of the treatment which he had received. It is to be remembered, to the honour of the gentleman by whom this letter was drawn up, that he yielded to Mr. Savage's reasons, and agreed that it ought to be suppressed.

After many alterations and delays, a subscription was at length raised, which did not amount to fifty pounds a year, though twenty were paid by one gentleman; such was the generosity of mankind, that what had been done by a player without solicitation, could not now be effected by application and interest; and Savage had a great number to court and to obey for a pension less than that which Mrs. Oldfield paid him without exacting any servilities.

Mr. Savage however was satisfied, and willing to retire, and was convinced that the allowance, though scanty, would be more than sufficient for him, being now determined to commence a rigid economist, and to live according to the exactest rules of frugality; for nothing was in his opinion more contemptible than a man, who, when he knew his income, exceeded it; and yet he confessed, that instances of such folly were too common, and lamented that some men were not to be trusted with their own money.

Full of these salutary resolutions, he left London in July 1739, having taken leave with great tenderness of his friends, and parted from the author of this narrative with tears in his eyes. He was furnished with fifteen guineas, and informed, that they would be sufficient, not only for the expence of his journey, but for his support in Wales for some time; and that there remained but little more of the first collection. He promised a strict adherence to his maxims of parsimony, and went away in the stage-coach; nor did his friends expect to hear from him, till he informed them of his arrival at Swansea.

But when they least expected, arrived a letter dated the fourteenth day after his departure, in which he sent them word, that he was yet upon the road, and without money; and that he therefore could not proceed without a remittance. They then sent him the money that was in their hands, with which he was enabled to reach Bristol, from whence he was to go to Swansea by water.

At Bristol he found an embargo laid upon the shipping, so that he could not immediately obtain a passage; and being therefore obliged to stay there some time, he with his usual felicity, ingratiated himself with many of the principal inhabitants, was invited to their houses, distinguished at their publick feasts, and treated with a regard that gratified his vanity, and therefore easily engaged his affection.

He began very early after his retirement to complain of the conduct of his friends in London, and irritated many of them so much by his letters, that they withdrew, however honourably, their contributions; and it is believed, that little more was paid than the twenty pounds a year, which were allowed him by the gentleman who proposed the subscription.

After some stay at Bristol he retired to Swansea, the place originally proposed for his residence, where he lived about a year, very much dissatisfied with the diminution of his salary; but contracted, as in other places, acquaintance with those who were most distinguished in that country, among whom he has celebrated Mr. Powel and Mrs. Jones, by some verses which he inserted in *The Gentleman's Magazine*.

Here he completed his tragedy, of which two acts were wanting when he left London, and was desirous of coming to town to bring it upon the stage. This design was very warmly opposed, and he was advised by his chief benefactor to put it into the hands of Mr. Thomson and Mr. Mallet, that it might be fitted for the stage, and to allow his friends to receive the profits, out of which an annual pension should be paid him.

This proposal he rejected with the utmost contempt.[32] He was by no means convinced that the judgement of those, to whom he was required to submit, was superior to his own. He was now determined, as he expressed it, to be "no longer kept in leading-strings," and had no elevated idea of "his bounty, who proposed to pension him out of the profits of his own labours."

He attempted in Wales to promote a subscription for his works, and had once hopes of success; but in a short time afterwards formed a resolution of leaving that part of the country, to which he thought it not reasonable to be confined for the gratification of those, who, having promised him a liberal income, had no sooner banished him to a remote corner, than they reduced his allowance to a salary scarcely equal to the necessities of life.

His resentment of this treatment, which, in his own opinion at least, he had not deserved, was such, that he broke off all correspondence with most of his contributors, and appeared to consider them as persecutors and oppressors; and in the latter part of his life declared, that their conduct toward him, since his departure from London, "had been perfidiousness improving on perfidiousness, and inhumanity on inhumanity."

It is not to be supposed, that the necessities of Mr. Savage did not sometimes incite him to satirical exaggeration of the behaviour of those by whom he thought himself reduced to them. But it must be granted, that the diminution of his allowance was a great hardship, and that those who withdrew their subscription from a man, who, upon the faith of their promise, had gone into a kind of banishment, and abandoned all those by whom he had been before relieved in his distress, will find it no easy task to vindicate their conduct.

It may be alleged, and perhaps justly, that he was petulant and contemptuous; that he more frequently reproached his subscribers for not giving him more, than thanked them for what he received; but it is to be remembered, that his conduct, and this is the worst charge that can be drawn up against him, did them no real injury; and that it therefore ought rather to have been pitied than resented; at least, the resentment it might provoke ought to have been generous and manly; epithets which his conduct will hardly deserve that starves the man whom he has persuaded to put himself into his power.

It might have been reasonably demanded by Savage, that they should, before they had taken away what they promised, have replaced him in his former state, that they should have taken no advantages from the situation to which the appearance of their kindness had reduced him, and that he should have been recalled to London before he was abandoned. He might justly represent, that he ought to have been considered as a lion in the toils, and demand to be released before the dogs should be loosed upon him.

He endeavoured, indeed, to release himself, and, with an intent to return to London, went to Bristol, where a repetition of the kindness which he had formerly found invited him to stay. He was not only caressed and treated, but had a collection made for him of about thirty pounds, with which it had been happy if he had immediately departed for London; but his negligence did not suffer him to consider, that such proofs of kindness were not often to be expected, and that this ardour of benevolence was in a great degree the effect of novelty, and might, probably, be every day less; and therefore he took no care to improve the happy time, but was encouraged by one favour to hope for another, till at length generosity was exhausted, and officiousness wearied.

Another part of his misconduct was the practice of prolonging his visits to unseasonable hours, and disconcerting all the families into which he was admitted. This was an error in a place of commerce which all the charms of his conversation could not compensate; for what trader would purchase such airy satisfaction by the loss of solid gain, which must be the consequence of midnight merriment, as those hours which were gained at night were generally lost in the morning?

Thus Mr. Savage, after the curiosity of the inhabitants was gratified, found the number of his friends daily decreasing, perhaps without suspecting for what reason their conduct was altered; for he still continued to harass, with his nocturnal intrusions, those that yet countenanced him, and admitted him to their houses.

But he did not spend all the time of his residence at Bristol in visits or at taverns, for he sometimes returned to his studies, and began several considerable designs. When he felt an inclination to write, he always retired from the knowledge of his friends, and lay hid in an obscure part of the suburbs, till he found himself again desirous of company, to which it is likely that intervals of absence made him more welcome.

He was always full of his design of returning to London, to bring his tragedy upon the stage; but, having neglected to depart with the money that was raised for him, he could not afterwards procure a sum sufficient to defray the expences of his journey; nor perhaps would a fresh supply have had any other effect, than, by putting immediate pleasures in his power, to have driven the thoughts of his journey out of his mind.

While he was thus spending the day in contriving a scheme for the morrow, distress stole upon him by imperceptible degrees. His conduct had already wearied some of those who were at first enamoured of his conversation; but he might, perhaps, still have devolved to others, whom he might have entertained with equal success, had not the decay of his clothes made it no longer consistent with their vanity to admit him to their tables, or to associate with him in publick places. He now began to find every man from home at whose house he called; and was therefore no longer able to procure the necessaries of life, but wandered about the town, slighted and neglected, in quest of a dinner, which he did not always obtain.

To complete his misery, he was pursued by the officers for small debts which he had contracted; and was therefore obliged to withdraw from the small number of friends from whom he had still reason to hope for favours. His custom was to lie in bed the greatest part of the day, and to go out in the dark with the utmost privacy, and after having paid his visit return again before morning to his lodging, which was in the garret of an obscure inn.

Being thus excluded on one hand, and confined on the other, he suffered the utmost extremities of poverty, and often fasted so long that he was seized with faintness, and had lost his appetite, not being able to bear the smell of meat, till the action of his stomach was restored by a cordial.

In this distress, he received a remittance of five pounds from London,[33] with which he provided himself a decent coat, and determined to go to London, but unhappily spent his money at a favourite tavern. Thus was he again confined to Bristol, where he was every day hunted by bailiffs. In this exigence he once more found a friend, who sheltered him in his house, though at the usual inconveniences with which his company was attended; for he neither could be persuaded to go to bed in the night, nor to rise in the day.

It is observable, that in these various scenes of misery, he was always disengaged and cheerful: he at some times pursued his studies, and at others continued or enlarged his epistolary correspondence; nor was he ever so far dejected as to endeavour to procure an increase of his allowance by any other methods than accusations and reproaches.

He had now no longer any hopes of assistance from his friends at Bristol, who as merchants, and by consequence sufficiently studious of profit, cannot be supposed to have looked with much compassion upon negligence and extravagance, or to think any excellence equivalent to a fault of such consequence as neglect of economy. It is natural to imagine, that many of those, who would have relieved his real wants, were discouraged from the exertion of their benevolence by observation of the use which was made of their favours, and conviction that relief would only be momentary, and that the same necessity would quickly return.

At last he quitted the house of his friend, and returned to his lodging at the inn, still intending to set out in a few days for London; but on the 10th of January 1742–3, having been at supper with two of his friends, he was at his return to his lodgings arrested for a debt of about eight pounds, which he owed at a coffee-house, and conducted to the house of a sheriff's officer. The account which he gives of this misfortune, in a letter to one of the gentlemen with whom he had supped, is too remarkable to be omitted.

"It was not a little unfortunate for me, that I spent yesterday's evening with you; because the hour hindered me from entering on my new lodging; however, I have now got one, but such a one as I believe nobody would choose.

"I was arrested at the suit of Mrs. Read, just as I was going up stairs to bed, at Mr. Bowyer's; but taken in so private a manner, that I believe nobody at the White Lion is apprised of it. Though I let the officers know the strength (or rather weakness) of my pocket, yet they treated me with the utmost civility; and even when they conducted me to confinement, it was in such a manner, that I verily believe I could have escaped, which I would rather be ruined than have done, notwithstanding the whole amount of my finances was but three pence halfpenny.

"In the first place I must insist, that you will industriously conceal this from Mrs. S——s, because I would not have her good-nature suffer that pain, which, I know, she would be apt to feel on this occasion.

"Next, I conjure you, dear Sir, by all the ties of friendship, by no means to have one uneasy thought on my account; but to have the same pleasantry of countenance, and unruffled serenity of mind, which (God be praised!) I have in this, and have had in a much severer calamity. Furthermore, I charge you, if you value my friendship as truly as I do yours, not to utter, or even harbour, the least resentment against Mrs. Read. I believe she has ruined me, but I freely forgive her; and (though I will never more have any intimacy with her) I would, at a due distance, rather do her an act of good, than ill will. Lastly (pardon the expression), I absolutely command you not to offer me any pecuniary assistance, nor to attempt getting me any from any one of your friends. At another time, or on any other occasion, you may, dear friend, be well assured, I would rather write to you in the submissive style of a request, than that of a peremptory command.

"However, that my truly valuable friend may not think I am too proud to ask a favour, let me entreat you to let me have your boy to attend me for this day, not only for the sake of saving me the expence of porters, but for the delivery of some letters to people whose names I would not have known to strangers.

"The civil treatment I have thus far met from those whose prisoner I am, makes me thankful to the Almighty, that, though he has thought fit to visit me (on my birth-night) with affliction, yet (such is his great goodness!) my affliction is not without alleviating circumstances. I murmur not; but am all resignation to the divine will. As to the world, I hope that I shall be endued by Heaven with that presence of mind, that serene dignity in misfortune, that constitutes the character of a true nobleman; a dignity far beyond that of coronets; a nobility arising from the just principles of philosophy, refined and exalted by those of Christianity."——

He continued five days at the officer's, in hopes that he should be able to procure bail, and avoid the necessity of going to prison. The state in which he passed his time, and the treatment which he received, are very justly expressed by him in a letter which he wrote to a friend: "The whole day," says he, "has been employed in various peoples' filling my head with their foolish chimerical systems, which has obliged me coolly (as far as nature will admit) to digest, and accommodate myself to, every different person's ways of thinking; hurried from one wild system to another, till it has quite made a chaos of my imagination, and nothing done——promised——disappointed——ordered to send, every hour, from one part of the town to the other."——

When his friends, who had hitherto caressed and applauded, found that to give bail and pay the debt was the same, they all refused to preserve him from a prison at the expence of eight pounds; and therefore, after having been some time at the officer's house, "at an immense expense," as he observes in his letter, he was at length removed to Newgate.

This expence he was enabled to support by the generosity of Mr. Nash[34] at Bath, who, upon receiving from him an account of his condition, immediately sent him five guineas, and promised to promote his subscription at Bath with all his interest.

By his removal to Newgate, he obtained at least a freedom from suspense, and rest from the disturbing vicissitudes of hope and disappointment; he now found that his friends were only companions, who were willing to share his gaiety, but not to partake of his misfortunes; and therefore he no longer expected any assistance from them.

It must however be observed of one gentleman, that he offered to release him by paying the debt; but that Mr. Savage would not consent, I suppose because he thought he had before been too burthensome to him.

He was offered by some of his friends, that a collection should be made for his enlargement; but he "treated the proposal," and declared, "he should again treat it, with disdain. As to writing any mendicant letters, he had too high a spirit, and determined only to write to some ministers of state, to try to regain his pension."

He continued to complain of those that had sent him into the country, and objected to them, that he had "lost the profits of his play, which had been finished three years;" and in another letter declares his resolution to publish a pamphlet, that the world might know how "he had been used."

This pamphlet was never written; for he in a very short time recovered his usual tranquillity, and cheerfully applied himself to more inoffensive studies. He indeed steadily declared, that he was promised a yearly allowance of fifty pounds, and never received half the sum; but he seemed to resign himself to that as well as to other misfortunes, and lose the remembrance of it in his amusements and employments.

The cheerfulness with which he bore his confinement, appears from the following letter, which he wrote, January the 30th, to one of his friends in London:

"I now write to you from my confinement in Newgate, where I have been ever since Monday last was se'nnight, and where I enjoy myself with much more tranquillity than I have known for upwards of a twelvemonth past; having a room entirely to myself, and pursuing the amusement of my poetical studies, uninterrupted, and agreeable to my mind. I thank the Almighty, I am now all collected in myself; and, though my person is in confinement, my mind can expatiate on ample and useful subjects with all the freedom imaginable. I am now more conversant with the Nine than ever; and if, instead of a Newgate-bird, I may be allowed to be a bird of the Muses, I assure you Sir, I sing very freely in my cage; sometimes indeed in the plaintive notes, of the nightingale; but, at others, in the cheerful strains of the lark."

In another letter he observes, that he ranges from one subject to another, without confining himself to any particular task; and that he was employed one week upon one attempt, and the next upon another.

Surely the fortitude of this man deserves, at least, to be mentioned with applause; and, whatever faults may be imputed to him, the virtue of suffering well cannot be denied him. The two powers which, in the opinion of Epictetus, constituted a wise man, are those of bearing and forbearing, which cannot indeed be affirmed to have been equally possessed by Savage; and indeed the want of one obliged him very frequently to practise the other.

He was treated by Mr. Dagg, the keeper of the prison, with great humanity supported by him at his own table without any certainty of recompence; had a room to himself, to which he could at any time retire from all disturbance; was allowed to stand at the door of the prison, and sometimes taken out into the fields; so that he suffered fewer hardships in prison than he had been accustomed to undergo in the greatest part of his life.[35]

The keeper did not confine his benevolence to a gentle execution of his office, but made some overtures to the creditor for his release, though without effect; and continued, during the whole time of his imprisonment, to treat him with the utmost tenderness and civility.

Virtue is undoubtedly most laudable in that state which makes it most difficult; and therefore the humanity of a gaoler certainly deserves this public attestation; and the man, whose heart has not been hardened by such an employment, may be justly proposed as a pattern of benevolence. If an inscription was once engraved "to the honest toll-gatherer," less honours ought not to be paid "to the tender gaoler."

Mr. Savage very frequently received visits, and sometimes presents, from his acquaintances: but they did not amount to a subsistence, for the greater part of which he was indebted to the generosity of this keeper; but these favours, however they might endear to him the particular persons from whom he received them, were very far from impressing upon his mind any advantageous ideas of the people of Bristol, and therefore he thought he could not more properly employ himself in prison, than in writing a poem called "London and Bristol Delineated."[36]

When he had brought this poem to its present state, which, without considering the chasm, is not perfect, he wrote to London an account of his design, and informed his friend, that he was determined to print it with his name; but enjoined him not to communicate his intention to his Bristol acquaintance. The gentleman,[37] surprised at his resolution, endeavoured to dissuade him from publishing it, at least from prefixing his name; and declared, that he could not reconcile the injunction of secrecy with his resolution to own it at its first appearance. To this Mr. Savage returned an answer agreeable to his character in the following terms:

"I received yours this morning; and not without a little surprise at the contents. To answer a question with a question, you ask me concerning London and Bristol, Why will I add delineated? Why did Mr. Woolaston add the same word to his *Religion of Nature?* I suppose that it was his will and pleasure to add it in his case; and it is mine to do so in my own. You are pleased to tell me, that you understand not why secrecy is enjoined, and yet I intend to set my name to it. My answer is—I have my private reasons, which I am not obliged to explain to any one. You doubt my friend Mr. S——[38] would not approve of it—And what is it to me whether he does or not? Do you imagine that Mr. S—— is to dictate to me? If any man who calls himself my friend should assume such an air, I would spurn at his friendship with contempt. You say, I seem to think so by not letting him know it—And suppose I do, what then? Perhaps I can give reasons for that disapprobation, very foreign from what you would imagine. You go on in saying, Suppose I should not put my name to it—My answer is, that I will not suppose any such thing, being determined to the contrary: neither, Sir, would I have you suppose, that I applied to you for want of another press: nor would I have you imagine, that I owe Mr. S ———— obligations which I do not."

Such was his imprudence, and such his obstinate adherence to his own resolutions, however absurd. A prisoner! supported by charity! and whatever insults he might have received during the latter part of his stay in Bristol, once caressed, esteemed, and presented with a liberal collection, he could forget on a sudden his danger and his obligations, to gratify the petulance of his wit, or the eagerness of his resentment, and publish a satire, by which he might reasonably expect that he should alienate those who then supported him, and provoke those whom he could neither resist nor escape.

This resolution, from the execution of which it is probable that only his death could have hindered him, is sufficient to shew, how much he disregarded all considerations that opposed his present passions, and how readily he hazarded all future advantages for any immediate gratifications. Whatever was his predominant inclination, neither hope nor fear hindered him from complying with it; nor had opposition any other effect than to heighten his ardour, and irritate his vehemence.

This performance was however laid aside, while he was employed in soliciting assistance from several great persons; and one interruption succeeding another, hindered him from supplying the chasm, and perhaps from retouching the other parts, which he can hardly be imagined to have finished in his own opinion; for it is very unequal, and some of the lines are rather inserted to rhyme to others, than to support or improve the sense; but the first and last parts are worked up with great spirit and elegance.

His time was spent in the prison for the most part in study, or in receiving visits; but sometimes he descended to lower amusements, and diverted himself in the kitchen with the conversation of the criminals; for it was not pleasing to him to be much without company; and though he was very capable of a judicious choice, he was often contented with the first that offered: for this he was sometimes reproved by his friends, who found him surrounded with felons; but the reproof was on that, as on other occasions, thrown away; he continued to gratify himself, and to set very little value on the opinion of others.

But here, as in every other scene of his life, he made use of such opportunities as occurred of benefiting those who were more miserable than himself, and was always ready to perform any office of humanity to his fellow-prisoners.

He had now ceased from corresponding with any of his subscribers except one, who yet continued to remit him the twenty pounds a year which he had promised him, and by whom it was expected that he would have been in a very short time enlarged, because he had directed the keeper to enquire after the state of his debts.[39]

However, he took care to enter his name according to the forms of the court, that the creditor might be obliged to make him some allowance, if he was continued a prisoner, and when on that occasion he appeared in the hall was treated with very unusual respect.

But the resentment of the city was afterwards raised by some accounts that had been spread of the satire, and he was informed that some of the merchants intended to pay the allowance which the law required, and to detain him a prisoner at their own expence. This he treated as an empty menace; and

196

perhaps might have hastened the publication, only to shew how much he was superior to their insults, had not all his schemes been suddenly destroyed.

When he had been six months in prison, he received from one of his friends,[40] in whose kindness he had the greatest confidence, and on whose assistance he chiefly depended, a letter, that contained a charge of very atrocious ingratitude, drawn up in such terms as sudden resentment dictated.[41] Henley, in one of his advertisements, had mentioned Pope's treatment of Savage. This was supposed by Pope to be the consequence of a complaint made by Savage to Henley, and was therefore mentioned by him with much resentment. Mr. Savage returned a very solemn protestation of his innocence, but however appeared much disturbed at the accusation. Some days afterwards he was seized with a pain in his back and side, which, as it was not violent, was not suspected to be dangerous; but growing daily more languid and dejected, on the 25th of July he confined himself to his room, and a fever seized his spirits. The symptoms grew every day more formidable, but his condition did not enable him to procure any assistance. The last time that the keeper saw him was on July the 31st, 1743; when Savage, seeing him at his bed-side, said, with an uncommon earnestness, "I have something to say to you, Sir;" but, after a pause, moved his hand in a melancholy manner; and, finding himself unable to recollect what he was going to communicate, said, "Tis gone!" The keeper soon after left him; and the next morning he died. He was buried in the church-yard of St. Peter, at the expence of the keeper.

Such were the life and death of Richard Savage, a man equally distinguished by his virtues and vices; and at once remarkable for his weaknesses and abilities.

He was of a middle stature, of a thin habit of body, a long visage, coarse features, and melancholy aspect; of a grave and manly deportment, a solemn dignity of mien; but which, upon a nearer acquaintance, softened into an engaging easiness of manners. His walk was slow, and his voice tremulous and mournful. He was easily excited to smiles, but very seldom provoked to laughter.

His mind was in an uncommon degree vigorous and active. His judgment was accurate, his apprehension quick, and his memory so tenacious, that he was frequently observed to know what he had learned from others in a short time, better than those by whom he was informed; and could frequently recollect incidents, with all their combination of circumstances, which few would have regarded at the present time, but which the quickness of his apprehension impressed upon him. He had the peculiar felicity, that his attention never deserted him; he was present to every object, and regardful of the most trifling occurrences. He had the art of escaping from his own reflections, and accommodating himself to every new scene.

To this quality is to be imputed the extent of his knowledge, compared with the small time which he spent in visible endeavours to acquire it. He mingled in cursory conversation with the same steadiness of attention as others apply to a lecture; and, amidst the appearance of thoughtless gaiety, lost no new idea that was started, nor any hint that could be improved. He had therefore made in coffee-houses the same proficiency as others in their closets: and it is remarkable, that the writings of a man of little education and little reading have an air of learning scarcely to be found in any other performances, but which perhaps as often obscures as embellishes them.

His judgement was eminently exact both with regard to writings and to men. The knowledge of life was indeed his chief attainment; and it is not without some satisfaction, that I can produce the suffrage of Savage in favour of human nature, of which he never appeared to entertain such odious ideas as some, who perhaps had neither his judgement nor experience, have published, either in ostentation of their sagacity, vindication of their crimes, or gratification of their malice.

His method of life particularly qualified him for conversation, of which he knew how to practise all the graces. He was never vehement or loud, but at once modest and easy, open and respectful; his language was vivacious and elegant, and equally happy upon grave or humourous subjects. He was generally censured for not knowing when to retire; but that was not the defect of his judgement, but of his fortune: when he left his company, he was frequently to spend the remaining part of the night in the street, or at least was abandoned to gloomy reflections, which it is not strange that he delayed as long as he could; and sometimes forgot that he gave others pain to avoid it himself.

It cannot be said, that he made use of his abilities for the direction of his own conduct: an irregular and dissipated manner of life had made him the slave of every passion that happened to be excited by the presence of its object, and that slavery to his passions reciprocally produced a life irregular and dissipated. He was not master of his own motions, nor could promise any thing for the next day.

With regard to his oeconomy, nothing can be added to the relation of his life. He appeared to think himself born to be supported by others, and dispensed from all necessity of providing for himself; he therefore never prosecuted any scheme of advantage, nor endeavoured even to secure the profits which his writings might have afforded him. His temper was, in consequence of the dominion of his passions, uncertain and capricious; he was easily engaged, and easily disgusted; but he is accused of retaining his hatred more tenaciously than his benevolence.

He was compassionate both by nature and principle, and always ready to perform offices of humanity; but when he was provoked (and small offences were sufficient to provoke him), he would prosecute his revenge with the utmost acrimony till his passion had subsided.

His friendship was therefore of little value; for though he was zealous in the support or vindication of those whom he loved, yet it was always dangerous to trust him, because he considered himself as discharged by the first quarrel from all ties of honour or gratitude; and would betray those secrets which, in the warmth of confidence, had been imparted to him. This practice drew upon him an universal accusation of ingratitude: nor can it be denied that he was very ready to set himself free from the load of an obligation; for he could not bear to conceive himself in a state of dependence, his pride being equally powerful with his other passions, and appearing in the form of insolence at one time, and of vanity at another. Vanity, the most innocent species of pride, was most frequently predominant: He could not easily leave off, when he had once begun to mention himself or his works; nor ever read his verses without stealing his eyes from the page, to discover, in the faces of his audience, how they were affected with any favourite passage.

A kinder name than that of vanity ought to be given to the delicacy with which he was always careful to separate his own merit from every other man's, and to reject that praise to which he had no claim. He did not forget, in mentioning his performances, to mark every line that had been suggested or amended; and was so accurate, as to relate that he owed three words in *The Wanderer* to the advice of his friends.

His veracity was questioned, but with little reason; his accounts, though not indeed always the same, were generally consistent. When he loved any man, he suppressed all his faults; and, when he had been offended by him, concealed all his virtues: but his characters were generally true, so far as he proceeded; though it cannot be denied, that his partiality might have sometimes the effect of falsehood.

In cases indifferent, he was zealous for virtue, truth, and justice: he knew very well the necessity of goodness to the present and future happiness of mankind; nor is there perhaps any writer, who has less endeavoured to please by flattering the appetites, or perverting the judgement.

As an author, therefore, and he now ceases to influence mankind in any other character, if one piece which he had resolved to suppress be excepted, he has very little to fear from the strictest moral or religious censure. And though he may not be altogether secure against the objections of the critic, it must however be acknowledged, that his works are the productions of a genius truly poetical; and, what many writers who have been more lavishly applauded cannot boast, that they have an original air, which has no resemblance of any foregoing work, that the versification and sentiments have a cast peculiar to themselves, which no man can imitate with success, because what was nature in Savage, would in another be affectation. It must be confessed, that his descriptions are striking, his images animated, his fictions justly imagined, and his allegories artfully pursued; that his diction is elevated, though sometimes forced, and his numbers sonorous and majestic, though frequently sluggish and encumbered. Of his style, the general fault is harshness, and its general excellence is dignity; of his sentiments, the prevailing beauty is sublimity, and uniformity the prevailing defect.

For his life, or for his writings, none, who candidly consider his fortune, will think an apology either necessary or difficult. If he was not always sufficiently instructed in his subject, his knowledge was at least greater than could have been attained by others in the same state. If his works were sometimes unfinished, accuracy cannot reasonably be exacted from a man oppressed with want, which he has no hope of relieving but by a speedy publication. The insolence and resentment of which he is accused were not easily to be avoided by a great mind, irritated by perpetual hardships, and constrained hourly to return the spurns of contempt, and repress the insolence of prosperity; and vanity may surely readily be pardoned in him, to whom life afforded no other comforts than barren praises, and the consciousness of deserving them.

Those are no proper judges of his conduct, who have slumbered away their time on the down of plenty; nor will any wise man presume to say, "Had I been in Savage's condition, I should have lived or written better than Savage."

This relation will not be wholly without its use, if those, who languish under any part of his sufferings, shall be enabled to fortify their patience, by reflecting that they feel only those afflictions from which the abilities of Savage did not exempt him; or those, who, in confidence of superior capacities or attainments, disregard the common maxims of life, shall be reminded, that nothing will supply the want of prudence; and that negligence, and, irregularity, long continued, will make knowledge useless, wit ridiculous, and genius contemptible.

Endnotes

1. I.e., beguiled.
2. Benjamin Hoadley, at that time (1717–20) Bishop of Bangor. His discourses denying absolute authority to institutions divine as well as secular gave rise to the so-called Bangorian Controversy, "one of the most intricate tangles of fruitless logomachy in the language" (Leslie Stephen, *History of English Thought in the Eighteenth Century*, ch. X, par. 31). Savage's poem was "The Convocation," 1717.

3. Christopher Bullock was joint manager of Lincoln's Inn Fields theatre. The play appeared 1716.

4. At Drury Lane Theatre, 1718, according to Jacob, *Poetical Register*, I, 298.

5. Robert Wilks (1665?–1732), one of the leading actors of his day, long popular in London (Drury Lane and Haymarket theatres) and in Dublin.

6. This I write upon the credit of the author of his life, which was published 1727. JOHNSON.

7. Anne Oldfield (1683–1730), a great actress, celebrated in both tragic and comic roles.

8. I.e., the house profits of an evening's theatrical performance.

9. In 1724. JOHNSON.

10. Aaron Hill (1685–1750), poet, dramatist, and critical journalist, conducted *The Plain Dealer* (1724), wrote the libretto for Handel's *Rinaldo* (1711), was ridiculed by Pope, whom he attacked.

11. The *Plain Dealer* was a periodical paper, written by Mr. Hill and Mr. Bond, whom Mr. Savage called the two contending powers of light and darkness. They wrote by turns each six Essays; and the character of the work was observed regularly to rise in Mr. Hill's weeks, and fall in Mr. Bond's. JOHNSON.

12. Quoted from the *Life of Savage*, 1727 [p. 23], on which see the note further on.

13. Written by Mr. Beckingham and another gentleman. JOHNSON. Charles Beckingham (1699–1731), poet and dramatist, had two plays performed (by the age of twenty) at Lincoln's Inn Fields theatre.

14. Reprinted as "A Character," in *The Poetical Works of Richard Savage*, ed. Clarence Tracy, 1962, p. 243.

15. Tyrconnel's mother and Savage's putative mother were sisters.

16. "If," here, is equivalent to "Considering that." Hill (*Lives*, II, 360, par. 107) omits it, and begins a new sentence at "The enumeration."

17. I.e., initials of proper names affixed to quotations.

18. Johnson prints in a footnote Savage's cruel epigram, believing it yet unpublished. Hill reprints it (II, 362), noting that it had appeared in *Gent. Mag.*, 1731, p. 306, slightly varied, and again in Washington's edition of Pope. Tracy does not include it in his edition of Savage's Poetry, though he gives another, on p. 182.

19. Sir Robert Walpole.

20. Lawrence Eusden died Sept. 27, 1730.

21. On March 14, 1734. The poem was entitled "The Genius of Liberty."

22. The Bishop of London was Edmund Gibson (1669–1748); the Chancellor, Charles Talbot (1685–1737): the quarrel was about appointing Thomas Rundle Bishop of Gloucester. Rundle was made Bishop of Derry in the event.

23. Thomson was the poet; James Foster a Nonconformist minister, "a man of mean ability," said Johnson elsewhere, "and of no original thinking." (*Johnsonian Miscellanies*, ed. Hill, II, 41).

24. "Satire on False Historians," in *The Gentleman's Magazine*, 1741, p. 491.

25. Johnson himself discusses these topics in his *Journey to the Western Isles*.

26. Hill surmises that James Miller, author of *The Coffee House*, 1737, is meant, but finds nothing in this or his other plays to substantiate the charge.

27. Queen Caroline made Stephen Duck (1705–1756), the "thresher poet," her librarian at Richmond. He later became Rector of Byfleet, but, in a fit of depression, drowned himself.

28. The writer was Pope.

29. An area surrounding Fleet Prison, made free to the debtors consigned to it.

30. By Mr. Pope. JOHNSON

31. Lemon, or Leman, was the son-in-law of Mrs. Brett (Savage's "mother's" name by a later marriage).

32. In a letter from Pope to Savage, 15 Sept., 1742, Pope writes defensively: "What mortal would take your play . . . out of your hands, if you could come, and attend it yourself? It was only in defect of that, these offices of the two gentlemen you are so angry at, were offered. What interest but trouble could they have had in it?" (Pope's *Correspondence*, ed. Sherburn, IV, 418.)

33. Again from Pope.

34. I.e., "Beau" Nash, "King of Bath." For his charitable conduct, see Goldsmith's Life of him.

35. In the Spring of 1739, George Whitefield and John Wesley began the Methodist open-air preaching at Bristol, and Dagg, who permitted Whitefield to speak to the prisoners every day, appears to have been an early convert.

36. In the first edition of the *Life*, 1744, Johnson printed the poem.

37. Edward Cave, the Printer, originator of *The Gentleman's Magazine*.

38. Strong, Bristol Post-Master, from whom Cave obtained letters and other information about Savage which Johnson was able to use.

39. Pope again.

40. Mr. Pope. JOHNSON

41. The following two sentences were not in the earlier text. John Henley gave weekly public orations, advertised beforehand in a flamboyant manner; he was no friend of Pope's.

William Wordsworth

From Preface to *Lyrical Ballads*

The Subject and Language of Poetry

The first volume of these poems has already been submitted to general perusal. It was published, as an experiment, which, I hoped, might be of some use to ascertain, how far, by fitting to metrical arrangement a selection of the real language of men in a state of vivid sensation, that sort of pleasure and that quantity of pleasure may be imparted, which a poet may rationally endeavour to impart.

I had formed no very inaccurate estimate of the probable effect of those poems: I flattered myself that they who should be pleased with them would read them with more than common pleasure: and, on the other hand, I was well aware, that by those who should dislike them they would be read with more than common dislike. The result has differed from my expectation in this only, that I have pleased a greater number than I ventured to hope I should please.

For the sake of variety, and from a consciousness of my own weakness, I was induced to request the assistance of a friend, who furnished me with the poems of the *Ancient Mariner*, the *Foster-Mother's Tale*, the *Nightingale*, and the poem entitled *Love*. I should not, however, have requested this assistance, had I not believed that the poems of my friend would in a great measure have the same tendency as my own, and that, though there would be found a difference, there would be found no discordance in the colours of our style; as our opinions on the subject of poetry do almost entirely coincide.

Several of my friends are anxious for the success of these poems from a belief, that, if the views with which they were composed were indeed realized, a class of poetry would be produced, well adapted to interest mankind permanently, and not unimportant in the multiplicity, and in the quality of its moral relations: and on this account they have advised me to prefix a systematic defence of the theory upon which the poems were written. But I was unwilling to undertake the task, because I knew that on this occasion the reader would look coldly upon my arguments, since I might be suspected of having been principally influenced by the selfish and foolish hope of *reasoning* him into an approbation of these particular poems: and I was still more unwilling to undertake the task, because, adequately to display my opinions, and fully to enforce my arguments, would require a space wholly disproportionate to the nature of a preface. For to treat the subject with the clearness and coherence of which I believe it susceptible, it would be necessary to give a full account of the present state of the public taste in this country, and to determine how far this taste is healthy or depraved; which, again, could not be determined, without pointing out, in what manner language and the human mind act and re-act on each other, and without retracing the revolutions, not of literature alone, but likewise of society itself. I have therefore altogether declined to enter regularly upon this defence; yet I am sensible, that there would be some impropriety in abruptly obtruding upon the

From *Preface to Lyrical Ballads, with Pastoral and Other Poems by William Wordsworth*.

public, without a few words of introduction, poems so materially different from those upon which general approbation is at present bestowed.

It is supposed, that by the act of writing in verse an author makes a formal engagement that he will gratify certain known habits of association; that he not only thus apprizes the reader that certain classes of ideas and expressions will be found in his book, but that others will be carefully excluded. This exponent or symbol held forth by metrical language must in different eras of literature have excited very different expectations: for example, in the age of Catullus, Terence, and Lucretius and that of Statius or Claudian, and in our own country, in the age of Shakespeare and Beaumont and Fletcher, and that of Donne and Cowley, or Dryden, or Pope. I will not take upon me to determine the exact import of the promise which by the act of writing in verse an author, in the present day, makes to his reader; but I am certain, it will appear to many persons that I have not fulfilled the terms of an engagement thus voluntarily contracted. They who have been accustomed to the gaudiness and inane phraseology of many modern writers, if they persist in reading this book to its conclusion, will, no doubt, frequently have to struggle with feelings of strangeness and awkwardness: they will look round for poetry, and will be induced to inquire by what species of courtesy these attempts can be permitted to assume that title. I hope therefore the reader will not censure me, if I attempt to state what I have proposed to myself to perform; and also (as far as the limits of a preface will permit) to explain some of the chief reasons which have determined me in the choice of my purpose: that at least he may be spared any unpleasant feeling of disappointment, and that I myself may be protected from the most dishonorable accusation which can be brought against an author, namely, that of an indolence which prevents him from endeavouring to ascertain what is his duty, or, when this duty is ascertained, prevents him from performing it.

"The principal object, then, which I proposed to myself in these poems was to choose incidents and situations from common life and to relate or describe them, throughout, as far as was possible, in a selection of language really used by men; and, at the same time, to throw over them a certain colouring of imagination, whereby ordinary things should be presented to the mind in an unusual way; and, further, and above all, to make these incidents and situations interesting by tracing in them, truly though not ostentatiously, the primary laws of our nature: chiefly, as far as regards the manner in which we associate ideas in a state of excitement. Low and rustic life was generally chosen, because in that condition, the essential passions of the heart find a better soil in which they can attain their maturity, are less under restraint, and speak a plainer and more emphatic language; because in that condition of life our elementary feelings co-exist in a state of greater simplicity, and, consequently, may be more accurately contemplated, and more forcibly communicated; because the manners of rural life germinate from those elementary feelings; and, from the necessary character of rural occupations, are more easily comprehended; and are more durable; and lastly, because in that condition, the passions of men are incorporated with the beautiful and permanent forms of nature. The language, too, of these men is adopted (purified indeed from what appear to be its real defects, from all lasting and rational causes of dislike or disgust) because such men hourly communicate with the best objects from which the best part of language is originally derived; and because, from their rank in society and the sameness and narrow circle of their intercourse, being less under the influence of social vanity they convey their feelings and notions in simple and unelaborated expressions. Accordingly, such a language, arising out of repeated experience and regular feelings, is a more permanent, and a far more philosophical language, than that which is frequently substituted for it by poets, who think that they are conferring honour upon themselves and their art, in proportion as they separate themselves from the sympathies of men, and indulge in arbitrary and capricious habits of expression, in order to furnish food for fickle tastes, and fickle appetites, of their own creation.

I cannot, however, be insensible of the present outcry against the triviality and meanness both of thought and language, which some of my contemporaries have occasionally introduced into their metrical compositions; and I acknowledge, that this defect, where it exists, is more dishonorable to the writer's own character than false refinement or arbitrary innovation, though I should contend at the same time that it is far less pernicious in the sum of its consequences. From such verses the poems in these volumes will be found distinguished at least by one mark of difference, that each of them has a worthy *purpose*. Not that I mean to say, that I always began to write with a distinct purpose formally conceived; but I believe that my habits of meditation have so formed my feelings, as that my descriptions of such objects as strongly excite those feelings, will be found to carry along with them a *purpose*. If in this opinion I am mistaken, I can have little right to the name of a poet. For all good poetry is the spontaneous overflow of powerful feelings: but though this be true, poems to which any value can be attached, were never produced on any variety of subjects but by a man who, being possessed of more than usual organic sensibility, had also thought long and deeply. For our continued influxes of feeling are modified and directed by our thoughts, which are indeed the representatives of all our past feelings; and, as by contemplating the relation of these general representatives to each other we discover what is really important to men, so, by the repetition and continuance of this act, our feelings will be connected with important subjects, till at length, if we be originally possessed of much sensibility, such habits of mind will be produced, that, by obeying blindly and mechanically the impulses of those habits, we shall describe objects, and utter sentiments, of such a nature and in such connection with each other, that the understanding of the being to whom we address ourselves, if he be in a healthful state of association, must necessarily be in some degree enlightened, and his affections ameliorated.

I have said that each of these poems has a purpose. I have also informed my reader what this purpose will be found principally to be: namely, to illustrate the manner in which our feelings and ideas are associated in a state of excitement. But, speaking in language somewhat more appropriate, it is to follow the fluxes and refluxes of the mind when agitated by the great and simple affections of our nature. This object I have endeavored in these short essays to attain by various means; by tracing the maternal passion through many of its more subtile windings, as in the poems of the *Idiot Boy* and the *Mad Mother*; by accompanying the last struggles of a human being, at the approach of death, cleaving in solitude to life and society, as in the poem of the *Forsaken Indian*; by shewing, as in the stanzas entitled *We Are Seven*, the perplexity and obscurity which in childhood attend our notion of death, or rather our utter inability to admit that notion; or by displaying the strength of fraternal, or to speak more philosophically, of moral attachment when early associated with the great and beautiful objects of nature, as in *The Brothers*; or, as in the *Incident of Simon Lee*, by placing my reader in the way of receiving from ordinary moral sensations another and more salutary impression than we are accustomed to receive from them. It has also been part of my general purpose to attempt to sketch characters under the influence of less impassioned feelings, as in the *Two April Mornings, The Fountain, The Old Man Travelling, The Two Thieves*, &c., characters of which the elements are simple, belonging rather to nature than to manners, such as exist now, and will probably always exist, and which from their constitution may be distinctly and profitably contemplated. I will not abuse the indulgence of my reader by dwelling longer upon this subject; but it is proper that I should mention one other circumstance which distinguishes these poems from the popular poetry of the day; it is this, that the feeling therein developed gives importance to the action and situation, and not the action and situation to the feeling. My meaning will be rendered perfectly intelligible by referring my reader to the poems entitled *Poor Susan* and the *Childless Father*, particularly to the last stanza of the latter poem.

I will not suffer a sense of false modesty to prevent me from asserting, that I point my reader's attention to this mark of distinction, far less for the sake of these particular poems than from the general importance of the subject. The subject is indeed important! For the human mind is capable of being excited without the application of gross and violent stimulants; and he must have a very faint perception of its beauty and dignity who does not know this, and who does not further know, that one being is elevated above another, in proportion as he possesses this capability. It has therefore appeared to me, that to endeavour to produce or enlarge this capability is one of the best services in which, at any period, a writer can be engaged; but this service, excellent at all times, is especially so at the present day. For a multitude of causes, unknown to former times, are now acting with a combined force to blunt the discriminating powers of the mind, and, unfitting it for all voluntary exertion, to reduce it to a state of almost savage torpor. The most effective of these causes are the great national events which are daily taking place, and the increasing accumulation of men in cities, where the uniformity of their occupations produces a craving for extraordinary incident, which the rapid communication of intelligence hourly gratifies. To this tendency of life and manners the literature and theatrical exhibitions of the country have conformed themselves. The invaluable works of our elder writers, I had almost said the works of Shakespeare and Milton, are driven into neglect by frantic novels, sickly and stupid German tragedies, and deluges of idle and extravagant stories in verse.—When I think upon this degrading thirst after outrageous stimulation, I am almost ashamed to have spoken of the feeble effort with which I have endeavoured to counteract it; and, reflecting upon the magnitude of the general evil, I should be oppressed with no dishonorable melancholy, had I not a deep impression of certain inherent and indestructible qualities of the human mind, and likewise of certain powers in the great and permanent objects that act upon it which are equally inherent and indestructible; and did I not further add to this impression a belief, that the time is approaching when the evil will be systematically opposed, by men of greater powers, and with far more distinguished success.

Having dwelt thus long on the subjects and aim of these poems, I shall request the reader's permission to apprize him of a few circumstances relating to their style, in order, among other reasons, that I may not be censured for not having performed what I never attempted. The reader will find that personifications of abstract ideas rarely occur in these volumes; and, I hope, are utterly rejected as an ordinary device to elevate the style, and raise it above prose. I have proposed to myself to imitate, and, as far as is possible, to adopt the very language of men; and assuredly such personifications do not make any natural or regular part of that language. They are, indeed, a figure of speech occasionally prompted by passion, and I have made use of them as such; but I have endeavoured utterly to reject them as a mechanical device of style, or as a family language which writers in metre seem to lay claim to by prescription. I have wished to keep my reader in the company of flesh and blood, persuaded that by so doing I shall interest him. I am, however, well aware that others who pursue a different track may interest him likewise; I do not interfere with their claim, I only wish to prefer a different claim of my own. There will also be found in these volumes little of what is usually called poetic diction; I have taken as much pains to avoid it as others ordinarily take to produce it; this I have done for the reason already alleged, to bring my language near to the language of men, and further, because the pleasure which I have proposed to myself to impart is of a kind very different from that which is supposed by many persons to be the proper object of poetry. I do not know how, without being culpably particular, I can give my reader a more exact notion of the style in which I wished these poems to be written than by informing him that I have at all times endeavoured to look steadily at my subject, consequently, I hope that there is in these poems little falsehood of description, and that my ideas are expressed in language fitted to their respective importance. Something I must have gained by this practice, as it is friendly to one property of all good poetry, namely, good sense; but it has necessarily cut me off from a large portion of phrases and figures of speech which from father to son have long been regarded as the common inheritance of poets. I have also thought it expedient to restrict myself still further, having abstained from the use of many expressions, in themselves proper and beautiful, but which have been foolishly repeated by bad poets, till such feelings of disgust are connected with them as it is scarcely possible by any art of association to overpower.

If in a poem there should be found a series of lines, or even a single line, in which the language, though naturally arranged and according to the strict laws of metre, does not differ from that of prose, there is a numerous class of critics, who, when they stumble upon these prosaisms as they call them, imagine that they have made a notable discovery, and exult over the poet as over a man ignorant of his own profession. Now these men would establish a canon of criticism which the reader will conclude he must utterly reject, if he wishes to be pleased with these volumes. And it would be a most easy task to prove to him, that not only the language of a large portion of every good poem, even of the most elevated character, must necessarily, except with reference to the metre, in no respect differ from that of good prose, but likewise that some of the most interesting parts of the best poems will be found to be strictly the language of prose, when prose is well written. The truth of this assertion might be demonstrated by innumerable passages from almost all the poetical writings, even of Milton himself. I have not space for much quotation; but, to illustrate the subject in a general manner, I will here adduce a short composition of Gray, who was at the head of those who by their reasonings have attempted to widen the space of separation betwixt prose and metrical composition, and was more than any other man curiously elaborate in the structure of his own poetic diction.

> In vain to me the smiling mornings shine,
> And reddening Phoebus lifts his golden fire:
> The birds in vain their amorous descant join,
> Or cheerful fields resume their green attire:
> These ears, alas! for other notes repine;
> *A different object do these eyes require;*
> *My lonely anguish melts no heart but mine;*
> *And in my breast the imperfect joys expire;*

> Yet Morning smiles the busy race to cheer,
> And new-born pleasure brings to happier men;
> The fields to all their wonted tribute bear;
> To warm their little loves the birds complain.
> *I fruitless mourn to him that cannot hear*
> *And weep the more because I weep in vain.*

It will easily be perceived that the only part of this sonnet which is of any value is the lines printed in italics: it is equally obvious, that, except in the rhyme, and in the use of the single word "fruitless" for fruitlessly, which is so far a defect, the language of these lines does in no respect differ from that of prose.

By the foregoing quotation I have shewn that the language of prose may yet be well adapted to poetry; and I have previously asserted that a large portion of the language of every good poem can in no respect differ from that of good prose. I will go further. I do not doubt that it may be safely affirmed, that there neither is, nor can be, any essential difference between the language of prose and metrical composition. We are fond of tracing the resemblance between poetry and painting, and, accordingly, we call them sisters: but where shall we find bonds of connection sufficiently strict to typify the affinity betwixt metrical and prose composition? They both speak by and to the same organs; the bodies in which both of them are clothed may be said to be of the same substance, their affections are kindred and almost identical, not necessarily differing even in degree; poetry sheds no tears "such as Angels, weep," but natural and human tears; she can boast of no celestial ichor that distinguishes her vital juices from those of prose; the same human blood circulates through the veins of them both.

***

"What Is a Poet?"

Taking up the subject, then, upon general grounds, I ask what is meant by the word "poet"? What is a poet? To whom does he address himself? And what language is to be expected from him? He is a man speaking to men: a man, it is true, endued with more lively sensibility, more enthusiasm and tenderness, who has a greater knowledge of human nature, and a more comprehensive soul, than are supposed to be common among mankind; a man pleased with his own passions and volitions, and who rejoices more than other men in the spirit of life that is in him; delighting to contemplate similar volitions and passions as manifested in the goings-on of the universe, and habitually impelled to create them where he does not find them. To these qualities he has added a disposition to be affected more than other men by absent things as if they were present; an ability of conjuring up in himself passions, which are indeed far from being the same as those produced by real events, yet (especially in those parts of the general sympathy which are pleasing and delightful) do more nearly resemble the passions produced by real events, than any thing which, from the motions of their own minds merely, other men are accustomed to feel in themselves; whence, and from practice, he has acquired a greater readiness and power in expressing what he thinks and feels, and especially those thoughts and feelings which, by his own choice, or from the structure of his own mind, arise in him without immediate external excitement.

But, whatever portion of this faculty we may suppose even the greatest poet to possess, there cannot be a doubt but that the language which it will suggest to him, must, in liveliness and truth, fall far short of that which is uttered by men in real life, under the actual pressure of those passions, certain shadows of which the poet thus produces, or feels to be produced, in himself: However exalted a notion we would wish to cherish of the character of a poet, it is obvious, that, while he describes and imitates passions, his situation is altogether slavish and mechanical, compared with the freedom and power of real and substantial action and suffering. So that it will be the wish of the poet to bring his feelings near to those of the persons whose feelings he describes, nay, for short spaces of time perhaps, to let himself slip into an entire delusion, and even confound and identify his own feelings with theirs; modifying only the language which is thus suggested to him, by a consideration that he describes for a particular purpose, that of giving pleasure. Here, then, he will apply the principle on which I have so much insisted, namely, that of selection; on this he will depend for removing what would otherwise be painful or disgusting in the passion; he will feel that there is no necessity to trick out or to elevate nature: and, the more industriously he applies this principle, the deeper will be his faith that no words, which his fancy or imagination can suggest, will be to be compared with those which are the emanations of reality and truth.

But it may be said by those who do not object to the general spirit of these remarks, that, as it is impossible for the poet to produce upon all occasions language as exquisitely fitted for the passion as that which the real passion itself suggests, it is proper that he should consider himself as in the situation of a translator, who deems himself justified when he substitutes excellences of another kind for those which are unattainable by him; and endeavours occasionally to surpass his original, in order to make some amends for the general inferiority to which he feels that he must submit. But this would be to encourage idleness and unmanly despair. Further, it is the language of men who speak of what they do not understand; who talk of poetry as a matter of amusement and idle pleasure; who will converse with us as gravely about a taste for poetry, as they express it, as if it were a thing as indifferent as a taste for rope-dancing, or Frontiniac or sherry. Aristotle, I have been told, hath said, that poetry is the most philosophic of all writing; it is so: its object is truth, not individual and local, but general, and operative; not standing upon external testimony, but carried alive into the heart by passion; truth which is its own testimony, which gives strength and divinity to the tribunal to which it appeals, and receives them from the same tribunal. Poetry is the image of man and nature. The obstacles which stand in the way of the fidelity of the biographer and historian, and of their consequent utility, are incalculably greater than those which are to be encountered by the poet who has an adequate notion of the dignity of his art. The poet writes under one restriction only, namely, that of the necessity of giving immediate pleasure to a human being possessed of that information which may be expected from him, not as a lawyer, a physician, a mariner, an astronomer or a natural philosopher, but as a man. Except this one restriction, there is no object standing between the poet and the image of things; between this, and the biographer and historian there are a thousand.

Nor let this necessity of producing immediate pleasure be considered as a degradation of the poet's art. It is far otherwise. It is an acknowledgment of the beauty of the universe, an acknowledgment the more sincere because it is not formal, but indirect; it is a task light and easy to him who looks at the world in the spirit of love: further, it is a homage paid to the native and naked dignity of man, to the grand elementary principle of pleasure, by which he knows, and feels, and lives, and moves. We have no sympathy but what is propagated by pleasure: I would not be misunderstood; but wherever we sympathize with pain it will be found that the sympathy, is produced and carried on by subtle combinations with pleasure. We have no knowledge, that is, no general principles drawn from the contemplation of particular facts, but what has been built up by pleasure, and exists in us by pleasure alone. The man of science, the chemist and mathematician, whatever difficulties and disgusts they may have had to struggle with, know and feel this. However painful may be the objects with which the anatomist's knowledge is connected, he feels that his knowledge is pleasure; and where he has no pleasure he has no knowledge. What then does the poet? He considers man and the objects that surround him as acting and re-acting upon each other, so as to produce an infinite complexity of pain and pleasure; he considers man in his own nature and in his ordinary life as contemplating this with a certain quantity of immediate knowledge, with certain convictions, intuitions, and deductions which by habit become of the nature of intuitions; he considers him as looking upon this complex scene of ideas and sensations, and finding every where objects that immediately excite in him sympathies which, from the necessities of his nature, are accompanied by an overbalance of enjoyment.

To this knowledge which all men carry about with them, and to these sympathies in which without any other discipline than that of our daily life we are fitted to take delight, the poet principally directs his attention. He considers man and nature as essentially adapted to each other, and the mind of man as naturally the mirror of the fairest and most interesting qualities of nature. And thus the poet, prompted by this feeling of pleasure which accompanies him through the whole course of his studies, converses with general nature with affections akin to those, which, through labour and length of time, the man of science has raised up in himself, by conversing with those particular parts of nature which are the objects of his studies. The knowledge both of the poet and the man of science is pleasure; but the knowledge of the one cleaves to us as a necessary part of our existence, our natural and unalienable inheritance; the other is a personal and individual acquisition, slow to come to us, and by no habitual and direct sympathy connecting us with our fellow-beings. The man of science seeks truth as a remote and unknown benefactor; he cherishes and loves it in his solitude: the poet, singing a song in which all human beings join with him, rejoices in the presence of truth as our visible friend and hourly companion. Poetry is the breath and finer spirit of all knowledge; it is the impassioned expression which is in the countenance of all science. Emphatically may it be said of the poet, as Shakespeare hath said of man, "that he looks before and after." He is the rock of defence of human nature; an upholder and preserver, carrying everywhere with him relationship and love. In spite of difference of soil and climate, of language and manners, of laws and customs, in spite of things silently gone out of mind and things violently destroyed, the poet binds together by passion and knowledge the vast empire of human society, as it is spread over the whole earth, and over all time. The objects of the poet's thoughts are every where; though the eyes and senses of man are, it is true, his favorite guides, yet he will follow wheresoever he can find an atmosphere of sensation in which to move his wings. Poetry is the first and last of all knowledge—it is as immortal as the heart of man. If the labours of men of science should ever create any material revolution, direct or indirect, in our condition, and in the impressions which we habitually receive, the poet will sleep then no more than at present, but he will be ready to follow the steps of the man of science, not only in those general indirect effects, but he will be at his side, carrying sensation into the midst of the objects of the science itself. The remotest discoveries of the chemist, the botanist, or mineralogist, will be as proper objects of the poet's art as any upon which it can be employed, if the time should ever come when these things shall be familiar to us, and the relations under which they are contemplated by the followers of these respective sciences shall be manifestly and palpably material to us as enjoying and suffering beings. If the time should ever come when what is now called science, thus familiarized to men, shall be ready to put on, as it were, a form of flesh and blood, the poet will lend his divine spirit to aid the transfiguration, and will welcome the being thus produced, as a dear and genuine inmate of the household of man.—It is not, then, to be supposed that any one, who holds that sublime notion of poetry which I have attempted to convey, will break in upon the sanctity and truth of his pictures by transitory and accidental ornaments, and endeavour to excite admiration of himself by arts, the necessity of which must manifestly depend upon the assumed meanness of his subject.

What I have thus far said applies to poetry in general; but especially to those parts of composition where the poet speaks through the mouth of his characters; and upon this point it appears to have such weight that I will conclude, there are few persons, of good sense, who would not allow that the dramatic parts of composition are defective, in proportion as they deviate from the real language of nature, and are coloured by a diction of the poet's own, either peculiar to him as an individual poet, or belonging simply to poets in general, to a body of men who, from the circumstance of their compositions being in metre, it is expected will employ a particular language.

It is not, then, in the dramatic parts of composition that we look for this distinction of language; but still it may be proper and necessary where the poet speaks to us in his own person and character. To this I answer by referring my reader to the description which I have before given of a wet: Among the qualities which I have enumerated as principally conducing to form a poet, is implied nothing differing in kind from other men, but only in degree. The sum of what I have there said is, that the poet is chiefly distinguished from other men by a greater promptness to think and feel without immediate external excitement, and a greater power in expressing such thoughts and feelings as are produced in him in that manner. But these passions and thoughts and feelings are the general passions and thoughts and feelings of men. And with what are they connected? Undoubtedly with our moral sentiments and animal sensations, and with the causes which excite these; with the operations of the elements and the appearances of the visible universe; with storm and sun-shine, with the revolutions of the seasons, with cold and heat, with loss of friends and kindred, with injuries and resentments, gratitude and hope, with fear and sorrow. These, and the like, are the sensations and objects which the poet describes, as they are the sensations of other men, and the objects which interest them. The poet thinks and feels in the spirit of the passions of men. How, then, can his language differ in any material degree from that of all other men who feel vividly and see clearly? It might be proved that it is impossible. But supposing that this were not the case, the poet might then be allowed to use a peculiar language, when expressing his feelings for his own gratification, or that of men like himself. But poets do not write for poets alone, but for men. Unless therefore we are advocates for that admiration which depends upon ignorance, and that pleasure which arises from hearing what we do not understand, the poet must descend from this supposed height, and, in order to excite rational sympathy, he must express himself as other men express themselves.

* * *

"Emotion Recollected in Tranquillity"

I have said that poetry is the spontaneous overflow of powerful feelings: it takes its origin from emotion recollected in tranquility: the emotion is contemplated till by a species of reaction the tranquillity gradually disappears, and an emotion, kindred to that which was before the subject of contemplation, is gradually produced, and does itself actually exist in the mind. In this mood successful composition generally begins, and in a mood similar to this it is carried on; but the emotion, of whatever kind and in whatever degree, from various causes is qualified by various pleasures, so that in describing any passions whatsoever, which are voluntarily described, the mind will upon the whole be in a state of enjoyment. Now, if nature be thus cautious in preserving in a state of enjoyment a being thus employed the poet ought to profit by the lesson thus held forth to him, and ought especially to take care, that whatever passions he communicates to his reader, those passions, if his reader's mind be sound and vigorous, should always be accompanied with an overbalance of pleasure. Now the music of harmonious metrical language, the sense of difficulty overcome, and the blind association of pleasure which has been previously received from works of rhyme or metre of the same or similar construction, an indistinct perception perpetually renewed of language closely resembling that of real life, and yet, in the circumstance of metre, differing from it so widely, all these imperceptibly make up a complex feeling of delight, which is of the most important use in tempering the painful feeling which will always be found intermingled with powerful descriptions of the deeper passions. This effect is always produced in pathetic and impassioned poetry; while, in lighter compositions, the ease and gracefulness with which the poet manages his numbers are themselves confessedly a principal source of the gratification of the reader. I might perhaps include all which it is necessary to say upon this subject by affirming, what few persons will deny, that, of two descriptions, either of passions, manners, or characters, each of them equally well executed, the one in prose and the other in verse, the verse will be read a hundred times where the prose is read once.

* * *

I know that nothing would have so effectually contributed to further the end which I have in view, as to have shewn of what kind the pleasure is, and how the pleasure is produced, which is confessedly produced by metrical composition essentially different from that which I have here endeavoured to recommend: for the reader will say that he has been pleased by such composition; and what can I do more for him? The power of any art is limited; and he will suspect, that, if I propose to furnish him with new friends, it is only upon condition of his abandoning his old friends. Besides, as I have said, the reader is himself conscious of the pleasure which he has received from such composition, composition to which he has peculiarly attached the endearing name of poetry; and all men feel an habitual gratitude, and something of an honorable bigotry for the objects which have long continued to please them: we not only wish to be pleased, but to be pleased in that particular way in which we have been accustomed to be pleased. There is a host of arguments in these feelings; and I should be the less able to combat them successfully, as I am willing to allow, that, in order entirely to enjoy the poetry which I am recommending, it would be necessary to give up much of what is ordinarily enjoyed. But, would my limits have permitted me to point out how this pleasure is produced, I might have removed many obstacles, and assisted my reader in perceiving that the powers of language are not so limited as he may suppose; and that it is possible that poetry may give other enjoyments, of a purer, more lasting, and more exquisite nature. This part of my subject I have not altogether neglected; but it has been less my present aim to prove, that the interest excited by some other kinds of poetry is less vivid, and less worthy of the nobler powers of the mind, than to offer reasons for presuming, that, if the object which I have proposed to myself were adequately attained, a species of poetry would be produced, which is genuine poetry; in its nature well adapted to interest mankind permanently, and likewise important in the multiplicity and quality of its moral relations.

From what has been said, and from a perusal of the poems, the reader will be able clearly to perceive the object which I have proposed to myself: he will determine how far I have attained this object; and, what is a much more important question, whether it be worth attaining; and upon the decision of these two questions will rest my claim to the approbation of the public.

William Wordsworth

The Old Cumberland Beggar

The class of Beggars, to which the Old Man here described belongs, will probably soon be extinct. It consisted of poor, and, mostly, old and infirm persons, who confined themselves to a stated round in their neighbourhood, and had certain fixed days, on which, at different houses, they regularly received alms, sometimes in money, but mostly in provisions.

I Saw an aged Beggar in my walk;
And he was seated, by the highway side,
On a low structure of rude masonry
Built at the foot of a huge hill, that they
Who lead their horses down the steep rough road   5
May thence remount at ease. The aged Man
Had placed his staff across the broad smooth stone
That overlays the pile; and, from a bag
All white with flour, the dole of village dames,
He drew his scraps and fragments, one by one;   10
And scanned them with a fixed and serious look
Of idle computation. In the sun,
Upon the second step of that small pile,
Surrounded by those wild unpeopled hills,
He sat, and ate his food in solitude: 15
And ever, scattered from his palsied hand,
That, still attempting to prevent the waste,
Was baffled still, the crumbs in little showers
Fell on the ground; and the small mountain birds,
Not venturing yet to peck their destined meal,   20
Approached within the length of half his staff.

    Him from my childhood have I known; and then
He was so old, he seems not older now;
He travels on, a solitary Man,
So helpless in appearance, that for him   25
The sauntering Horseman throws not with a slack
And careless hand his alms upon the ground,
But stops,— that he may safely lodge the coin

From *Selected Poems and Prefaces by William Wordsworth*.

Within the old Man's hat; nor quits him so,

From Selected Poems and Prefaces by William Wordsworth.

But still, when he has given his horse the rein,   30
Watches the aged Beggar with a look
Sidelong, and half-reverted. She who tends
The toll-gate, when in summer at her door
She turns her wheel, if on the road she sees
The aged Beggar coming, quits her work,   35
And lifts the latch for him that he may pass.
The post-boy, when his rattling wheels o'ertake
The aged Beggar in the woody lane,
Shouts to him from behind; and, if thus warned
The old man does not change his course, the boy   40
Turns with less noisy wheels to the roadside,
And passes gently by, without a curse
Upon his lips, or anger at his heart.

    He travels on, a solitary Man;
His age has no companion. On the ground   45
His eyes are turned, and, as he moves along,
They move along the ground; and, evermore,
Instead of common and habitual sight
Of fields with rural works, of hill and dale,
And the blue sky, one little span of earth   50
Is all his prospect. Thus, from day to day,
Bow-bent, his eyes for ever on the ground,
He plies his weary journey; seeing still,
And seldom knowing that he sees, some straw,
Some scattered leaf, or marks which, in one track,   55
The nails of cart or chariot-wheel have left
Impressed on the white road,— in the same line,
At distance still the same. Poor Traveller!
His staff trails with him; scarcely do his feet
Disturb the summer dust; he is so still   60
In look and motion, that the cottage curs,
Ere he has passed the door, will turn away,
Weary of barking at him. Boys and girls,
The vacant and the busy, maids and youths,
And urchins newly breeched—all pass him by: 65
Him even the slow-paced waggon leaves behind.

But deem not this Man useless.—Statesmen! ye
Who are so restless in your wisdom, ye
Who have a broom still ready in your hands
To rid the world of nuisances; ye proud,   70
Heart-swoln, while in your pride ye contemplate
Your talents, power, or wisdom, deem him not
A burthen of the earth! 'Tis Nature's law
That none, the meanest of created things,
Of forms created the most vile and brute,   75
The dullest or most noxious, should exist
Divorced from good—a spirit and pulse of good,
A life and soul, to every mode of being
Inseparably linked. Then be assured
That least of all can aught—that ever owned   80
The heaven-regarding eye and front sublime
Which man is born to—sink, howe'er depressed,
So low as to be scorned without a sin;
Without offence to God cast out of view;
Like the dry remnant of a garden-flower   85
Whose seeds are shed, or as an implement
Worn out and worthless: While from door to door,
This old Man creeps, the villagers in him
Behold a record which together binds
Past deeds and offices of charity,   90
Else unremembered, and so keeps alive
The kindly mood in hearts which lapse of years,
And that half-wisdom half-experience gives,
Make slow to feel, and by sure steps resign
To selfishness and cold oblivious cares.   95
Among the farms and solitary huts,
Hamlets and thinly-scattered villages,
Where'er the aged Beggar takes his rounds,
The mild necessity of use compels
To acts of love; and habit does the work   100
Of reason; yet prepares that after-joy
Which reason cherishes. And thus the soul,
By that sweet taste of pleasure unpursued,
Doth find herself insensibly disposed
To virtue and true goodness.

Some there are,   105
By their good works exalted, lofty minds
And meditative, authors of delight
And happiness, which to the end of time
Will live, and spread, and kindle: even such minds
In childhood, from this solitary Being,   110
Or from like wanderer, haply have received
(A thing more precious far than all that books
Or the solicitudes of love can do!)
That first mild touch of sympathy and thought,
In which they found their kindred with a world   115
Where want and sorrow were. The easy man
Who sits at his own door,—and, like the pear
That overhangs his head from the green wall,
Feeds in the sunshine; the robust and young,
The prosperous and unthinking, they who live   120
Sheltered, and flourish in a little grove
Of their own kindred;—all behold in him
A silent monitor, which on their minds
Must needs impress a transitory thought
Of self-congratulation, to the heart   125
Of each recalling his peculiar boons,
His charters and exemptions; and, perchance,
Though he to no one give the fortitude
And circumspection needful to preserve
His present blessings, and to husband up   130
The respite of the season, he, at least,
And 'tis no vulgar service, makes them felt.

Yet further.— Many, I believe, there are
Who live a life of virtuous decency,
Men who can hear the Decalogue and feel   135
No self-reproach; who of the moral law
Established in the land where they abide
Are strict observers; and not negligent
In acts of love to those with whom they dwell,
Their kindred, and the children of their blood.   140
Praise be to such, and to their slumbers peace!
—But of the poor man ask, the abject poor;
Go, and demand of him, if there be here

In this cold abstinence from evil deeds,
And these inevitable charities, 145
Wherewith to satisfy the human soul?
No—man is dear to map; the poorest poor
Long for some moments in a weary life
When they can know and feel that they have been,
Themselves, the fathers and the dealers-out 150
Of some small blessings; have been kind to such
As needed kindness, for this single cause,
That we have all of us one human heart.
—Such pleasure is to one kind Being known,
My neighbour, when with punctual care, each week 155
Duly as Friday comes, though pressed herself
By her own wants, she from her store of meal
Takes one unsparing handful for the scrip
Of this old Mendicant, and, from her door
Returning with exhilarated heart, 160
Sits by her fire, and builds her hope in heaven.

Then let him pass, a blessing on his head!
And while in that vast solitude to which
The tide of things has borne him, he appears
To breathe and live but for himself alone, 165
Unblamed, uninjured, let him bear about
The good which the benignant law of Heaven
Has hung around him: and, while life is his,
Still let him prompt the unlettered villagers
To tender offices and pensive thoughts. 170
—Then let him pass, a blessing on his head!
And, long as he can wander, let him breathe
The freshness of the valleys; let his blood
Struggle with frosty air and winter snows;
And let the chartered wind that sweeps the heath 175
Beat his grey locks against his withered face.
Reverence the hope whose vital anxiousness
Gives the last human interest to his heart.
May never House, misnamed of INDUSTRY,
Make him a captive!—for that pent-up din, 180
Those life-consuming sounds that clog the air,
Be his the natural silence of old age!

Let him be free of mountain solitudes;
And have around him, whether heard or not,
The pleasant melody of woodland birds. 185
Few are his pleasures: if his eyes have now
Been doomed so long to settle upon earth
That not without some effort they behold
The countenance of the horizontal sun,
Rising or setting, let the light at least 190
Find a free entrance to their languid orbs.
And let him, *where* and *when* he will, sit down
Beneath the trees, or on a grassy bank
Of highway side, and with the little birds
Share his chance-gathered meal; and, finally, 195
As in the eye of Nature he has lived,
So in the eye of Nature let him die!

SAMUEL TAYLOR COLERIDGE

This Lime-tree Bower my Prison

Well, they are gone, and here must I remain,
This lime-tree bower my prison! I have lost
Beauties and feelings, such as would have been
Most sweet to my remembrance even when age
Had dimm'd mine eyes to blindness! They, meanwhile,   5
Friends, whom I never more may meet again,
On springy heath, along the hill-top edge,
Wander in gladness, and wind down, perchance,
To that still roaring dell, of which I told;
The roaring dell, o'erwooded, narrow, deep,   10
And only speckled by the mid-day sun;
Where its slim trunk the ash from rock to rock
Flings arching like a bridge;—that branchless ash,
Unsunn'd and damp, whose few poor yellow leaves
Ne'er tremble in the gale, yet tremble still,   15
Fann'd by the water-fall! and there my friends
Behold the dark green file of long lank weeds,
That all at once (a most fantastic sight!)
Still nod and drip beneath the dripping edge
Of the blue clay-stone.   20

     Now, my friends emerge
Beneath the wide wide Heaven—and view again
The many-steepled tract magnificent
Of hilly fields and meadows, and the sea,
With some fair bark, perhaps, whose sails light up   25
The slip of smooth clear blue betwixt two Isles
Of purple shadow! Yes! they wander on
In gladness all; but thou, methinks, most glad,
My gentle-hearted Charles! for thou hast pined
And hunger'd after Nature, many a year,   30
In the great City pent, winning thy way
With sad yet patient soul, through evil and pain
And strange calamity! Ah! slowly sink
Behind the western ridge, thou glorious Sun!

Shine in the slant beams of the sinking orb,   35
Ye purple heath-flowers! richlier burn, ye clouds!
Live in the yellow light, ye distant groves!
And kindle, thou blue Ocean! So my friend
Struck with deep joy may stand, as I have stood,
Silent with swimming sense; yea, gazing round   40
On the wide landscape, gaze till all doth seem
Less gross than bodily; and of such hues
As veil the Almighty Spirit, when yet he makes
Spirits perceive his presence.

　　　　　A delight   45
Comes sudden on my heart, and I am glad
As I myself were there! Nor in this bower,
This little lime-tree bower, have I not mark'd
Much that has sooth'd me. Pale beneath the blaze
Hung the transparent foliage; and I watch'd   50
Some broad and sunny leaf, and lov'd to see
The shadow of the leaf and stem above
Dappling its sunshine! And that walnut-tree
Was richly ting'd, and a deep radiance lay
Full on the ancient ivy, which usurps   55
Those fronting elms, and now, with blackest mass
Makes their dark branches gleam a lighter hue
Through the late twilight: and though now the bat
Wheels silent by, and not a swallow twitters,
Yet still the solitary humble-bee   60
Sings in the bean-flower! Henceforth I shall know
That Nature ne'er deserts the wise and pure;
No plot so narrow, be but Nature there,
No waste so vacant, but may well employ
Each faculty of sense, and keep the heart   65
Awake to Love and Beauty! and sometimes
'Tis well to be bereft of promis'd good,
That we may lift the soul, and contemplate
With lively joy the joys we cannot share.
My gentle-hearted Charles! when the last rook   70
Beat its straight path along the dusky air
Homewards, I blest it! deeming its black wing
(Now a dim speck, now vanishing in light)

Had cross'd the mighty Orb's dilated glory,
While thou stood'st gazing; or, when all was still, 75
Flew creeking o'er thy head, and had a charm
For thee, my gentle-hearted Charles, to whom
No sound is dissonant which tells of Life.

Edward Bulwer Lytton

Money

First produced at the Theatre Royal, Haymarket, London, 8 December 1840, with the following cast:

ALFRED EVELYN	Mr. Macready
SIR JOHN VESEY	Mr. Strickland
LORD GLOSSMORE	Mr. F. Vining
SIR FREDERICK BLOUNT	Mr. Walter Lacy
STOUT	Mr. D. Reece
GRAVES	Mr. Webster
CAPTAIN DUDLEY SMOOTH	Mr. Wrench
SHARP	Mr. Waldron
OLD MEMBER	Mr. Wilmott
TOKE	Mr. Oxberry
MACFINCH, *a silversmith*	Mr. Gough
CRIMSON, *a portrait painter*	Mr. Gallot
MACSTUCCO, *an architect*	Mr. Mathews
PATENT, *a coachmaker*	Mr. Clarke
FRANTZ, *a tailor*	Mr. O. Smith
TABOURET, *an upholsterer*	Mr. Howe
GRAB, *a publisher*	Mr. Caulfield
KITE, *a horse-dealer*	Mr. Santer
CLARA DOUGLAS	Miss H. Faucit
LADY FRANKLIN	Mrs. Glover
GEORGINA VESEY	Miss P. Horton

Officer, Club Members, Flat, Green, &c., Waiters at the Club, Servants.

First produced at the Theatre Royal, Haymarket, London, 1840

225

ACT I

SCENE 1. *A drawing-room in* SIR JOHN VESEY'S *house; folding doors at the back,
which open on another drawing- room. To the right a table with newspapers,
books, &c., to the left a sofa writing-table.*

Sir John, Georgina, R.C.

Sir John [*reading a letter edged with black*]. Yes, he says at two precisely. 'Dear Sir John,—As since the death of my sainted Maria,'—Hum—that's his wife; she made him a martyr, and now he makes her a saint!

Georgina. Well, as since her death?—

Sir John [*reading*]. 'I have been living in chambers, where I cannot so well invite ladies, you will allow me to bring Mr. Sharp, the lawyer, to read the will of the late Mr. Mordaunt (to which I am appointed executor) at your house—your daughter being the nearest relation. I shall be with you at two precisely. HENRY GRAVES.'

Georgina. And you really feel sure that poor Mr. Mordaunt has made me his heiress?

Sir John. Ay, the richest heiress in England. Can you doubt it? Are you not his nearest relation? Niece by your poor mother, his own sister. All the time he was making this enormous fortune in India did we ever miss sending him little reminiscences of our disinterested affection? When he was last in England, and you only so high, was not my house his home? Didn't I get a surfeit out of complaisance to his execrable curries and pilaws? Didn't he smoke his hookah—nasty old—that is, poor dear man—in my best drawing-room? And did you ever speak without calling him your 'handsome uncle'—for the excellent creature was as vain as a peacock?"

Georgina. And so ugly—

Sir John. The dear deceased! Alas, he was indeed, like a kangaroo in a jaundice! And *if,* after all these marks of attachment, you are *not* his heiress, why then the finest feeling of our nature—the ties of blood—the principles of justice—are implanted in us in vain.

Georgina. Beautiful, sir. Was not that in your last speech at the Freemasons' Tavern upon the great Chimney-sweep Question?

Sir John. Clever girl!—what a memory she has! Sit down, Georgy. Upon this most happy—I mean melancholy—occasion I feel that I may trust you with a secret. You see this fine house—our fine servants—our fine plate—our fine dinners: every one thinks Sir John Vesey a rich man.

Georgina. And are you not, papa?

Sir John. Not a bit of it—all humbug, child—all humbug, upon my soul! As you hazard a minnow to hook in a trout, so one guinea thrown out with address is often the best bait for a hundred. There are two rules in life—First, men are valued not for what they *are,* but what they *seem* to be. Secondly, if you have no merit or money of your own, you must trade on the merits and money of other people. My father got the title by services in the army, and died penniless. On the strength of his services I got a pension of £400 a year—on the strength of £400 a year, I took credit for £800; on the strength of £800 a year I married your mother with £10,000; on the strength of £10,000, I took credit for £40,000, and paid Dicky Gossip three guineas a week to go about everywhere calling me 'Stingy Jack.'

Georgina. Ha! ha! A disagreeable nickname.

Sir John. But a valuable reputation. When a man is called stingy, it is as much as calling him rich; and when a man's called rich, why he's a man universally respected. On the strength of my respectability I wheeled a constituency, changed my politics, resigned my seat to a minister, who to a man of such stake in the country could offer nothing less in return than a Patent Office of £2,000 a year. That's the way to succeed in life. Humbug, my dead—all humbug, upon my soul!

Georgina. I must say that you—

Sir John. Know the world, to be sure. Now, for your fortune; as I spend all that I have, I can have nothing to leave you; yet even without counting your uncle, you have always passed for an heiress on the credit of your expectations from the savings of 'Stingy Jack.' The same with your education. I never grudged anything to make a show—never stuffed your head with histories and homilies; but you draw, you sing, you dance, you walk well into a room; and that's the way young ladies are educated now-a-days in order to become a pride to their parents and a blessing to their husband—that is, when they have caught him. Apropos of a husband, you know we thought of Sir Frederick Blount.

Georgina. Ah, papa, he is charming.

Sir John. He *was* so, my dear, before we knew your poor uncle was dead; but an heiress, such as you will be, should look out for a duke. Where the deuce is Evelyn this morning?

Georgina. I've not seen him, papa. What a strange character he is—so sarcastic; and yet he can be agreeable.

Sir John. A humorist—a cynic! one never knows how to take him. My private secretary, a poor cousin, has not got a shilling, and yet, hang me if he does not keep us all at a sort of a distance.

Georgina. But why do you take him to live with us, papa, since there's no good to be got by it?

Sir John. There you are wrong: he has a great deal of talent: prepares my speeches, writes my pamphlets, looks up my calculations. My report on the last Commission has got me a great deal of fame, and has put me at the head of the new one. Beside, he *is* our cousin—he has no salary: kindness to a poor relation always tells well in the world; and benevolence is a useful virtue, particularly when you can have it for nothing. With our other cousin, Clara, it was different: her father thought fit to leave me her guardian, though she had not a penny—a mere useless encumbrance; so, you see, I got my half-sister, Lady Franklin, to take her off my hands.

Georgina. How much longer is Lady Franklin's visit to be?

Sir John. I don't know, my dear; the longer the better—for her husband left her a good deal of money at her own disposal. Ah, here she comes.

Enter Lady Franklin *and* Clara, R.

Sir John. My dear sister, we were just loud in your praise. But how's this?—not in mourning?

Lady Franklin. Why should I go into mourning for a man I never saw?

Sir John. Still there may be a legacy.

Lady Franklin. Then there'll be less cause for affliction. Ha! ha! my dear Sir John, I'm one of those who think feelings a kind of property, and never take credit for them upon false pretences. [*Retires up a little.*]

Sir John [*aside*]. Very silly woman! But, Clara, I see you are more attentive to the proper decorum; yet you are very, *very*, Very distantly connected with the deceased—a third cousin, I think.

Clara. Mr. Mordaunt once assisted my father, and these poor robes are all the gratitude I can show him.

Sir John. Gratitude! humph ! I am afraid the minx has got expectations.

Lady Franklin. So, Mr. Graves is the executor—the will is addressed to him? The same Mr. Graves who is always in black—always lamenting his ill fortune and his sainted Maria, who led him the life of a dog?

Sir John. The very same. His liveries are black—his carriage is black—he always rides a black Galloway—and, faith, if he ever marry again, I think he will show his respect to the sainted Maria by marrying a black woman.

Lady Franklin. Ha! ha! we shall see. [*Aside.*] Poor Graves, I always liked him; he made an excellent husband.

Enter EVELYN, *seats himself,* R.C., *and takes up a book unobserved.*

Sir John. What a crowd of relations this will brings to light: Mr. Stout, the Political Economist—Lord Glossmore—

Lady Franklin. Whose grandfather kept a pawn-broker's shop and who, accordingly, entertains the profoundest contempt for everything popular, *parvenu,* and plebeian.

Sir John. Sir Frederick Blount—

Lady Franklin. Sir Fwedewick Blount, who objects to the letter *R* as being too wough, and therefore dwops its acquaintance: one of the new class of prudent young gentlemen, who, not having spirits and constitution for the hearty excesses of their predecessors, entrench themselves in the dignity of a lady-like languor. A man of fashion in the last century was riotous and thoughtless—in this he is tranquil and egotistical. He never does anything that is silly, or says anything that is wise. I beg your pardon, my dear; I believe Sir Frederick is an admirer of yours, provided, on reflection, he does not see 'what harm it could do him' to fall in love with your beauty and expectations. Then, too, our poor cousin, the scholar. Oh, Mr. Evelyn, there you are! [*Crosses to* L. *corner.*

Sir John. Evelyn—the very person I wanted; where have you been all day? Have you seen to those papers? have you written my epitaph on poor Mordaunt?—Latin, you know! Have you reported my speech at Exeter Hall? have you looked out the debates on the Customs?—and, oh, have you mended up all the old pens in the study?

Georgina. And have you brought me the black floss silk?—have you been to Storr's for my ring?—and, as we cannot go out on this melancholy occasion, did you call at Hookham's for the last H. B. and the Comic Annual?

Lady Franklin. And did you see what was really the matter with my bay horse?—did you get me the Opera-box?—did you buy my little Charley his peg-top?

Evelyn [*always reading*]. Certainly Paley is right upon that point; for, put the syllogism thus—[*Looking up.*] Ma'am—Sir—Miss Vesey— you want something of me?—Paley observes, that to assist even the undeserving, tends to the better regulation of our charitable feelings—no apologies—I am quite at your service.

Sir John. Now he's in one of his humours!

Lady Franklin. You allow him strange liberties, Sir John.

228

Evelyn. You will be the less surprised at that, madam, when I inform you that Sir John allows me nothing else. I am now about to draw on his benevolence—

Lady Franklin. I beg your pardon, sir, and like your spirit. Sir John, I'm in the way, I see; for I know your benevolence is so delicate that you never allow any one to detect it! [*Walks aside a little,* L.

Evelyn. I could not do your commissions today; I have been to visit a poor woman who was my nurse and mother's last friend. She is very poor, *very*—sick—dying—and she owes six months' rent!

Sir John. You know I should be most happy to do anything for yourself. But the nurse—[*aside*] (some people's nurses are always ill!)—there are so many impostors about!—We'll talk of it tomorrow. This most mournful occasion takes up all my attention. [*Looking at his watch.*] Bless me, so late! I've letters to write, and—none of the pens are mended! [*Exit.* R.

Georgina [*taking out her purse*]. I think I will give it to him: and yet, if I don't get the fortune after all! papa allows me so little!—then I *must* have those ear-rings. [*Puts up the purse.*] Mr. Evelyn, what is the address of your nurse?

Evelyn [*writes and gives it*]. She has a good heart with all her foibles! Ah! Miss Vesey, if that poor woman had not closed the eyes of my lost mother, Alfred Evelyn had not been this beggar to your father.

[CLARA *looks over the address.*

Georgina. I will certainly attend to it [*aside*] if I get the fortune.

Sir John [*calling without*]. Georgy, I say.

Georgina. Yes, papa. [*Exit,* R.

Evelyn has seated himself again at the table (to the right) and leans his face on his hands.

Clara. His noble spirit bowed to this! Ah, at least here I may give him comfort. [*Sits down to write.*] But he will recognize my hand.

Lady Franklin [*looking over her shoulder*]. What bill are you paying, Clara?—putting up a bank note?

Clara. Hush! Oh, Lady Franklin, you are the kindest of human beings. This is for a poor person—I would not have her know whence it came, or she would refuse it. Would you?—No, he knows *her* handwriting also!

Lady Franklin. Will I—what? give the money myself? with pleasure! Poor Clara! Why this covers all your savings—and I am so rich!

Clara. Nay, I would wish to do all myself! It is a pride—a duty—it is a joy; and I have so few joys! But, hush!— this way.

[*They retire into the inner room and converse in dumb show.*

Evelyn. And thus must I grind out my life for ever!—I am ambitious, and Poverty drags me down!—I have learning, and Poverty makes me the drudge of fools!—I love, and Poverty stands like a spectre before the altar!—But no—if, as I believe, I am but loved again, I will—will—what?—turn opium-eater, and dream of the Eden I may never enter!

Lady Franklin [*to* CLARA]. Yes I'will get my maid to copy and direct this; she writes well, and her hand will never be discovered. I will have it done, and sent instantly. [*Exit,* R.

CLARA *advances to the front of the stage and seats herself.*
EVELYN *reading. Enter* SIR FREDERICK BLOUNT, R.C.

Blount. No one in the woom! Oh, Miss Douglas! Pway don't let me disturb you. Where is Miss Vesey—
Georgina? [*Taking* CLARA'S *chair as she rises.*

Evelyn [*looking up, gives* CLARA *a chair and re-seats himself aside*]. Insolent puppy!

Clara. Shall I tell her you are here, Sir Frederick?

Blount. Not for the *world*—[*aside*] vewy pwetty girl this companion!

Clara. What did you think of the panorama the other day, cousin Evelyn?

Evelyn [*reading*].

'I cannot talk with civet in the room,
A fine puss gentleman that's all perfume!'
Rather good lines these.

Blount. Sir!

Evelyn [*offering the book*]. Don't you think so?—Cowper.

Blount [*declining the book*]. Cowper!

Evelyn. Cowper.

Blount [*shrugging his shoulders; to* CLARA]. Stwange person, Mr. Evelyn!—quite a chawacter! Indeed the
panowama gives you no idea of Naples—a delightful place. I make it a wule to go there evewy second
year—I am vewy fond of travelling. You'd like Wome (Rome)—bad inns, but vewy fine wuins; gives
you quite a taste for that sort of thing!

Evelyn [*reading*].

'How much a dunce that has been sent to roam
Excels a dunce that has been kept at home.'

Blount [*aside*]. That fellow Cowper says vewy odd things! Humph! it is beneath me to quawwell. [*Aloud.*]
It will not take long to wead the will, I suppose. Poor old Mordaunt! I am his nearest male welation.
He was vewy eccentwic. [*Draws his chair nearer.*] By the way, Miss Douglas, did you wemark my
cuwicle? It is bwinging cuwicles into fashion. I should be most happy if you would allow me to dwive
you out. Nay—nay—I should upon my word. [*Trying to take her hand.*

Evelyn [*starting up*]. A wasp!—a wasp!—just going to settle. Take care of the wasp, Miss Douglas!

Blount. A wasp!—where?—don't bwing it this way!— some people don't mind them. I've a particular
dislike to wasps; they sting damnably!

Evelyn. I beg pardon—it's only a gad-fly.

Enter SERVANT, R.

Servant. Sir John will be happy to see you in his study, Sir Frederick.   [*Exit* SERVANT.

Blount. Vewy well. Upon my word, there is something vewy nice about this girl. To be sure, I love
Georgina—but if this one would take a fancy to me [*thoughtfully*] —Well, I don't see what harm it
could do me!—*Au plaisir!*   [*Exit,* R.

Evelyn. Clara!

Clara. Cousin!

Evelyn. And you too are a dependant!

Clara. But on Lady Franklin, who seeks to make me forget it.

Evelyn. Ay, but can the world forget it? This insolent condescension—this coxcombry of admiration—more galling than the arrogance of contempt! Look you now—robe Beauty in silk and cachemire—hand Virtue into her chariot—lackey their caprices—wrap them from the winds—fence them round with a golden circle—and Virtue and Beauty are as goddesses, both to peasant and to prince. Strip them of the adjuncts—see Beauty and Virtue poor—dependent—solitary—walking the world defenceless; oh *then* the devotion changes its character—the same crowd gather eagerly around—fools—fops—libertines—not to worship at the shrine, but to sacrifice the victim!

Clara. My cousin, you are cruel!

Evelyn. Forgive me! There is a something when a man's heart is better than his fortunes, that makes even affection bitter. Mortification for myself—it has ceased to chafe me—I can mock where I once resented. But *you*—You, so delicately framed and nurtured—one slight to you—one careless look—one disdainful tone—makes me feel the true curse of the poor man. His pride gives armour to his *own* breast, but it has no shield to protect another!

Clara. But I too have pride of my own—I too can smile at the pointless insolence.

Evelyn. Smile—and he took your hand! Oh, Clara, you know not the tortures that I suffer hourly! When others approach you, young—fair—rich—the sleek darlings of the world—I accuse you of your very beauty—I wither beneath every smile that you bestow. [CLARA *about to speak.*] No—speak not!—my heart has broken its silence, and you shall hear the rest. For you I have endured the weary bondage of this house—the fool's gibe—the hireling's sneer—the bread, purchased by toil, that should have led to loftier ends; yes, to see you—hear you; for this—for this I have lingered, suffered, and forborne. Oh, *Clara!* we are orphans both—friendless both; you are all in the world to me; [*she turns away*] turn not away! my very soul speaks in these words—I LOVE YOU!

Clara. No—Evelyn—Alfred—No! Say it not—think it not! it were madness.

Evelyn. Madness!—Nay, hear me yet. I *am* poor—penniless—a beggar for bread to a dying servant. True!—But I have a heart of iron! I have knowledge—patience—health,—and my love for you gives me at last ambition! I have trifled with my own energies till now, for I despised all things till I loved thee! With you to toil for—your step to support—your path to smooth,—and I—I, poor Alfred Evelyn—promise at last to win for you even fame and fortune. Do not withdraw your hand—*this* hand—shall it not be mine?   [*Kneels.*

Clara. Ah, Evelyn! Never—never!

Evelyn. Never!   [*Rises.*

Clara. Forget this folly; our union is impossible, and to talk of love were to deceive both!

Evelyn [*bitterly*]. Because I am poor!

Clara. And I *too*! A marriage of privation—of penury—of days that dread the morrow! I have seen such a lot! Never return to this again.   [*Crosses to* R.

Evelyn. Enough—you are obeyed. I deceived myself—ha!—ha!—I fancied that I too was loved. I whose youth is already half gone with care and toil!—whose mind is soured—whom nobody can love—who ought to have loved no one!

Clara [*aside*]. And if it were only I to suffer, or perhaps to starve!—Oh, what shall I say? Evelyn—Cousin!

Evelyn. Madam.

Clara. Alfred—I—I—

Evelyn. Reject me!

Clara. Yes! It is past!   [*Exit*, R.

Evelyn. Let me think. It was yesterday her hand trembled when mine touched it. And the rose I gave her—yes, she pressed her lips to it once when she seemed as if she saw me not. But it was a trap—a trick—for I was as poor then as now. This will be a jest for them all! Well! courage! it is but a poor heart that a coquette's contempt can break! And now that 1 care for no one, the world is but a great chess-board, and I will sit down in earnest and play with Fortune.   [*Retires up to the table*, R.

Enter LORD GLOSSMORE, *preceded by* SERVANT, R.

Servant. I will tell Sir John, my lord.   [*Exit*, R.

EVELYN *takes up the newspaper*.

Glossmore. The secretary—hum !—Fine day, sir; any news from the East?   [*To* EVELYN.

Evelyn. Yes !—all the wise men have gone back there.

Glossmore. Ha, ha!—not all, for here comes Mr. Stout, the great political economist.

Enter STOUT, R.

Stout. Good morning, Glossmore.

Glossmore. *Glossmore!*—the parvenu!

Stout. Afraid I might be late—been detained at the Vestry—astonishing how ignorant the English poor are!—took me an hour and a half to beat it into the head of a stupid old widow, with nine children, that to allow her three shillings a week was against all the rules of public morality!

Evelyn. Excellent!—admirable!—Your hand, sir!

Glossmore. What! You approve such doctrines, Mr. Evelyn! Are old women only fit to be starved?

Evelyn. Starved! popular delusion! Observe, my lord—to squander money upon those who starve is only to afford encouragement to starvation!

Stout. A very superior person that!

Glossmore. Atrocious principles! Give me the good old times, when it was the duty of the rich to succour the distressed.

Evelyn. On second thoughts *you* are right, my lord. I, too, know a poor woman—ill—dying—in want. Shall *she*, too, perish?

Glossmore. Perish! horrible!—in a Christian country. Perish! Heaven forbid!

Evelyn [*holding out his hand*]. What, then, will you give her?

Glossmore. Ehem! Sir—the parish ought to give.

Stout. No—No—No! Certainly not!   [*With vehemence*.

Glossmore. No! no! But I say yes! yes! And if the parish refuse to maintain the poor, the only way left to a man of firmness and resolution, holding the principles that I do, and adhering to the constitution of our fathers, is to force the poor *on* the parish by never giving them a farthing oneself.

Enter Sir John, Blount, Lady Franklin, *and* Georgina, R.

Sir John. How d'ye do!—Ah! How d'ye do, gentlemen? This is a most melancholy meeting! The poor deceased! what a man he was!

Blount. I was chwistened Fwedewick after him! He was my first cousin.

Sir John. And Georgina his own niece—next of kin!—an excellent man, though odd—a kind heart, but no liver! I sent him twice a year thirty dozen of the Cheltenham waters. It's a comfort to reflect on these little attentions at such a time.

Stout. And I, too, sent him the Parliamentary Debates regularly, bound in calf. He was my second cousin—sensible man—and a follower of Malthus; never married to increase the surplus population, and fritter away his money on his own children. And now—

Evelyn. He reaps the benefit of celibacy in the prospective gratitude of every cousin he had in the world!

Lady Franklin. Ha! ha! ha!

Sir John. Hush! hush! decency, Lady Franklin; decency!

Enter Servant, R.

Servant. Mr. Graves—Mr. Sharp.

Sir John. Oh, here's Mr. Graves; that's Sharp, the lawyer who brought the will from Calcutta.

Enter Graves *and* Sharp, R.

Chorus of Sir John, Glossmore, Blount, Stout. Ah, sir—Ah, Mr. Graves!

[Georgina *holds her handkerchief to her eyes.*

Sir John. A sad occasion!

Graves. But everything in life is sad. Be comforted Miss Vesey. True, you have lost an uncle; but I—I have lost a wife—such a wife!—the first of her sex—and the second cousin of the defunct! Excuse me, Sir John; at the sight of your mourning, my wounds bleed afresh.

[Servants *hand round wine and sandwiches.*

Sir John. Take some refreshment—a glass of wine.

Graves. Thank you!—(very fine sherry!)—Ah! my poor sainted Maria! Sherry was her wine: everything reminds me of Maria! Ah, Lady Franklin! you knew her. Nothing in life can charm me now. [*Aside.*] A monstrous fine woman that!

Sir John. And now to business. Evelyn, you may retire.

Sharp [*looking at his notes*]. Evelyn—any relation to Alfred Evelyn?

Evelyn. The same.

Sharp. Cousin to the deceased, seven times removed. Be seated, sir; there may be some legacy, though trifling; all the relations, however distant, should be present.

Lady Franklin. Then Clara is related—I will go for her. [*Exit*, R.

Georgina. Ah, Mr. Evelyn, I hope you will come in for something—a few hundreds, or even more.

Sir John. Silence! Hush! Whugh! ugh! Attention.

While the LAWYER *opens the will, re-enter* LADY FRANKLIN *and* CLARA.

Sharp. The will is very short, being all personal property. He was a man that always came to the point.

Sir John. I wish there were more like him! [*Groans, and shakes his head.*] [*Chorus groan and shake their heads.*

Sharp [*reading*]. 'I, Frederick James Mordaunt, of Calcutta, being at the present date of sound mind, though infirm body, do hereby give, will and bequeath, imprimis, to my second cousin, Benjamin Stout, Esq., of Pall Mall, London—[*chorus exhibit lively emotion*]—*being* the value of the Parliamentary Debates, with which he has been pleased to trouble me for some time past—deducting the carriage thereof, which he always forgot to pay—the sum of £14. 2s. 4d.' [*Chorus breathe more freely.*

Stout. Eh! what!—£14? Oh hang the old miser!

Sir John. Decency—decency! Proceed, sir.

Sharp. 'Item.—To Sir Frederick Blount, Baronet, my nearest male relative.' [*Chorus exhibit lively emotion.*

Blount. Poor old boy!

[GEORGINA *puts her arm over* BLOUNT'S *chair.*

Sharp. 'Being, as I am informed, the best dressed young gentleman in London, and in testimony to the only merit I ever heard he possessed, the sum of £500, to buy a dressing case.'

[*Chorus breathe more freely;* GEORGINA *catches her father's eye, and removes her arm.*

Blount [*laughing confusedly*]. Ha! ha! ha! Vewy poor wit—low!—vewy—vewy low!

Sir John. Silence, now, will you?

Sharp. 'Item.—To Charles Lord Glossmore—who asserts that he is my relation—my collection of dried butterflies, and the pedigree of the Mordaunts from the reign of King John.' [*Chorus as before.*

Glossmore. Butterflies!—pedigree I—I disown the plebeian!

Sir John [*angrily*]. Upon my word, this is too revolting! Decency—go on.

Sharp. 'Item.—To Sir John Vesey, Baron, Knight of the Guelph, F.R.S., F.S.A., etc.'— [*Chorus as before.*

Sir John. Hush! *Now* it is really interesting!

Sharp. 'Who married my sister, and who sends me every year the Cheltenham waters, which nearly gave me my death—I bequeath—the empty bottles.'

Sir John. Why the ungrateful, rascally, old—

Chorus. Decency, Sir John—decency!

Sharp. 'Item.—To Henry Graves, Esq., of the Albany——, [*Chorus as before.*

Graves. Pooh, gentlemen, my usual luck—not even a ring, I dare swear!

Sharp. 'The sum of £5,000 in the Three per Cents.'

Lady Franklin. I wish you joy!

Graves. Joy—pooh! Three per Cents!—Funds sure to go! Had it been *land* now—though only an acre!—just like my luck.

Sharp. 'Item.—To my niece Georgina Vesey—'

Sir John. Ah, now it comes!   [*Chorus as before.*

Sharp. The sum of £10,000 India stock, being, with her father's reputed savings, as much as a single woman ought to possess.'

Sir John. And what the devil, then, does the old fool do with all his money?

Chorus. Really, Sir John, this is too revolting. Decency! Hush!

Sharp. 'And with the aforesaid legacies and exceptions, I do bequeath the whole of my fortune, in India stock, bonds, Exchequer bills, Three per Cents, Consols and in the bank of Calcutta (constituting him hereby sole residuary legatee and joint executor with the aforesaid Henry Graves, Esq.), to Alfred Evelyn, now, or formerly of Trinity College, Cambridge—[*universal excitement*] being, I am told, an oddity, like myself—the only one of my relations who never fawned on me, and who, having known privation, may the better employ wealth.' [*All rise.*] And now, sir, I have only to wish you joy, and give you this letter from the deceased—I believe it is important.   [*Gives letter to* EVELYN.

Evelyn [*crossing over to* CLARA]. Ah, Clara, if you had but loved me!

Clara [*turning away*]. And his wealth, even more than poverty, separates us for ever!

[*All surround* EVELYN *with congratulations.*

Sir John [*to* GEORGINA]. Go child, put a good face on it—he's an immense match ! My dear fellow, I wish you joy; you are a great man now—a very great man!

Evelyn [*aside*]. And *her* voice alone is silent!

Glossmore. If I can be of any use to you—

Stout. Or I, sir—

Blount. Or I? Shall I put you up at the clubs?

Sharp. You will want a man of business. I transacted all Mr. Mordaunt's affairs.

Sir John. Tush, tush! Mr. Evelyn is at home *here*. Always looked on him as a son. Nothing in the world we would not do for him! Nothing!

Evelyn. Lend me £10 for my old nurse!

[*Chorus put their hands into their pockets.*

END OF ACT I

ACT II

SCENE I. *An anteroom in* EVELYN'S *new house; at one corner, behind a large screen,* MR. SHARP, *writing at a desk, books and parchments before him.* MR. CRIMSON, *the portrait painter;* MR. GRAB, *the publisher;* MR. MACSTUCCO, *the architect;* MR. TABOURET, *the upholsterer;* MR. MACFINCH, *the silversmith;* MR. PATENT, *the coachmaker;* MR. KITE, *the horse-dealer; and* MR. FRANTZ, *the tailor. Servants in livery cross to and fro the stage.*

Patent [*to* FRANTZ, *showing a drawing*]. Yes, sir, this is the Evelyn vis-à-vis! No one more the fashion than Mr. Evelyn. Money makes the man, sir.

Frantz. But de tailor, de schneider, make de gentleman! It is Mr. Frantz, of St. James's, who take his measure and his cloth, and who make de fine handsome noblemen and gentry, where de faders and de mutters make only de ugly little naked boys!

MacStucco. He's a mon o' teeste, Mr. Evelyn. He taulks o' boying a veela (villa), just to pool dune and build oop again. Ah, Mr. MacFinch, a design for a piece of pleete, eh!

MacFinch [*showing the drawing*]. yees, sir, the shield o' Alexander the Great, to hold ices and lemonade! It will cost two thousand poond!

MacStucco. And it's dirt cheap—ye're Scotch, aren't ye?

MacFinch. Aberdounshire!—scraitch me, and I'll scraitch you!

Doors at the back thrown open. Enter EVELYN.

Evelyn. A levee, as usual. Good day. Ah, Tabouret, your designs for the draperies; very well. And what do you want, Mr. Crimson?

Crimson. Sir, if you'd let me take your portrait, it would make my fortune. Every one says you're the finest judge of paintings.

Evelyn. Of paintings! paintings! Are you sure I'm a judge of paintings?

Crimson. Oh, sir, didn't you buy the great Correggio for £4,000?

Evelyn. True—I see. So £4,000 makes me an excellent judge of paintings. I'll call on you,

Mr. Crimson. Good day, Mr. Grab—oh, you're the publisher who once refused me £5 for my poem? you are right; it was sad doggerel.

Grab. Doggerel! Mr. Evelyn, it was sublime! But times were bad then.

Evelyn. Very bad times with me.

Grab. But, now, sir, if you give me the preference I'll push it, sir—I'll push it! I only publish for poets in high life, sir; and a gentleman of your station ought to be pushed!—£500 for the poem, sir!

Evelyn. £500 when I don't want it, where £5 once would have seemed a fortune.

'Now I am rich, what value in the lines!

How the wit brightens—how the sense refines!'

[*Turns to the rest who surround him.*

Kite. Thirty young horses from Yorkshire, sir!

Patent [*showing drawing*]. The Evelyn vis-à-vis!

MacFinch [*showing drawing*]. The Evelyn salver!

Frantz [*opening his bundle and with dignity*]. Sare, I have brought de coat—de great Evelyn coat.

Evelyn. Oh, go to—that is, go home! Make me as celebrated for vis-à-vis, salvers, furniture, and coats, as I already am for painting, and shortly shall be for poetry. I resign myself to you— go! [*Exeunt* PATENT, & C., R.

Enter STOUT, R.

Evelyn. Stout, you look heated?

Stout. I hear you have just bought the great Groginhole property.

Evelyn. It is true. Sharp says it's a bargain.

Stout. Well, my dear friend Hopkins, member for Groginhole, can't live another month—but the interests of mankind forbid regret for individuals! The patriot Popkins intends to start for the borough the instant Hopkins is dead!—your interest will secure his election!—now is your time!—put yourself forward in the march of enlightenment!—By all that is bigoted here comes Glossmore !   [*Crosses to* L.

Enter GLOSSMORE, R.; SHARP still at his desk.

Glossmore. So lucky to find you at home! Hopkins, of Groginhole, is not long for this world. Popkins the brewer, is already canvassing underhand (so very ungentlemanly like!) Keep your interest for young Lord Cipher—a valuable candidate. This is an awful moment—the CONSTITUTION depends on his return! Vote for Cipher!

Stout. Popkins is your man!

Evelyn [*musingly*]. Cipher and Popkins—Popkins and Cipher! Enlightenment and Popkins—Cipher and the Constitution! I AM puzzled! Stout, I am not known at Groginhole.

Stout. Your *property's* known there!

Evelyn. But purity of election—independence of votes—

Stout. To be sure: Cipher bribes abominably. Frustrate his schemes—preserve the liberties of the borough—turn every man out of his house who votes against enlightenment and Popkins!

Evelyn. Right!—down with those who take the liberty to admire any liberty except *our* liberty! That *is* liberty!

Glossmore. Cipher has a stake in the country—will have £50,000 a year. Cipher will never give a vote without considering beforehand how people of £50,000 a year will be affected by the motion.

Evelyn. Right: for as without law there would be no property, so to be the law for property is the only property of law!—That is law!

Stout. Popkins is all for economy; there's a sad waste of the public money; they give the Speaker £5,000 year when I've a brother-in-law who takes the chair at the vestry, and who assures me confidentially he'd consent to be Speaker for half the money!

Glossmore. Enough, Mr. Stout. Mr. Evelyn has too much at stake for a leveller.

Stout. And too much sense for a bigot.

Evelyn. Mr. Evelyn has no politics at all!—Did you ever play at *battledore?*

237

Both. Battledore!

Evelyn. Battledore!—that is, a contest between two parties; both parties knock about something with singular skill; something is kept up—high—low—here—there—everywhere—nowhere! How grave are the players! how anxious the bystanders! how noisy the battledores! But when this something falls to the ground, only fancy—it's nothing but cork and feather! Go and play by yourselves,—I'm no hand at it !   [*Crosses*, L

Stout [*aside*]. Sad ignorance!—Aristocrat!

Glossmore [*aside*]. Heartless principles!—Parvenu!

Stout. Then you don't go *against* us? I'll bring Popkins tomorrow.

Glossmore. Keep yourself free till I present Cipher to you.

Stout. I must go to inquire after Popkins. The return of Popkins will be an era in history.   [*Exit*, R.

Glossmore. I must be off to the club—the eyes of the country are upon Groginhole. If Cipher fail, the Constitution is gone!   [*Exit*, R.

Evelyn [*at table*, R.]. Both sides alike! Money versus Man! Sharp, come here, [Sharp *advances*] let me look at you! You are my agent, my lawyer, my man of business. I believe you honest; but what *is* honesty?—where does it exist?—in what part of us?

Sharp. In the heart, I suppose, sir.

Evelyn. Mr. Sharp, it exists in the breeches' pocket! Observe! I lay this piece of yellow earth on the table—I contemplate you both; the man there—the gold here! Now there is many a man in those streets, honest as you are, who moves, thinks, feels, and reasons as well as we do; excellent in form—imperishable in soul; who, if his pockets were three days empty, would sell thought, reason, body, and, soul too, for that little coin! Is that the fault of the man?—no! it is the fault of mankind! God made man—Behold what mankind have made a god! When I was poor I hated the world; now I am rich I despise it. [*Rises*.] Fools—knaves—hypocrites! By the by, Sharp, send £100 to the poor bricklayer whose house was burnt down yesterday.

Enter Graves, R.

Ah, Graves, my dear friend! What a world this is!—a cur of a world, that fawns on its master, and bites the beggar! Ha! ha! it fawns on *me* now, for the beggar has bought the cur!

Graves. *It* is an atrocious world!—But astronomers say that there is a travelling comet which must set it on fire one day,—and that's some comfort.

Evelyn. Every hour brings its gloomy lesson—the temper sours—the affections wither—the heart hardens into stone! Zounds! Sharp! what do you stand gaping there for? have you no bowels? why don't you go and see to the bricklayer? [*Exit* Sharp, R.] Graves, of all my new friends—and their name is Legion,—you are the only one I esteem; there is sympathy between us—we take the same views of life. I am cordially glad to see you.

Graves [*groaning*]. Ah! why should you be glad to see a man so miserable?

Evelyn [*sighs*]. Because I am miserable myself!

Graves. You! Pshaw! *you* have not been condemned to lose a wife!

Evelyn. But, plague on it, man, I may be condemned to take one! Sit down and listen. [*They seat themselves.*] I want a confidant. Left fatherless when yet a boy, my poor mother grudged herself food to give me education. Some one had told her that learning was better than house and land—that's a lie, Graves.

Graves. A scandalous lie, Evelyn.

Evelyn. On the strength of that lie I was put to school—sent to college, a sizar. Do you know what a sizar is? In pride he is a gentleman—in knowledge a scholar—and he crawls about, amidst gentlemen and scholars, with the livery of a pauper on his back! I carried off the great prizes—I became distinguished; I looked to a high degree, leading to a fellowship; that is, an independence for myself—a home for my mother. One day a lord insulted me—I retorted; he struck me—refused apology—refused redress. I was a sizar! a Pariah!—a thing to be struck! Sir, I was at least a man, and I horsewhipped him in the hall before the eyes of the whole college! A few days, and the lord's chastisement was forgotten. The next day the sizar was expelled—the career of a life blasted. That is the difference between rich and poor: it takes a whirlwind to move the one—a breath may uproot the other! I came to London. As long as my mother lived I had one to toil for; and I did toil—did hope—did struggle to be something yet. She died, and then somehow, my spirit broke. I resigned myself to my fate; the Alps above me seemed too high to ascend—I ceased to care what became of me. At last I submitted to be the poor relation—the hanger-on and gentleman-lackey of Sir John Vesey. But I had an object in that; there was one in that house whom I had loved at the first sight.

Graves. And were you loved again?

Evelyn. I fancied it, and was deceived. Not an hour before I inherited this mighty wealth, I confessed my love, and was rejected because I was poor. Now, mark: you remember the letter which Sharp gave me when the will was read?

Graves. Perfectly; what were the contents?

Evelyn. After hints, cautions and admonitions, half in irony, half in earnest, (ah, poor Mordaunt had known the world!) it proceeded—but I'll read it to you: 'Having selected you as my heir, because I think money a trust to be placed where it seems likely to be best employed, I now—not impose a condition, but ask a favour. If you have formed no other insuperable attachment, I could wish to suggest your choice. My two nearest female relations are my niece Georgina and my third cousin, Clara Douglas, the daughter of a once dear friend. If you could see in either of these one whom you could make your wife, such would be a marriage that if I live long enough to return to England, I would seek to bring about before I die.' My friend, this is not a legal condition; the fortune does not rest on it; yet, need I say, that my gratitude considers it a moral obligation? Several months have elapsed since thus called upon—I ought now to decide; you hear the names—Clara Douglas is the woman who rejected me!

Graves. But now she would accept you!

Evelyn. And do you think I am so base a slave to passion that I would owe to my gold what was denied to my affection?

Graves. But you must choose one in common gratitude; you *ought* to do so—yes, there you are right. Besides, you are constantly at the house—the world observes it: you must have raised hopes in one of the girls—Yes; it is time to decide between her whom you love, and her whom you do not!

Evelyn. Of the two, then, I would rather marry where I should exact the least. A marriage to which each can bring sober esteem and calm regard, may not be happiness, but it may be content. But to marry one whom you could adore, and whose heart is closed to you—to yearn for the treasure, and only to claim the casket—to worship the statue that you may never warm to life—Oh! such a marriage would be a hell the more terrible because Paradise was in sight !

Graves. Georgina is pretty, but vain and frivolous. [*Aside.*] But he has no right to be fastidious—he has never known Maria! [*Aloud.*] Yes, my dear friend, now I think on it, you *will* be as wretched as myself! When you are married we will mingle our groans together!

Evelyn. You may misjudge Georgina; she may have a nobler nature than appears on the surface. On the day, but before the hour, in which the will was read, a letter, in a strange or disguised hand, *'from an unknown Friend to Alfred Evelyn,'* and enclosing what to a girl would have been a considerable sum, was sent to a poor woman for whom I had implored charity, and whose address I had given only to Georgina.

Graves. Why not assure yourself?

Evelyn. Because I have not dared. For sometimes, against my reason, I have hoped that it might be Clara! [*Taking a letter from his bosom and looking at it.*] No, I can't recognize the hand. Graves, I detest that girl!   [*Rises.*

Graves. Who? Georgina?

Evelyn. No; but I've already, thank heaven! taken some revenge upon her. Come nearer. [*Whispers.*] I've bribed Sharp to say that Mordaunt's letter to me contained a codicil leaving Clara Douglas £20,000.

Graves. And didn't it? How odd, then, not to have mentioned her in his will.

Evelyn. One of his caprices: besides, Sir John wrote him word that Lady Franklin adopted her. But I'm glad of it—I've paid the money—she's no more a dependant. No one can insult her now; she owes it all to me, and does not guess it, man, does not guess it! owes it to me whom she rejected;—me, the poor scholar! Ha! ha! There's some spite in that, eh?

Graves. You're a fine fellow, Evelyn, and we understand each other. Perhaps Clara may have seen the address, and dictated this letter, after all!

Evelyn. Do you think so? I'll go to the house this instant.

Graves. Eh? Humph! Then I'll go with you. That Lady Franklin is a fine woman. If she were not so gay, I think—I could—

Evelyn. No, no; don't think any such thing: women are even worse than men.

Graves. True; to love is a boy's madness!

Evelyn. To feel is to suffer!

Graves. To hope is to be deceived.

Evelyn. I have done with romance!

Graves. Mine is buried with Maria!

Evelyn. If Clara did but write this!—

Graves. Make haste, or Lady Franklin will be out!—A vale of tears—a vale of tears!   [*Exeunt*, R.

Evelyn. A vale of tears, indeed!   [*Exeunt*, R.

Re-enter Graves *for his hat*.

Graves. And I left my hat behind me! Just like my luck! If I had been bred a hatter, little boys would have come into the world without heads!   [*Exit*, R.

SCENE II. *Drawing-rooms at* Sir John Vesey's,
as in Act I, Scene I. Lady Franklin, Clara, Servant.

Lady Franklin. Past two, and I have so many places to go to. Tell Philipps I want the carriage directly— instantly.

Servant. I beg pardon, my lady; Philipps told me to say the young horse had fallen lame, and could not be used today.   [*Exit*.

Lady Franklin. Well, on second thoughts, that is lucky; now I have an excuse for not making a great many tedious visits. I must borrow Sir John's horses for the ball tonight. Oh, Clara, you must see my new turban from Carson's—the prettiest thing in the world, and so becoming!

Clara. Ah, Lady Franklin, you'll be so sorry—but—but—

Lady Franklin. But what?

Clara. Such a misfortune! poor Smith is in tears—I promised to break it to you. Your little Charley had been writing his copy, and spilt the ink on the table; and Smith not seeing it—and taking out the turban to put in the pearls as you desired—she—she—

Lady Franklin. Ha! ha! laid it on the table, and the ink spoilt it. Ha! ha! how well I can fancy the face she made! Seriously, on the whole, it is fortunate; for I think I look best, after all, in the black hat and feathers.

Clara. Dear Lady Franklin, you really have the sweetest temper!

Lady Franklin. I hope so—for it's the most becoming thing a woman can wear! Think of that when you marry. Oh, talking of marriage, I've certainly made a conquest of Mr. Graves.

Clara. Mr. Graves! I thought he was inconsolable.

Lady Franklin. For his sainted Maria! Poor man! not contented with plaguing him while she lived, she must needs haunt him now she is dead.

Clara. But why does he regret her?

Lady Franklin. Why? Because he has everything to make him happy. Easy fortune, good health, respectable character. And since it is his delight to be miserable, he takes the only excuse the world will allow him. For the rest, it's the way with widowers; that is, whenever they mean to marry again. But, my dear Clara, you seem absent—pale—unhappy;—tears, too!

Clara. No—no—not tears. No!

Lady Franklin. Ever since Mr. Mordaunt left you £20,000 every one admires you. Sir Frederick is desperately smitten.

Clara [*with disdain*]. Sir Frederick !

Lady Franklin. Ah! Clara, be comforted—I know your secret; I am certain that Evelyn loves you, Clara. He did—it is past now. He misconceived me when he was poor; and now he is rich, it is not for me to explain.

Lady Franklin. My dear child, happiness is too rare to be sacrificed to a scruple. Why does he come here so often?

Clara. Perhaps for Georgina!

Enter SIR JOHN, R.C., *and turns over the books, &c.,*
on the table, as if to look for the newspaper.

Lady Franklin. Pooh! Georgina is my niece; she is handsome and accomplished, but her father's worldliness has spoilt her nature—she is not worthy of Evelyn! Behind the humour of his irony there is something noble—something that may yet be great. For his sake as well as yours, let me at least—

Clara. Recommend me to his pity! Ah, Lady Franklin! if he addressed me from dictation, I should again refuse him. No; if he cannot read my heart—if he will not seek to read it, let it break unknown.

Lady Franklin. You mistake me, my dear child: let me only tell him that you dictated that letter—that you sent that money to his old nurse. Poor Clara, it was your little all. He will then know, at least, if avarice be your sin.

Clara. He would have guessed it, had *his* love been like *mine*.

Lady Franklin. Guessed it—nonsense! The handwriting unknown to him—every reason to think it came from Georgina.

Sir John [*aside*, R. *at table*]. Hum! came from Georgina.

Lady Franklin. Come, *let* me tell him *this*. I know the effect it would have upon his choice.

Clara. Choice! oh, that humiliating word! No, Lady Franklin, no! Promise me!

Lady Franklin. But—

Clara. No! Promise—faithfully—sacredly.

Lady Franklin. Well, I promise.

Clara. You know how fearful is my character—no infant is more timid—if a poor spider cross the floor, you often laugh to see me grow pale and tremble; and yet I would lay this hand upon the block—I would walk barefoot over the ploughshare of the old ordeal—to save Alfred Evelyn one moment's pain. But I have refused to share his poverty, and I should die with shame if he thought I had now grown enamoured of his wealth. My kind friend, you will keep your promise?

Lady Franklin. Yes, since it must be so.

Clara. Thanks. I—I—forgive me—I am not well.   [*Exit*, R.

Lady Franklin. What fools these girls are! they take as much pains to lose a husband as a poor widow does to get one!

Sir John. Have you seen *The Times* newspaper? Where the deuce is the newspaper? I can't find *The Times* newspaper.

Lady Franklin. I think it is in my room. Shall I fetch it?

Sir John. My dear sister, you're the best creature. Do! [*Exit* LADY FRANKLIN, R.

Ugh! you unnatural conspirator against your own family! What can this *letter* be? Ah! I recollect something.

Enter GEORGINA, R.C.

242

Georgina. Papa, I want—

Sir John. Yes, I know what you want, well enough! Tell me—were you aware that Clara had sent money to that old nurse Evelyn bored us about the day of the will?

Georgina. No! He gave me the address, and I promised, if—

Sir John. Gave you the *address*?—*that's* lucky. Hush!

Enter Servant, R.

Servant. Mr. Graves—Mr. Evelyn.   [*Exit* Servant, R.

Enter Graves *and* Evelyn, R.

Lady Franklin [*returning*]. Here is the newspaper.

Graves. Ay—read the newspapers!—they'll tell you what this world is made of. Daily calendars of roguery and woe! Here, advertisements from quacks, money-lenders, cheap warehouses, and spotted boys with two heads! So much for dupes and impostors! Turn to the other column—police reports, bankruptcies, swindling, forgery, and a biographical sketch of the snub-nosed man who murdered his own three little cherubs at Pentonville. Do you fancy these but exceptions to the *general* virtue and health of the nation?—Turn to the leading article! and your hair will stand on end at the horrible wickedness or melancholy idiotism of that half of the population who think differently from yourself. In my day I have seen already eighteen crises, six annihilations of agriculture and commerce, four overthrows of the Church, and three last, final, awful, and irremediable destructions of the entire Constitution! And that's a newspaper—a newspaper—a newspaper.

Lady Franklin. Ha! ha! your usual vein! always so amusing and good humoured!

Graves [*frowning and very angry*]. Ma'am—good humoured!

Lady Franklin. Ah! you should always wear that agreeable smile; you look so much younger—so much handsomer, when you smile!

Graves [*softened*]. Ma'am—a charming creature, upon my word!   [*Aside.*

Lady Franklin. You have not seen the last of H. B.? it is excellent, I think it might make you laugh. But, by the by, I don't think you can laugh.

Graves. Ma'am—I have not laughed since the death of my sainted Ma—

Lady Franklin. Ah! and that spiteful Sir Frederick says you never laugh, because—but you'll be angry?

Graves. Angry! pooh! I despise Sir Frederick too much to let anything he says have the smallest influence over me! He says I don't laugh, because—

Lady Franklin. You have lost your front teeth!

Graves. Lost my front teeth! Upon my word! ha! ha! ha! That's too good—capital! Ha! ha! ha!   [*Laughing from ear to ear.*

Lady Franklin. Ha! ha! ha!

[*They retire to the table in the inner drawing-room.*

Evelyn [*aside at R. table*]. Of course Clara will not appear—avoids me as usual! But what do I care?

what is she to me? Nothing! I'll swear this is her glove! no one else has so small a hand. She'll miss it—so—so! Nobody's looking—I'll keep it just to vex her.

Sir John [*to* GEORGINA]. Yes, yes—leave me to manage; you took his portrait, as I told you? Georgina. Yes, but I could not catch the expression. I got Clara to touch it up.

Sir John. That girl's always in the way!

Enter CAPTAIN DUDLEY SMOOTH, R.

Smooth. Good morning, dear John. Ah, Miss Vesey, you have no idea of the conquests you made at Almack's last night!

Evelyn [*examining him curiously while* SMOOTH *is talking to* GEORGINA, R. *at table*]. And that's the celebrated Dudley Smooth!

Sir John. More commonly called Deadly Smooth!—the finest player at whist, écarté, billiards, chess, and piquet between this and the Pyramids—the sweetest manners!—always calls you by your Christian name. But take care how you play cards with him!

Evelyn. He does not cheat, I suppose?

Sir John. No! but he always *wins!* Eats up a brace of lords and a score or two of guardsmen every season, and runs through a man's fortune like a course of the Carlsbad waters. He's an uncommonly clever fellow!

Evelyn. Clever? yes! When a man steals a loaf, we cry down the knavery; when a man diverts his neighbour's mill-stream to grind his own corn, we cry up the cleverness! and every one courts Captain Dudley Smooth!

Sir John. Why, who could offend him? the best bred, civilest creature—and a dead shot! There is not a cleverer man in the three kingdoms.

Evelyn. A study—a study!—let me examine him! Such men are living satires on the world.

Smooth [*passing his arm caressingly over* SIR JOHN'S *shoulder*]. My dear John, how well you are looking! A new lease of life! Introduce me to Mr. Evelyn.

Evelyn. Sir, it's an honour I've long ardently desired. [*Crosses to him; they bow and shake hands.*

Enter SIR FREDERICK BLOUNT, R.

Blount. How d'ye do, Sir John? Ah, Evelyn, I wish so much to see you!

Evelyn. 'Tis my misfortune to be visible!

Blount. A little this way. You know, perhaps, that I once paid my addwesses to Miss Vesey; but since that vewy eccentwic will Sir John has shuffled me off, and hints at a pwior attachment—[*aside*] which I know to be false.

Evelyn [*seeing* CLARA]. A prior attachment !—(Ha! Clara!) Well well, another time, my dear Blount.

Enter CLARA, R.

Blount. Stay a moment—I want you to do me a favour with wegard to Miss Douglas!

Evelyn. Miss Douglas!

244

Blount. Yes;—you see, though Georgina has gweat expectations, and Stingy Jack will leave her all that he has, yet she has only her legacy of £10,000 at the moment—no doubt closely settled on herself too. Clawa has £20,000. And I think, Clawa always liked me a little.

Evelyn. You! I dare say she did!

Blount. It is whispered about that you mean to pwopose to Georgina. Nay, Sir John more than hinted that was her pwior attachment!

Evelyn. Indeed!

Blount. Now, as you are all in all with the family, if you could say a word for me to Miss Douglas, I don't see what harm it could do me! [*Aside.*] I will punish Georgina for her perfidy.

Evelyn. 'Sdeath, man ! speak for yourself; you are just the sort of man for young ladies to like—they understand you. You're of their own level. Pshaw ! you're too modest—you want no mediator!

Blount. My dear fellow, you flatter me. I'm well enough in my way. But you, you know, would cawwy evewything before you!—you're so confoundedly wich!

Evelyn [*turning to* CLARA]. Miss Douglas, what do you think of Sir Frederick Blount? Observe him. He is well dressed—young—tolerably handsome—[BLOUNT *bowing*]—bows with an air—has plenty of small talk—everything to captivate. Yet he thinks that if he and I were suitors to the same lady, I should be more successful because I am richer? What say you? Is love an auction? and do women's hearts go to the highest bidder?

Clara. Their hearts? No!

Evelyn. But their hands—yes! [*She turns away.*] You turn away. Ah, you dare not answer that question!

Georgina [*aside*]. Sir Frederick flirting with Clara! I'll punish him for his perfidy. *You* are the last person to talk so, Mr. Evelyn!—you, whose wealth is your smallest attraction—you, whom every one admires, so witty, such taste! such talent! Ah! I'm very foolish!

Sir John [*clapping him on the shoulder*]. You must not turn my little girl's head. Oh, you're a sad fellow! Apropos, I must show you Georgina's last drawings. She has wonderfully improved since you gave her lessons in perspective.

Georgina. No, papa—No! pray, no! Nay, don't!

Sir John. Nonsense, child!—it's very odd, but she's more afraid of *you* than of anyone!

Smooth [*to* BLOUNT, *taking snuff*]. He's an excellent father, our dear John, and supplies the place of a mother to her. [*Turns away to* LADY FRANKLIN *and* GRAVES].

[EVELYN *and* GEORGINA *seat themselves and look over the drawings;*
SIR JOHN *leans over them;* SIR FREDERICK *converses with* CLARA; EVELYN *watches them.*

Evelyn. Beautiful! a view from Tivoli. (Death! she looks down while he speaks to her!) Is there not a little fault in that colouring? (She positively blushes!) This Jupiter is superb. (What a d—d coxcomb it is!) [*Rising.*] Oh, she certainly loves him—I too can be loved elsewhere—I too can see smiles and blushes on the face of another!

Georgina. Are you not well?

Evelyn. I beg pardon. Yes, you are indeed improved. Ah! who so accomplished as Miss Vesey?

245

[Takes up drawings; pays her marked attention in dumb show.

Clara. Yes, Sir Frederick, the concert was very crowded! (Ah, I see that Georgina consoles him for the past! He has only praises for her, nothing but taunts for me!)

Blount. I wish you would take my opewa box next Saturday—'tis the best in the house. I'm not wich, but I spend what I have on myself! I make a point to have evewything the best in a quiet way. Best opewa box—best dogs —best horses—best house of its kind. I want nothing to complete my establishment but the best wife!

Clara [*abstractedly*]. That will come in good time, Sir Frederick.

Evelyn. Oh, it will come—will it? Georgina refused the trifler—she courts him. [*Taking up a portrait.*] Why, what is this?—my own—

Georgina. You must not look at that—you must not, indeed. I did not know it was there!

Sir John. Your own portrait, Evelyn! Why, child! I was not aware you took likenesses? That's something new! Upon my word, it's a strong resemblance.

Georgina. Oh, no—it does not do him justice. Give it to me. I will tear it. [*Aside.*] That odious Sir Frederick!

Evelyn. Nay, you shall not.

Clara. (So—so—he loves her then! Misery—misery! But he shall not perceive it! No—no—I can be proud too.) Ha! ha!—Sir Frederick—excellent—excellent! you are so entertaining—ha! ha! [*Laughs hysterically.*

Evelyn. Oh, the affectation of coquettes—they cannot even laugh naturally! [CLARA *looks at him reproachfully, and walks aside with* SIR FREDERICK.] But where is the new guitar you meant to buy, Miss Vesey—the one inlaid with tortoise shell? It is near a year since you set your heart on it, and I don't see it yet.

Sir John [*taking him aside confidentially*] The guitar—oh, to tell you a secret, she applied the money I gave her for it to a case of charity several months ago—the very day the will was read. I saw the letter lying on the table, with the money in it. Mind, not a word to her—she'd never forgive me!

Evelyn. Letter!—money! What was the name of the person she relieved?—not Stanton?

Sir John. I don't remember, indeed.

Evelyn [*taking out the letter*]. This is not her hand.

Sir John. No, I observed at the time it was not her hand, but I got out from her that she did not wish the thing *to be known*, and had employed someone else to copy it. May I see the letter? Yes, I think this is the wording. But I did not mean to tell you what case of charity it was. I promised Georgy I would not. Still, how did she know Mrs. Stanton's address? you never gave it to me.

Evelyn. I gave it to her, Sir John.

Clara [*at a distance*]. Yes, I'll go to the opera if Lady Franklin will. Do go, dear Lady Franklin!—on Saturday, then, Sir Frederick.

Evelyn. Sir John, to a man like me, this simple act of unostentatious generosity is worth all the accomplishments in the world. A good heart—a tender disposition—a charity that shuns the day—a modesty that blushes at its own excellence—an impulse towards something more divine than Mammon such are the true accomplishments which preserve beauty for ever young. Such I have sought in the partner I would take for life;—such I have found—alas! not where I had dreamed!—Miss Vesey, I will be honest—[Georgina *advances* L.] I say, then, frankly [*as* Clara *approaches, raising his voice and looking fixedly at her*]—I have loved another—deeply—truly—bitterly—vainly. I cannot offer to you, as I did to her, the fair first love of the human heart, rich with all its blossoms and its verdure. But if esteem—if gratitude—if an earnest resolve to conquer every recollection that would wander from your image; if these can tempt you to accept my hand and fortune, my life shall be a study to deserve your confidence.

[Clara *stands motionless, clasping her hands, and then slowly seats herself.*

Sir John. The happiest day of my life!

[Clara *falls back in her chair.*

Evelyn [*darting forward; aside*]. She is pale! she faints! What have I done? Clara!

Clara [*rising with a smile*]. Be happy, my cousin—be happy! Yes, with my whole heart I say it—be happy. Alfred Evelyn!

END OF ACT II

ACT III

SCENE I. *The drawing-rooms of* Sir John Vesey's *house.*

Enter Sir John *and* Georgina.

Sir John. And he has not pressed you to fix the wedding-day!

Georgina. No; and since he proposed he comes here so seldom, and seems so gloomy. Heigho! Poor Sir Frederick was twenty times more amusing.

Sir John. But Evelyn is fifty times as rich!

Georgina. Sir Frederick *dresses* so well!

Sir John. You'll have magnificent diamonds! But a word with you: I saw you yesterday in the square with Sir Frederick; that must not happen again. When a young lady is engaged to one man, nothing is so indecorous as to flirt with another. It might endanger your marriage itself. Oh, it's highly indecorous!

Georgina. Don't be afraid, papa—he takes up with Clara.

Sir John. Who? Evelyn?

Georgina. Sir Frederick. Heigho!—I hate artful girls.

Sir John. The settlement will be splendid! If anything happens, nothing can be handsomer than your jointure.

Georgina. My own kind papa, you always put things so pleasantly. Do you not fear lest he discover that Clara wrote the letter?

Sir John. No; and I shall get Clara out of the house. But there is something else that makes me very uneasy.

You know that no sooner did Evelyn come into possession of his fortune than he launched out in the style of a prince. His house in London is a palace, and he has bought a great estate in the country. Look how he lives!—Balls—banquets—fine arts—fiddlers—charities—and the devil to pay!

Georgina. But if he can afford it—

Sir John. Oh, so long as he stopped *there* I had no apprehension, but since he proposed for you he is more extravagant than ever. They say he has taken to gambling; and he is always with Captain Smooth. No fortune can stand Deadly Smooth! if he gets into a scrape he may fall off from the settlement. We must press the marriage at once.

Georgina. Heigho! Poor Frederick! You don't think he is *really* attached to Clara?

Sir John. Upon my word I can't say. Put on your bonnet, and come to Storr and Mortimer's to choose the jewels

Georgina. —yes—the drive will do me good. So you'll send away Clara? she's so very deceitful.

Sir John. Never fear—yes—tell her to come to me.

[*Exit* GEORGINA, R.

Yes; I must press on this marriage; Georgina has not wit enough to manage him—at least till he's her husband, and then all women find it smooth sailing. This match will make me a man of prodigious importance. I suspect he'll give me up her ten thousand pounds. I can't think of his taking to gambling, for I love him as a son—and I look to his money as my own.

Enter CLARA, R.

Sir John. Clara, my love!

Clara. Sir—

Sir John. My dear, what I am going to say may appear a little rude and unkind, but you know my character is frankness. To the point then: my poor child, I'm aware of your attachment to Mr. Evelyn—

Clara. Sir! *my attachment?*

Sir John. It is generally remarked. Lady Kind says you are falling away. Poor girl, I pity you—I do, indeed! Now there's that letter you wrote to his old nurse—it has got about somehow—and the world is so ill natured. I don't know if I did right; but, after he had proposed to Georgy—(of course not before!)—I thought it so unpleasant for you, as a young lady, to be suspected of anything forward with respect to a man who was not attached to you, that I rather let it be supposed that Georgy *herself* wrote the letter.

Clara. Sir, I don't know what right you had to—

Sir John. That's very true, my dear; and I've been thinking since that I ought perhaps to tell Mr. Evelyn that the letter was yours—shall I?

Clara. No, Sir; I beg you will not. I—I   [*Weeps.*

Sir John. My dear Clara, don't take on; I would not have said this for the world, if I was not a little anxious about my own girl. Georgina is so unhappy at what every one says of your attachment—

Clara. Every one?—Oh, torture!

Sir John. That it preys on her spirits—it even irritates her temper! In a word, I fear these little jealousies and suspicions will tend to embitter their future union—I'm a father; forgive me.

Clara. Embitter their union! Oh, never! What would you have me to do, sir?

Sir John. Why, you're now independent. Lady Franklin seems resolved to stay in town. Surely she can't mean to take her money out of the family by some foolish inclination for Mr. Graves! He's always purring and whining about the house, like a black cat in the megrims. What think you, eh?

Clara. Sir, it was of myself—my unhappy self—you were speaking.

Sir John. Sly !—True, true! What I meant to say was this: Lady Franklin persists in staying *here*; you are your own mistress. Mrs. Carlton, aunt to my late wife, is going abroad for a short time, and would be delighted if you would accompany her.

Clara. It is the very favour I would have asked of you. [*Aside.*] I shall escape at least the struggle and the shame. When does she go?

Sir John. In five days—next Monday. You forgive me?

Clara. Sir, thank you.

Sir John [*drawing the table*, R.]. Suppose, then, you write a line to her yourself, and settle it at once?

Enter SERVANT, R.C.

Servant. The carriage, Sir John; Miss Vesey is quite ready.

Sir John. Wait a moment. Shall I tell Evelyn you wrote the letter?

Clara. No, Sir, I implore you.

Sir John. But it would be awkward for Georgy if discovered.

Clara. It never shall be.

Sir John. Well, well, as you please. I know nothing could be so painful to a young lady of pride and delicacy. James, if Mr. Serious, the clergyman, calls, say I am gone to the great meeting at Exeter Hall; if Lord Spruce calls, say you believe I'm gone to the rehearsal of Cinderella. Oh! and if MacFinch should come—MacFinch, who duns me three times a week—say I've hurried off to Garraway's to bid for the great Bulstrode estate. Just put the Duke of Lofty's card carelessly on the hall table. And I say, James, I expect two gentlemen a little before dinner—Mr. Squab, the Radical, and Mr. Qualm of the great Marylebone Conservative Association. Show Squab into the study, and be sure to give him the *Weekly True Sun*,—Qualm into the back parlour with *The Times*, and the *Morning Post*. [*Exit* SERVANT, R.C.] One must have a little management in this world. All humbug!—all humbug, upon my soul!   [*Exit*, door C.

Clara [*folding the letter*]. There—it is decided! A few days, and we are parted for ever !—a few weeks, and another will bear his name—his wife! Oh, happy fate! She will have the right to say to him—though the whole world should hear her— 'I am thine!' And I embitter their lot—I am the cloud upon their joyous sunshine! And yet, O Alfred! if she loves thee—if she knows thee—if she values thee—and, when thou wrongst her, if she can forgive thee, as I do, I can bless her when far away, and join her name in my prayers for thee!

Evelyn [*without*]. Miss Vesey just gone? Well, I will write a line. [*Enters*, R.C.] [*Aside.*] So—Clara! [*Aloud.*] Do not let me disturb you, Miss Douglas.

Clara. Nay, I have done.   [*Going, R.

249

Evelyn. I see that my presence is always odious to you. It is a reason why I come so seldom. But be cheered, madam; I am here but to fix the day of my marriage, and I shall then go into the country—till—till—In short, this is the last time my visit will banish you from the room I enter.

Clara [*aside*]. The last time!—and we shall then meet no more! And to part thus for ever—in scorn—in anger—I cannot bear it! [*Approaching him.*] Alfred, my cousin, it is true this may be the last time we shall meet; I have made arrangements to quit England.

Evelyn. To quit England?

Clara. But, before I go, let me thank you for many a past kindness, which it is not for an orphan easily to forget.

Evelyn [*mechanically*]. To quit England!

Clara. I have long wished it: but enough of me—Evelyn, now that you are betrothed to another, now, without recurring to the past—now, without the fear of mutual error and mistake—something of our old friendship may at least return to us. And if, too, I dared, I have that on my mind which only a friend—a sister—might presume to say to you.

Evelyn [*moved*]. Miss Douglas—Clara—if there is aught that I could do—if, while hundreds—strangers—beggars—tell me that I have the power, by opening or shutting this worthless hand, to bid sorrow rejoice or poverty despair; if—if my life—my heart's blood—could render to you one such service as my gold can give to others—why, speak! and the past you allude to,—yes, even that bitter past,—I will cancel and forget!

Clara [*holding out her hand*]. We are friends, then!—you are again my cousin!—my brother!

Evelyn [*dropping her hand*]. Ah! say on!

Clara. I speak then as a sister—herself weak, inexperienced, ignorant, nothing—might speak to a brother, in whose career she felt the ambition of a man. Oh, Evelyn! when you inherited this vast wealth I pleased myself with imagining how you would wield the power delegated to your hands. I knew your benevolence—your intellect—your genius!—the ardent mind couched beneath the cold sarcasm of a long-baffled spirit! I saw before me the noble and bright career open to you at last—and I often thought that, in after years, when far away, I should hear your name identified—not with what fortune can give the base, but with deeds and ends to which, for the great, fortune is but the instrument; I often thought that I should say to my own heart—weeping proud and delicious tears— 'And once this man loved me!'

Evelyn. No more, Clara! (oh heavens)—no more!

Clara. But *has* it been so? have you been true to your own self? Pomp, parade, luxuries, follies—all these might distinguish others, they do but belie the ambition and the soul of Alfred Evelyn! Oh, pardon me—I am too bold—I pain—I offend you,—Ah, I should not have dared thus much had I not thought at times, that—that—

Evelyn. That these follies—these vanities—this dalliance with a loftier fate, were your own work! You thought that, and you were right! Perhaps indeed, after a youth steeped to the lips in the hyssop and gall of penury—perhaps, I might have wished royally to know the full value of that dazzling and starry life which, from the last step in the ladder, I had seen indignantly and from afar. But a month—a week would have sufficed for that experience. Experience!—Oh, how soon we learn that hearts are as cold and souls as vile—no matter whether the sun shine on the noble in his palace, or the rain drench the rags of the beggar cowering at the porch. The extremes of life differ but in this:—Above, *Vice* smiles and revels—below, *Crime* frowns and starves. But you—did not you reject me because I was poor? Despise me if you please! My revenge might be unworthy—I wished to show you the luxuries, the gaud, the splendour I thought you prized—to surround with the attributes your sex seems most to value, the station that, had you loved me, it would have been yours to command. But vain—vain alike my poverty and my wealth! You loved me not in either, and my fate is sealed.

Clara. A happy fate, Evelyn! you love!

Evelyn. And at last I am beloved. [*After a pause, and turning to her abruptly.*] Do you doubt it? Clara. No, I believe it firmly! [*Aside.*] Were it possible for her not to love him?

Evelyn. Georgina, perhaps, is vain, and light—and—

Clara. No—think it not! Once removed from the worldly atmosphere of her father's councils, and you will form and raise her to your own level. She is so young yet—she has beauty, cheerfulness, and temper; the rest you will give her, if you will but yet do justice to your own nature. And, now there is nothing unkind between us—not even regret—and surely [*with a smile*] not revenge, my cousin; you will rise to our nobler self—and so, farewell!

Evelyn. No; stay—one moment; you still feel an interest in my fate. Have I been deceived? Oh, why, why did you spurn the heart whose offerings were lavished at your feet? Could you still—still?—Distraction—I know not what to say! my honour pledged to another—my vows accepted and returned! Go, Clara; it is best so! Yet you will miss some one, perhaps, more than me—some one to whose follies you have been more indulgent—some one to whom you would permit a yet tenderer name than that of brother!

Clara [*aside*]. It will make him, perhaps, happier to think it!—Think so, if you will!—but part friends.

Evelyn. Friends—and is that all! Look you, this is life! The eyes that charmed away every sorrow—the hand whose lightest touch thrilled to the very core—the presence that, like moonlight, shed its own hallowing beauty over the meanest things—a little while—a year—a month—a day—and we smile that we could dream so idly. All—all the sweet enchantment, known but once, never to return again, vanished from the world! And the one who forgets the soonest—the one who robs your earth for ever of its summer, comes to you with a careless lip and says, 'Let us part friends!' Go, go, Clara, go—and be happy if you can!

Clara [*weeping*]. Cruel, cruel, to the last! Heaven forgive you, Alfred!   [*Exit*, R.

Evelyn. Soft!—Let me recall her words, her tones, her looks. *Does she love me?* She defends her rival— she did not deny it when I charged her with attachment to another: and yet—and yet—there is a voice at my heart which tells me I have been the rash slave of a jealous anger. But I have made my choice—I must abide the issue!

Enter GRAVES, *preceded by* SERVANT, R.C.

Servant. Lady Franklin is dressing, sir.

Graves. Well, I'll wait.   [*Exit* SERVANT, R.

She was worthy to have known the lost Maria! So considerate to ask me hither—not to console me—

that is impossible—but to indulge the luxury of woe. It will be a mournful scene. [*Seeing* Evelyn.] Is that you, Evelyn? I have just heard that the borough of Groginhole is vacant at last. Why not stand yourself?—with your property you might come in without even a personal canvass.

Evelyn. I who despise these contests for the colour of a straw—this everlasting litigation of Authority *versus* Man—I to be one of the wranglers?—never!

Graves. You are quite right, and I beg your pardon.

Evelyn [*aside*]. And yet Clara spoke of ambition. She would regret me if I could be distinguished. [*Aloud*.] To be sure, after all, Graves, corrupt as mankind are, it is our duty to try at least to make them a little better. An Englishman owes something to his country.

Graves. He does, indeed!—[*Counting on his fingers*.] East winds, fogs, rheumatism, pulmonary complaints, and taxes. [Evelyn *walks about in disorder*.] You seem agitated—a quarrel with your intended? Oh! when you've been married a month, you won't know what to do with one!

Evelyn. You are a pleasant comforter. [*Crosses*, L.]

Graves. Do you deserve a comforter? One morning you tell me you love Clara, or at least detest her, which is the same thing—(poor Maria often said she detested *me*), and that very afternoon you propose to Georgina!

Evelyn. Clara will easily console herself—thanks to Sir Frederick!

Graves. He is young!

Evelyn. Good looking!

Graves. A coxcomb!

Evelyn. And therefore irresistible!

Graves. Nevertheless, Clara has had the bad taste to refuse him. I have it from Lady Franklin, to whom he confided his despair in re-arranging his neckcloth.

Evelyn. My dear friend, is it possible?

Graves. But what then? You *must* marry Georgina, who, to believe Lady Franklin, is sincerely attached to—your fortune. Go and hang yourself, Evelyn; you have been duped by them.

Evelyn. By them—bah! If deceived, I have been my own dupe. Is it not a strange thing that in matters of reason—of the arithmetic and logic of life—we are sensible, shrewd, prudent men? But touch our hearts—move our passions—take us for an instant from the hard safety of worldly calculation—and the philosopher is duller than the fool! Duped—if I thought it—

Graves. To be sure! you tried Clara in your *poverty*, it was a safe experiment to try Georgina in your *wealth*.

Evelyn. Ha! that is true; very true. Go on.

Graves. You'll have an excellent father-in-law. Sir John positively weeps when he talks of your income!

Evelyn. Sir John possibly—but Georgina?

Graves. Plays affection to you in the afternoon, after practising first with Sir Frederick in the morning.

Evelyn. On your life, sir, be serious; what do you mean?

Graves. That in passing this way I see her very often walking in the square with Sir Frederick.

Evelyn. Ha! say you so?

Graves. What then? Man is born to be deceived: You look nervous—your hand trembles; that comes of gaming. They say at the clubs that you play deeply.

Evelyn. Ha! ha! Do they say that?—a few hundreds lost or won—a cheap opiate—anything that can lay the memory to sleep. The poor man drinks, and the rich man gambles—the same motive to both! But you are right, it is a base resource—I will play no more.

Graves. I am delighted to hear it, for your friend Captain Smooth has ruined half the young heirs in London—to play with him is to advertise yourself a bankrupt. Even Sir John is alarmed. I met him just now in Pall Mall; he made me stop, and implored me to speak to you. By the by, I forgot—do you bank with Flash, Brisk, Credit and Co.?

Evelyn. So, Sir John is alarmed? [*Aside.*] Gulled by this cogging charlatan? I may beat him yet at his own weapons! Humph! Bank with Flash! Why do you ask me?

Graves. Because Sir John has just heard that they are in a very bad way, and begs you to withdraw anything you have in their hands.

Evelyn. I'll see to it. So Sir John is *alarmed* at my gambling!

Graves. Terribly! He even told me he should go himself to the club this evening to watch you.

Evelyn. To watch me! Good—I will be there.

Graves. But you will promise not to play.

Evelyn. Yes—to play. I feel it is impossible to give it up!

Graves. No—no! 'Sdeath, man! be as wretched as you please—break your heart, that's nothing! but damme, take care of your pockets!

Evelyn. I will be there—I will play with Captain Smooth, I will lose as much as I please—thousands—millions—billions; and if he presume to spy on my losses, hang me if I don't lose Sir John himself into the bargain! [*Going out and returning.*] I am so absent! What was the bank you mentioned? Flash, Brisk, and Credit. Bless me, how unlucky! and it's too late to draw out today! Tell Sir John I'm very much obliged to him, and he'll find me at the club any time before daybreak hard at work with my friend Smooth.   [*Exit*, R.

Graves. He's certainly crazy! but I don't wonder at it. What the approach of the dog-days is to the canine species, the approach of the honeymoon is to the human race.

Enter SERVANT, R.

Servant. Lady Franklin's compliments; she will see you in the boudoir, sir.

Graves. In the *boudoir!*—go, go—I'll come directly.

[*Exit* SERVANT.

My heart beats—it must be for grief. Poor *Maria!*—[*Searching his pockets for his handkerchief.*] Not a white one—just like my luck! I call on a lady to talk of the dear departed, and I've nothing about me but a cursed gaudy, flaunting, red, yellow, and blue abomination from India, which it's even indecent for a disconsolate widower to exhibit. Ah! Fortune never ceases to torment the susceptible. The *boudoir!* Ha! ha! the *boudoir!*   [*Exit*, R.

253

SCENE II. *A boudoir in the same house. Two chairs on.*

Lady Franklin. I take so much compassion on this poor man, who is determined to make himself wretched, that I am equally determined to make him happy! Well, if my scheme does not succeed, he shall laugh, he shall sing, he shall—Mum!—here he comes!

Enter GRAVES, R.

Graves [*sighing*]. Ah, Lady Franklin!

Lady Franklin [*sighing*]. Ah, Mr. Graves! [*They seat themselves.*] Pray excuse me for having kept you so long. Is it not a charming day?

Graves. An east wind, ma'am! but nothing comes amiss to you!—it's a happy disposition! Poor Maria!—she, too, was naturally gay.

Lady Franklin [*aside*]. Yes, she was gay. So much life, and a great deal of spirit.

Graves. Spirit? Yes!—nothing could master it. She would have her own way; ah, there was nobody like her!

Lady Franklin. And then, when her spirit was up, she looked so handsome! Her eyes grew so brilliant!

Graves. Did not they? Ah! ah! ha! ha! ha! And do you remember her pretty trick of stamping her foot?—the tiniest little foot—I think I see her now. Ah! this conversation is very soothing.

Lady Franklin. How well she acted in your private theatricals!

Graves. You remember her Mrs. Oakely in 'The Jealous Wife?' Ha! ha! how good it was!—ha! ha! Lady Franklin. Ha! ha! Yes, in the very first scene, when she came out with [*mimicking*] 'Your unkindness and barbarity will be the death of me!'

Graves. No—no! that's not it! more energy. [*Mimicking.*] 'Your unkindness and barbarity will be the DEATH of me.' Ha! ha! I ought to know how she said it, for she used to practise it on me twice a day. Ah! poor dear lamb!   [*Wipes his eyes.*

Lady Franklin. And then she sang so well! was such a composer! What was the little French air she was so fond of?

Graves. Ha! ha! sprightly! was it not? Let me see—let me see.

Lady Franklin [*humming*]. Turn ti—ti—tum—ti—ti—ti. No, that's not it.

Graves [*humming*]. Turn ti—ti—tum ti—ti—turn turn turn.

Both. Turn ti—ti—turn ti—ti—tum—tum—tum. Ha! ha!

Graves [*throwing himself back*]. Ah, what recollections it revives! It is too affecting.

Lady Franklin. It is affecting, but we are all mortal. [*Sighs.*] And at your Christmas party, at Cyprus Lodge, do you remember her dancing the Scotch reel with Captain Macnaughten?

Graves. Ha! ha! ha! To be sure—to be sure.

Lady Franklin. Can you think of the step?—somehow thus, was it not?   [*Dancing.*

Graves. No—no, quite wrong!—just stand there. Now then, [*humming the tune*] La—la-la-la—La-la, &c. [*They dance.*] That's it—excellent—admirable!

Lady Franklin [*aside*]. Now it's coming.

Enter SIR JOHN, BLOUNT, *and* GEORGINA, R.
They stand amazed. LADY FRANKLIN *continues to dance.*

Graves. Bewitching—irresistible! It's Maria herself that I see before me! Thus, let me clasp—Oh, the devil! Just like my luck! [*Stopping opposite* SIR JOHN].

[LADY FRANKLIN *runs off* L.

Sir John. Upon my word, Mr. Graves!

Georgina and Blount. Encore—encore! Bravo—bravo!

Graves. It's all a mistake! I—I—Sir John—Lady Franklin, you see—that is to say I—Sainted Maria! you are spared at least this affliction!

Georgina. Pray go on!

Blount. Don't let us intewwupt you.

Graves. Interrupt me! I must say that this rudeness—this gross impropriety—to pry into the sorrows of a poor bereaved sufferer, seeking comfort from a sympathizing friend—But such is human nature!

Georgina. But, Mr. Graves—   [*Following him.*

Graves. Heartless!

Blount. My dear Mr. Gwaves!   [*Following him.*

Graves. Frivolous!

Sir John. Stay and dine!   [*Following him.*

Graves. Unfeeling!

Omnes. Ha!—ha!—ha!

Graves. Monsters! Good day to you.

[*Exit, followed by* SIR JOHN, &C.

SCENE III. *The interior of * * * * *'s Club; night; lights, &c. Small sofa-tables, with books, papers, tea, coffee, &c. Several members grouped by the fire-place; one member with his legs over the back of his chair; another with his legs over his table; a third with his legs on the chimney-piece. To the left, and in front of the stage, an old member reading the newspaper, seated by a small round table; to the right a card table, before which* CAPTAIN DUDLEY SMOOTH *is seated and sipping lemonade; at the bottom of the stage another card table.*

GLOSSMORE *and* STOUT, C.

Glossmore. You don't come often to the club, Stout?

Stout. No; time is money. An hour spent at a club is unproductive capital.

Old Member [*reading the newspaper*]. Waiter!—the snuff-box.

WAITER *brings it.*

Glossmore. So, Evelyn has taken to play? I see Deadly Smooth, 'hushed in grim repose, awaits his evening prey.' Deep work tonight, I suspect, for Smooth is drinking lemonade—keeps his head clear—monstrous clever dog!

Enter Evelyn; *salutes and shakes hands with different*
members in passing up the stage, C.

Evelyn. How do you do, Glossmore? How are you, Stout? *You* don't play, I think! Political economy never plays at cards, eh?—never has time for anything more frivolous than rents and profits, wages and labour, high price and low—corn laws, poor laws, tithes, currency—dot-and-go-one—rates, puzzles, taxes, riddles, and botheration! Smooth is the man. Aha! Smooth. Piquet, eh? You owe me my revenge.

[*Members touch each other significantly.* Stout *walks away with the snuff-box;*
Old Member *looks at him savagely.*

Smooth. My dear Alfred, anything to oblige.

[*They seat themselves.*

Old Member. Waiter!—the snuff-box.

[Waiter *takes it from* Stout *and brings it back to* Old Member.
Enter Blount, C.

Blount. So, so! Evelyn at it again—eh, Glossmore?

Glossmore. Yes, Smooth sticks to him like a leech. Clever fellow, that Smooth.

Blount. Will you make up a wubber?

Glossmore. Have you got two others?

Blount. Yes; Flat and Gween.

Glossmore. Bad players.

Blount. I make it a wule to play with bad players; it is five per cent. in one's favour. I hate gambling. But a quiet wubber, if one is the best player out of four, can't do one any harm.

Glossmore. Clever fellow, that Blount !

[Blount *takes up the snuff-box and walks off with it;* Old Member *looks at him savagely.*
Blount, Glossmore, Flat, *and* Green, *make up a table at the bottom of the stage.*

Smooth. A thousand pardons, my dear Alfred, —ninety repique—ten cards!—game!

Evelyn [*passing a note to him*]. Game! Before we go on, one question. This is Thursday-how much do you calculate to win of me before Tuesday next?

Smooth. Ce cher Alfred! He is so droll!

Evelyn [*writing in his pocket-book*]. Forty games a night,—four nights, minus Sunday—our usual stakes —that would be right, I think?

Smooth [*glancing over the account*]. Quite—if I win all—which is next to impossible.

Evelyn. It shall be possible to win twice as much, on one condition. Can you keep a secret?

Smooth. My dear Alfred, I have kept myself! I never inherited a farthing—I never spent less than £4,000 a year—and I never told a soul how I managed it.

Evelyn. Hark ye then, a word with you.   [*They whisper.*

Old Member. Waiter!—the snuff-box.   [Waiter *takes it from* Blount, &c.

Enter Sir John, C.

Evelyn. You understand?

Smooth. Perfectly; anything to oblige.

Evelyn [*cutting*]. It is for you to deal.   [*They go on playing.*

Sir John [*groaning*]. There's my precious son-in-law that is to be, spending *my* consequence, and making a fool of himself.

[*Taking up the snuff-box;* Old Member *looks at him savagely.*

Blount. I'm out. Flat, a pony on the odd twick. That's wight. [*Coming up counting his money.*] Well, Sir John, you don't play?

Sir John. Play, no! [Evelyn *passes money to* Smooth.] Confound him—lost again!

Evelyn. Hang the cards!—double the stakes!

Smooth. Just as you please—done! Anything to oblige.

Sir John. Done, indeed!

Old Member. Waiter!—the snuff-box.   [Waiter *takes it from* Sir John.

Blount. I've won eight pounds and the bets—I never lose—I never play in the Deadly Smooth set!

[*Takes up the snuff-box.* Old Member *as before.*

Sir John [*looking over* Smooth's *hand and fidgeting backwards and forwards*]. Lord have mercy on us! Smooth has seven for his point. What's the stakes?

Evelyn. Don't disturb us—I only throw out four. Stakes, Sir John?—immense! Was ever such luck?—not a card for my point. Do stand back, Sir John—I'm getting irritable!

Old Member. Waiter!—the snuff-box.

[Waiter *brings it back.*

Blount. One hundred pounds on the next game, Evelyn?

Sir John. Nonsense—nonsense—don't disturb him! All the fishes come to the bait! Sharks and minnows all nibbling away at my son-in-law!

Evelyn. One hundred pounds, Blount? Ah, the finest gentleman is never too fine a gentleman to pick up a guinea. Done! Treble the stakes, Smooth!

Sir John. I'm on the rack! [*Seizing the snuff-box.*] Be cool, Evelyn! Take care, my dear boy!—now don't ye—now don't!

Evelyn. What—what? You have four queens! five to the king. Confound the cards!—a fresh pack.

[*Throws the cards behind him over* Sir John.
Waiter *brings a new pack of cards to* Evelyn.

Old Member. Waiter, the snuff-box.

[*Different* Members *gather round*

First Member [*with back to audience*]. I never before saw Evelyn out of temper. He must be losing immensely!

Second Member. Yes, this is interesting!

Sir John. Interesting! There's a wretch!

First Member. Poor fellow, he'll be ruined in a month!

Sir John. I'm in a cold sweat.

Second Member. Smooth is the very devil.

Sir John. The devil's a joke to him!

Glossmore [*slapping* Sir John *on the back*]. A clever fellow, that Smooth, Sir John, eh? [*Takes up the snuff-box;* Old Member *as before.*] £100 on this game, Evelyn?

Evelyn [*half turning round*]. You! well done the Constitution! yes, £100.

Old Member. Waiter!—the snuff-box.

Stout. I think I'll venture! £200 on this game, Evelyn?

Evelyn [*quite turning round*]. Ha! ha! ha! Enlightenment and the Constitution on the same side of the question at last! O, Stout, Stout!—greatest happiness of the greatest number—greatest number, number one! Done, Stout !—£200!—ha! ha! ha!—I deal, Stout. Well done, Political Economy——Ha! ha! ha!

Sir John. Quite hysterical—drivelling! Aren't you ashamed of yourselves? His own cousins!—all in a conspiracy—a perfect gang of them. [Members *indignant*.

Stout [*to* Members]. Hush! He's to marry Sir John's daughter.

First Member. What, Stingy Jack's? Oh!

Chorus of Members. Oh! oh!

Old Member. Waiter!—the snuff-box.

Evelyn [*rising in great agitation*]. No more, no more—I've done!—quite enough. Glossmore, Stout, Blount—I'll pay you tomorrow. I—I—. Death! this is ruinous!

[*Seizes the snuff-box;* Old Member *as before*.

Sir John. Ruinous! I dare say it is! What has he lost? What *has* he lost, Smooth? Not much? eh? eh?

[Omnes *gather round* Smooth.

Smooth. Oh, a trifle, dear John!—excuse me! we never tell our winnings. [*To* Blount.] How d'ye do, Fred? [*To* Glossmore.] By the by, Charles, don't you want to sell your house in Grosvenor Square?—£12,000, eh?

Glossmore. Yes, and the furniture at a valuation. About £3,000 more.

Smooth [*looking over his pocket-book*]. Um!—well, we'll talk of it.

Sir John. Twelve and three—£15,000. What a cold-blooded rascal it is!—£15,000, Smooth?

Smooth. Oh, the house itself is a trifle, but the establishment—I'm considering whether I have enough to keep it up, my dear John.

Old Member. Waiter, the snuff-box! [*Scraping it round, and with a wry face.*] And it's all gone!

[*Gives it to the* Waiter *to fill*.

Sir John [*turning round*]. And it's all gone!

Evelyn [*starting up and laughing hysterically*]. Ha! ha! ha! all gone? not a bit of it. Smooth, this club is so noisy. Sir John, you are always in the way. Come to my house! come! Champagne and a broiled bone. Nothing venture, nothing have! The luck must turn, and by Jupiter, we'll make a night of it.

Sir John. A night of it!!! For Heaven's sake, Evelyn, EVELYN!—think what you are about!—think of Georgina's feelings!—think of your poor mother!—think of the babes unborn!—think of—

Evelyn. I'll think of nothing! Zounds!—you don't know what I have lost, man; it's all your fault, distracting my attention! Pshaw—pshaw! Out of the way, do! Come, Smooth. Ha! ha! a night of it, my boy—a night of it!

[*Exeunt* SMOOTH *and* EVELYN.

Sir John [*following*]. You must not, you shall not! Evelyn, my dear Evelyn!—he's drunk—he's mad! Will no one send for the police?

Members. Ha! ha! ha!—Poor old Stingy Jack!

Old Member [*rising for the first time in a great rage*). Waiter, the snuff-box!

END OF ACT III

ACT IV

SCENE I. *The anteroom in Evelyn's house as in Act II, Scene I.*
TABOURET, MACFINCH, FRANTZ *and other tradesmen.*

Tabouret [*half whispers*]. So, I hear that Mr. Evelyn is turned gamester! There are strange reports about today—I don't know what to make of it! We must look sharp, and make hay while the sun shines.

MacFinch. I wuish those geeming-houses were aw at the deevill—it's a sheam and a sin for gentlemen to gang and ruin themselves, when we honest tradesmen could do it for them with sae muckle advantage to the arts and commerce o' the country!

[OMNES *shake their heads approvingly.*
Enter SMOOTH, R.C., *from the inner room, with a pocketbook and pencil in his hand.*

Smooth [*looking round*]. Hum! ha! Fine pictures! [*Feel the curtains.*] The new-fashioned velvet, hem!—good proportioned rooms! Yes, this house is better than Glossmore's! Oh, Mr. Tabouret, the upholsterer! you furnished these rooms. All of the best, eh?

Tabouret. Oh! the Very best! Mr. Evelyn is not a man to grudge expense, sir!

Smooth. He is not indeed. You've been paid, I suppose, Tabouret?

Tabouret. No, sir, no—I never send in my bills when a customer is rich. [*Aside.*] Bills are like trees, and grow by standing.

Smooth. Humph! Not Paid? humph!

OMNES *gather round.*

MacFinch. I dinna like that hoomph, there's something vara suspeecious about it.

Tabouret [*to the tradesmen*]. It's the great card-player, Captain Smooth—finest player in Europe—cleaned out the Duke of Silly Val. Uncommonly clever man!

Smooth [*pacing about the room*]. Thirty-six feet by twenty-eight—Um! I think a bow-window there would be an improvement; could it be done easily, Tabouret?

MacFinch. If Mr. Evelyn wishes to pool about his house, there's no mon like my friend, Mr. MacStucco.

Smooth. Evelyn? I was speaking of *myself*, Mr. MacStucco—humph!

Tabouret. Yourself? Have you bought the house, sir?

Smooth. Bought it!—hum!—ha!—it depends. So you have not been paid yet?—um! Nor you—nor you— nor you? Hum! ah!

Tabouret. No, sir—what *then?* No fear of Mr. Evelyn? Ha! ha!

Omnes [*anxiously*]. Ha! ha!—what then?

MacFinch. Ah, sir, what then? I'm a puir mon with a family; this way, Captain! You've a leetle account in the buiks; an' we'll e'en wipe it out altogether, gin you'll say what you mean by that Hoom ha!

Smooth. MacFinch, my dear fellow, don't oblige me to cane you; I would not have Mr. Evelyn distressed for the world. Poor fellow! he holds very bad cards. So you've not been paid yet? Don't send in your bills on any account—mind! Yes; I don't dislike the house with some alteration. Good day to you— Hum! ha!

[*Exit, looking about him, examining the chairs, tables, &c.*

Tabouret. Plain as a pikestaff! staked his very house on an odd trick!

Enter SHARP, C., *agitated and in a hurry.*

Sharp. O Lord! O Lord!—who'd have thought it? Cards are the devil's book! John!—Thomas!—Harris! [*Ringing the bell that was on the table.*]

Enter Two SERVANTS, C.

Tom, take this letter to Sir John Vesey's. If not at home, find him—he will give you a cheque. Go to his banker's, and get it cashed instantly. Quick—quick—off with you.

Tabouret [*seizing* SERVANT]. What's the matter?—What's the matter? How's Mr. Evelyn?

Servant. Bad—very bad! Sat up all night with Captain Smooth! [*Runs off* R.

Sharp [*to the other* SERVANT]. Yes, Harris, your poor master! O dear! O dear ! You will take this note to the Belgian Minister, Portland Place. Passport for Ostend! Have the travelling carriage ready at a moment's notice!

Tabouret [*stopping* SERVANT]. Passport! Hark ye, my man; is he going to put the salt seas between us and our money?

Servant. Don't stop me—something wrong in the chest—change of air—late hours—and Captain Smooth!   [*Exit*, R.

Sharp [*walking about*]. And if the bank should break!—if the bank is broke, and he can't draw out!— bound to Smooth!

Tabouret. Bank !—what bank?

Sharp. Flash's bank! Flash, brother-in-law to Captain Smooth! What have *you* heard?—eh?—eh?

Tabouret. That there's an awful run on it!

Sharp. I must be off. Go—go—you can't see Mr. Evelyn today!

Tabouret. My account, sir!

MacFinch. I've a muckle bairns and a sma' bill!

Frantz. O sare, de great gentlemen a'ways tink first of the tailor!

Sharp. Call again—call again at Christmas. The bank, the cards—the cards, the bank! O dear! O dear!   [*Exit*, C.

Tabouret. The bank!

MacFinch. The passport!

Frantz. And all dat vill be seen of de great Evelyn coat is de back of it. Donner und Hagel!—I vil arrest him—I vil put de salt on de tail of it!

Tabouret [*aside*]. I'll slip down to the City and see how the bank goes!

MacFinch [*aside*]. I'll e'en gang to my coosin the la'yer. Nothing but peetience for us, Mr. Tabouret.

Tabouret. Ay, ay, stick by each other—share and share alike—that's my way, sir.

Omnes. Share and share alike.   *Exeunt*, R.

Enter SERVANT, GLOSSMORE, and BLOUNT, C.

Servant. My master is not very well, my lord; but I'll let him know.   [*Exit*, C.

Glossmore. I'm very curious to learn the result of his gambling tête-à-tête with Deadly Smooth!

Blount. Oh, he's so howwidly wich, he can afford even a tête-à-tête with Deadly Smooch!

Glossmore. Poor old Stingy Jack! why, Georgina was *your* intended.

Blount. Yes; and I weally liked the girl, though out of pique I pwoposed to her cousin. But what can a man do against money?

Enter EVELYN, C.

It we could start fair, you'd see whom Georgina would pwefer; but she's sacwificed by her father! She as much as told me so!   [*Crosses*, R.

Evelyn. So, so, gentlemen, we've a little account to settle—one hundred each.

Both. Don't talk of it.

Evelyn. Well, I won't! [*Taking* BLOUNT *aside*.] Ha! ha! you'd hardly believe it, but I'd rather not pay you just at present; my money is locked up, and I must wait, you know, for the Groginhole rents. So! instead of owing you one hundred pounds, suppose I owe you five? You can give me a cheque for the other four. And, hark ye, not a word to Glossmore.

Blount. Glossmore! the gweatest gossip in London! I shall be delighted! [*Aside*.] It never does harm too to lend to a wich man! one gets it back somehow. [*Aloud*.] By the way, Evelyn, if you want my gwey cab-horse, you may have him for two hundred pounds, and that will make seven!

Evelyn [*aside*]. That's the fashionable usury; your friend does not take interest—he sells you a horse. [*Aloud*.] Blount, it's a bargain.

Blount [*writing the cheque, and musingly*]. No; I don't see what harm it can do to me; that off leg must end in a spavin.

Evelyn [*to* GLOSSMORE]. That hundred pounds I owe you is rather inconvenient at present; I've a large sum to make up for the Groginhole property; perhaps you would lend me five or six hundred more—just to go on with?

Glossmore. Certainly! Hopkins is dead; your interest for Cipher would—

Evelyn. Why, I can't promise *that* at this moment. But as a slight mark of friendship and gratitude, I shall be very much flattered if you'll accept a splendid grey cab-horse I bought today—cost two hundred pounds!

Glossmore. Bought today!—then I'm safe. My dear fellow! You're always so princely!

Evelyn. Nonsense! just write the cheque; and, hark ye!— not a syllable to Blount!

Glossmore. He's the town-crier!   [*Goes to write.*

Blount [*giving* EVELYN *the cheque*]. Wansom's, Pall Mall East.

Evelyn. Thank you. So you proposed to Miss Douglas!

Blount. Hang it! yes; I could have sworn that she fancied me; her manner, for instance, that vewy day you pwoposed for Miss Vesey—otherwise Georgina—

Evelyn. Has only half what Miss Douglas has.

Blount. You forget how much Stingy Jack must have saved! But I beg your pardon.

Evelyn. Never mind; but not a word to Sir John, or he'll fancy I'm ruined.

Glossmore [*giving the cheque*]. Ransom's, Pall Mall East. Tell me, did you win or lose last night?

Evelyn. Win! lose! Oh! no more of that, if you love me. I must send off at once to the banker's.   [*Looking at the two cheques.*

Glossmore [*aside*]. Why! He's borrowed from Blount, too!

Blount [*aside*]. That's a cheque from Lord Glossmore!

Evelyn. Excuse me; I must dress! I have not a moment to lose. You remember you dine with me today— seven o'clock. You'll see Smooth. [*With tears in his eyes.*] It may be the last time I shall ever welcome you here!—My—what am I saying?—Oh, merely a joke!—good-bye—good-bye. [*Shaking them heartily by the hand.*]

[*Exit,* C.

Blount. Glossmore!

Glossmore. Blount!

Blount. I am afwaid all's not wight!

Glossmore. I incline to your opinion!

Blount. But I've sold my gwey cab-horse.

Glossmore. Grey cab-horse! you! What is he really worth now?

Blount. Since he is sold, I will tell you—Not a sixpence!

Glossmore. Not a sixpence! he gave it to me!

EVELYN *at the door, giving directions to a* SERVANT *in dumb show.*

Blount. That was devilish unhandsome! Do you know I feel nervous?

Glossmore. Nervous! Let us run and stop payment of our cheques.

EVELYN *shuts the door, and* SERVANT *runs across the stage.*

Blount. Hallo, John! where so fast?

Servant [*in great haste*]. Beg pardon, Sir Frederick, to Pall Mall East—Messrs. Ransom.   [*Exit*, R.

Blount [*solemnly*] Glossmore, we are floored!

Glossmore. Sir, the whole town shall know of it!   [*Exeunt*, R.

Enter TOKE *and other* SERVANTS, C.

Toke. Come, come, stir yourselves! We've no time to lose. This room is to be got ready for the shawls. Mrs. Crump and the other ladies of our household are to wait here on the women before they go up to the drawing-room. Take away that desk; don't be lazy! and give me the newspaper. [TOKE *seats himself; the* SERVANTS *bustle about*.] Strange reports about my patron! and the walley is gone for the passport!

Enter FRANTZ *with a bundle*, R.

Frantz. Mr. Toke, my goot Mr. Toke, I've brought you von leetel present.

Toke. John and Charles, vanish! [*Exeunt* SERVANTS, C.] I scorns to corrupt them 'ere working classes!

Frantz [*producing a pair of smallclothes, which* TOKE *examines*). Your master is von beggar! He vants to run away; ye are all in de same vat-you-call-it—de same leetel nasty boat, Mr. Toke! Just let my friend Mr. Clutch up through the area, and I vill arrest him dis very day.

Toke. I accept the abridgments; but you've forgotten to line the pockets.

Frantz. Blesh my soul, so I have!   [*Giving a note.*

Toke. The area gate shall be left undefended. Do it quietly; no *claw*, as the French say.

Frantz. Goot Mr. Toke—tomorrow I vill line de oter pocket.   [*Exit*, R.

Toke. My patron does not give me satisfaction!

Enter FOOTMAN, C.

Footman. What chandeliers are to be lighted, Mr. Toke?—it's getting late.

Toke. Don't disturb me—rum-mynating!—yes, yes, there's no doubt of it! Charles, the area gate is open?

Footman. And all the plate in the pantry! I'll run and—

Toke. Not a step! leave it open.

Footman. But—

Yoke [*with dignity*]. It's for the sake of wentilation.

[*Exeunt*, C.

SCENE II. *A splendid saloon in* EVELYN'S *house.*

Enter EVELYN *and* GRAVES.

Graves. You've withdrawn your money from Flash and Brisk?

Evelyn. No.

Graves. No!—then

Enter SIR JOHN, LADY FRANKLIN, GEORGINA, *and* STOUT, R.

Sir John. You got the cheque for £500 safely ?—too happy to—

Evelyn [*interrupting him*]. My best thanks! my warmest gratitude! So kind in you! so seasonable!—that £500— you don't know the value of that £500. I shall never forget your nobleness of conduct.

Sir John. Gratitude! Nobleness!—[*Aside.*] I can't have been taken in!

Evelyn. And in a moment of such distress!

Sir John [*aside*]. Such distress! He picks out the ugliest words in the whole dictionary!

Evelyn. I've done with Smooth. But I'm still a little crippled, and you must do me *another* favour. I've only as yet paid the deposit of ten per cent, for the great Groginhole property. I am to pay the rest this week—nay, I fear, tomorrow. I've already sold out of the Funds; the money lies at the bankers', and of course I can't touch it; for if I don't pay by a certain day, I forfeit the estate and the deposit.

Sir John. What's coming now, I wonder?

Evelyn. Georgina's fortune is £10,000. I always meant, my dear Sir John, to present you with that little sum.

Sir John. Oh, Evelyn! your generosity is positively touching. [*Wipes his eyes.*

Evelyn. But the news of my losses has frightened my tradesmen! I have so many heavy debts at this moment—that—that—But I see Georgina is listening, and I'll say what I have to say to her. [*Crosses to her.*

Sir John. No, no—no, no. Girls don't understand business!

Evelyn. The very reason I speak to her. This is an affair, not of business but of *feeling*. Stout, show Sir John my Correggio.

Sir John [*aside*]. Devil take his Correggio! The man is born to torment me! [STOUT *takes him in.*

Evelyn. My dear Georgina, whatever you may hear said of me, I flatter myself that you feel confidence in my honour.

Georgina. Can you doubt it?

Evelyn. I confess that I am embarrassed at this moment; I have been weak enough to lose money at play, and there are other demands on me. I promise you never to gamble again as long as I live. My affairs can be retrieved, but for the first few years of our marriage it may be necessary to retrench.

Georgina. Retrench!

Evelyn. To live perhaps altogether in the country!

Georgina. Altogether in the country!

Evelyn. To confine ourselves to a modest competence!

Georgina. Modest competence! I knew something horrid was coming.

Enter BLOUNT, R.

Evelyn. And now, Georgina, you may have it in your power at this moment to save me from much anxiety and humiliation. My money is locked up—my debts of honour must be settled—you are of age—your £10,000 in your own hands—

Sir John [STOUT *listening as well as* SIR JOHN]. I'm standing on hot iron!

Evelyn. If you could lend it to me for a few weeks.—You hesitate! oh! believe the honour of the man you will call your husband before all the calumnies of the fools whom we call the world!—Can you give me this proof of your confidence? Remember, without confidence, what is wedlock?

Sir John [*aside to her*). No! [*Aloud, pointing his glass at the Correggio.*] Yes, the picture may be fine.

Stout. But you don't like the subject!

Georgina [*aside*]. He may be only trying me! Best leave it to papa.

Evelyn. Well—

Georgina. You—you shall hear from me tomorrow. [*Aside*] Ah, there's that dear Sir Frederick.

[*Goes to* BLOUNT.

Enter GLOSSMORE *and* SMOOTH, R. EVELYN *salutes them, paying* SMOOTH *servile respect.*

Lady Franklin [*to* GRAVES]. Ha! ha! To be so disturbed yesterday—was it not droll?

Graves. Never recur to that humiliating topic.

Glossmore [*to* STOUT]. See how Evelyn fawns upon Smooth!

Stout. How mean in him! *Smooth*—a professional gambler—a fellow who lives by his wits! I would not know such a man on any account!

Smooth [*to* GLOSSMORE]. So Hopkins is dead; you want Cipher to come in for Groginhole, eh?

Glossmore. What!—could *you* manage it?

Smooth. Ce cher Charles—anything to oblige!

Stout. Groginhole! What can he have to do with Groginhole? Glossmore, present me to Smooth.

Glossmore. What! the gambler—the fellow who lives by his wits?

Stout. Why his wits seem to be an uncommonly productive capital! I'll introduce myself. How d'ye do, Captain Smooth? We have met at the club, I think—I am charmed to make your acquaintance in private. I say, sir, what do you think of the affairs of the nation? Bad! very bad!— no enlightenment!— great fall off in the revenue!—no knowledge of finance! There's only one man who can save the country—and that's POPKINS!

Smooth. Is he in Parliament, Mr. Stout? What's your Christian name, by the by?

Stout. Benjamin. No; constituencies are so ignorant, they don't understand his value. He's no orator; in fact, he stammers so much—but devilish profound. Could not we ensure him for Groginhole?

Smooth. My dear Benjamin, it's a thing to be thought on.

Evelyn [*advancing*]. My friends, I wish to consult you. This day twelvemonth I succeeded to an immense income, and as, by a happy coincidence, on the same day I secured your esteem, so now I wish to ask you if you think I could have spent that income in a way more worthy of your good opinion?

Glossmore. Impossible! excellent taste—beautiful house!

Blount. Vewy good horses— [*aside to* GLOSSMORE] especially the gwey cab!

Lady Franklin. Splendid pictures!

Graves. And a magnificent cook, ma'am!

Smooth [*thrusting his hands in his pockets*]. It's my opinion, Alfred—and I'm a judge—that you could not have spent your money better.

Omnes [*except* SIR JOHN]. Very true!

Evelyn. What say *you*, Sir John?—You may think me a little extravagant; but you know that in this world the only way to show oneself thoroughly respectable is to make a thoroughly respectable show.

Sir John. Certainly—certainly. No, you could not have done better. [*Aside*.] I don't know what to make of it.

Georgina. Certainly. [*Coaxingly.*] Don't retrench, my dear Alfred!

Glossmore. Retrench! nothing so plebeian!

Stout. Plebeian, sir!—worse than plebeian!—it is against all the rules of public morality.

Everyone knows, nowadays, that extravagance is a benefit to the population—encourages art—employs labour, and multiplies spinning-jennies.

Evelyn. You reassure me! I own I did think that a man worthy of friends so sincere, might have done something better than feast—dress—drink—play

Glossmore. Nonsense! we like you the better for it. [*Aside.*] I wish I had my £600 back, though.

Evelyn. And you are as much my friends now as when you offered me £10 for my old nurse.

Sir John. A thousand times more so, my dear boy.

[Omnes *approve. Enter* Sharp, R.

Smooth. But who's our new friend?

Evelyn. Who? the very man who first announced to me the wealth which you allow I have spent so well. But what's the matter, Sharp?

Sharp *whispering* Evelyn.

[*Aloud.*] The bank's broke!

Sir John. Broke!—what bank?

Evelyn. Flash, Brisk and Co.

Glossmore [to Smooth]. And Flash was your brother-in-law. I'm very sorry.

Smooth [*taking snuff*]. Not at all, Charles—I did not bank there.

Sir John. But I warned you—you withdrew?

Evelyn. Alas! no!

Sir John. Oh!—not much in their hands?

Evelyn. Why, I told you the purchase money for Groginhole was at my bankers'. But, no, no; don't look so frightened! It was not placed with Flash—it is at Hoare's—it is indeed. Nay, I assure you it is! A mere trifle at Flash's—upon my word, now! Tomorrow, Sharp, we'll talk of this! One day more—one day at least for enjoyment!

Sir John. Oh! a pretty enjoyment!

Blount. And he borrowed £700 of me!

Glossmore. And £600 of me!

Sir John. And £500 of me!

Stout. Oh! a regular Jeremy Diddler!

Smooth [to Sir John]. John, do you know, I think I would take a handsome offer for this house just as it stands—furniture, plate, pictures, books, bronzes, and statues!

Sir John. Powers above!

Stout [to Sir John]. I say, you have placed your daughter in a very unsafe investment. Transfer the stock in hand to t'other speculation.

Sir John [*going to* Georgina]. Ha! I'm afraid we've been very rude to Sir Frederick. A monstrous fine young man!

Enter Toke, R.

Toke [*to* Evelyn]. Sir, I beg your pardon, but Mr. MacFinch insists on my giving up this letter instantly.

Evelyn [*reading*]. How! Sir John, this fellow, MacFinch, has heard of my misfortunes, and insists on being paid;—a lawyer's letter—quite insolent!

Toke. And, sir, Mr. Tabouret is below, and declares he won't stir till he's paid. [*Exit*, R. Evelyn. Won't stir till he's paid! What's to be done, Sir John!—Smooth, what is to be done? Smooth. If he won't stir till he's paid, make him up a bed, and I'll take him in the inventory as one of the fixtures, Alfred!

Evelyn. It is very well for you to joke, Mr. Smooth. But—

Enter Servant *and* Officer, *giving a paper to* Evelyn, *and whispering.*

What's this? Frantz, the tailor. Why, you impudent scoundrel! Faith! this is more than I bargained for—Sir John, I'm arrested.

Enter Servant, R.

Stout [*slapping* Sir John *on the back with glee*]. He's arrested, old gentleman! But I didn't lend him a farthing!

Evelyn. And for a mere song—£150. Sir John, pay this fellow, will you? or bail me, or something— while we go to dinner.

Sir John. Pay—bail—I'll be d—d if I do! Oh, my £500! my £500! Mr. Alfred Evelyn, I want my £500!

Graves. I'm going to do a very silly thing, I shall lose both my friend and my money;—just like my luck!—Evelyn, go to dinner—I'll settle this for you.

Lady Franklin. I love you for that!

Graves. Do you? then I am the happiest—Ah! Ma'am, I don't know what I am saying!

[*Exeunt* Graves *and* Officer, R.

Evelyn [*to* Georgina]. Don't go by these appearances! I repeat, £10,000 will more than cover all my embarrassments. I shall hear from you tomorrow?

[*Going up*, R.

Georgina. Yes—yes!

Evelyn. But you're not going?—You, too, Glossmore?—you, Blount?—you, Stout?—you, Smooth?

Smooth. No; I'll stick by you—as long as you've a guinea to stake!

Glossmore. Oh, this might have been expected from a man of such ambiguous political opinions.

Stout. Don' stop me, sir. No man of common enlightenment would have squandered his substance in this way. Pictures and statues!—baugh!

Evelyn. Why, you all said I could not spend my money better! Ha! ha! ha!—the absurdest mistake. You don't fancy I'm going to prison? Ha! ha! Why don't you laugh, Sir John? Ha! ha! ha!

Sir John. Sir, this is horrible levity!—Take Sir Frederick's arm, my poor injured, innocent child!—Mr. Evelyn, after this extraordinary scene, you can't be surprised that I—I—Zounds, I'm suffocating!

Smooth. But, my dear John, they've no right to arrest the dinner!

Stout [*aside*]. But the election at Groginhole is tomorrow. This news may not arrive before the poll closes!—[*Rushing to* EVELYN.] Sir, Popkins never bribes; but Popkins will bet you £1,000 that he don't come in for Groginhole.

Glossmore. This is infamous, Mr. Stout! Cipher is a man who scorns every subterfuge! [*Aside to* EVELYN.] But for the sake of the Constitution, name your price.

Evelyn. I know the services of Cipher—I know the profundity of Popkins: but it's too late—the borough's engaged!

Enter TOKE, C.

Toke. Dinner is served.

Glossmore [*pausing*]. Dinner!

Stout. Dinner?—it's a very good smell!

Evelyn [*to* SIR JOHN]. Turtle and venison too.

[*They stop irresolute.*

That's right—come along. But, I say, Blount—Stout—Glossmore—Sir John—one word first; will you lend me £10 for my old nurse?   [*Exeunt* OMNES, *indignantly,* R.

Smooth and Evelyn. Ha! ha! ha!

END OF ACT IV

ACT V

SCENE I. * * * *'s CLUB.

SMOOTH *and* GLOSSMORE *discovered.*

Glossmore. Will his horses be sold, think you?

Smooth. Very possibly, Charles!—a fine stud—hum, ha. Waiter, a glass of sherry!

Enter WAITER, C., *with sherry.*

Glossmore. They say he must go abroad.

Smooth. Well! It's the best time of year for travelling, Charles.

Glossmore. We are all to be paid today; and that looks suspicious!

Smooth. Very suspicious, Charles! Hum!—ah!

Glossmore. My dear fellow, you must know the rights of the matter: I wish you'd speak out. What have you really won? Is the house itself gone?

Smooth. The house itself is certainly not gone, Charles, for I saw it exactly in the same place this morning at half-past ten—it has not moved an inch!

268

[WAITER *gives a letter to* GLOSSMORE.

Glossmore [*reading*]. From Groginhole—an express! What's this? I'm amazed!!! [*Reading.*] 'They've actually at the eleventh hour started Mr. Evelyn; and nobody knows what his politics are! We shall be beat!—the constitution is gone!—Cipher!' Oh! this is infamous in Evelyn! Gets into Parliament just to keep himself out of the Bench!

Smooth. He's capable of it!

Glossmore. Not a doubt of it, sir!—not a doubt of it!

Enter SIR JOHN *and* BLOUNT, C., *talking.*

Sir John My dear boy, I'm not flint! I am but a man! If Georgina really loves you—and I am sure that she does—I will never think of sacrificing her happiness to ambition—she is yours; I told her so this very morning.

Blount [*aside*]. The old humbug!

Sir John. She's the best of daughters!—the most obedient, artless creature! Oh! She's been properly brought up: a good daughter makes a good wife. Dine with me at seven, and we'll talk of the settlements.

Blount. Yes; I don't care for fortune; but—

Sir John. Her £10,000 will be settled on herself—that of course.

Blount. All of it, Sir? Weally I—

Sir John. What then, my dear boy? I shall leave you both all I've laid by. Ah! you know I'm a close fellow! 'Stingy Jack'—eh? After all, worth makes the man!

Smooth. And the more a man's worth, John, the worthier man he must be!   [*Exit.*

Blount [*aside*]. Yes; he has no other child! She must have all his savings; I don't see what harm it could do me. Still that £10,000—I want that £10,000: if she would but wun off now, one could get wid of the settlements.

Enter STOUT, C., *wiping his forehead, and takes* SIR JOHN *aside.*

Stout. Sir John, we've been played upon! My secretary is brother to Flash's head clerk; Evelyn had not £300 in the bank!

Sir John. Bless us and save us! you take away my breath! But then—Deadly Smooth—the arrest—the—oh, he must be done up!

Stout. As to Smooth, he'd do 'anything to oblige.' All a trick, depend on it! Smooth has already deceived me, for before the day's over Evelyn will be member for Groginhole!

Sir John. But what could be Evelyn's object?

Stout. Object? Do you look for an object in a whimsical creature like that? A man who has not even any political opinions! Object! Perhaps to break off his match with your daughter! Take care, Sir John, or the borough will be lost to your family!

Sir John. Aha! I begin to smell a rat! But it's not too late yet.

Stout. My interest in Popkins made me run to Lord Spendquick, the late proprietor of Groginhole. I told him that Evelyn could not pay the rest of the money; and he told me that—

Sir John. What?

Stout. Mr. Sharp had just paid it him; there's no hope for Popkins! England will rue this day! [*Goes up stage*

Sir John. Georgina shall lend him the money! I'll lend him—every man in the house shall lend him—I feel again what it is to be a father-in-law! [*Aside.*] But stop; I'll be cautious. Stout may be on his side—a trap—not likely; but I'll go first to Spendquick myself. Sir Frederick, excuse me—you can't dine with me today. And, on second thoughts, I see that it would be very unhandsome to desert poor Evelyn now he's down in the world. Can't think of it, my dear boy—can't think of it. Very much honoured, and happy to see you as a friend. Waiter! my carriage! Urn! What, humbug *Stingy Jack*, will they? Ah! a good joke, indeed!   [*Exit*, C.

Blount. Mr. Stout, what have you been saying to Sir John? Something against my chawacter, I know you have; don't deny it. Sir, I shall expect satisfaction!

Stout. Satisfaction, Sir Frederick? as if a man of enlightenment had any satisfaction in fighting! Did not mention your name; we were talking of Evelyn. Only think! he's no more ruined than you are.

Blount. Not wuined? Aha, now I understand!—So, so! Stay, let me see—she's to meet me in the square. [*Pulls out his watch; a very small one.*

Stout [*pulling out his own; a very large one*]. I must be off to the Vestry.

Blount. Just in time!—ten thousand pounds! Gad, my blood's up, and I won't be tweated in this way, if he were fifty times Stingy Jack!   [*Exit*, C.

SCENE II. *The drawing-rooms in* Sir John Vesey's *house.*

Enter Lady Franklin *and* Graves, R.

Graves. Well, well, I am certain that poor Evelyn loves Clara still; but you can't persuade me that she cares for him.

Lady Franklin. She has been breaking her heart ever since she heard of his distress. Nay, I am sure she would give all she has, could it save him from the consequence of his own folly.

Graves [*half aside*]. She would give him his own money if she did. I should like just to sound her.

Lady Franklin [*ringing the bell*]. And you shall. I take so much interest in her that I forgive your friend everything but his offer to Georgina.

Enter Servant, R.

Where are the young ladies?

Servant. Miss Vesey is, I believe, still in the square; Miss Douglas is just come in, my lady.

Lady Franklin. What, did not she go out with Miss Vesey?

Servant. No, my lady; I attended her to Drummond's, the banker.   [*Exit*, R.

Lady Franklin. Drummond's?

Enter Clara, R.

Why, child, what on earth could take you to Drummond's at this hour of the day?

Clara [*confused*]. Oh, I—that is—I—Ah, Mr. Graves! How is Mr. Evelyn? How does he bear up against so sudden a reverse?

Graves. With an awful calm. I fear all is not right here! [*Touching his head.*] The report in the town is that he must go abroad instantly—perhaps today!   [*Crosses to* C.

Clara. Abroad!—today!

 Graves. But all his creditors will be paid; and he only seems anxious to know if Miss Vesey remains true in his misfortunes.

Clara. Ah! he loves her so *much* then!

Graves. Um!—that's more than I can say.

Clara. She told me, last night, that he said to the last that £10,000 would free him from all liabilities—that was the sum, was it not?

Graves. Yes; he persists in the same assertion. Will Miss Vesey lend it?

Lady Frankin [*aside*]. If she does I shall not think so well of her poor dear mother; for I am sure she'd be no child of Sir John's!

Graves. I should like to convince myself that my poor friend has nothing to hope from a woman's generosity.

Lady Frankin. Civil! And are men, then, less covetous?

Graves. I know one man, at least, who, rejected in his poverty by one as poor as himself, no sooner came into sudden fortune than he made his lawyer invent a codicil which the testator never dreamt of, bequeathing independence to the woman who had scorned him. Lady Franklin. And never told her?

Graves. Never! There's no such document at Doctors' Commons, depend on it! You seem incredulous, Miss Clara. Good day!   [*Crosses,* R.

Clara [*following him*]. One word, for mercy's sake! Do I understand you right? Ah, how could I be so blind! Generous Evelyn!

Graves. *You* appreciate, and Georgina will desert him. Miss Douglas, he loves you still—If that's not just like me! Meddling with other people's affairs, as if they were worth it—hang them.   [*Exit,* R.

Clara. Georgina will desert him. Do you think so? [*Aside.*] Ah, he will soon discover that she never wrote that letter.

Lady Frankin. She told me, last night, that she would never see him again. To do her justice, she's less interested than her father, and as much attached as she can be to another. Even while engaged to Evelyn she has met Sir Frederick every day in the square.

Clara. And he is alone—sad—forsaken—ruined. And I, whom he enriched—I, the creature of his bounty—I, once the woman of his love—I stand idly here to content myself with tears and prayers! Oh, Lady Franklin, have pity on me—on him! We are both of kin to him—as relations we have both a right to comfort! Let us go to him—come!

Lady Frankin. No! it would scarcely be right—remember the world—I cannot.

Clara. All abandon him—then I will go alone!

Lady Frankin. You!—so proud—so sensitive?

Clara. Pride—when he wants a friend?

Lady Frankin. His misfortunes are his own fault—a gambler!

Clara. Can you think of his faults now? *I* have no right to do so. All I have—all—his gift!—and I never to have dreamed it!

Lady Franklin. But if Georgina do indeed release him—if she has already done so—what will he think? What but—

Clara. What but—that, if he loves me still, I may have enough for both, and I am by his side. But that is too bright a dream. He told me I might call him brother! Where, now, should a sister be?—But—but—I—I—I tremble! If, after all—if—if—In one word—Am I too bold? The world—my conscience can answer *that*—but do you think that HE could despise me?

Lady Franklin. No, Clara, no! Your fair soul is too transparent for even libertines to misconstrue. Something tells me that this meeting may make the happiness of both! You cannot go alone. My presence justifies all. Give me your hand—we will go together!   [*Exeunt*, R.

SCENE III. *A room in* EVELYN'S *house*.

Enter EVELYN, R.

Evelyn. Yes; as yet, all surpasses my expectations. I am sure of Smooth—I have managed even Sharp; my election will seem but an escape from a prison. Ha! ha! True, it cannot last long; but a few hours more are all I require—and for that time at least I shall hope to be thoroughly ruined.

Enter GRAVES, R.

Well, Graves, what do the people say of me?

Graves. Everything that's bad!

Evelyn. Three days ago I was universally respected. I awake this morning to find myself singularly infamous. Yet I am the same man.

Graves. Humph! why, gambling—

Evelyn. Come! it was not criminal to gamble—it was criminal to lose. Tut!—will you deny that, if I had ruined Smooth instead of myself, every hand would have grasped mine yet more cordially, and every lip would have smiled congratulations on my success? Man—man! I've not been rich and poor for nothing! The Vices and the Virtues are written in a language the World cannot construe; it reads them in a vile translation, and the translators are FAILURE and SUCCESS! You alone are unchanged.

Graves. There's no merit in that. I am always ready to mingle my tears with any man. [*Aside*.] I know I'm a fool, but I can't help it. Hark ye, Evelyn! I like you—I'm rich; and anything I can do to get you out of your hobble will give me an excuse to grumble for the rest of my life. There, now it's out.

Evelyn [*touched*]. There's something good in human nature after all! My dear friend, did I want your aid I would accept it, but I can extricate myself yet. Do you think Georgina will give me the same proof of confidence and affection?

Graves. Would you break your heart if she did not?

Evelyn. It is in vain to deny that I still love Clara—our last conversation renewed feelings which would task all the energies of my soul to conquer. What then? I am not one of those, the Sybarites of sentiment, who deem it impossible for humanity to conquer love—who call their own weakness the voice of a resistless destiny. Such is the poor excuse of every woman who yields her honour, of every adulterer who betrays his friend. No! the heart was given to the soul as its ally, not as its traitor.

Graves. What do you tend to?

272

Evelyn. This:—If Georgina still adheres to my fortunes (and I will not put her to too harsh a trial), if she can face the prospect, not of ruin and poverty, for reports wrong me there, but of a moderate independence; if, in one word, she loves me for myself, I will shut Clara for ever from my thought. I am pledged to Georgina, and I will carry to the altar a soul resolute to deserve her affection and fulfil its vows.

Graves. And if she rejects you?

Evelyn [*joyfully*]. If she do, I am free once more! And then—then I will dare to ask, for I can ask without dishonour, if Clara can explain the past and bless the future!

Enter SERVANT, R., *with a letter.*

[*Crosses to meet him, after reading it.*] The die is cast—the dream is o'er! Generous girl! Oh, Georgina! I will deserve you yet.

Graves. Georgina! is it possible?

Evelyn. And the delicacy, the womanhood, the exquisite grace of this! How we misjudge the depth of the human heart! I imagined her incapable of this devotion.

Graves. And I too!

Evelyn. It were base in me to continue this trial a moment longer; I will write at once to undeceive that generous heart.   [*Writing.*

Graves. I would have given £1,000 if that little jade Clara had been beforehand; but just like my luck! if I want a man to marry one woman, he's sure to marry another on purpose to vex me!   [EVELYN *rings the bell.*

Enter SERVANT, R.

Evelyn. Take this instantly to Miss Vesey; say I will call in an hour. [*Exit* SERVANT.] And now Clara is resigned for ever! Why does my heart sink within me? Why, why, looking to the fate to come, do I see only the memory of what has been?

Graves. You are re-engaged then to Georgina!

Evelyn. Irrevocably.

Enter SERVANT, R., *announcing* LADY FRANKLIN *and* MISS DOUGLAS.

Lady Franklin. My dear Evelyn, you may think it strange to receive such visitors at this moment; but indeed, it is no time for ceremony. We are your relations—it is reported you are about to leave the country—we come to ask frankly what we can do to serve you? Evelyn. Madam,—I—

Lady Franklin. Come, come—do not hesitate to confide in us; Clara is less a stranger to you than I am; your friend here will perhaps let me consult with him. [*Crosses and speaks, aside, to* GRAVES.] Let us leave them to themselves.

Graves. You're an angel of a widow; but you come too late, as whatever is good for anything generally does.

[*Goes up with* LADY FRANKLIN.

Evelyn. Miss Douglas, I may well want words to thank you; this goodness—this sympathy—

Clara [*abandoning herself to her emotion*]. Evelyn! Evelyn! Do not talk thus!—Goodness! sympathy!—I have learned *all—all*! It is for ME to speak of *gratitude!* What! even when I had so wounded you— when you believed me mercenary and cold—when you thought that I was blind and base enough not to know you for what you are;—even at that time you thought but of my happiness—my fortunes—my fate!—And to you—you—I owe all that has raised the poor orphan from servitude and dependence! While your words were so bitter, your deeds so gentle! Oh! noble Evelyn, this, then, was your revenge!

Evelyn. You owe me no thanks; that revenge was sweet! Think you it was nothing to feel that my presence haunted you, though you knew it not? That in things, the pettiest as the greatest, which that gold could buy—the very jewels you wore—the very robe in which, to other eyes, you might seem more fair—in all in which you took the woman's young and innocent delight—I had a part—a share?—that even if separated for ever—even if another's—even in distant years—perhaps in a happy home, listening to sweet voices, that might call you 'mother!'—even then, should the uses of that dross bring to your lips one smile, that smile was mine—due to me—due, as a sacred debt, to the hand that you rejected—to the love that you despised!

Clara. Despised! See the proof that I despised you! see, in this hour, when they say you are again as poor as before, I forget the world—my pride—perhaps too much my sex; I remember but your sorrow—I am here!

Evelyn. And is this the same voice that, when I knelt at your feet, and asked but one day the hope to call you mine, spoke only of poverty, and answered 'Never'?

Clara. Because I had been unworthy of your love if I had ensured your misery. Evelyn, hear me! My father, like you, was poor—generous; gifted, like you, with genius, ambition; sensitive, like you, to the least breath of insult. He married as you would have done—married one whose dowry was penury and care! Alfred, I saw that genius the curse to itself!—I saw that ambition wither to despair!—I saw the struggle—the humiliation—the proud man's agony—the bitter life—the early death!—and heard over his breathless clay my mother's groan of self-reproach! Alfred Evelyn, now speak! Was the woman you loved so nobly to repay you with such a doom?

Evelyn. Clara, we should have shared it?

Clara. Shared? Never let the woman who really loves comfort her selfishness with such delusion! In marriages like this the wife cannot share the burden; it is he—the husband—to provide, to scheme, to work, to endure—to grind out his strong heart at the miserable wheel! The wife, also, cannot share the struggle—she can but witness despair! And therefore, Alfred, I rejected you.

Evelyn. Yet you believe me as poor now as I was then.

Clara. But / am not poor; we are not so poor! Of this fortune, which is all your own—if, as I hear, one half would free you from your debts, why, we have the other half still left, Evelyn! It is humble—but it is not penury.

Evelyn. Cease, cease! you know not how you torture me. Oh, that when hope was possible!—oh, that you had bid me take it to my breast and wait for a brighter day.

Clara. And so have consumed your life of life upon a hope perhaps delayed till age—shut you from a happier choice, from fairer fortunes—shackled you with vows that, as my youth and its poor attributes decayed, would only have irritated and galled—made your whole existence one long suspense! No, Alfred, even yet you do not know me!

Evelyn. Know you! Fair angel, too excellent for man's harder nature to know!—at least it is permitted me to revere. Why were such blessed words not vouchsafed to me before?—why, why come they now—too late? Oh, heaven—too late!

274

Clara. Too late! What then have I said?

Evelyn. Wealth! what is it without you? With you, I recognize its power; to forestall your every wish—to smooth your every path—to make all that life borrows from Grace and Beauty your ministrant and handmaid; and then, looking to those eyes, to read there the treasures of a heart that excelled all that kings could lavish;—why that were to make gold indeed a god! But vain—vain—vain! Bound by every tie of faith, gratitude, loyalty, and honour, to another!

Clara. Another! Is she, then, true to your reverses? I did not know this—indeed, I did not! And I have thus betrayed myself! O, shame! he must despise me now! [*Goes up.*

Enter SIR JOHN; *at the same time* GRAVES *and* LADY FRANKLIN *come down.*

Sir John [*with dignity and frankness*]. Evelyn, I was hasty yesterday. You must own it natural that I should be so. But Georgina has been so urgent in your defence, that [*as* LADY FRANKLIN *comes up to listen*]—sister, just shut the door will you?—that I cannot resist her. What's money without happiness? So give me your security; for she insists on lending you the £10,000.

Evelyn. I know, and have already received it.

Sir John. Already received it! Is he joking! Faith, for the last two days I believe I have been living amongst the Mysteries of Udolpho! Sister, have you seen Georgina?

Lady Franklin. Not since she went out to walk in the square.

Sir John [*aside*]. She's not in the square nor the house. Where the deuce can the girl be?

Evelyn. I have written to Miss Vesey—I have asked her to fix the day for our wedding.

Sir John [*joyfully*]. Have you? Go, Lady Franklin, find her instantly—she must be back by this time; take my carriage, it is but a step—you won't be two minutes gone. [*Aside.*] I'd go myself, but I'm afraid of leaving him a moment while he's in such excellent dispositions.

Lady Franklin [*repulsing* CLARA]. No, no: stay till I return.   [*Exit*, R.

Sir John. And don't be down-hearted, my dear fellow; if the worst come to the worst, you will have everything I can leave you. Meantime, if I can in any way help you—

Evelyn. Ha!—you!—*you*, too? Sir John, you have seen my letter to Miss Vesey?—[*aside*] or could she have learned the truth before she ventured to be so generous?

Sir John. No; on my honour. I only just called at the door on my way from Lord Spend—that is from the City. Georgina was out;—was ever anything so unlucky? [*Without.* Hurrah— hurrah! Blue for ever!] [*Enter* SHARP, R.] What's that?

Sharp. Sir, a deputation from Groginhole—poll closed in the first hour—you are returned! Hallo, sir—hallo!

Evelyn. And it was to please Clara!

Sir John. Mr. Sharp—Mr. Sharp—I say, how much has Mr. Evelyn lost by Messrs. Flash and Co.?

Sharp. Oh, a great deal, sir—a great deal.

Sir John [*alarmed*]. How!—a great deal!

Evelyn. Speak the truth, Sharp—concealment is all over.

Sharp. £223. 6s. 3d.—a great sum to throw away.

Graves. Ah, I comprehend now! Poor Evelyn, caught in his own trap!

Sir John. Eh! what, my dear boy?—what? Ha! ha! all humbug, was it?—all humbug, upon my soul! So, Mr. Sharp, isn't he ruined after all?—not the least wee, rascally little bit in the world, ruined?

Sharp. Sir, he has never lived up to his income.

Sir John. Worthy man! I could jump up to the ceiling! I am the happiest father-in-law in the three kingdoms. [*Knocking*, R.] And that's my sister's knock, too.

Clara. Since I was mistaken, cousin—since, now, you do not need me—forget what has passed; my business here is over. Farewell!

Evelyn. Could you but see my heart at this moment, with what love, what veneration, what anguish it is filled, you would know how little, in the great calamities of life, fortune is really worth. And must we part now,—now, when—when—I never wept before, since my mother died!

Enter LADY FRANKLIN *and* GEORGINA, *followed by* BLOUNT, *who looks shy and embarrassed.*

Graves. Georgina herself—then there's no hope!

Sir John. What the deuce brings that fellow Blount here? Georgy, my dear Georgy, I want to——

Evelyn. Stand back, Sir John.

Sir John. But I must speak a word to her—I want to——

Evelyn. Stand back, I say—not a whisper—not a sign. If your daughter is to be my wife, to *her* heart only will I look for a reply to *mine*.

Lady Franklin [to GEORGINA]. Speak the truth, niece.

Evelyn. Georgina, it is true, then, that you trust me with your confidence—your fortune? Is it also true, that, when you did so, you believed me ruined? O pardon the doubt! Answer as if your father stood not there—answer me from that truth the world cannot yet have plucked from your soul—answer as if the woe or weal of a life trembled in the balance—answer as the woman's heart, yet virgin and unpolluted, should answer to one who has trusted to it his all!

Georgina. What can he mean?

Sir John [*making signs*]. She won't look this way, she won't!—hang her—HEM!

Evelyn. You falter. I implore—I adjure you, answer!

Lady Franklin. The truth!

Georgina. Mr. Evelyn, your fortune might well dazzle me, as it dazzled others. Believe me, I sincerely pity your reverses.

Sir John. Good girl! you hear her, Evelyn?

Georgina. What's money without happiness?

Sir John. Clever creature!—my own sentiments!

Georgina. And, so, as our engagement is now annulled—papa told me so this very morning—I have promised my hand where I have given my heart—to Sir Frederick Blount.

Sir John. I told you—I? No such thing—no such thing. You frighten her out of her wits—she don't know what she's saying.

Evelyn. Am I awake? But this letter—this letter, received today——

Lady Franklin [*looking over letter*]. Drummond's!—from a banker!

Evelyn. Read—read.

Lady Franklin. 'Ten thousand pounds placed to your account, from the same unknown friend to Alfred Evelyn!' Oh, Clara, I know now why you went to Drummond's this morning!

Evelyn. Clara! What!—and the former one with the same signature—on the faith of which I pledged my hand and sacrificed my heart—

Lady Franklin. Was written under my eyes, and the secret kept that—

Evelyn. Look up, look up, Clara—I am free! I am, released! you forgive me? you love me?—you are mine! We are rich—rich! I can give you fortune, power—I can devote to you my whole life, thought, heart, soul—I am all yours, Clara—my own, my wife!

Sir John. A pretty mess you've made of it, to humbug your own father! And you, too, Lady Franklin, I am to thank you for this!

Lady Franklin. You've to thank me that she's not now on the road to Scotland with Sir Frederick; I chanced on them by the Park just in time to dissuade and save her. But to do her justice, a hint of your displeasure was sufficient.

Georgina [*half sobbing*]. And you know, papa, you said this very morning that poor Frederick had been very ill used, and you would settle it all at the club.

Blount. Come, Sir John, you can only blame yourself and Evelyn's cunning device! After all, I'm no such vewy bad, bad match; and as for the £10,000—

Evelyn. I'll double it. Ah, Sir John, what's money without happiness?

Sir John. Pshaw—nonsense—stuff! Don't humbug me.

Lady Franklin. But if you don't consent, she'll have no husband at all.

Sir John. Hum! There's something in that. [*Aside to* Evelyn.] Double it, will you? Then settle it all tightly on her. Well—well—my foible is not avarice. Blount, make her happy. Child, I forgive you. [*Pinching her arm.*] Ugh, you fool!   [Blount *and* Georgina *go up.*

Graves [*to* Lady Franklin]. I'm afraid it's catching. What say you? I feel the symptoms of matrimony creeping all over me. Shall we? eh? Frankly, now, frankly—

Lady Franklin. Frankly, now, there's my hand, on one condition—that we finish our reel on the wedding day.

Graves. Accepted! Is it possible? Sainted Maria! thank Heaven you are spared this affliction.

Enter Smooth, R.

Smooth. How d'ye do, Alfred?—I intrude, I fear! Quite a family party.

Blount. Wish us joy, Smooth—Georgina's mine, and—

Smooth. And our four friends there apparently have made up another rubber. John, my dear boy, you look as if you had something at stake on the odd trick.

Sir John. Sir, you're very—Confound the fellow! and he's a dead shot too!

Enter Stout *and* Glossmore *hastily, talking with each other.*

Stout. I'm sure he's of our side; we've all the intelligence.

Glossmore. I'm sure he's of ours if his fortune is safe, for we've all the property.

Stout. Just heard of your return, Evelyn! Congratulate you. The great motion of the Session is fixed for Friday. We count on your vote. Progress with the times!

Glossmore. Preserve the Constitution!

Stout. Your money will do wonders for the party!—Advance!

Glossmore. The party respects men of your property! Stick fast!

Evelyn. I have the greatest respect, I assure you, for the worthy and intelligent flies upon both sides of the wheel; but whether we go too fast or too slow, does not, I fancy, depend so much on the flies as on the Stout Gentleman who sits inside and pays the post-boys. Now all my politics as yet is to consider what's best for the Stout Gentleman!

Smooth. Meaning John Bull. *Ce cher* old John!

Stout. I'm as wise as I was before.

Glossmore. Sir, he's a trimmer!

Evelyn. Smooth, we have yet to settle our first piquet account and our last! And I sincerely thank you for the service you have rendered to me, and the lesson you have given these gentlemen. [*Turning to* CLARA.] Ah, Clara, you—you have succeeded where wealth had failed! You have reconciled me to the world and to mankind. My friends—we must confess it—amidst the humours and the follies, the vanities, deceits, and vices that play their part in the Great Comedy of life—it is our own fault if we do not find such natures, though rare and few, as redeem the rest, brightening the shadows that are flung from the form and body of the TIME with glimpses of the everlasting holiness of truth and love.

Graves. But for the truth and the love, when found, to make us tolerably happy, we should not be without—

Lady Franklin. Good health;

Graves. Good spirits;

Clara. A good heart;

Smooth. An innocent rubber;

Georgina. Congenial tempers;

Blount. A pwoper degwee of pwudence;

Stout. Enlightened opinions;

Glossmore. Constitutional principles;

Sir John. Knowledge of the world;

Evelyn. And—plenty of Money.

CURTAIN

Robert Browning

Fra Lippo Lippi[1]

I am poor brother Lippo, by your leave!
You need not clap your torches to my face.
Zooks,[2] what's to blame? you think you see a monk!
What, 'tis past midnight, and you go the rounds,
5   And here you catch me at an alley's end
Where sportive ladies leave their doors ajar?
The Carmine's[3] my cloister: hunt it up,
Do,—harry out, if you must show your zeal,
Whatever rat, there, haps on his wrong hole,
10   And nip each softling of a wee white mouse,
Weke, weke, that's crept to keep him company!
Aha, you know your betters! Then, you'll take
Your hand away that's fiddling on my throat,
And please to know me likewise. Who am I?
15   Why, one, sir, who is lodging with a friend
Three streets off—he's a certain . . . how d'ye call?
Master—a ...Cosimo of the Medici,[4]
I' the house that caps the corner. Boh! you were best!
Remember and tell me, the day you're hanged,
20   How you affected such a gullet's-gripe![5]
But you,[6] sir, it concerns you that your knaves
Pick up a manner nor discredit you:
Zooks, are we pilchards,° that they sweep the streets   *small fish*
And count fair price what comes into their net?
25   He's Judas to a tittle, that man is![7]
Just such a face! Why, sir, you make amends.
Lord, I'm not angry! Bid your hang-dogs go
Drink out this quarter-florin to the health
Of the munificent House that harbours me
30   (And many more beside, lads! more beside!)
And all's come square again. I'd like his face—
His, elbowing on his comrade in the door
With the pike and lantern,—for the slave that holds

John Baptist's head a-dangle by the hair

35 With one hand ("Look you, now," as who should say)

And his weapon in the other, yet unwiped!

It's not your chance to have a bit of chalk,

A wood-coal or the like? or you should see!

Yes, I'm the painter, since you style me so.

40 What, brother Lippo's doings, up and down,

You know them and they take you? like enough!

I saw the proper twinkle in your eye—

'Tell you, I liked your looks at very first.

Let's sit and set things straight now, hip to haunch.

45 Here's spring come, and the nights one makes up bands

To roam the town and sing out carnival,[8]

And I've been three weeks shut within my mew,°   *private den*

A-painting for the great man, saints and saints

And saints again. I could not paint all night—

50 Ouf! I leaned out of window for fresh air.

There came a hurry of feet and little feet,

A sweep of lute strings, laughs, and whiffs of song, —

Flower o' the broom,

Take away love, and our earth is a tomb!

55 *Flower o' the quince,*

I let Lisa go, and what good in life since?[9]

Flower o' the thyme—and so on. Round they went.

Scarce had they turned the corner when a titter

Like the skipping of rabbits by moonlight,—three slim shapes,

60 And a face that looked up . . . zooks, sir, flesh and blood,

That's all I'm made of! Into shreds it went,

Curtain and counterpane and coverlet,

All the bed-furniture—a dozen knots,

There was a ladder! Down I let myself,

65 Hands and feet, scrambling somehow, and so dropped,

And after them. I came up with the sun

Hard by Saint Laurence,[10] hail fellow, well met,—

Flower o' the rose,

If I've been merry, what matter who knows?

70 And so as I was stealing back again

To get to bed and have a bit of sleep

Ere I rise up to-morrow and go work

On Jerome knocking at his poor old breast

With his great round stone to subdue the flesh,[11]

75   You snap me of the sudden. Ah, I see!

Though your eye twinkles still, you shake your head—

Mine's shaved—a monk, you say—the sting 's in that!

If Master Cosimo announced himself,

Mum's the word naturally; but a monk!

80   Come, what am I a beast for? tell us, now!

I was a baby when my mother died

And father died and left me in the street.

I starved there, God knows how, a year or two

On fig-skins, melon-parings, rinds and shucks,

85   Refuse and rubbish. One fine frosty day,

My stomach being empty as your hat,

The wind doubled me up and down I went.

Old Aunt Lapaccia trussed me with one hand,

(Its fellow was a stinger as I knew)

90   And so along the wall, over the bridge,

By the straight cut to the convent. Six words there,

While I stood munching my first bread that month:

"So, boy, you're minded," quoth the good fat father

Wiping his own mouth, 'twas refection-time,°—   *mealtime*

95   "To quit this very miserable world?

Will you renounce" . . . "the mouthful of bread?" thought I;

By no means! Brief, they made a monk of me;

I did renounce the world, its pride and greed,

Palace, farm, villa, shop, and banking-house,

100   Trash, such as these poor devils of Medici

Have given their hearts to—all at eight years old.

Well, sir, I found in time, you may be sure,

'Twas not for nothing—the good bellyful,

The warm serge and the rope that goes all round,

105   And day-long blessed idleness beside!

"Let's see what the urchin's fit for"—that came next.

Not overmuch their way, I must confess.

Such a to-do! They tried me with their books:

Lord, they'd have taught me Latin in pure waste!

110   *Flower o' the clove.*

All the Latin I construe is, "amo" I love!

But, mind you, when a boy starves in the streets

Eight years together, as my fortune was,

281

Watching folk's faces to know who will fling

115 The bit of half-stripped grape-bunch he desires,
And who will curse or kick him for his pains,—
Which gentleman processional and fine,
Holding a candle to the Sacrament,
Will wink and let him lift a plate and catch

120 The droppings of the wax to sell again,
Or holla for the Eight° and have him whipped,—   *Florentine magistrates*
How say I?—nay, which dog bites, which lets drop
His bone from the heap of offal in the street,—
Why, soul and sense of him grow sharp alike,

125 He learns the look of things, and none the less
For admonition from the hunger-pinch.
I had a store of such remarks, be sure,
Which, after I found leisure, turned to use.
I drew men's faces on my copy-books,

130 Scrawled them within the antiphonary's marge,[12]
Joined legs and arms to the long music-notes,
Found eyes and nose and chin for A's and B's,
And made a string of pictures of the world
Betwixt the ins and outs of verb and noun,

135 On the wall, the bench, the door. The monks looked black.
"Nay," quoth the Prior,[13] "turn him out, d'ye say?
In no wise. Lose a crow and catch a lark.
What if at last we get our man of parts,
We Carmelites, like those Camaldolese

140 And Preaching Friars,[14] to do our church up fine
And put the front on it that ought to be!"
And hereupon he bade me daub away.
Thank you! my head being crammed, the walls a blank,
Never was such prompt disemburdening.

145 First, every sort of monk, the black and white,
I drew them, fat and lean: then, folk at church,
From good old gossips waiting to confess
Their cribs of barrel-droppings, candle-ends,—
To the breathless fellow at the altar-foot,

150 Fresh from his murder, safe and sitting there
With the little children round him in a row
Of admiration, half for his beard and half
For that white anger of his victim's son

Shaking a fist at him with one fierce arm,

155 Signing himself with the other because of Christ

(Whose sad face on the cross sees only this

After the passion° of a thousand years) *sufferings*

Till some poor girl, her apron o'er her head,

(Which the intense eyes looked through) came at eve

160 On tiptoe, said a word, dropped in a loaf,

Her pair of earrings and a bunch of flowers

(The brute took growling), prayed, and so was gone.

I painted all, then cried "'Tis ask and have;

Choose, for more's ready!"—laid the ladder flat,

165 And showed my covered bit of cloister-wall.

The monks closed in a circle and praised loud

Till checked, taught what to see and not to see,

Being simple bodies,—"That's the very man!

Look at the boy who stoops to pat the dog!

170 That woman's like the Prior's niece who comes

To care about his asthma: it's the life!"

But there my triumph's straw-fire flared and funked;[15]

Their betters took their turn to see and say:

The Prior and the learned pulled a face

175 And stopped all that in no time. "How? what's here?

Quite from the mark of painting, bless us all!

Faces, arms, legs, and bodies like the true

As much as pea and pea! it's devil's-game!

Your business is not to catch men with show,

180 With homage to the perishable clay,

But lift them over it, ignore it all,

Make them forget there's such a thing as flesh.

Your business is to paint the souls of men—

Man's soul, and it's a fire, smoke . . . no, it's not . . .

185 It's vapour done up like a new-born babe—

(In that shape when you die it leaves your mouth)

It's . . . well, what matters talking, it's the soul!

Give us no more of body than shows soul!

Here's Giotto,[16] with his Saint a-praising God,

190 That sets us praising—why not stop with him?

Why put all thoughts of praise out of our head

With wonder at lines, colours, and what not?

Paint the soul, never mind the legs and arms!

Rub all out, try at it a second time.

195   Oh, that white smallish female with the breasts,

She's just my niece . . . Herodias,[17] I would say,—

Who went and danced and got men's heads cut off!

Have it all out!" Now, is this sense, I ask?

A fine way to paint soul, by painting body

200   So ill, the eye can't stop there, must go further

And can't fare worse! Thus, yellow does for white

When what you put for yellow's simply black,

And any sort of meaning looks intense

When all beside itself means and looks naught.

205   Why can't a painter lift each foot in turn,

Left foot and right foot, go a double step,

Make his flesh liker and his soul more like,

Both in their order? Take the prettiest face,

The Prior's niece . . . patron-saint—is it so pretty

210   You can't discover if it means hope, fear,

Sorrow or joy? won't beauty go with these?

Suppose I've made her eyes all right and blue,

Can't I take breath and try to add life's flash,

And then add soul and heighten them three-fold?

215   Or say there's beauty with no soul at all—

(I never saw it—put the case the same—)

If you get simple beauty and nought else,

You get about the best thing God invents:

That's somewhat: and you'll find the soul you have missed,

220   Within yourself, when you return him thanks.

"Rub all out!" Well, well, there's my life, in short,

And so the thing has gone on ever since.

I'm grown a man no doubt, I've broken bounds:

You should not take a fellow eight years old

225   And make him swear to never kiss the girls.

I'm my own master, paint now as I please—

Having a friend, you see, in the Corner-house![18]

Lord, it's fast holding by the rings in front—

Those great rings serve more purposes than just

230   To plant a flag in, or tie up a horse!

And yet the old schooling sticks, the old grave eyes

Are peeping o'er my shoulder as I work,

The heads shake still—"It's art's decline, my son!

You're not of the true painters, great and old;

235 Brother Angelico's the man, you'll find;

Brother Lorenzo[19] stands his single peer:

Fag on at flesh, you'll never make the third!"

Flower o' the pine,

You keep your mistr ... manners, and I'll stick to mine!

240 I'm not the third, then: bless us, they must know!

Don't you think they're the likeliest to know,

They with their Latin? So, I swallow my rage,

Clench my teeth, suck my lips in tight, and paint

To please them—sometimes do and sometimes don't;

245 For, doing most, there's pretty sure to come

A turn, some warm eve finds me at my saints—

A laugh, a cry, the business of the world—

(Flower o' the peach

Death for us all, and his own life for each!)

250 And my whole soul revolves, the cup runs over,

The world and life's too big to pass for a dream,

And I do these wild things in sheer despite,

And play the fooleries you catch me at,

In pure rage! The old mill-horse, out at grass

255 After hard years, throws up his stiff heels so,

Although the miller does not preach to him

The only good of grass is to make chaff.°   *straw*

What would men have? Do they like grass or no—

May they or mayn't they? all I want's the thing

260 Settled for ever one way. As it is,

You tell too many lies and hurt yourself:

You don't like what you only like too much,

You do like what, if given you at your word,

You find abundantly detestable.

265 For me, I think I speak as I was taught;

I always see the garden and God there

A-making man's wife: and, my lesson learned,

The value and significance of flesh,

I can't unlearn ten minutes afterwards.

270   You understand me: I'm a beast, I know.

But see, now—why, I see as certainly

As that the morning-star's about to shine,

What will hap some day. We've a youngster here
Comes to our convent, studies what I do,
275   Slouches and stares and lets no atom drop:
His name is Guidi[20]—he'll not mind the monks—
They call him Hulking Tom, he lets them talk—
He picks my practice up—he'll paint apace.
I hope so—though I never live so long,
280   I know what's sure to follow. You be judge!
You speak no Latin more than I, belike;
However, you're my man, you've seen the world
—The beauty and the wonder and the power,
The shapes of things, their colours, lights and shades,
285   Changes, surprises,—and God made it all!
—For what? Do you feel thankful, ay or no,
For this fair town's face, yonder river's line,
The mountain round it and the sky above,
Much more the figures of man, woman, child,
290   These are the frame to? What's it all about?
To be passed over, despised? or dwelt upon,
Wondered at? oh, this last of course!—you say.
But why not do as well as say,—paint these
Just as they are, careless what comes of it?
295   God's works—paint any one, and count it crime
To let a truth slip. Don't object, "His works
Are here already; nature is complete:
Suppose you reproduce her—(which you can't)
There's no advantage! you must beat her, then."
300   For, don't you mark? we're made so that we love
First when we see them painted, things we have passed
Perhaps a hundred times nor cared to see;
And so they are better, painted—better to us,
Which is the same thing. Art was given for that;
305   God uses us to help each other so,
Lending our minds out. Have you noticed, now,
Your cullion's° hanging face? A bit of chalk,   *rascal's*
And trust me but you should, though! How much more,
If I drew higher things with the same truth!
310   That were to take the Prior's pulpit-place,
Interpret God to all of you! Oh, oh,
It makes me mad to see what men shall do

And we in our graves! This world's no blot for us,
Nor blank; it means intensely, and means good:
315 To find its meaning is my meat and drink.
"Ay, but you don't so instigate to prayer!"
Strikes in the Prior: "when your meaning's plain
It does not say to folk—remember matins,
Or, mind you fast next Friday!" Why, for this
320 What need of art at all? A skull and bones,
Two bits of stick nailed crosswise, or, what's best,
A bell to chime the hour with, does as well.
I painted a Saint Laurence[21] six months since
At Prato, splashed the fresco[22] in fine style:
325 "How looks my painting, now the scaffold's down?"
I ask a brother: "Hugely," he returns—
"Already not one phiz of your three slaves
Who turn the Deacon off his toasted side,
But's scratched and prodded to our heart's content,
330 The pious people have so eased their own
With coming to say prayers there in a rage:
We get on fast to see the bricks beneath.
Expect another job this time next year,
For pity and religion grow i' the crowd—
335 Your painting serves its purpose!" Hang the fools!

　　　—That is—you'll not mistake an idle word
Spoke in a huff by a poor monk, God wot,
Tasting the air this spicy night which turns
340 The unaccustomed head like Chianti wine!
Oh, the church knows! don't misreport me, now!
It's natural a poor monk out of bounds
Should have his apt word to excuse himself:
And hearken how I plot to make amends.
I have bethought me: I shall paint a piece
345 . . . There's for you! Give me six months, then go, see
Something in Sant' Ambrogio's![23] Bless the nuns!
They want a cast o' my office.[24] I shall paint
God in the midst, Madonna and her babe,
Ringed by a bowery, flowery angel-brood,
350 Lilies and vestments and white faces, sweet
As puff on puff of grated orris-root[25]

When ladies crowd to Church at midsummer.
And then i' the front, of course a saint or two——
Saint John' because he saves the Florentines,

355 Saint Ambrose, who puts down in black and white
The convent's friends and gives them a long day,
And Job, I must have him there past mistake,
The man of Uz (and Us without the z,
Painters who need his patience). Well, all these

360 Secured at their devotion, up shall come
Out of a corner when you least expect,
As one by a dark stair into a great light,
Music and talking, who but Lippo! I!—
Mazed, motionless, and moonstruck—I'm the man!

365 Back I shrink—what is this I see and hear?
I, caught up with my monk's-things by mistake,
My old serge gown and rope that goes all round,
I, in this presence, this pure company!
Where's a hole, where's a corner for escape?

370 Then steps a sweet angelic slip of a thing
Forward, puts out a soft palm—"Not so fast!"
—Addresses the celestial presence, "nay—
He made you and devised you, after all,
Though he's none of you! Could Saint John there draw—

375 His camel-hair[26] make up a painting brush?
We come to brother Lippo for all that,
Iste perfecit opus![27] So, all smile—
I shuffle sideways with my blushing face
Under the cover of a hundred wings

380 Thrown like a spread of kirtles° when you're gay   *skirts*
And play hot cockles,[28] all the doors being shut,
Till, wholly unexpected, in there pops
The hothead husband! Thus I scuttle off
To some safe bench behind, not letting go

385 The palm of her, the little lily thing
That spoke the good word for me in the nick,
Like the Prior's niece . . . Saint Lucy, I would say.
And so all's saved for me, and for the church
A pretty picture gained. Go, six months hence!

390   Your hand, sir, and good-bye: no lights, no lights!
      The street's hushed, and I know my own way back,
      Don't fear me! There's the grey beginning. Zooks!

ca. 1853-1855

Endnotes

1. This monologue portrays the dawn of the Renaissance in Italy at a point when the medieval attitude toward life and art was about to be displaced by a fresh appreciation of earthly pleasures. It was from Giorgio Vasari's *Lives of the Painters* that Browning derived most of his information about the life of the Florentine painter and friar Lippo Lippi (1406-1469). However, the theory of art propounded by Lippi in the poem was developed by the poet himself.
2. A shortened version of *Gadzooks*, a mild oath now obscure in meaning but perhaps resembling a phrase still in use: "God's truth."
3. Santa Maria del Carmine, a church and cloister of the Carmelite order of friars to which Lippi belonged.
4. Lippi's patron, banker and virtual ruler of Florence.
5. I.e., how you had the arrogance to choke the gullet of someone with my connections.
6. The officer in charge of the patrol of policemen or watchmen.
7. I.e., one of the watchmen has a face that would serve as a model for a painting of Judas.
8. Season of revelry before the commencement of Lent.
9. This and other interspersed flower songs are called *stornelli* in Italy.
10. San Lorenzo, a church in Florence.
11. A picture of Saint Jerome (ca. 340-420), whose ascetic observances were hardly a congenial subject for such a painter as Lippi.
12. Margin of music book used for choral singing.
13. Head of a Carmelite convent.
14. Benedictine and Dominican religious orders, respectively.
15. Went up in smoke.
16. Great Florentine painter (1276–1337), whose stylized pictures of religious subjects were admired as models of pre-Renaissance art.
17. Also called Salome, had the same name as her mother (Herodias), sister-in-law of King Herod. The daughter's dance coincided with the beheading of John the Baptist, who had aroused her mother's displeasure (Matthew 14.6–11).
18. The Medici palace.
19. Fra Angelico (1387–1455) and Lorenzo Monaco (1370–1425), whose paintings were in the approved traditional manner.
20. Guidi or Masaccio (1401–1428), a painter who may have been Lippi's master rather than his pupil, although Browning, in a letter to the press in 1870, argued that Lippi had been born earlier. Like

Lippi, Masaccio was in revolt against the medieval theory of art. His frescoes in the chapel of Santa Maria del Carmine are considered his masterpiece.

21. A scene representing the fiery martyrdom of Saint Laurence.

22. Painted on a freshly plastered surface. It must be painted quickly before the plaster dries. Prato is a town near Florence.

23. A convent church in Florence.

24. Sample of my work. The completed painting, which Browning saw in Florence, is Lippi's *Coronation of the Virgin*.

25. Powder (like talcum) made from sweet-smelling roots of a flower.

26. Cf. Mark 1.6: "And John was clothed with camel's hair."

27. This man made the work! (Latin). In this painting, as later completed, these words appear beside a figure that Browning took to be Lippi's self-portrait.

28. A game in which a player wears a blindfold.

General William Booth

In Darkest England

CHAPTER I

Why "Darkest England"?

This summer the attention of the civilized world has been arrested by the story which Mr. Stanley has told of "Darkest Africa" and his journeyings across the heart of the Lost Continent. In all that spirited narrative of heroic endeavor, nothing has so much impressed the imagination, as his description of the immense forest, which offered an almost impenetrable barrier to his advance. The intrepid explorer, in his own phrase, "marched, tore, ploughed, and cut his way for one hundred and sixty days through this inner womb of the true tropical forest." The mind of man with difficulty endeavors to realize this immensity of wooded wilderness, covering a territory half as large again as the whole of France, where the rays of the sun never penetrate, where in the dark, dank air, filled with the steam of the heated morass, human beings dwarfed into pygmies and brutalized into cannibals lurk and live and die. Mr. Stanley vainly endeavors to bring home to us the full horror of that awful gloom. He says:

Take a thick Scottish copse dripping with rain; imagine this to be a mere undergrowth nourished under the impenetrable shade of ancient trees ranging from 100 to 180 feet high; briars and thorns abundant; lazy creeks meandering through the depths of the jungle, and sometimes a deep affluent of a great river. Imagine this forest and jungle in all stages of decay and growth, rain pattering on you every other day of the year; an impure atmosphere with its dread consequences, fever and dysentery; gloom throughout the day and darkness almost palpable throughout the night; and then if you can imagine such a forest extending the entire distance from Plymouth to Peterhead, you will have a fair idea of some of the inconveniences endured by us in the Congo forest.

The denizens of this region are filled with a conviction that the forest is endless—interminable. In vain did Mr. Stanley and his companions endeavor to convince them that outside the dreary wood were to be found sunlight, pasturage and peaceful meadows.

They replied in a manner that seemed to imply that we must be strange creatures to suppose that it would be possible for any world to exist save their illimitable forest. "No," they replied, shaking their heads compassionately, and pitying our absurd questions, "all like this," and they moved their hands sweepingly to illustrate that the world was all alike, nothing but trees, trees and trees—great

Published The Salvation Army, 1890

trees rising as high as an arrow shot to the sky, lifting their crowns intertwining their branches, pressing and crowding one against the other, until neither the sunbeam nor shaft of light can penetrate it.

"We entered the forest," says Mr. Stanley, "with confidence: forty pioneers in front with axes and bill hooks to clear a path through the obstructions, praying that God and good fortune would lead us." But before the conviction of the forest dwellers that the forest was without end, hope faded out of the hearts of the natives of Stanley's company. The men became sodden with despair, preaching was useless to move their brooding sullenness, their morbid gloom.

The little religion they knew was nothing more than legendary lore, and in their memories there dimly floated a story of a land which grew darker and darker as one travelled towards the end of the earth and drew nearer to the place where a great serpent lay supine and coiled round the whole world. Ah! then the ancients must have referred to this, where the light is so ghastly, and the woods are endless, and are so still and solemn and grey; to this oppressive loneliness, amid so much life, which is so chilling to the poor distressed heart; and the horror grew darker with their fancies; the cold of early morning, the comfortless grey of dawn, the dead white mist, the ever-dripping tears of the dew, the deluging rains, the appalling thunder bursts and the echoes, and the wonderful play of the dazzling lightning. And when the night comes with its thick palpable darkness, and they lie huddled in their damp little huts, and they hear the tempest overhead, and the howling of the wild winds, the grinding and groaning of the storm-tost trees, and the dread sounds of the falling giants, and the shock of the trembling earth which sends their hearts with fitful leaps to their throats, and the roaring and a rushing as of a mad overwhelming sea—oh, then the horror is intensified! When the march has begun once again, and the files are slowly moving through the woods, they renew their morbid broodings, and ask themselves: How long is this to last? Is the joy of life to end thus? Must we jog on day after day in this cheerless gloom and this joyless duskiness, until we stagger and fall and rot among the toads? Then they disappear into the woods by twos, and threes, and sixes; and after the caravan has passed they return by the trail, some to reach Yambuya and upset the young officers with their tales of woe and war; some to fall sobbing under a spear-thrust; some to wander and stray in the dark mazes of the woods, hopelessly lost; and some to be carved for the cannibal feast. And those who remain compelled to it by fears of greater danger, mechanically march on, a prey to dread and weakness.

That is the forest. But what of its denizens? They are comparatively few; only some hundreds of thousands living in small tribes from ten to thirty miles apart, scattered over an area on which ten thousand million trees put out the sun from a region four times as wide as Great Britain. Of these pygmies there are two kinds; one a very degraded specimen with ferretlike eyes, close-set nose, more nearly approaching the baboon than was supposed to be possible, but very human; the other very handsome, with frank open innocent features, very prepossessing. They are quick and intelligent, capable of deep affection and gratitude, showing remarkable industry and patience. A pygmy boy of eighteen worked with consuming zeal; time with him was too precious to waste in talk. His mind seemed ever concentrated on work. Mr. Stanley said:

"When I once stopped him to ask him his name, his face seemed to say, 'Please don't stop me. I must finish my task.'

"All alike, the baboon variety and the handsome innocents, are cannibals. They are possessed with a perfect mania for meat. We were obliged to bury our dead in the river, lest the bodies should be exhumed and eaten, even when they had died from smallpox."

Upon the pygmies and all the dwellers of the forest has descended a devastating visitation in the shape of the ivory raiders of civilization. The race that wrote the Arabian Nights, built Bagdad and Granada, and invented Algebra, sends forth men with the hunger for gold in their hearts, and Enfield muskets in their hands, to plunder and to slay. They exploit the domestic affections of the forest dwellers in order to strip them of all they possess in the world. That has been going on for years. It is going on to-day. It has come to be regarded as the natural and normal law of existence. Of the religion of these hunted pygmies, Mr. Stanley tells us nothing, perhaps because there is nothing to tell. But an earlier traveler, Dr. Kraff, says that one of these tribes, by name Doko, had some notion of a Supreme Being, to whom, under the name of Yer, they sometimes addressed prayers in moments of sadness or terror. In these prayers they say; "Oh Yer, if Thou dost really exist why dost Thou let us be slaves? We ask not for food or clothing, for we live on snakes, ants, and mice. Thou hast made us, wherefore dost Thou let us be trodden down?"

It is a terrible picture, and one that has engraved itself deep on the heart of civilization. But while brooding over the awful presentation of life as it exists in the vast African forest, it seemed to me only too vivid a picture of many parts of our own land. As there is a darkest Africa is there not also a darkest England? Civilization, which can breed its own barbarians, does it not also breed its own pygmies? May we not find a parallel at our own doors, and discover within a stone's throw of our cathedrals and palaces similar horrors to those which Stanley has found existing in the great Equatorial forest?

The more the mind dwells upon the subject, the closer the analogy appears. The ivory raiders who brutally traffic in the unfortunate denizens of the forest glades, what are they but the publicans who flourish on the weakness of our poor? The two tribes of savages, the human baboon and the handsome dwarf, who will not speak lest it impede him in his task, may be accepted as the two varieties who are continually present with us—the vicious, lazy lout, and the toiling slave. They, too, have lost all faith of life being other than it is and has been. As in Africa, it is all trees, trees, trees with no other world conceivable; so is it here—it is all vice and poverty and crime. To many the world is all slum, with the Workhouse as an intermediate purgatory before the grave. And just as Mr. Stanley's Zanzibaris lost faith, and could only be induced to plod on in brooding sullenness of dull despair, so the most of our social reformers, no matter how cheerily they may have started off, with forty pioneers swinging blithely their axes as they force their way into the wood, soon become depressed and despairing. Who can battle against the ten thousand million trees? Who can hope to make headway against the innumerable adverse conditions which doom the dweller in Darkest England to eternal and immutable misery? What wonder is it that many of the warmest hearts and enthusiastic workers feel disposed to repeat the lament of the old English chronicler, who, speaking of the evil days which fell upon our forefathers in the reign of Stephen, said "It seemed to them as if God and his Saints were dead."

An analogy is as good as a suggestion; it becomes wearisome when it is pressed too far. But before leaving it, think for a moment how close the parallel is, and how strange it is that so much interest should be excited by a narrative of human squalor and human heroism in a distant continent, while greater squalor and heroism not less magnificent may be observed at our very doors.

The Equatorial Forest traversed by Stanley resembles that Darkest England of which I have to speak, alike in its vast extent—both stretch, in Stanley's phrase, "as far as from Plymouth to Peterhead"; its monotonous darkness, its malaria and its gloom, its dwarfish de-humanized inhabitants, the slavery to which they are subjected, their privations and their misery. That which sickens the stoutest heart, and causes many of our bravest and best to fold their hands in despair, is the apparent impossibility of doing more than merely to peck at the outside of the endless tangle of monotonous undergrowth, to let light into it, to make a road clear through it, that shall not be immediately choked up by the ooze of the morass and the luxuriant parasitical growth of the forest—who dare hope for that? At present, alas, it would seem as though no one dares even to hope! It is the great Slough of Despond of our time.

And what a slough it is no man can gauge who has not waded therein, as some of us have done, up to the very neck for long years. Talk about Dante's Hell, and all the horrors and cruelties of the torture-chamber of the lost! The man who walks with open eyes and with bleeding heart through the shambles of our civilization needs no such fantastic images of the poet to teach him horror. Often and often, when I have seen the young and the poor and the helpless go down before my eyes into the morass, trampled underfoot by beasts of prey in human shape that haunt these regions, it seemed as if God were no longer in His world, but that in His stead reigned a fiend, merciless as Hell, ruthless as the grave. Hard it is, no doubt, to read in Stanley's pages of the slave-traders coldly arranging for the surprise of a village, the capture of the inhabitants, the massacre of those who resist, and the violation of all the women; but the stony streets of London, if they could but speak, would tell of tragedies as awful, of ruin as complete, of ravishments as horrible, as if we were in Central Africa; only the ghastly devastation is covered, corpse-like, with the artificialities and hypocrisies of modern civilization.

The lot of a negress in the Equatorial Forest is not, perhaps, a very happy one, but is it so very much worse than that of many a pretty orphan girl in our Christian capital? We talk about the brutalities of the dark ages, and we profess to shudder as we read in books of the shameful exaction of the rights of feudal superior. And yet here, beneath our very eyes, in our theaters, in our restaurants, and in many other places, unspeakable though it be but to name it, the same hideous abuse flourishes unchecked. A young penniless girl, if she be pretty, is often hunted from pillar to post by her employers, confronted always by the alternative—Starve or Sin. And when once the poor girl has consented to buy the right to earn her living by the sacrifice of her virtue, then she is treated as a slave and an outcast by the very men who have ruined her. Her word becomes unbelievable, her life an ignomi

ny, and she is swept downward ever downward, into the bottomless perdition of prostitution. But there, even in the lowest depths, excommunicated by Humanity and outcast from God, she is far nearer the pitying heart of the One true Saviour than all the men who forced her down, aye, and than all the Pharisees and Scribes who stand silently by while these fiendish wrongs are perpetrated before their very eyes.

The blood boils with impotent rage at the sight of these enormities, callously inflicted, and silently borne by these miserable victims. Nor is it only women who are the victims, although their fate is the most tragic. Those firms which reduce sweating to a fine art, who systematically and deliberately defraud the workman of his pay, who grind the faces of the poor, and who rob the widow and the orphan, and who for a pretense make great professions of public-spirit and philanthropy, these men nowadays are sent to Parliament to make laws for the people. The old prophets sent them to Hell—but we have changed all that. They send their victims to Hell, and are rewarded by all that wealth can do to make their lives comfortable. Read the House of Lords' Report on the Sweating System, and ask if any African slave system, making due allowance for the superior civilization, and therefore sensitiveness, of the victims, reveals more misery.

Darkest England, like Darkest Africa, reeks with malaria. The foul and fetid breath of our slums is almost as poisonous as that of the African swamp. Fever is almost as chronic there as on the Equator. Every year thousands of children are killed off by what is called defects of our sanitary system. They are in reality starved and poisoned, and all that can be said is that, in many cases, it is better for them that they were taken away from the trouble to come.

Just as in Darkest Africa it is only a part of the evil and misery that comes from the superior race who invade the forest to enslave and massacre its miserable inhabitants, so with us, much of the misery of those whose lot we are considering arises from their own habits. Drunkenness and all manner of uncleanness, moral and physical, abound. Have you ever watched by the bedside of a man in delirium tremens? Multiply the sufferings of that one drunkard by the hundred thousand, and you have some idea of what scenes are being witnessed in all our great cities at this moment. As in Africa streams intersect the forest in every direction, so the gin-shop stands at every corner with its River of the Water of Death flowing seventeen hours out of the twenty-four for the destruction of the people. A population sodden with drink, steeped in vice, eaten up by every social and physical malady, these are the denizens of Darkest England amidst whom my life has been spent, and to whose rescue I would now summon all that is best in the manhood and womanhood of our land.

But this book is no mere lamentation of despair. For Darkest England, as for Darkest Africa, there is a light beyond. I think I see my way out, a way by which these wretched ones may escape from the gloom of their miserable existence into a higher and happier life. Long wandering in the Forest of the Shadow of Death at our doors, has familiarized me with its horrors; but while the realization is a vigorous spur to action it has never been so oppressive as to extinguish hope. Mr. Stanley never succumbed to the terrors which oppressed his followers. He had lived in a larger life, and knew that the forest, though long, was not interminable. Every step forward brought him nearer his destined goal, nearer to the light of the sun, the clear sky, and the rolling uplands of the grazing land. Therefore he did not despair. The Equatorial Forest was, after all, a mere corner of one quarter of the world. In the knowledge of the light outside, in the confidence begotten by past experience of successful endeavor, he pressed forward: and when the 160 days' struggle was over, he and his men came out into a pleasant place where the land smiled with peace and plenty, and their hardships and hunger were forgotten in the joy of a great deliverance.

So I venture to believe it will be with us. But the end is not yet. We are still in the depths of the depressing gloom. It is in no spirit of light-heartedness that this book is sent forth into the world. The magnitude of the evils and the difficulty of dealing with them are immense.

If this were the first time that this wail of hopeless misery had sounded on our ears the matter would have been less serious. It is because we have heard it so often that the case is so desperate. The exceeding bitter cry of the disinherited has become to be as familiar in the ears of men as the dull roar of the streets or as the moaning of the wind through the trees. And so it rises unceasing, year in and year out, and we are too busy or too idle, too indifferent or too selfish, to spare it a thought. Only now and then, on rare occasions, when some clear voice is heard giving more articulate utterance to the miseries of the miserable men, do we pause in the regular routine of our daily duties, and shudder as we realize for one brief moment what life means to the inmates of the Slums. But one of the grimmest social problems of our time should be sternly faced, not with a view to the generation of profitless emotion, but with a view to its solution.

Is it not time? There is, it is true, an audacity in the mere suggestion that the problem is not insoluble that is enough to take away the breath. But can nothing be done? If, after full and exhaustive consideration, we come to the deliberate conclusion that nothing can be done, and that it is the inevitable and inexorable destiny of thousands of Englishmen to be brutalized into worse than beasts by the condition of their environment, so be it. But if, on the contrary, we are unable to believe that this "awful slough," which engulfs the manhood and womanhood of generation after generation, is incapable of removal; and if the heart and intellect of mankind alike revolt against the fatalism of despair, then, indeed, it is time, and high time, that the question were faced in no mere dilettante spirit, but with a resolute determination to make an end of the crying scandal of our age.

What a satire it is upon our Christianity and our civilization, that the existence of these colonies of heathens and savages in the heart of our capital should attract so little.attention! It is no better than a ghastly mockery—theologians might use a stronger word—to call by the name of One who came to seek and to save that which was lost those Churches which in the midst of lost multitudes either sleep in apathy or display a fitful interest in a chasuble. Why all this apparatus of temples and meeting-houses to save men from perdition in a world which is to come, while never a helping hand is stretched out to save them from the inferno of their present life? Is it not time that, forgetting for a moment their wranglings about the infinitely little or infinitely obscure, they should concentrate all their energies on a united effort to break this terrible perpetuity of perdition, and to rescue some at least of those for whom they profess to believe their Founder came to die?

Before venturing to define the remedy, I begin by describing the malady. But even when presenting the dreary picture of our social ills, and describing the difficulties which confront us, I speak not in despondency but in hope. "I know in whom I have believed." I know, therefore do I speak. Darker England is but a fractional part of "Greater England." There is wealth enough abundantly to minister to its social regeneration so far as wealth can, if there be but heart enough to set about the work in earnest. And I hope and believe that the heart will not be lacking when once the problem is manfully faced, and the method of its solution plainly pointed out.

CHAPTER II

The Submerged Tenth

In setting forth the difficulties which have to be grappled with, I shall endeavor in all things to understate rather than overstate my case. I do this for two reasons: first, any exaggeration would create a reaction; and secondly, as my object is to demonstrate the practicability of solving the problem, I do not wish to magnify its dimensions. In this and in subsequent chapters I hope to convince those who read them that there is no overstraining in the representation of the facts, and nothing Utopian in the presentation of remedies.

I appeal neither to hysterical emotionalists nor headlong enthusiasts; but having tried to approach the examination of this question in a spirit of scientific investigation, I put forth my proposals with the view of securing the support and co-operation of the sober, serious, practical men and women who constitute the saving strength and moral backbone of the country. I fully admit that there is much that is lacking in the diagnosis of the disease, and, no doubt, in this first draft of the prescription there is much room for improvement, which will come when we have the light of fuller experience. But with all its drawbacks and defects, I do not hesitate to submit my proposals to the impartial judgment of all who are interested in the solution of the social question as an immediate and practical mode of dealing with this, the greatest problem of our time.

The first duty of an investigator in approaching the study of any question is to eliminate all that is foreign to the inquiry, and to concentrate his attention upon the subject to be dealt with. Here I may remark that I make no attempt in this book to deal with Society as a whole. I leave to others the formulation of ambitious programs for the reconstruction of our entire social system: not because I may not desire its reconstruction, but because the elaboration of any plans which are more or less visionary and incapable of realization for many years would stand in the way of the consideration of this Scheme for dealing with the most urgently pressing aspect of the question, which I hope may be put into operation at once.

In taking this course I am aware that I cut myself off from a wide and attractive field; but as a practical man, dealing with sternly prosaic facts, I must confine my attention to that particular section of the problem which clamors most pressingly for a solution. Only one thing I may say in passing. There is nothing in my scheme which will bring it into collision either with Socialists of the State, or Socialists of the Municipality, with Individualists or Nationalists, or any of the various schools of thought in the great field of social economics—excepting only those anti-Christian economists who hold that it is an offense against the doctrine of the survival of the fittest to try to save the weakest from going to the wall, and who believe that when once a man is down the supreme duty of a self-regarding Society is to jump upon him. Such economists will naturally be disappointed with this book. I venture to believe that all others will find nothing in it to offend their favorite theories, but perhaps something of helpful suggestion which they may utilize hereafter.

What, then, is Darkest England? For whom do we claim that "urgency" which gives their case priority over that of all other sections of their countrymen and countrywomen?

I claim it for the Lost, for the Outcast, for the Disinherited of the World.

These, it may be said, are but phrases. Who are the Lost? I reply, not in a religious, but in a social sense, the lost are those who have gone under, who have lost their foothold in Society, those to whom the prayer to our Heavenly Father, "Give us day by day our daily bread," is either unfulfilled, or only fulfilled by the Devil's agency: by the earnings of vice, the proceeds of crime, or the contribution enforced by the threat of the law.

But I will be more precise. The denizens in Darkest England, for whom I appeal, are (1) those who, having no capital or income of their own, would in a month be dead from sheer starvation were they exclusively dependent upon the money earned by their own work; and (2) those who by their utmost exertions are unable to attain the regulation allowance of food which the law prescribes as indispensable even for the worst criminals in our jails.

I sorrowfully admit that it would be Utopian in our present social arrangements to dream of attaining for every honest Englishman a jail standard of all the necessaries of life. Some time, perhaps, we may venture to hope that every honest worker on English soil will always be as warmly clad, as healthily housed, and as regularly fed as our criminal convicts—but that is not yet.

Neither is it possible to hope for many years to come that human beings generally will be as well cared for as horses. Mr. Carlyle long ago remarked that the four-footed worker has already got all that this two-handed one is clamoring for: "There are not many horses in England, able and willing to work, which have not due food and lodging and go about sleek coated, satisfied in heart." You say it is impossible: but, said Carlyle, "The human brain, looking at these sleek English horses, refuses to believe in such impossibility for English men." Nevertheless, forty years have passed since Carlyle said that, and we seem to be no nearer the attainment of the four-footed standard for the two-handed worker. "Perhaps it might be nearer realization," growls the cynic, "if we could only produce 'men according to demand, as we do horses, and promptly send them to the slaughter-house when past their prime"—which, of course, is not to be thought of.

What, then, is the standard towards which we may venture to aim with some prospect of realization in our time? It is a very humble one, but if realized it would solve the worst problems of modern Society.

It is the standard of the London Cab Horse.

When in the streets of London a Cab Horse, weary or careless or stupid, trips and falls and lies stretched out in the midst of the traffic, there is no question of debating how he came to stumble before we try to get him on his legs again. The Cab Horse is a very real illustration of poor broken-down humanity; he usually falls down because of overwork and underfeeding. If you put him on his feet without altering his conditions, it would only be to give him another dose of agony; but first of all you'll have to pick him up again. It may have been through overwork or underfeeding, or it may have been all his own fault that he has broken his knees and smashed the shafts, but that does not matter. If not for his own sake, then merely in order to prevent an obstruction of the traffic, all attention is concentrated upon the question of how we are to get him on his legs again. The load is taken off, the harness is unbuckled, or, if need be, cut, and everything is done to help him up. Then he is put in the shafts again and once more restored to his regular round of work. That is the first point. The second is that every Cab Horse in London has three things; a shelter for the night, food for its stomach, and work allotted to it by which it can earn its corn.

These are the two points of the Cab Horse's Charter. When he is down he is helped up, and while he lives he has food, shelter and work. That, although a humble standard, is at present absolutely unattainable by millions—literally by millions—of our fellow-men and women in this country. Can the Cab Horse Charter be gained for human beings? I answer yes. The Cab Horse standard can be attained on the Cab Horse terms. If you get your fallen fellow on his feet again, Docility and Discipline will enable you to teach the Cab Horse ideal, otherwise it will remain unattainable. But Docility seldom fails where Discipline is intelligently maintained. Intelligence is more frequently lacking to direct, than obedience to follow direction. At any rate it is not for those who possess the intelligence to despair of obedience, until they have done their part. Some, no doubt, like the bucking horse that will never be broken in, will always refuse to submit to any guidance but their own lawless will. They will remain either the Ishmaels or the Sloths of Society. But man is naturally neither an Ishmael nor a Sloth.

The first question, then, which confronts us is, what are the dimensions of the Evil? How many of our fellow-men dwell in this Darkest England? How can we take the census of those who have fallen below the Cab Horse standard to which it is our aim to elevate the most wretched of our countrymen?

The moment you attempt to answer this question, you are confronted by the fact that the Social Problem has scarcely been studied at all scientifically. Go to Mudie's and ask for all the books that have been written on the subject, and you will be surprised to find how few there are. There are probably more scientific books treating of diabetes or of gout than there are dealing with the great social malady which eats out the vitals of such numbers of our people. Of late there has been a change for the better. The Report of the Royal Commission on the Housing of the Poor, and the Report of the Committee of the House of Lords on Sweating, represent an attempt at least to ascertain the facts which bear upon the Condition of the People question. But, after all, more minute, patient, intelligent observation has been devoted to the study of Earthworms, than to the evolution, or rather the degradation, of the Sunken Section of our people. Here and there in the immense field individual workers make notes, and occasionally emit a wail of despair, but where is there any attempt even so much as to take the first preliminary step of counting those who have gone under?

One book there is, and so far as I know at present, only one, which even attempts to enumerate the destitute. In his "Life and Labor in the East of London," Mr. Charles Booth attempts to form some kind of an idea as to the numbers of those with whom we have to deal. With a large staff of assistants, and provided with all the facts in possession of the School Board Visitors, Mr. Booth took an industrial census of East London. This district, which comprises Tower Hamlets, Shoreditch, Bethnal Green and Hackney, contains a population of 908,000; and that is to say, less than one-fourth of the population of London.

How do his statistics work out? If we estimate the number of the poorest class in the rest of London as being twice as numerous as those in the Eastern District, instead of being thrice as numerous, as they would be if they were calculated according to the population in the same proportion, the following is the result:—

	East London	Estimate For Rest of London	Total
PAUPERS			
Inmates of Workhouses, Asylums, and Hospitals	17,000	34,000	51,000
HOMELESS			
Loafers, Casuals, and some Criminals	11,000	22,000	33,000
STARVING			
Casual earnings between 18s. per week and chronic want	100,000	200,000	300,000
THE VERY POOR			
Intermittent earnings 18s. to 21s. per week	74,000	148,000	222,000
Small regular earnings 18s. to 21s. per week	129,000	258,000	387,000
	331,000	662,000	993,000
Regular wages, artisans, etc., 22s. to 30s. per week	377,000		
Higher class labor, 30s. to 50s. per week	121,000		
Lower middle class, shopkeepers, clerks, etc.	34,000		
Upper middle class (servant keepers)	45,000		
	908,000		

It may be admitted that East London affords an exceptionally bad district from which to generalize for the rest of the country. Wages are higher in London than elsewhere, but so is rent, and the number of the homeless and starving is greater in the human warren at the East End. There are 31 millions of people in Great Britain, exclusive of Ireland. If destitution existed everywhere in East London proportions, there would be 31 times as many homeless and starving people as there are in the district round Bethnal Green.

But let us suppose that the East London rate is double the average for the rest of the country. That would bring out the following figures:—

	East London	United Kingdom
HOUSELESS		
Loafers, Casuals, and some Criminals	11,000	165,500
STARVING		
Casual earnings or chronic want	100,000	1,550,000
Total Houseless and Starving	111,000	1,715,500
In Workhouses, Asylums, etc.:	170,000	190,000
	128,000	1,905,500

Of those returned as homeless and starving, 870,000 were in receipt of outdoor relief.

To these must be added the inmates of our prisons. In 1889, 174,779 persons were received in the prisons, but the average number in prison at any one time did not exceed 60,000. The figures, as given in the Prison Returns, are as follows:—

In Convict Prisons	11,600
In Local Prisons	20,883
In Reformatories	1,270
In Industrial Schools	21,413
Criminal Lunatics	910
	56,136

Add to this the number of indoor paupers and lunatics (excluding criminals) 78,966—and we have an army of nearly two millions belonging to the submerged classes. To this there must be added, at the very least, another million, representing those dependent upon the criminal, lunatic and other classes, not enumerated here, and the more or less helpless of the class immediately above the houseless and starving. This brings my total to three millions, or, to put it roughly to one-tenth of the population. According to Lord Brabazon and Mr. Samuel Smith, "between two and three millions of our population are always pauperized and degraded." Mr. Chamberlain says there is a "population equal to that of the metropolis,"—that is, between four and five millions—"which has remained constantly in a state of abject destitution and misery." Mr. Giffen is more moderate. The submerged class, according to him, comprises one in five of manual laborers, six in 100 of the population. Mr. Giffen does not add the third million which is living on the border line. Between Mr. Chamberlain's four millions and a half, and Mr. Giffen's 1,800,000, I am content to take three millions as representing the total strength of the destitute army.

Darkest England, then, may be said to have a population about equal to that of Scotland. Three million men, women, and children, a vast despairing multitude in a condition nominally free, but really enslaved:—these it is whom we have to save.

It is a large order. England emancipated her negroes sixty years ago, at a cost of £40,000,000, and has never ceased boasting about it since. But at our own doors, from "Plymouth to Peterhead," stretches this waste Continent of humanity—three million human beings who are enslaved—some of them to taskmasters as merciless as any West Indian overseer, all of them to destitution and despair.

Is anything to be done with them? Can anything be done for them? Or is this million-headed mass to be regarded as offering a problem as insoluble as that of the London sewage, which, feculent and festering, swings heavily up and down the basin of the Thames with the ebb and flow of the tide?

This Submerged Tenth—is it, then, beyond the reach of the nine-tenths in the midst of whom they live, and around whose homes they rot and die? No doubt, in every large mass of human beings there will be some incurably diseased in morals and in body, some for whom nothing can be done, some of whom even the optimist must despair, and for whom he can prescribe nothing but the beneficiently stern restraints of an asylum or a jail.

But is not one in ten a proportion scandalously high? The Israelites of old set apart one tribe in twelve to minister to the Lord in the service of the 'Temple; but must we doom one in ten of "God's Englishmen" to the service of the great Twin Devils—Destitution and Despair?

CHAPTER III

The Homeless

Darkest England may be described as consisting broadly of three circles, one within the other. The outer and widest circle is inhabited by the starving and the homeless, but honest, Poor. The second by those who live by Vice; and the third and innermost region at the center is peopled by those who exist by Crime. The whole of the three circles is sodden with Drink. Darkest England has many more public-houses than the Forest of the Aruwimi has rivers, of which Mr. Stanley sometimes had to cross three in half-an-hour.

The borders of this great lost land are not sharply defined. They are continually expanding or contracting. Whenever there is a period of depression in trade, they stretch; when prosperity returns, they contract. So far as individuals are concerned, there are none among the hundreds of thousands who live upon the outskirts of the dark forest who can truly say that they or their children are secure from being hopelessly entangled in its labyrinth. The death of the bread-winner, a long illness, a failure in the City, or any one of a thousand other causes which might be named, will bring within the first circle those who at present imagine themselves free from all danger of actual want. The death-rate in Darkest England is high. Death is the great jail-deliverer of the captives. But the dead are hardly in the grave before their places are taken by others. Some escape, but the majority, their health sapped by their surroundings, become weaker and weaker, until at last they fall by the way, perishing without hope at the very doors of the palatial mansions which, maybe, some of them helped to build.

Some seven years ago a great outcry was made concerning the Housing of the Poor. Much was said, and rightly said—it could not be said too strongly—concerning the disease-breeding, manhood-destroying character of many of the tenements in which the poor herd in our large cities. But there is a depth below that of the dweller in the slums. It is that of the dweller in the street, who has not even a lair in the slums which he can call his own. The houseless Out-of-Work is in one respect at least like Him of whom it was said, "Foxes have holes, and birds of the air have nests, but the Son of Man hath not where to lay His head."

The existence of these unfortunates was somewhat rudely forced upon the attention of Society in 1887, when Trafalgar Square became the camping ground of the Homeless Outcasts of London. Our Shelters have done something, but not enough, to provide for the outcasts, who this night and every night are walking about the streets, not knowing where they can find a spot on which to rest their weary frames.

Here is the return of one of my Officers who was told off this summer to report upon the actual condition of the Homeless who have no roof to shelter them in all London:—

There are still a large number of Londoners and a considerable percentage of wanderers from the country in search of work, who find themselves at nightfall destitute. These now betake themselves to the seats under the plane trees on the Embankment. Formerly they endeavored to occupy all the seats, but the lynx-eyed Metropolitan Police declined to allow any such proceedings, and the dossers, knowing the invariable kindness of the City Police, made tracks for that portion of the Embankment which, lying east of the Temple, comes under the control of the Civic Fathers. Here, between the Temple and Black friars, I found the poor wretches by the score; almost every seat contained its full complement of six—some men, some women—all reclining in various postures and nearly all fast asleep. Just as Big Ben strikes two, the moon, flashing across the Thames and lighting up the stone work of the Embankment, brings into relief a pitiable spectacle. Here on the stone abutments, which afford a slight protection from the biting wind, are scores of men lying side by side, huddled together for warmth, and, of course, without any other covering than their ordinary clothing, which is scanty enough at the best. Some have laid down a few pieces of waste paper, by way of taking the chill off the stones, but the majority are too tired, even for that, and the nightly toilet of most consists of first removing the hat, swathing the head in whatever old rag may be doing duty as a handkerchief, and then replacing the hat.

The intelligent-looking elderly man, who was just fixing himself up on a seat, informed me that he frequently made that his night's abode. "You see," quoth he, "there's nowhere else so comfortable. I was here last night, and Monday and Tuesday as well, that's four nights this- week. I had no money for lodgings, couldn't earn any, try as I might. I've had one bit of bread today, nothing else whatever, and I've earned nothing today or yesterday; I had threepence the day before. Gets my living by carrying parcels, or minding horses, or odd jobs of that sort. You see I haven't got my health, that's where it is. I used to work on the London General omnibus Company and after that on the Road Car Company, but I had to go to the infirmary with bronchitis and couldn't get work after that. What's the good of a man what's got bronchitis and just left the infirmary? Who'll engage him, I'd like to know? Besides, it makes me short of breath at times, and I can't do much. I'm a widower; wife died long ago. I have one boy, abroad, a sailor, but he's only lately started and can't help me. Yes! It's very fair out here of nights, seats rather hard, but a bit of waste paper makes it a lot softer. We have women sleep here often, and children, too. They're very well conducted, and there's seldom many rows here, you see, because everybody's tired out. We're too sleepy to make a row."

Another party, a tall, dull, helpless-looking individual, had walked up from the country; would prefer not to mention the place. He had hoped to have obtained a hospital letter at the Mansion House so as to obtain a truss for a bad rupture, but failing, had tried various other places, also in vain, winding up minus money or food on the Embankment.

In addition to these sleepers, a considerable number walk about the streets up till the early hours of the morning to hunt up some job which will bring a copper into the empty exchequer, and save them from actual starvation. I had some conversation with one such, a stalwart youth lately discharged from the militia, and unable to get work.

"You see," said he, pitifully, "I don't know my way about like most of the London fellows. I'm so green, and don't know how to pick up jobs like they do. I've been walking the streets almost day and night these two weeks and can't get work. I've got the strength, though I shan't have it long at this rate. I only want a job. This is the third night running that I've walked the streets all night; the only money I get is by minding blacking-boys' boxes while they go into Lockhart's for their dinner. I got a penny yesterday at it, and twopence for carrying a parcel, and today I've had a penny. Bought a ha'porth of bread and a ha'penny mug of tea."

Poor lad! probably he would soon get into thieves' company, and sink into the depths, for there is no other means of living for many like him; it is starve or steal, even for the young. There are gangs of lad thieves in the low Whitechapel lodging-houses, varying in age from thirteen to fifteen, who live by thieving eatables and other easily obtained goods from shop fronts.

In addition to the Embankment, al fresco lodgings are found in the seats outside Spitalfields Church, and many homeless wanderers have their own little nooks and corners of resort in many sheltered yards, vans, etc., all over London. Two poor women I observed making their home in a shop door-way in Liverpool Street. Thus they manage in the summer; what it's like in winter time is terrible to think of In many cases it means the pauper's grave, as in the case of a young woman who was wont to sleep in a van in Bedfordbury. Some men who were aware of her practice surprised her by dashing a bucket of water on her. The blow to her weak system caused illness, and the inevitable sequel—a coroner's jury came to the conclusion that the water only hastened her death, which was due, in plain English, to starvation.

The following are some statements taken down by the same Officer from twelve men whom he found sleeping on the Embankment on the nights of June 13th and 14th, 1890:—

No. 1. *"I've slept here two nights; I'm a confectioner by trade; I come from Dartford. I got turned off because I'm getting elderly. They can get young men cheaper, and I have the rheumatism so bad. I've earned nothing these two days; I thought I could get a job at Woolwich, so I walked there, but could get nothing. I found a bit of bread in the road wrapped up in a bit of newspaper. That did me for yesterday. I had a bit of bread and butter today. I'm 54 years old. When its wet we stand about all night under the arches."*

No. 2. *"Been sleeping out three weeks all but one night; do odd jobs, mind horses, and that sort of thing. Earned nothing today, or shouldn't be here. Have had a pen'orth of bread today. That's all. Yesterday had some pieces given to me at a cook-shop. Two days last week had nothing at all from morning till night. By trade I'm a feather-bed dresser, but it's gone out of fashion, and besides that, I've a cataract in one eye, and have lost the sight of it completely. I'm a widower, have one child, a soldier, at Dover. My last regular work was eight months ago, but the firm broke. Been doing odd jobs since."*

No. 3. *"I'm a tailor; have slept here four nights running. Can't get work. Been out of a job three weeks. If I can muster cash I sleep at a lodging-house in Vere Street, Clare Market. It was very wet last night. I left these seats and went to Covent Garden Market and slept under cover. There were about thirty of us. The police moved us on, but we went back as soon as they had gone. I've had a pen'orth of bread and pen'orth of soup during the last two days—often goes without altogether. There are women sleep out here. They are decent people, mostly charwomen and such like who can't get work."*

No. 4. *Elderly man; trembles visibly with excitement at mention of work; produces a card carefully wrapped in old newspaper, to the effect that Mr. I. R. is a member of the Trade Protection League. He is a waterside laborer; last job at that was a fortnight since. Has earned nothing for five days. Had a bit of bread this morning, but not a scrap since. Had a cup of tea and two slices of bread yesterday, and the same the day before; the deputy at a lodging house gave it to him. He is fifty years old, and is still damp from sleeping out in the wet last night.*

No. 5. *Sawyer by trade, machinery cut him out. Had a job, haymaking near Uxbridge. Had been on same job lately for a month; got 2s. 6d. a day. (Probably spent it in drink, seems a very doubtful worker.) Has been odd jobbing a long time, earned 2d. today, bought a pen'orth of tea an(ditto of sugar (produces same from pocket) but can't get any place to make the tea; was hoping to get to a lodging house where he could borrow a teapot, but had no money. Earned nothing yesterday, slept at a casual ward; very poor place, get insufficient food, considering the labor. Six ounces of bread and a pint of skilly for breakfast, one ounce of cheese and six or seven ounces of bread for dinner (bread cut by guess). Tea same as breakfast,—no supper. For this you have to break 10 cwt. of stones, or pick 4 lbs. of oakum.*

No. 6. *Had slept out four nights running. Was a distiller by trade; been out four months; unwilling to enter into details of leaving, but it was his own fault. (Very likely; a heavy, thick, stubborn, and senseless-looking fellow, six feet high, thick neck, strong limbs, evidently destitute of ability.) Does odd jobs; earned 3d. for minding a horse, bought a cup of coffee and pen'orth of bread and butter. Has no money now. Slept under Waterloo Bridge last night.*

No. 7. *Good-natured looking man; one who would suffer and say nothing; clothes shining with age, grease, and dirt; they hang on his joints as on pegs; awful rags! I saw him endeavoring to walk. He lifted his feet very slowly and put them down carefully in evident pain. His legs are bad; been in infirmary several times with them. His uncle and grandfather were clergymen; both dead now. He was once in a good position in a money office, and afterwards in the London and County Bank for nine years. Then he went with an auctioneer who broke, and he was left ill, old, and without any trade. "A clerk's place," says he, "is never worth having, because there are so many of them, and once out you can only get another place with difficulty. I have a brother-in-law on the Stock Exchange but he won't own me. Look at my clothes? Is it likely?"*

No. 8. *Slept here four nights running. Is a builder's laborer by trade, that is, a handyman. Had a settled job for a few weeks which expired three weeks since. Has earned nothing for nine days. Then helped wash down a shop front and got 2s. 6d. for it. Does anything he can get. Is 46 years old. Earns about 2d. or 3d. a day at horse minding. A cup of tea and a bit of bread yesterday, and same today, is all he has had.*

No. 9. *A plumber's laborer (all these men who are somebody's "laborers" are poor samples of humanity, evidently lacking in grit, and destitute of ability to do any work which would mean decent wages). Judging from appearances, they will do nothing well. They are a kind of automaton, with the machinery rusty; slow, dull, and incapable. The man of ordinary intelligence leaves them in the rear. They could doubtless earn more even at odd jobs, but lack the energy. Of course, this means little food, exposure to weather, and increased incapability day by day. ("From him that hath not," etc.) Out, of work through slackness, .does odd jobs; slept here three nights running. Is a dock laborer when he can get work. Has 6d, an hour; works so many hours, according as he is wanted. Gets 2s., 3s., or 4s. 6d. a day. Has to work very hard for it. Casual ward life is also very hard, he says, for those who are not used to it, and there is not enough to eat. Has had today a pen'orth of bread, for minding a cab. Yesterday he spent 3½d. on a breakfast, and that lasted him all day. Age 25.*

No. 10. *Been out of work a month. Carman by trade. Arm withered, and cannot do work properly. Has slept here all the week; got an awful cold through the wet. Lives at odd jobs (they all do). Got sixpence yesterday for minding a cab and carrying a couple of parcels. Earned nothing today, but has one good meal; a lady gave it him. Has been walking about all day looking for work, and is tired out.*

No. 11. *Youth, aged 16. Sad case; Londoner. Works at odd jobs and matches selling. Has taken 3d. today, i.e., net profit 1½d. Has five boxes still. Has slept here every night for a month. Before that slept in Covent Garden Market or on doorsteps. Been sleeping out six months, since he left Feltham Industrial School. Was sent there for playing truant. Has had one bit of bread today; yesterday had only some gooseberries and cherries, i.e., bad ones that had been thrown away. Mother is alive. She "chucked him out" when he returned home on leaving Feltham because he couldn't find her money for drink.*

No. 12. *Old man, age 67. Seems to take rather a humorous view of the position. Kind of Mark Tapley. Says he can't say he does like it, but then he must like it! Ha, ha! Is a slater by trade. Been out of work for some time; younger men naturally get the work. Gets a bit of bricklaying sometimes; can turn his hand to anything. Goes miles and gets nothing. Earned one and two-pence this week at holding horses. Finds it hard, certainly. Used to care once, and get downhearted, but that's no good; don't trouble now. Had a bit of bread and butter and cup of coffee today. Health is awful bad, not half the size he was; exposure and want of food is the cause; got wet last night, and is very stiff in consequence. Has been walking about since it was light, that is 3 A.M. Was so cold and wet and weak, scarcely knew what to do. Walked to Hyde Park, and got a little sleep there on a dry seat as soon as the park opened.*

These are fairly typical cases of the men who are now wandering homeless through the streets. That is the way in which the nomads of civilization are constantly being recruited from above.

Such are the stories gathered at random one Midsummer night this year under the shade of the plane trees of the Embankment. A month later, when one of my staff took the census of the sleepers out of doors along the line of the Thames from Blackfriars to Westminster, he found three hundred and sixty-eight persons sleeping in the open air. Of these, two hundred and seventy were on the Embankment proper, and ninety-eight in and about Covent Garden Market, while the recesses of Waterloo and Blackfriars Bridges were full of human misery.

This, be it remembered, was not during a season of bad trade. The revival of business has been attested on all hands, notably by the barometer of strong drink. England is prosperous enough to drink rum in quantities which appall the Chancellor of the Exchequer, but she is not prosperous enough to provide other shelter than the midnight sky for these poor outcasts on the Embankment.

To very many even of those who live in London it may be news that there are so many hundreds who sleep out of doors every night. There are comparatively few people stirring after midnight, and when we are snugly tucked into our own beds we are apt to forget the multitude outside in the rain and the storm who are shivering the long hours through on the hard stone seats in the open or under the arches of the railway. These homeless, hungry people are, however, there, but being broken-spirited folk for the most part they seldom make their voices audible in the ears of their neighbors. Now and again, however, a harsh cry from the depths is heard for a moment, jarring rudely upon the ear and then all is still. The inarticulate classes speak as seldom as Balaam's ass. But they sometimes find a voice. Here for instance is one such case which impressed me much. It was reported in one of the Liverpool papers some time back. The speaker was haranguing a small knot of twenty or thirty men:—

"My lads," he commenced, with one hand in the breast of his ragged vest, and the other, as usual, plucking nervously at his beard, "This kind o' work can't last for ever." (Deep and earnest exclamations, "It can't! It shan't!") "Well, boys," continued the speaker, "Somebody'll have to find a road out o' this. What we.want is work, not work'us bounty, though the parish has been busy enough amongst us lately, God knows! What we want is honest work. (Hear, hear.) Now, what I propose is that each of you gets fifty mates to join you; that's make about 1,200 starving chaps—" "And then?" asked several very gaunt and hungry-looking men excitedly. "Why, then, continued the leader. "Why, then," interrupted a cadaverous-looking man from the farther and darkest end of the cellar, "of course we'll make a — London job of it, eh?" "No, no," hastily interposed my friend, and holding up his hands deprecatingly, "we'll go peaceably about it, chaps; we'll go in a body to the Town Hall, and show our poverty and ask for work. We'll take the women and children with us too." ("Too ragged! Too starved! They can't walk it!") "The women's rags is no disgrace, the staggerin' children '11 show what we come to. Let's go a thousand strong, and ask for work and bread!"

Three years ago, in London, there were some such processions. Church parades to the Abbey and St. Paul's, bivouacs in Trafalgar Square, etc. But Lazarus showed his rags and his sores too conspicuously for the convenience of Dives, and was summarily dealt with in the name of law and order. But as we have Lord Mayor's Days, when all the well-fed fur-clad City Fathers go in State Coaches through the town, why should we not have a Lazarus Day, in which the starving Out-of-Works, and the sweated half-starved "in-works" of London should crawl in their tattered raggedness, with their gaunt, hungry faces, and emaciated wives and children, a Procession of Despair through the main thoroughfares, past the massive houses and princely palaces of luxurious London?

For these men are gradually, but surely, being sucked down into the quicksand of modern life. They stretch out their grimy hands to us in vain appeal, not for charity, but for work.

Work, work! it is always work that they ask. The Divine curse is to them the most blessed of benedictions. "In the sweat of thy brow thou shalt eat thy bread," but alas for these forlorn sons of Adam, they fail to find the bread to eat, for Society has no work for them to do. They have not even leave to sweat. As well as discussing how these poor wanderers should in the second Adam "all be made alive," ought we not to put forth some effort to effect their restoration to that share in the heritage of labor which is theirs by right of descent from the first Adam?

CHAPTER IV

The Out-of-Works

There is hardly any more pathetic figure than that of the strong, able worker crying plaintively in the midst of our palaces and churches, not for charity, but for work, asking only to be allowed the privilege of perpetual hard labor, that thereby he may earn wherewith to fill his empty belly and silence the cry of his children for food. Crying for it and not getting it, seeking for labor as lost treasure and finding it not, until at last, all spirit and vigor worn out in the weary quest, the once willing worker becomes a broken-down drudge, sodden with wretchedness and despairing of all help in this world or in that which is to come. Our organization of industry certainly leaves much to be desired. A problem which even slave owners have solved ought not to be abandoned as insoluble by the Christian civilization of the Nineteenth Century.

I have already given a few life stories taken down from the lips of those who were found homeless on the Embankment which suggest somewhat of the hardships and the misery of the fruitless search for work. But what a volume of dull, squalid horror—a horror of great darkness gradually obscuring all the light of day from the life of the sufferer—might be written from the simple prosaic experiences of the ragged fellows whom you meet every day in the street. These men, whose labor is their only capital, are allowed, nay compelled, to waste day after day by the want of any means of employment, and then when they have seen days and weeks roll by during which their capital has been wasted by pounds and pounds, they are lectured for not saving the pence. When a rich man cannot employ his capital he puts it out at interest but the bank for the labor capital of the poor man has yet to be invented. Yet it might be worth while inventing one. A man's labor is not only his capital, but his life. When it passes it returns never more. To utilize it, to prevent its wasteful squandering, to enable the poor man to bank it up for use hereafter, this surely is one of the most urgent tasks before civilization.

Of all heart-breaking toil the hunt for work is surely the worst. Yet at any moment let a workman lose his present situation, and he is compelled to begin anew the dreary round of fruitless calls. Here is the story of one among thousands of the nomads, taken down from his own lips, of one who was driven by sheer hunger into crime.

A bright Spring morning found me landed from a western colony. Fourteen years had passed since I embarked from the same spot. They were fourteen years, as far as results were concerned, of non-success, and here I was again in my own land, a stranger, with a new career to carve for myself and the battle of life to fight over again.

My first thought was work. Never before had I felt more eager for a downright good chance to win my way by honest toil; but where was I to find work? With firm determination I started in search. One day passed without success, and another, and another, but the thought cheered me, "Better luck tomorrow." It has been said, "Hope springs eternal in the human breast." In my case it was to be severely tested. Days soon ran into weeks, and still I was on the trail patiently and hopefully. Courtesy and politeness so often met me in my enquiries for employment that I often wished they would kick me out, and so vary the monotony of the sickly veneer of consideration that so thinly overlaid the indifference and the absolute unconcern they had to my needs. A few cut up rough and said, "No; we don't want you." "Please don't trouble us again (this after the second visit). We have no vacancy; and if we had, we have plenty of people on hand to fill it."

Who can express the feeling that comes over one when the fact begins to dawn that the search for work is a failure? All my hopes and prospects seemed to have turned out false. Helplessness, I had often heard of it, had often talked about it, thought I knew all about it. Yes! in others, but now I began to understand it for myself. Gradually my personal appearance faded. My once faultless linen became unkempt and unclean. Down further and further went the heels of my shoes, and I drifted into that distressing condition, "shabby gentility." If the odds were against me before, how much more so now, seeing that I was too shabby even to command attention, much less a reply to my enquiry for work.
Hunger now began to do its work, and I drifted to the dock gates, but what chance had I among the hungry giants there? And so down the stream I drifted until "Grim Want" brought me to the last

shilling, the last lodging, and the last meal. What shall I do? Where shall I go? I tried to think. Must I starve? Surely there must be some door still open for honest willing endeavor, but where? What can I do? "Drink," said the Tempter; but to drink to drunkenness needs cash, and oblivion by liquor demands an equivalent in the currency.

Starve or steal. "You must do one or the other," said the Tempter. But I recoiled from being a thief "Why be so particular?" says the Tempter again. "You are down now, who will trouble about you? Why trouble about yourself? The choice is between starving and stealing." And I struggled until hunger stole my judgment, and then I became a Thief.

No one can pretend that it was an idle fear of death by starvation which drove this poor fellow to steal. Deaths from actual hunger are more common than is generally supposed. Last year, a man, whose name was never known, was walking through St. James's Park, when three of our Shelter men saw him suddenly stumble and fall. They thought he was drunk, but found he had fainted. They carried him to the bridge and gave him to the police. They took him to St. George's Hospital, where he died. It appeared that he had, according to his own tale, walked up from Liverpool, and had been without food for five days. The doctor, however, said he had gone longer than that. The jury returned a verdict of "Death from Starvation."

Without food for five days or longer! Who that has experienced the sinking sensation that is felt when even a single meal has been sacrificed may form some idea of what kind of slow torture killed that man!

In 1888 the average daily number of unemployed in London was estimated by the Mansion House Committee at 20,000. This vast reservoir of unemployed labor is the bane of all efforts to raise the scale of living, to improve the condition of labor. Men hungering to death for lack of opportunity to earn a crust are the materials from which "blacklegs" are made, by whose aid the laborer is constantly defeated in his attempts to improve his condition.

This is the problem that underlies all questions of Trades Unionism, and all Schemes for the Improvement of the Condition of the Industrial Army. To rear any stable edifice that will not perish when the first storm rises and the first hurricane blows, it must be built not upon sand, but upon a rock. And the worst of all existing Schemes for social betterment by organization of the skilled workers and the like is that they are founded, not upon "rock," nor even upon "sand," but upon the bottomless bog of the stratum of the Workless. It is here where we must begin. The regimentation of industrial workers who have got regular work is not so very difficult. That can be done, and is being done, by themselves. The problem that we have to face is the regimentation, the organization, of those who have not got work, or who have only irregular work, and who from sheer pressure of absolute starvation are driven irresistibly into cut-throat competition with their better employed brothers and sisters. Skin for skin, all that a man hath, will be given for his life; much more, then, will those who experimentally know not God give all that they might hope hereafter to have—in this world or in the world to come.

There is no gainsaying the immensity of the problem. It is appalling enough to make us despair. But those who do not put their trust in man alone, but in One who is Almighty, have no right to despair. To despair is to lose faith; to despair is to forget God. Without God we can do nothing in this frightful chaos of human misery. But with God we can do all things, and in the faith that He has made in His image all the children of men we face even this hideous wreckage of humanity with a cheerful confidence that if we are but faithful to our own high calling He will not fail to open up a way of deliverance.

I have nothing to say against those who are endeavoring to open up a way of escape without any consciousness of God's help. For them I feel only sympathy and compassion. In so far as they are endeavoring to give bread to the hungry, clothing to the naked, and above all, work to the workless, they are to that extent endeavoring to do the will of our Father which is in Heaven, and woe be unto all those who say them nay! But to be orphaned of all sense of the Fatherhood of God is surely not a secret source of strength. It is in most cases—it would be in my own—the secret of paralysis. If I did not feel my Father's hand in the darkness, and hear His voice in the silence of the-night watches bidding me put my hand to this thing, I would shrink back dismayed;—but as it is I dare not.

How many are there who have made similar attempts and have failed, and we have heard of them no more! Yet none of them proposed to deal with more than the mere fringe of the evil which, God helping me, I will try to face in all its immensity. Most Schemes that are put forward for the Improvement of the Circumstances of the People are either avowedly or actually limited to those whose condition least needs amelioration. The Utopians, the economists, and most of the philanthropists propound remedies, which if adopted tomorrow, would only affect the aristocracy of the miserable. It is the thrifty, the industrious, the sober, the thoughtful who can take advantage of these plans. But the thrifty, the industrious, the sober, and the thoughtful are already very well able for the most part to take care of themselves. No one will ever make even a visible dint on the Morass of Squalor who does not deal with the improvident, the lazy, the vicious, and the criminal. The Scheme of Social Salvation is not worth discussion which is not as wide as the Scheme of Eternal Salvation set forth in the Gospel. The Glad Tidings must be to every creature, not merely to an elect few who are to be saved while the mass of their fellows are predestined to a temporal damnation. We have had this doctrine of an inhuman cast-iron pseudo-political economy too long enthroned amongst us. It is now time to fling down the false idol, and proclaim a Temporal Salvation as full, free, and universal, and with no other limitations than the "Whosoever will," of the Gospel.

To attempt to save the Lost, we must accept no limitations to human brotherhood. If the Scheme which I set forth in these and the following pages is not applicable to the Thief, the Harlot, the Drunkard, and the Sluggard, it may as well be dismissed without ceremony. As Christ came to call not the saints but sinners to repentance, so the New Message of Temporal Salvation, of salvation from pinching poverty, from rags and misery, must be offered to all.

They may reject it, of course. But we who call ourselves by the name of Christ are not worthy to profess to be His disciples until we have set an open door before the least and worst of these who are now apparently imprisoned for life in a horrible dungeon of misery and despair. The responsibility for its rejection must be theirs, not ours. We all know the prayer "Give me neither poverty nor riches, feed me with food convenient for me"—and for every child of man on this planet, thank God the prayer of Agur, the son of Jakeh, may be fulfilled.

At present how far it is from being realized may be seen by anyone who will take the trouble to go down to the docks and see the struggle for work. Here is a sketch of what was found there this summer:—

London Docks, 7.25 a. m. The three pairs of huge wooden doors are closed. Leaning against them, and standing about, there are perhaps a couple of hundred men. The public house opposite is full, doing a heavy trade. All along the road are groups of men, and from each direction a steady stream increases the crowd at the gate.

7:30. Doors open, there is a general rush to the interior. Everybody marches about a hundred yards along to the iron barrier—a temporary chain affair, guarded by the dock police. Those men who have previously (i.e., night before) been engaged, show their ticket and pass through, about six hundred. The rest—some five hundred—stand behind the barrier, patiently waiting the chance of a job, but less than twenty of these get engaged. They are taken on by a foreman who appears next the barrier and proceeds to pick his men. No sooner is the foreman seen, than there is a wild rush to the spot and a sharp, mad fight to "catch his eye." The men picked out, pass the barrier, and the excitement dies away until another lot of men are wanted.

They wait until eight o'clock strikes, which is the signal to withdraw. The barrier is taken down and all those hundreds of men, wearily disperse to "find a job." Five hundred applicants, twenty acceptances! No wonder one tired-out looking individual ejaculates, "Oh dear, Oh dear! Whatever shall I do?" A few hang about until mid-day on the slender chance of getting taken on then for a half day.

Ask the men and they will tell you something like the following story, which gives the simple experiences of a dock laborer.

R. P. said:—"I was in regular work at the South West India Docks before the strike. We got 5d. an hour. Start work 8 a. m. summer and 9 a. m. winter. Often there would be five hundred go, and only twenty get taken on (that is besides those engaged the night previous.) The foreman stood in his box, and called out the men he wanted. He would know quite five hundred by name. It was a regular fight to get work, I have known nine hundred to be taken on, but there's always hundreds turned away. You see they get to know -when ships come in, and when they're consequently likely to be wanted, and turn up then in greater numbers. I would earn 30s. a week sometimes and then perhaps nothing for a fortnight That's what °makes it so hard. You get nothing to eat for a week scarcely, and then when you get taken on, you are so weak that you can't do it properly. I've stood in the crowd at the gate and had to go away without work, hundreds of times. Still I should go at it again if I could. I got tired of the little work and went away into the country to get work on a farm, but couldn't get it, so I'm without the 10s. that it costs to join the Dockers' Union. I'm going to the country again in a day or two to try again. Expect to get 3s. a day perhaps. Shall come back to the docks again. There is a chance of getting regular dock work, and that is, to lounge about the pubs, where the foremen go, and treat them. Then they will very likely take you on next day."

R. P. was a non-Unionist. Henry F. is a Unionist. His history is much the same.

"I worked at St. Katherine's Docks five months ago. You have to get to the gates at 6 o'clock for the first call. There's generally about 400 waiting. They will take on one to two hundred. Then at 7

o'clock there's a second call. Another 400 will have gathered by then, and another hundred or so will be taken on. Also there will probably be calls at nine and one o'clock. About the same number turn up but there's no work for many hundreds of them. I was a Union man. That means 10s. a week sick pay, or 8s. a week for slight accidents; also some other advantages. The Docks won't take men on now unless they are Unionists. The point is that there's too many men. I would often be out of work a fortnight to three weeks at a time. Once earned £3 in a week working day and night, but then had a fortnight out directly after. Especially when there don't happen to be any ships in for a few days, which means, of course, nothing to unload. That's the time; there's plenty of men almost starving then. They have no trade to go to, or can get no work at it, and they swoop down to the docks for work, when they had much better stay away."

But it is not only at the dock-gates that you come upon these unfortunates who spend their lives in the vain hunt for work. Here is the story of another man whose case has only too many parallels.

C. is a fine built man, standing nearly six feet. He has been in the Royal Artillery for eight years and held very good situations whilst in it. It seems that he was thrifty and consequently steady. He bought his discharge, and being an excellent cook opened a refreshment house, but at the end of five months he was compelled to close his shop on account of slackness in trade, which was brought about by the closing of a large factory in the locality.

After having worked in Scotland and Newcastle-on-Tyne for a few years, and through ill health having to give up his situation, he came to London with the hope that he might get something to do in his native town. He has had no regular employment for the past eight months. His wife and family are in a state of destitution, and he remarked, "We only had 1 lb. of bread between us yesterday." He is six weeks in arrears of rent, and is afraid that he will be ejected. The furniture which is in his home is not worth 3s. and the clothes of each member of his family are in a tattered state and hardly fit for the rag bag. He assured us he had tried everywhere to get employment and would be willing to take anything. His characters are very good indeed.

Now, it may seem a preposterous dream that any arrangement can be devised by which it may be possible, under all circumstances, to provide food, clothes, and shelter for all these Out-of-Works without any loss of self respect; but I am convinced that it can be done, providing only that they are willing to Work, and, God helping me, if the means are forthcoming, I mean to try to do it; how, and where, and when, I will explain in subsequent chapters.

All that I need to say here is, that so long as a man or woman is willing to submit to the discipline indispensable in every campaign against any formidable foe, there appears to me nothing impossible about this ideal; and the great element of hope before us is that the majority are, beyond all gainsaying, eager for work. Most of them now do more exhausting work in seeking for employment than the regular toilers do in their workshops, and do it, too, under the darkness of hope deferred which maketh the heart sick.

CHAPTER V

On the Verge of the Abyss

There is, unfortunately, no need for me to attempt to set out, however imperfectly, any statement of the evil case of the sufferers whom we wish to help. For years past the Press has been filled with echoes of the "Bitter Cry of Outcast London," with pictures of "Horrible Glasgow," and the like. We have had several volumes describing "How the Poor Live," and I may therefore assume that all my readers are more or less cognizant of the main outlines of "Darkest England." My slum officers are living in the midst of it; their reports are before me, and one day I may publish some more detailed account of the actual facts of the social condition of the Sunken Millions. But not now. All that must be taken as read. I only glance at the subject in order to bring into clear relief the salient points of our new Enterprize.

I have spoken of the houseless poor. Each of these represents a point in the scale of human suffering below that of those who have still contrived to keep a shelter over their heads. A home is a home, be it ever so low; and the desperate tenacity with which the poor will cling to the last wretched semblance of one is very touching. There are vile dens, fever-haunted and stenchful crowded courts, where the return of summer is dreaded because it means the unloosing of myriads of vermin which render night unbearable, which, nevertheless, are regarded at this moment as havens of rest by their hard-working occupants. They can scarcely be said to be furnished. A chair, a mattress, and a few miserable sticks constitute all the furniture of the single room in which they have to sleep, and breed, and die; but they cling to it as a drowning man to a half-submerged raft. Every week they contrive by pinching and scheming to raise the rent, for with them it is pay or go; and they struggle to meet the collector as the sailor nerves himself to avoid being sucked under by the foaming wave. If at any time work fails or sickness comes they are liable to drop helplessly into the ranks of the homeless. It is bad for a single man to have to confront the struggle for life in the streets and Casual Wards. But how much more terrible must it be for the married man with his wife and children to be turned out into the streets. So long as the family has a lair into which it can creep at night, he keeps his footing; but when he loses that solitary foothold then arrives the time if there be such a thing as Christian compassion, for the helping hand to be held out to save him from the vortex that sucks him downward—ay, downward to the hopeless under-strata of crime and despair.

"The heart knoweth its own bitterness and the stranger intermeddleth not therewith." But now and then out of the depths there sounds a bitter wail as of some strong swimmer in his agony as he is drawn under by the current. A short time ago a respectable man, a chemist in Holloway, fifty years of age, driven hard to the wall, tried to end it all by cutting his throat. His wife also cut her throat, and at the same time they gave strychnine to their only child. The effort failed, and they were placed on trial for attempted murder. In the Court a letter was read which the poor wretch had written before attempting his life:—

MY DEAREST GEORGE,—Twelve months have I now passed of a most miserable and struggling existence, and I really cannot stand it any more. I am completely worn out, and relations who could assist me won't do any more, for such was uncle's last intimation. Never mind; he can't take his money and comfort with him, and in all probability will find himself in the same boat as myself. He never enquires whether I am starving or not. £3—a mere flea-bite to him—would have put us straight, and with his security and good interest might have obtained me a good situation long ago. I can face poverty and degradation no longer, and would sooner die than go to the workhouse, whatever may be the awful consequences of the steps we have taken. We have, God forgive us, taken our darling Arty with us out of pure love and affection, so that the darling should never be cuffed about, or reminded or taunted with his heartbroken parents' crime. My poor wife has done her best at needle-work, washing, house-minding, etc., in fact, anything and everything that would bring in a shilling; but it would only keep us in semi-starvation. I have now done six weeks' travelling from morning till night, and not received one farthing for it. If that is not enough to drive you mad—wickedly mad—I don't know what is. No bright prospect anywhere; no ray of hope.

May God Almighty forgive us for this heinous sin, and have mercy on our sinful souls, is the prayer of your miserable, broken-hearted, but loving brother, Arthur. We have now done everything that we can possibly think of to avert this wicked proceeding, but can discover no ray of hope. Fervent prayer has availed us nothing; our lot is cast, and we must abide by it. It must be God's will or He would have ordained it differently. Dearest Georgy, I am exceedingly sorry to leave you all, but I am mad—thoroughly mad. You, dear, must try and forget us, and, if possible, forgive us; for I do not consider it our own fault we have not succeeded. If you could get £3 for our bed it will pay our rent, and our scanty furniture may fetch enough to bury us in a cheap way. Don't grieve over us or follow us, for we shall not be worthy of such respect. Our clergyman has never called on us or given us the least consolation, though I called on him a month ago. He is paid to preach, and there he considers his responsibility ends, the rich excepted. We have only yourself and a very few others who care one pin what becomes of us, but you must try and forgive us, is the last fervent prayer of your devotedly fond and affectionate but broken-hearted and persecuted brother. (Signed) R. A. O—.

That is an authentic human document—a transcript from the life of one among thousands who go down inarticulate into the depths. They die and make no sign, or, worse still, they continue to exist, carrying about with them, year after year, the bitter ashes of a life from which the furnace of misfortune has burnt away all joy, and hope, and strength. Who is there who has not been confronted by many despairing ones, who come, as Richard 0—went, to the clergyman, crying for help, and how seldom have we been able to give it them? It is unjust, no doubt, for them to blame the clergy and the comfortable well-to-do—for what can they do but preach and offer good advice? To assist all the Richard O—'s by direct financial advance would drag even Rothschild into the gutter. And what else can be done? Yet something else must be done if Christianity is not to be a mockery to perishing men. Here is another case, a very common case, which illustrates how the Army of Despair is recruited.

Mr. T., Margaret Place, Gascoign Place, Bethnal Green, is a boot-maker by trade. Is a good hand,

and has earned three shillings and sixpence to four shillings and sixpence a day. He was taken ill last Christmas, and went to the London Hospital; was there three months. A week after he had gone Mrs. T. had rheumatic fever, and was taken to Bethnal Green Infirmary, where she remained about three months. Directly after they had been taken ill, their furniture was seized for the three weeks' rent which was owing. Consequently, on becoming convalescent, they were homeless. They came out about the same time. He went out to a lodging-house for a night or two, until she came out. He then had twopence, and she had sixpence, which a nurse had given her. They went to a lodging-house together, but the society there was dreadful. Next day he had a day's work, and got two shillings and sixpence, and on the strength of this they took a furnished room at tenpence per day (payable nightly). His work lasted a few weeks, when he was again taken ill, lost his job, and spent all their money. Pawned a shirt and apron for a shilling; spent that, too. At last pawned their tools for three shillings, which got them a few days' food and lodging. He is now minus tools and cannot work at his own job, and does anything he can. Spent their last twopence on a pen'orth each of tea and sugar. In two days they had a slice of bread and butter each, that's all. They are both very weak through want of food.

"Let things alone," the laws of supply and demand, and all the rest of the excuses by which those who stand on firm ground salve their consciences when they leave their brother to sink, how do they look when we apply them to the actual loss of life at sea? Does "Let things alone" man the lifeboat? Will the inexorable laws of political economy save the shipwrecked sailor from the boiling surf? They often enough are responsible for his disaster. Coffin ships are a direct result of the wretched policy of non-interference with the legitimate operations of commerce, but no desire to make it pay created the National Lifeboat Institution, no law of supply and demand actuates the volunteers who risk their lives to bring the shipwrecked to shore.

What we have to do is to apply the same principle to society. We want a Social Lifeboat Institution, a Social Lifeboat Brigade, to snatch from the abyss those who, if left to themselves, will perish as miserably as the crew of a ship that founders in mid-ocean.

The moment that we take in hand this work we shall be compelled to turn our attention seriously to the question whether prevention is not better than cure. It is easier and cheaper, and in every way better, to prevent the loss of home than to have to re-create that home. It is better to keep a man out of the mire than to let him fall in first and then risk the chance of plucking him out. Any Scheme, therefore, that attempts to deal with the reclamation of the lost must tend to develop into an endless variety of ameliorative measures, of some of which I shall have somewhat to say hereafter. I only mention the subject here in order that no one may say I am blind to the necessity of going further and adopting wider plans of operation than those which I put forward in this book. The renovation of our Social System is a work so vast that no one of us, nor all of us put together, can define all the measures that will have to be taken before we attain even the Cab-Horse Ideal of existence for our children and children's children. All that we can do is to attack, in a serious, practical spirit the worst and most pressing evils, knowing that if we do our duty we obey the voice of God. He is the Captain of our Salvation. If we but follow where He leads we shall not want for marching orders, nor need we imagine that He will narrow the field of operations.

I am laboring under no delusions as to the possibility of inaugurating the Millennium by any social specific. In the struggle of life the weakest will go to the wall, and there are so many weak. The fittest, in tooth and claw, will survive. All that we can do is to soften the lot of the unfit and make their suffering less horrible than it is at present. No amount of assistance will give a jellyfish a backbone. No outside propping will make some men stand erect. All material help from without is useful only in so far as it develops moral strength within. And some men seem to have lost even the very faculty of self-help. There is an immense lack of common sense and of vital energy on the part of multitudes.

It is against Stupidity in every shape and form that we have to wage our eternal battle. But how can we wonder at the want of sense on the part of those who have had no advantages, when we see such plentiful absence of that commodity on the part of those who have had all the advantages?

How can we marvel if, after leaving generation after generation to grow up uneducated and underfed, there should be developed a heredity of incapacity, and that thousands of dull-witted people should be born into the world, disinherited before their birth of their share in the average intelligence of mankind?

Besides those who are thus hereditarily wanting in the qualities necessary to enable them to hold their own, there are the weak, the disabled, the aged, and the unskilled; worse than all, there is the want of character. Those who have the best of reputation, if they lose their foothold on the ladder, find it difficult enough to regain their place. What, then, can men and women who have no character do? When a master has the choice of a hundred honest men, is it reasonable to expect that he will select a poor fellow with tarnished reputation?

All this is true, and it is one of the things that makes the problem almost insoluble. And insoluble it is, I am absolutely convinced, unless it is possible to bring new moral life into the soul of these people. This should be the first object of every social reformer, whose work will only last if it is built on the solid foundation of a new birth, to cry "You must be born again."

To get a man soundly saved it is not enough to put on him a pair of new breeches, to give him regular work, or even to give him a University education. These things are all outside a man, and if the inside remains unchanged you have wasted your labor. You must in some way or other graft upon the man's nature a new nature, which has in it the element of the Divine. All that I propose in this book is governed by that principle.

The difference between the method which seeks to regenerate the man by ameliorating his circumstances and that which ameliorates his circumstances in order to get at the regeneration of his heart, is the difference between the method of the gardener who grafts a Ribstone Pippin on a crab-apple tree and one who merely ties apples with string upon the branches of the crab. To change the nature of the individual, to get at the heart, to save his soul is the only real, lasting method of doing him any good. In many modern schemes of social regeneration it is forgotten that "'it takes a soul to move a body, e'en to a cleaner sty," and at the risk of being misunderstood and misrepresented, I must assert in the most unqualified way that it is primarily and mainly for the sake of saving the soul that I seek the salvation of the body.

But what is the use of preaching the Gospel to men whose whole attention is concentrated upon a mad, desperate struggle to keep themselves alive? You might as well give a tract to a shipwrecked sailor who is battling with the surf which has drowned his comrades and threatens to drown him. He will not listen to you. Nay, he cannot hear you any more than a man whose head is under water can listen to a sermon. The first thing to do is to get him at least a footing on firm ground, and to give him room to live. Then you may have a chance. At present you have none. And you will have all the better opportunity to find a way to his heart, if he comes to know that it was you who pulled him out of the horrible pit and the miry clay in which he was sinking to perdition.

CHAPTER VI

The Vicious

There are many vices and seven deadly sins. But of late years many of the seven have contrived to pass themselves off as virtues. Avarice, for instance; and Pride, when re-baptized thrift and self-respect, have become the guardian angels of Christian civilization; and as for Envy, it is the corner-stone upon which much of our competitive system is founded. There are still two vices which are fortunate, or unfortunate, enough to remain undisguised, not even concealing from themselves the fact that they are vices and not virtues. One is drunkenness; the other fornication. The viciousness of these vices is so little disguised, even from those who habitually practice them, that there will be a protest against merely describing one of them by the right Biblical name. Why not say prostitution? For this reason: prostitution is a word applied to only one half of the vice, and that the most pitiable. Fornication hits both sinners alike. Prostitution applies only to the woman.

When, however, we cease to regard this vice from the point of view of morality and religion, and look at it solely as a factor in the social problem, the word prostitution is less objectionable: For the social burden of this vice is borne almost entirely by women. The male sinner does not, by the mere fact of his sin, find himself in a worse position in obtaining employment, in finding a home, or even in securing a wife. His wrong-doing only hits him in his purse, or, perhaps, in his health. His incontinence, excepting so far as it relates to the woman whose degradation it necessitates, does not add to the number of those for whom society has to provide. It is an immense addition to the infamy of this vice in man that its consequences have to be borne almost exclusively by woman.

The difficulty of dealing with drunkards and harlots is almost insurmountable. Were it not that I utterly repudiate as a fundamental denial of the essential principle of the Christian religion the popular pseudo-scientific doctrine that any man or woman is past saving by the grace of God and the power of the Holy Spirit, I would sometimes be disposed to despair when contemplating these victims of the Devil. The doctrine of Heredity and the suggestion of Irresponsibility come perilously near re-establishing, on scientific bases, the awful dogma of Reprobation which has cast so terrible a shadow over the Christian Church. For thousands upon thousands of these poor wretches are, as Bishop South truly said, "not so much born into this world as damned into it." The bastard of a harlot, born in a brothel, suckled on gin, and familiar from earliest infancy with all the bestialities of debauch, violated before she is twelve, and driven out into the streets by her mother a year or two later, what chance is there for such a girl in this world—I say nothing about the next? Yet such a case is not exceptional. There are many such differing in detail, but in essentials the same. And with boys it is almost as bad. There are thousands who were begotten when both parents were besotted with drink, whose mothers saturated themselves with alcohol every day of their pregnancy, who may be said to have sucked in a taste for strong drink with their mothers' milk, and who were surrounded from childhood with opportunities and incitements to drink. How can we marvel that the constitution thus disposed to intemperance finds the stimulus of drink indispensable? Even if they make a stand against it, the increasing pressure of exhaustion and of scanty food drives them back to the cup. Of these poor wretches, born slaves of the bottle, predestined to drunkenness from their mother's womb, there are—who can say how many? Yet they are all men; all with what the Russian peasants call "a spark of God" in them, which can never be wholly obscured and destroyed while life exists, and if any social scheme is to be comprehensive and practical it must deal with these men. It must provide for the drunkard and the harlot as it provides for the improvident and the out-of-work. But who is sufficient for these things?

I will take the question of the drunkard, for the drink difficulty lies at the root of everything. Nine-tenths of our poverty, squalor, vice, and crime spring from this poisonous taproot. Many of our social evils, which overshadow the land like so many upas trees, would dwindle away and die if they were not constantly watered with strong drink. There is universal agreement on that point; in fact, the agreement as to the evils of intemperance is almost as universal as the conviction that politicians will do nothing practical to interfere with them. In Ireland, Mr. Justice Fitzgerald says that intemperance leads to nineteen-twentieths of the crime in that country, but no one proposes a Coercion Act to deal with that evil. In England, the judges all say the same thing. Of course it is a mistake to assume that a murder, for instance, would never be committed by sober men, because murderers in most cases prime themselves for their deadly work by a glass of Dutch courage. But the facility of securing a reinforcement of passion undoubtedly tends to render always dangerous, and sometimes irresistible, the temptation to violate the laws of God and man.

Mere lectures against the evil habit are, however, of no avail. We have to recognize that the gin-palace, like many other evils, although a poisonous, is still a natural outgrowth of our social conditions. The tap-room in many cases is the poor man's only parlor. Many a man takes to beer, not from the love of beer, but from a natural craving for the light, warmth, company, and comfort which is thrown in along with the beer, and which he cannot get excepting by buying beer. Reformers will never get rid of the drink shop until they can outbid it in the subsidiary attractions which it offers to its customers. Then, again, let us never forget that the temptation to drink is strongest when want is sharpest and misery the most acute. A well-fed man is not driven to drink by the craving that torments the hungry; and the comfortable do not crave for the boon of forgetfulness. Gin is the only Lethe of the miserable. The foul and poisoned air of the dens in which thousands live predisposes to a longing for stimulant. Fresh air, with its oxygen and its ozone, being lacking, a man supplies the want with spirit. After a time the longing for drink becomes a mania. Life seems as insupportable without alcohol as without food. It is a disease often inherited, always developed by indulgence, but as clearly a disease as ophthalmia or stone.

All this should predispose us to charity and sympathy. While recognizing that the primary responsibility must always rest upon the individual, we may fairly insist that society, which, by its habits, its customs, and its laws, has greased the slope down which these poor creatures slide to perdition, shall seriously take in hand their salvation.

How many are there who are, more or less, under the dominion of strong drink? Statistics abound, but they seldom tell us what we want to know. We know how many public-houses there are in the land, and how many arrests for drunkenness the police make in a year; but beyond that we know little. Everyone knows that for one man who is arrested for drunkenness there are at least ten—and often twenty—who go home intoxicated. In London, for instance, there are 14,000 drink shops, and every year 20,000 persons are arrested for drunkenness. But who can for a moment believe that there are only 20,000, more or less, habitual drunkards in London? By habitual drunkard I do not mean one who is always drunk, but one who is so much under the dominion of the evil habit that he cannot be depended upon not to get drunk whenever the opportunity offers.

In the United Kingdom there are 190,000 public-houses, and every year there are 200,000 arrests for drunkenness. Of course, several of these arrests refer to the same person, who is locked up again and again. Were this not so, if we allowed six drunkards to each house as an average, or five habitual drunkards for one arrested for drunkenness, we should arrive at a total of a million adults who are more or less prisoners of the publican—as a matter of fact, Isaac Hoyle gives 1 in 12 of the adult population. This may be an excessive estimate, but, if we take half of a million, we shall not be accused of exaggeration. Of these some are in the last stage of confirmed dipsomania; others are but over the verge; but the procession tends ever downwards.

The loss which the maintenance of this huge standing army of a half of a million of men who are more or less always besotted men whose intemperance impairs their working power, consumes their earnings, and renders their homes wretched, has long been a familiar theme of the platform. But what can be done for them? Total abstinence is no doubt admirable, but how are you to get them to be totally abstinent? When a man is drowning in mid-ocean the one thing that is needful, no doubt, is that he should plant his feet firmly on terra firma. But how is he to get there? It is just what he cannot do. And so it is with the drunkards. If they are to be rescued there must be something more done for them than at present is attempted, unless, of course, we decide definitely to allow the iron laws of nature to work themselves out in their destruction. In that case it might be more merciful to facilitate the slow workings of natural law. There is no need of establishing a lethal chamber for drunkards like that into which the lost dogs of London are driven, to die in peaceful sleep under the influence of carbonic oxide. The State would only need to go a little further than it goes at present in the way of supplying poison to the community. If, in addition to planting a flaming gin palace at each corner, free to all who enter, it were to supply free gin to all who have attained a certain recognized standard of inebriety, delirium tremens would soon reduce our drunken population to manageable proportions. I can imagine a cynical millionaire of the scientific philanthropic school making a clearance of all the drunkards in a district by the simple expedient of an unlimited allowance of alcohol. But that for us is out of the question. The problem of what to do with our half of a million drunkards remains to be solved, and few more difficult questions confront the social reformer.

The question of the harlots is, however, quite as insoluble by the ordinary methods. For these unfortunates no one who looks below the surface can fail to have the deepest sympathy. Some there are, no doubt, perhaps many, who—whether from inherited passion or from evil education—have deliberately embarked upon a life of vice, but with the majority it is not so. Even those who deliberately and of free choice adopt the profession of a prostitute, do so under the stress of temptations which few moralists seem to realize. Terrible as the fact is, there is no doubt it is a fact that there is no industrial career in which for a short time a beautiful girl can make as much money with as little trouble as the profession of a courtesan. The case recently tried at the Lewes assizes, in which the wife of an officer in the army admitted that while living as a kept mistress she had received as much as £4,000 a year, was no doubt very exceptional. Even the most successful adventuresses seldom make the income of a Cabinet Minister. But take women in professions and in businesses all round, and the number of young women who have received £500 in one year for the sale of their person is larger than the number of women of all ages who make a similar sum by honest industry. It is only the very few who draw these gilded prizes, and they only do it for a very short time. But it is the few prizes in every profession which allure the multitude, who think little of the many blanks. And speaking broadly, vice offers to every good-looking girl during the first bloom of her youth and beauty more money than she can earn by labor in any field of industry open to her sex. The penalty exacted afterwards is disease, degradation and death, but these things at first are hidden from her sight.

The profession of a prostitute is the only career in which the maximum income is paid to the newest apprentice. It is the one calling in which at the beginning the only exertion is that of self-indulgence; all the prizes are at the commencement. It is the ever-new embodiment of the old fable of the sale of the soul to the Devil. The tempter offers wealth, comfort, excitement, but in return the victim must sell her soul, nor does the other party forget to exact his due to the uttermost farthing. Human nature, however, is short-sighted. Giddy girls, chafing against the restraints of uncongenial industry, see the glittering bait continually before them. They are told that if they will but "do as others do" they will make more in a night, if they are lucky, than they can make in a week at their sewing; and who can wonder that in many cases the irrevocable step is taken before they realize that it is irrevocable, and that they have bartered away the future of their lives for the paltry chance of a year's ill-gotten gains?

Of the severity of the punishment there can be no question. If the premium is high at the beginning, the penalty is terrible at the close. And this penalty is exacted equally from those who have deliberately said, "Evil, be thou my Good," and for those who have been decoyed, snared, trapped into the life which is a living death. When you see a girl on the street you can never say without enquiry whether she is one of the most-to-be condemned, or the most-to-be pitied of her sex. Many of them find themselves where they are because of a too trusting disposition, confidence born of innocence being often the unsuspecting ally of the procuress and seducer. Others are as much the innocent victims of crime as if they had been stabbed or maimed by the dagger of the assassin. The records of our Rescue Homes abound with life stories, some of which we have been able to verify to the letter—which prove only too conclusively the existence of numbers of innocent victims whose entry upon this dismal life can in no way be attributed to any act of their own will. Many are orphans or the children of depraved mothers, whose one idea of a daughter is to make money out of her prostitution. Here are a few cases on our register:—

E. C., aged 18, a soldier's child, born on the sea. Her father died, and her mother, a thoroughly depraved woman, assisted to secure her daughter's prostitution.

P. S., aged 20, illegitimate child. Went to consult a doctor one time about some ailment. The doctor abused his position and took advantage of his patient, and when she complained, gave her £4 as compensation. When that was spent, having lost her character, she came on the town. We looked the doctor up, and he fled.

E. A., aged 17, was left an orphan very early in life, and adopted by her godfather, who himself was the means of her ruin at the age of 10.

A girl in her teens lived with her mother in the "Dusthole," the lowest part of Woolwich. This woman forced her out upon the streets, and profited by her prostitution up to the very night of her confinement. The mother had all the time been the receiver of the gains.

E., neither father nor mother, was taken care of by a grandmother till, at an early age, accounted old enough. Married a soldier; but shortly before the birth of her first child, found that her deceiver had a wife and family in a distant part of the country, and she was soon left- friendless and alone. She sought an asylum in the Workhouse for a few weeks, after which she vainly tried to get honest employment. Failing that, and being on the very verge of starvation, she entered a lodging-house in Westminster and "did as other girls." Here our lieutenant found and persuaded her to leave and enter one of our Homes, where she soon gave abundant proof of her conversion by a thoroughly changed life. She is now a faithful and trusted servant in a clergyman's family.

A girl was some time ago discharged from a city hospital after an illness. She was homeless and friendless, an orphan, and obliged to work for her living. Walking down the street and wondering what she should do next, she met a girl, who came up to her in a most friendly fashion and speedily won her confidence.

"Discharged ill, and nowhere to go, are you?" said her new friend. "Well, come home to my mother's; she will lodge you, and we'll go to work together, when you are quite strong."

The girl consented gladly, but found herself conducted to the very lowest part of Woolwich and ushered into a brothel; there was no mother in the case. She was hoaxed, and powerless to resist. Her protestations were too late to save her, and having had her character forced from her she became hopeless, and stayed on to live the life of her false friend.

There is no need for me to go into the details of the way in which men and women, whose whole livelihood depends upon their success in disarming the suspicions of their victims and luring them to their doom, contrive to overcome the reluctance of the young girl without parents, friends, or helpers to enter their toils. What fraud fails to accomplish, a little force succeeds in effecting; and a girl who has been guilty of nothing but imprudence finds herself an outcast for life.

The very innocence of a girl tells against her. A woman of the world, once entrapped, would have all her wits about her to extricate herself from the position in which she found herself. A perfectly virtuous girl is often so overcome with shame and horror that there seems nothing in life worth struggling for. She accepts her doom without further struggle, and treads the long and torturing path-way of "the streets" to the grave.

"Judge not, that ye be not judged" is a saying that applies most appropriately of all to these unfortunates. Many of them would have escaped their evil fate had they been less innocent. They are where they are because they loved too utterly to calculate consequences, and trusted too absolutely to dare to suspect evil, And others are there because of the false education which confounds ignorance with virtue, and throws our young people into the midst of a great city, with all its excitements and all its temptations, without more preparation or warning than if they were going to live in the Garden of Eden.

Whatever sin they have committed, a terrible penalty is exacted. While the man who caused their ruin passes as a respectable member of society, to whom virtuous matrons gladly marry—if he is rich—their maiden daughters, they are crushed beneath the millstone of social excommunication.

Here let me quote from a report made to me by the head of our Rescue Homes as to the actual life of these unfortunates.

The following hundred cases are taken as they come from our Rescue Register. The statements are those of the girls themselves. They are certainly frank, and it will be noticed that only two out of the hundred allege that they took to the life out of poverty:—

CAUSE OF FALL		CONDITION WHEN APPLYING	
Drink	14		
Seduction	33		
Wilful choice	24	Rags	25
Bad company	27	Destitution	27
Poverty	2	Decently dressed	48
Total	100		100

Out of these girls twenty-three have been in prison.

The girls suffer so much that the shortness of their miserable life is the only redeeming feature. Whether we look at the wretchedness of the life itself; their perpetual intoxication; the cruel treatment to which they are subjected by their taskmasters and mistresses or bullies; the hopelessness, suffering and despair induced by their circumstances and surroundings; the depths of misery, degradation and poverty to which they eventually descend; or their treatment in sickness, their friendlessness and loneliness in death, it must be admitted that a more dismal lot seldom falls to the fate of a human being. I will take each of these in turn.

HEALTH.—This life induces insanity, rheumatism, consumption, and all forms of syphilis. Rheumatism and gout are the commonest of these evils. Some were quite crippled by both—young though they were. Consumption sows its seeds broadcast. The life is a hot-bed for the development of any constitutional and hereditary germs of the disease. We have found girls in Piccadilly at midnight who are continually prostrated by hemorrhage, yet who have no other way of life open, so struggle on in this awful manner between whiles.

DRINK.—This is an inevitable part of the business. All confess that they could never lead their miserable lives if it were not for its influence.

A girl, who was educated at college, and who had a home in which was every comfort, but who, when ruined, had fallen even to the depth of Woolwich "Dusthole," exclaimed to us indignantly—"Do you think I could ever, ever do this if it weren't for the drink? I always have to be in drink if I want to sin." No girl has ever come into our Homes *from street-life* but has been more or less a prey to drink.

323

CRUEL TREATMENT.—The devotion of these women to their bullies is as remarkable as the brutality of their bullies is abominable. Probably the primary cause of the fall of numberless girls of the lower class, is their great aspiration to the dignity of wifehood;—they are never "somebody" until they are married, and will link themselves to any creature, no matter how debased, in the hope of being ultimately married by him. This consideration, in addition to their helpless condition when once character has gone, makes them suffer cruelties which they would never otherwise endure from the men with whom large numbers of them live.

One case in illustration of this is that of a girl who was once a respectable servant, the daughter of a police sergeant. She was ruined, and shame led her to leave home. At length she drifted to Woolwich, where she came across a man who persuaded her to live with him, and for a considerable length of time she kept him, although his conduct to her was brutal in the extreme.

The girl living in the next room to her has frequently heard him knock her head against the wall, and *pound* it, when he was out of temper, through her gains of prostitution being less than usual. He lavished upon her every sort of cruelty and abuse, and at length she grew so wretched, and was reduced to so dreadful a plight, that she ceased to attract. At this he became furious, and pawned all her clothing but one thin garment of rags. The week before her first confinement he kicked her black and blue from neck to knees, and she was carried to the police station in a pool of blood, but she was so loyal to the wretch that she refused to appear against him.

She was going to drown herself in desperation, when our Rescue Officers spoke to her, wrapped their own shawl around her shivering shoulders, took her home with them, and cared for her. The baby was born dead—a tiny, shapeless mass.

This state of things is all too common.

HOPELESSNESS—SURROUNDINGS.—The state of hopelessness and despair in which these girls live continually, makes them reckless of consequences, and large numbers commit suicide who are never heard of. A West End policeman assured us that the number of prostitute-suicides was terribly in advance of anything guessed at by the public.

DEPTHS TO WHICH THEY SINK.—There is scarcely a lower class of girls to be found than the girls of Woolwich "Dusthole"—where one of our Rescue Slum Homes is established. The women living and following their dreadful business in this neighborhood are so degraded that even abandoned men will refuse to accompany them home. Soldiers are forbidden to enter the place, or to go down the street, on pain of twenty-five days' imprisonment; pickets are stationed at either end to prevent this. The streets are much cleaner than many of the rooms we have seen.

One public house there is shut up three or four times in a day sometimes for fear of losing the license through the terrible brawls which take place within. A policeman never goes down this street alone at night—one having died not long ago from injuries received there—but our two lasses go unharmed and loved at all hours, spending every other night always upon the streets.

The girls sink to the "Dusthole" after coming down several grades. There is but one on record who came there with beautiful clothes, and this poor girl, when last seen by the officers, was a pauper in the workhouse infirmary in a wretched condition.

The lowest class of all is the girls who stand at the pier-head—these sell themselves literally for a bare crust of bread and sleep in the streets.

Filth and vermin abound to an extent to which no one who has not seen it can have any idea.

The "Dusthole" is only one, alas, of many similar districts in this highly civilized land.

SICKNESS, FRIENDLESSNESS—DEATH.—In hospitals it is a known fact that these girls are not treated at all like other cases; they inspire disgust, and are most frequently discharged before being really cured.

Scorned by their relations, and ashamed to make their case known even to those who would help them, unable longer to struggle out on the streets to earn the bread of shame, there are girls lying in many a dark hole in this big city positively rotting away, and maintained by their old companions on the streets.

Many are totally friendless, utterly cast out and left to perish by relatives and friends. One of this class came to us, sickened and died, and we buried her, being her only followers to the grave.

It is a sad story, but one that must not be forgotten, for these women constitute a large standing army whose numbers no one can calculate. All estimates that I have seem purely imaginary. The ordinary figure given for London is from 60,000 to 80,000. This may be true if it is meant to include all habitually unchaste women. It is a monstrous exaggeration if it is meant to apply to those who make their living solely and habitually by prostitution. These figures, however, only confuse. We shall have to deal with hundreds every month, whatever estimate we take. How utterly unprepared society is for any such systematic reformation may be seen from the fact that even now at our Homes we are unable to take in all the girls who apply. They cannot escape, even if they would, for want of funds whereby to provide them a way of release.

Information and Terms

Information for Anglo-Saxon and Middle English

1. Anglo-Saxon (or Old English [OE])—about 450 to about 1066 (date of the Norman Conquest)

Celts	Angles
Irish	Saxons
Britons	Jutes

   "Angle-ish" became distinguishable from the forms of Indo-European spoken by the invading tribes around 700.

   Anglo-Saxon alphabet identical to the modern English alphabet, with the addition of three letters:

   "ash" — æ
   "thorn" — þ
   "eth" — ð

2. Norman Conquest—1066

3. Middle English—about 1066 to 1400 (year of Chaucer's death) or 1476 (year Caxton introduced printing into England)

   Norman influence most clearly perceivable in changes in vocabulary.
   Grammar and syntax of the language still cleave to Anglo-Saxon (generally Germanic) origins.

4. Significant event distinguishing Middle English from modern English is the Great Vowel Shift.

Terms for Chaucer

1. Traits that characterize Chaucer's pilgrims in the General Prologue:

   their clothes (coats, shoes, jewelry)
   their eyes
   their hair
   their horses and how they ride them
   the saints associated with them
   the animals to which they are compared

2. Caritas

3. Amor vincit omnia

4. Papal bull of 1272 (Pope Gregory X)

5. Royal Edict of 1290

Terms for Shakespeare

1. Reformation

2. Martin Luther, Wittenberg, 1517

3. Henry VIII broke with Roman Catholic Church, 1535

4. Elizabeth I (Tudor)

5. Old Poor Law

6. 43 Elizabeth I (1601)

7. Actors as vagrants

8. "Kind"

9. "Natural"

Dates of Reigns (and Other Matters)

Henry VIII–1533—broke with Rome

Elizabeth 1-1558–1603

James 1-1603–1625

Charles 1-1625–1649 (beheaded)

Commonwealth Period-1641–1660 (Cromwell)
    Stuarts in exile in France

Restoration–1660

Charles II-1660–1685

James 11-1685–1689

William III and Mary 11-1689–1702 (Mary dies in 1694)

Anne-1702–1714

George 1-1714–1727

George 11-1727–1760

George 111-1760–1820

Terms for the 18th Century and Barrow

1. English Civil War

2. Oliver Cromwell

3. Restoration (1660)

4. Charles II (Stuart)

5. Bank of England, 1697

6. South Sea Bubble, 1720

7. Latitudinarian

8. Law of Settlement and Removal

9. Captain Coram

10. William Hogarth

11. Jonas Hanway

12. Sir Isaac Newton

13. Lucasian Chair of Mathematics, Cambridge

14. Sympathy
as a term in physics (sympathetic attractions, sympathetic cures)
as a term in ethics

Terms for Mandeville and Steele

1. *The Fable of the Bees: or, Private Vices, Publick Benefits* (1714)

2. Menippean satire

3. "An Essay on Charity, and Charity Schools" added in 1723

4. *The Tatler* and *The Spectator*

5. Terence, *Andria* (The Woman of Andros)

6. Roman comedy and romantic comedy

7. Sentiment(s)

8. "Conscious" = "SELF-conscious"

Terms for Swift

1. Dean of the Anglican Church in Ireland

2. Irony

3. Satire (a work that ridicules human vice and folly, with the aim of correcting it)

4. Ironic satire

5. "the wealth of nations"

6. Salmanaazor (George Psalamanazar)

7. Reprehensio

8. "A Proposal for giving Badges to the Beggars" (1737)

Cicero and "A Modest Proposal"

I. The classical model, taken from Cicero.

1. Exordium (proem) – introduction

2. Narratio – general description of the subject and background

3. Digressio – digression, an expansion on a smaller point or issue

4. Confirmatio – chief evidence in support of the thesis; body of the essay

5. Reprehensio – defeat of the opposition

6. Peroratio – conclusion

II. Swift's use of the Ciceronian model.

1. Exordium – paragraphs 1–7

2. Narratio – paragraphs 8–16

3. Digressio – paragraphs 17–19

4. Confirmatio – paragraphs 20–28

5. Reprehensio – paragraphs 29–30

6. Peroratio – paragraphs 31–33

Terms for Johnson

1. *Life of Savage* (1744)

2. *A Dictionary of the English Language* (1755)

3. Johnson edited the works of Shakespeare (1765)

4. *Lives of the English Poets* (1779-81)

5. Gratitude, "gratefulness"

6. Benevolence and gratitude as the essential bonds of social order

Terms for Sterne

1. Sterne an Anglican clergyman

2. *The Life and Opinions of Tristram Shandy* (1759–1767)

3. The Seven Years' War (1756–1763)
   (The fighting in North America was known as The French and Indian War.)

4. Epistemology

5. Sensibility

6. "sentimental" and "sentimentalism"

7. "benevolent" and "benevolence"

Terms for Bentham and Malthus

1. French Revolution, 1789

2. Jeremy Bentham, *Outline of a Work Entitled Pauper Management Improved* (1797-1798)

3. Utilitarianism

4. The greatest good for the greatest number

5. Thomas Robert Malthus, *An Essay on the Principle of Population* (1798)

6. The New Poor Law Amendment Act of 1834 (the "New Poor Law")

7. Indoor vs. outdoor relief

8. Less eligibility

9. The workhouse test

10. William Holman Hunt

11. Adam Smith: *The Theory of Moral Sentiments* (1759); *The Wealth of Nations* (1776)

Terms for Wordsworth and Coleridge

1. Hobbes, *Leviathan* (1651): imagination is "decayed sense"

2. Addison, *The Spectator* (1711):
   Pleasures of the Imagination:
   > Primary = looking at or seeing objects
   > Secondary = remembering or creating objects (more enjoyable, the more the objects resemble those found in nature)

3. Preface to *Lyrical Ballads* (1798):
   Imagination is creative, original
   Imagination works by sympathy ("sympathetic imagination")

4. Charles Lamb

5. The Quantock Hills (The Quantocks)

Terms for Bulwer Lytton and Dickens

1. "It was a dark and stormy night."

2. "pursuit of the almighty dollar"

3. Charles Macready

4. *Oliver Twist* (1838)

5. ragged schools

6. Urania Cottage

7. Angela Burdett-Coutts

8. Materialism

Terms for Browning

1. Dramatic monologue

2. Cosimo de' Medici

3. Giotto

4. Caravaggio

Terms for Booth and Stead

1. Jonas Hanway, "climbing boys" (1750s and after)

2. Henry Mayhew, *London Labour and the London Poor* (1861)

3. General William Booth

4. The Salvation Army

5. W. T. Stead

6. Crusading journalism

7. Henry Morton Stanley, *In Darkest Africa* (1890)

8. David Livingston

Terms for Shaw

1. Fabian socialism

2. The Life Force

3. *Mrs. Warren's Profession*

4. Beatrice and Sidney Webb

5. "Shavian"

6. Shaw as feminist

7. Relief and reform